GROWING OLD
IN AMERICA

ISSN 1538-6686

GROWING OLD IN AMERICA

Barbara Wexler

INFORMATION PLUS® REFERENCE SERIES
Formerly Published by Information Plus, Wylie, Texas

GALE
A Cengage Company

Farmington Hills, Mich • San Francisco • New York • Waterville, Maine
Meriden, Conn • Mason, Ohio • Chicago

Growing Old in America

Barbara Wexler

Kepos Media, Inc.: Steven Long and
Janice Jorgensen, Series Editors

Project Editor: Laura Avery

Rights Acquisition and Management:
  Ashley Maynard, Carissa Poweleit

Composition: Evi Abou-El-Seoud, Jeff Sumner,
  Mary Beth Trimper

Manufacturing: Rita Wimberley

Product Design: Kristin Julien

For product information and technology assistance, contact us at
Gale Customer Support, 1-800-877-4253.
For permission to use material from this text or product,
submit all requests online at **www.cengage.com/permissions.**
Further permissions questions can be emailed to
permissionrequest@cengage.com

Cover photograph: © Robert Kneschke/Shutterstock.com.

Gale
27500 Drake Rd.
Farmington Hills, MI 48331-3535

ISBN-13: 978-0-7876-5103-9 (set)
ISBN-13: 978-1-4103-2551-8

ISSN 1538-6686

This title is also available as an e-book.
ISBN-13: 978-1-4103-2583-9
Contact your Gale sales representative for ordering information.

Printed in the United States of America
1 2 3 4 5   22 21 20 19 18

TABLE OF CONTENTS

of health care reform legislation on older adults. The challenges of long-term care are highlighted along with in-home services that enable older adults to remain in the community.

    This chapter enumerates the rates and types of crime against older Americans, including characteristics of older crime victims.

It also delves into the types of frauds that are perpetrated against the older population, domestic and institutional abuse, and mistreatment.

PREFACE

Growing Old in America is part of the *Information Plus Reference Series*. The purpose of each volume of the series is to present the latest facts on a topic of pressing concern in modern American life. These topics include the most controversial and studied social issues of the 21st century: abortion, capital punishment, crime, the environment, health care, immigration, national security, social welfare, weight, women, youth, and many more. Although this series is written for high school and undergraduate students, it is an excellent resource for anyone in need of factual information on current affairs.

By presenting the facts, it is the intention of Gale, a Cengage Company, to provide its readers with everything they need to reach an informed opinion on current issues. To that end, there is a particular emphasis in this series on the presentation of scientific studies, surveys, and statistics. These data are generally presented in the form of tables, charts, and other graphics placed within the text of each book. Every graphic is directly referred to and carefully explained in the text. The source of each graphic is presented within the graphic itself. The data used in these graphics are drawn from the most reputable and reliable sources, such as from the various branches of the US government and from private organizations and associations. Every effort has been made to secure the most recent information available. Readers should bear in mind that many major studies take years to conduct and that additional years often pass before the data from these studies are made available to the public. Therefore, in many cases the most recent information available in 2018 is dated from 2015 or 2016. Older statistics are sometimes presented as well if they are landmark studies or of particular interest and no more-recent data are available.

Although statistics are a major focus of the *Information Plus Reference Series*, they are by no means its only content. Each book also presents the widely held positions and important ideas that shape how the book's subject is discussed in the United States. These positions are explained in detail and, where possible, in the words of their proponents. Some of the other material to be found in these books includes historical background, descriptions of major events related to the subject, relevant laws and court cases, and examples of how these issues play out in American life. Some books also feature primary documents or have pro and con debate sections that provide the words and opinions of prominent Americans on both sides of a controversial topic. All material is presented in an evenhanded and unbiased manner; readers will never be encouraged to accept one view of an issue over another.

HOW TO USE THIS BOOK

The percentage of Americans over the age of 65 years has increased over the past century, and will continue to increase as children born during the mid-20th-century baby boom age. This book explores the current condition of aging in the United States. Included is a general overview on growing old in the United States, the economic status of older people, the Social Security program, Medicare and Medicaid, the living arrangements of older adults, working and retirement, and the education levels and political behavior of older Americans. Physical and mental health problems, drug and alcohol abuse, care for older adults, and crime and victimization of older adults are also covered.

Growing Old in America consists of 11 chapters and 3 appendixes. Each chapter is devoted to a particular aspect of aging. For a summary of the information that is covered in each chapter, please see the synopses that are provided in the Table of Contents. Chapters generally begin with an overview of the basic facts and background information on the chapter's topic, then proceed to examine subtopics of particular interest. For example, Chapter 6: On the Road: Older Adult Drivers begins by explaining that readily available transportation is a vital factor in the quality of life of older adults. This is followed by a discussion of the number of older drivers and their involvement in motor vehicle accidents. The chapter concludes with a discussion of transportation alternatives for older adults who do not drive and technological advances that help improve older drivers' safety. Readers can find their way through a chapter by looking for the section and subsection headings, which are clearly set off from the text. They can also refer to the book's extensive Index if they already know what they are looking for.

Statistical Information

The tables and figures featured throughout *Growing Old in America* will be of particular use to readers in learning about this issue. These tables and figures represent an extensive collection of the most recent and important statistics on growing old and related issues—for example, graphics cover the living arrangements of older adults, the marital status of older Americans, chronic health conditions, crimes against older Americans, national health expenditures, health insurance coverage, and the percentage of workers with retirement plan benefits. Gale, a Cengage Company, believes that making this information available to readers is the most important way to fulfill the goal of this book: to help readers understand the issues and controversies surrounding growing old in the United States and to reach their own conclusions.

Each table or figure has a unique identifier appearing above it for ease of identification and reference. Titles for the tables and figures explain their purpose. At the end of each table or figure, the original source of the data is provided.

To help readers understand these often-complicated statistics, all tables and figures are explained in the text. References in the text direct readers to the relevant statistics. Furthermore, the contents of all tables and figures are fully indexed. Please see the opening section of the Index at the back of this volume for a description of how to find tables and figures within it.

Appendixes

Besides the main body text and images, *Growing Old in America* has three appendixes. The first is the Important Names and Addresses directory. Here, readers will find contact information for a number of government and private organizations that can provide further information on growing old. The second appendix is the Resources section, which can also assist readers in conducting their own research. In this section, the author and editors of *Growing Old in America* describe some of the sources that were most useful during the compilation of this book. The final appendix is the detailed Index. It has been greatly expanded from previous editions and should make it even easier to find specific topics in this book.

COMMENTS AND SUGGESTIONS

The editors of the *Information Plus Reference Series* welcome your feedback on *Growing Old in America*. Please direct all correspondence to:

Editors
Information Plus Reference Series
27500 Drake Rd.
Farmington Hills, MI 48331-3535

CHAPTER 1

OLDER AMERICANS: A DIVERSE AND GROWING POPULATION

Old age is the most unexpected of all the things that happen to a man.

—Leon Trotsky

THE US POPULATION GROWS OLDER

The US population is aging. Throughout the second half of the 20th century and the first two decades of the 21st century the country's older population (adults aged 65 years and older) increased significantly. According to the US Census Bureau, in 2016 the number of adults aged 65 years and older reached 49.2 million, an increase of 3 million over 2014. During this period the population of older adults as a percentage of the total US population also grew, from 14.5% to 15.2%. In "Older Americans Month: May 2017" (April 10, 2017, https://www.census .gov/newsroom/facts-for-features/2017/cb17-ff08.html), the Census Bureau projects that by 2060 people aged 65 years and older will number 98.2 million and make up a quarter of the US population. Figure 1.1 shows projected growth in the population of older adults between 2015 and 2060. During that time the number of older adults is expected to increase more than 105%.

The Census Bureau observes that throughout the world, the growth in the population of older adults will outpace the growth of any other segment of the population. Figure 1.2 compares young children (under five years old) and adults aged 65 years and older as a percentage of the global population between 1950 and 2050. It reveals a steady decline in the percentage of children and a sharp increase in the percentage of older adults between 2000 and 2050. By 2020, for the first time in history, people aged 65 and older will outnumber children under age five.

Fewer children per family and longer life spans have shifted the proportion of older adults in the population. Growth in the population segment of older adults in the United States, often called "the graying of America," is

considered to be one of the most significant issues facing the country in the 21st century. The swelling population of people aged 65 years and older affects every aspect of society, challenging policy makers, health care providers, employers, families, and others to meet the needs of older Americans.

Many of the findings and statistics cited in this chapter are drawn from data collected by the following federal entities: Administration on Aging (AoA; a unit of the Administration for Community Living); Agency for Healthcare Research and Quality; Census Bureau; Centers for Medicare and Medicaid Services; Employee Benefits Security Administration; National Center for Health Statistics (part of the Centers for Disease Control and Prevention); National Institute on Aging; Office of Statistical and Science Policy; Office of the Assistant Secretary for Planning and Evaluation (US Department of Health and Human Services); Substance Abuse and Mental Health Services Administration; US Bureau of Labor Statistics; US Department of Housing and Urban Development; US Department of Veterans Affairs; US Environmental Protection Agency; and the Social Security Administration. These organizations are dedicated to encouraging cooperation and collaboration among federal agencies to improve the quality and utility of data on the aging population. One study cited is the AoA's *A Profile of Older Americans: 2016* (April 2017, https://www.acl .gov/sites/default/files/Aging%20and%20Disability%20in %20America/2016-Profile.pdf).

To understand the aging of the US population, it is important to not only consider the current population of older adults but also to look at how the older population will fare over time. To anticipate the needs of this growing segment of society, policy makers, planners, and researchers rely on projections and population estimates. Population estimates and projections are made at different times and are based on different assumptions. Therefore, considerable variation may be seen in the statistics cited by different agencies and investigators. This chapter contains estimates and projections of demographic changes from several different sources, and as a result there is some variability in the data presented.

HOW DO POPULATIONS AGE?

Unlike individuals, populations can age or become younger. There are key indicators of the age structure of a given population. Populations age or grow younger because of changes in fertility (birth rates expressed as the number of births per 1,000 population per year) and/or mortality (death rates expressed as the number of deaths per 1,000 population per year) or in response to migration (people entering or leaving the population).

The aging of the United States in the early 21st century resulted from changes in fertility and mortality that occurred over the past century. Such shifts in birth rates and death rates are called demographic transitions. Population aging is primarily a response to long-term declines in fertility, and declining fertility is the basic cause of the aging of the US population. Reduced infant and child mortality, chiefly as a result of public health measures, fueled the decline in the fertility rate; that is, the increased survival of children prompted families to have fewer offspring. The birth of fewer babies resulted in fewer young people.

According to the Central Intelligence Agency (CIA), in *The World Factbook: United States* (January 23, 2018, https://www.cia.gov/library/publications/the-world-factbook/geos/us.html), in 2017 the total fertility rate in the United States was an estimated 1.87 children born per woman. This rate is sharply lower than the fertility rates between 1946 and 1964, following the end of World War II (1939–1945). Victorious service members returning home after the war were eager to start families, and this was facilitated by the relatively prosperous postwar economy.

Census Bureau statistics indicate that during this period, which came to be known as the baby boom, US fertility rates exploded, at one point approaching four children born per woman. People born during the baby

FIGURE 1.1

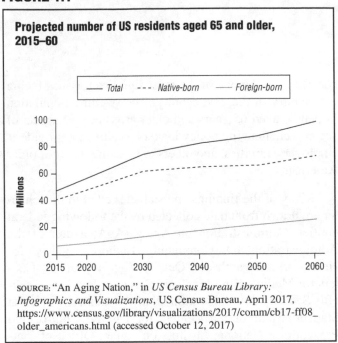

Projected number of US residents aged 65 and older, 2015–60

SOURCE: "An Aging Nation," in *US Census Bureau Library: Infographics and Visualizations*, US Census Bureau, April 2017, https://www.census.gov/library/visualizations/2017/comm/cb17-ff08_older_americans.html (accessed October 12, 2017)

FIGURE 1.2

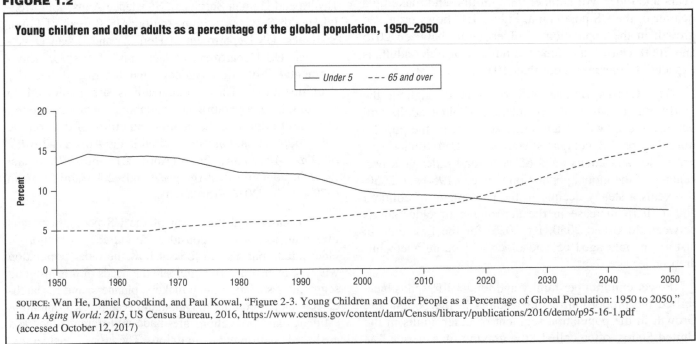

Young children and older adults as a percentage of the global population, 1950–2050

SOURCE: Wan He, Daniel Goodkind, and Paul Kowal, "Figure 2-3. Young Children and Older People as a Percentage of Global Population: 1950 to 2050," in *An Aging World: 2015*, US Census Bureau, 2016, https://www.census.gov/content/dam/Census/library/publications/2016/demo/p95-16-1.pdf (accessed October 12, 2017)

boom (1946–1964) became known as baby boomers, and it is this cohort (a group of individuals that shares a common characteristic such as birth years and is studied over time) that is responsible for the tremendous increase projected in the number of people aged 65 years and older, and especially aged 65 to 74 years. The older adult segment of the population is expected to swell until 2030, as the baby boom cohort completes its transition from middle age to old age. In 2033 the population of adults aged 65 years and older is expected to outnumber the population aged 18 years and younger for the first time.

The decline in death rates, especially at the older ages, has also contributed to the increase in the number of older adults. The death rates of older adults began to decrease during the late 1960s and continued to decline through the first decade of the 21st century. Advances in medical care have produced declining death rates for three of the leading causes of death among older people: heart disease, malignancies (cancer), and cerebrovascular diseases that cause strokes. Kenneth D. Kochanek et al. report in *Mortality in the United States, 2016* (December 2017, https://www.cdc.gov/nchs/data/databriefs/db293.pdf) that the age-adjusted death rate in the United States was 728.8 deaths per 100,000 population in 2016. This was consistent with a long-term decrease in the death rate, which was 869 deaths per 100,000 population in 2000, according to the Centers for Disease Control and Prevention.

Projections of an increasing proportion of older adults between 2015 and 2030 are based on three assumptions: historic low fertility and the prospect of continuing low fertility until 2030, aging of the baby boom cohort, and continued declines in mortality at older ages and low mortality until 2030. Demographers (those who study population statistics) expect that when the entire baby boom generation has attained age 65 (or older) in 2030, the proportion of older people in the US population will stabilize. Figure 1.3 shows how the baby boomers will be a smaller proportion of the population, decreasing from about 25% in 2012 to 0.6% in 2060.

DEFINING OLD AGE

Forty is the old age of youth; fifty the youth of old age.

—Victor Hugo

When does old age begin? The challenge of defining old age is reflected in the terminology that is used to describe adults aged 50 years and older: for example, middle aged, elder, elderly, older, aged, mature, or senior. The AARP (formerly the American Association of Retired Persons), a national advocacy organization for older adults, invites people to join its ranks at age 50. Many retailers offer senior discounts to people aged 50 or 55 years and older, and federal entitlement programs such as Medicare (a medical insurance program for older adults and people with disabilities) extend benefits to people at age 65, while Social Security (a program that provides retirement income and health care for older adults) benefits may begin as early as age 62. Despite these varying definitions, in this text, unless otherwise specified, the term *older adults* refers to people aged 65 years and older.

Gerontology (the field of study that considers the social, psychological, and biological aspects of aging) distinguishes three groups of older adults: the young-old are those aged 65 to 74 years, the middle-old includes those aged 75 to 84 years, and the oldest-old are those aged 85 years and older. Figure 1.4 shows that in the United States the oldest segment of older adults, the oldest-old, grew from just over 100,000 people in 1900 to 6 million in 2014 and is projected to increase to 20 million by 2060.

LIFE EXPECTANCY

Life expectancy (the anticipated average length of life) has increased dramatically since 1900, when the average age of death for men and women combined was 47.3 years. The Centers for Disease Control and Prevention (May 3, 2017, http://www.cdc.gov/nchs/fastats/life-expectancy.htm) reports that life expectancy rose to 78.8 years in 2012 and then plateaued for the next three years. In 2016 it dropped slightly to 78.6 years (as reported in *Mortality in the United States, 2016*). Most projections see life expectancy continuing to rise.

Life expectancy in the United States varies by geography. For example, Laura Dwyer-Lindgren et al. find in "Inequalities in Life Expectancy among US Counties, 1980 to 2014: Temporal Trends and Key Drivers" (*JAMA Internal Medicine*, vol. 177, no. 7, July 1, 2017) that much of the variation in life expectancy among counties can be explained by a combination of socioeconomic and race/ethnicity factors, behavioral and metabolic risk factors, and health care factors. Nearly three-quarters (74%) of the variation was explained by behavioral and metabolic risk factors, such as smoking, substance abuse, obesity, high blood pressure, and diabetes.

Global Life Expectancy

The more developed regions of the world have lower death rates than the less developed regions and, as such, have higher life expectancies. In *World Factbook*, the CIA observes that some nations more than doubled their life expectancy during the 20th century. Table 1.1 shows the ranks of the top-50 countries in terms of life expectancy in 2016. The United States was number 42. The country with the longest projected life expectancy at birth was Monaco, where it was 89.5 years. The life expectancy was at least 79 years in many developed countries. Many less-developed countries have also seen a steady increase in life expectancy, except for countries in Africa that have been hard hit by the human immunodeficiency virus (HIV)/acquired immunodeficiency syndrome epidemic.

FIGURE 1.3

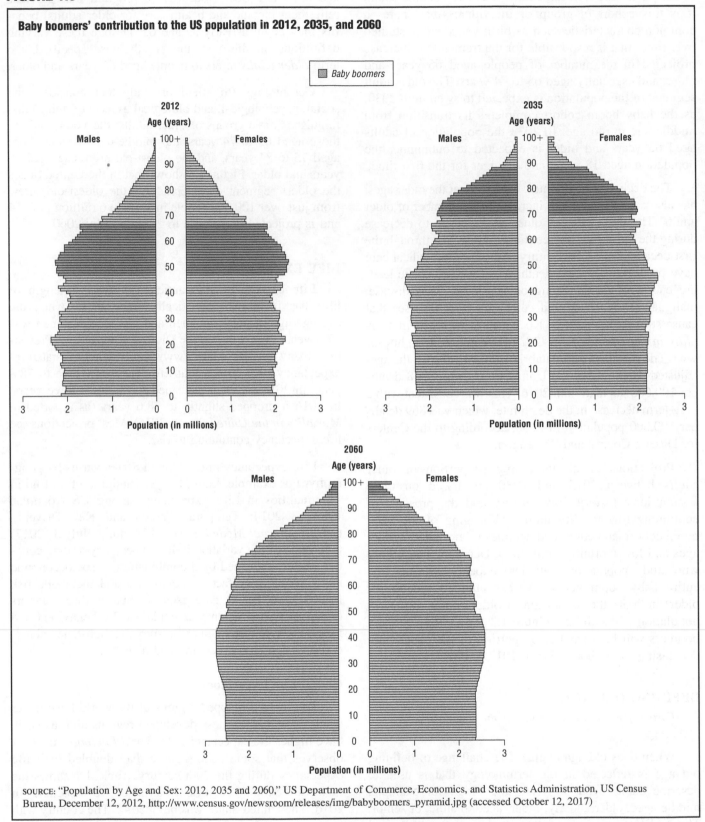

Baby boomers' contribution to the US population in 2012, 2035, and 2060

SOURCE: "Population by Age and Sex: 2012, 2035 and 2060," US Department of Commerce, Economics, and Statistics Administration, US Census Bureau, December 12, 2012, http://www.census.gov/newsroom/releases/img/babyboomers_pyramid.jpg (accessed October 12, 2017)

Table 1.2 shows the ranks of the 30 countries with the lowest estimates of life expectancy in 2016. Chad at 50.2 years had the lowest life expectancy. Nazrul Islam Mondal and Mahendran Shitan explain in "Relative Importance of Demographic, Socioeconomic and Health Factors on Life Expectancy in Low- and Lower-Middle-Income Countries" (*Journal of Epidemiology*, vol. 24, no. 2, March 2014) that many factors contribute to lower life expectancy in developing countries. Chief among them are poverty, inadequate medical care, lack of education, and HIV prevalence.

FIGURE 1.4

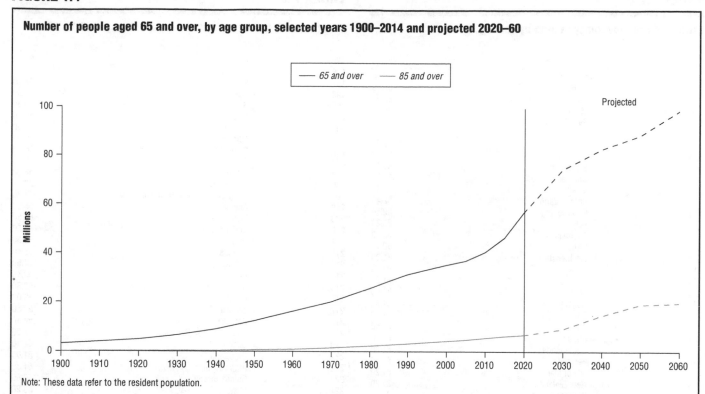

Number of people aged 65 and over, by age group, selected years 1900–2014 and projected 2020–60

Note: These data refer to the resident population.

SOURCE: "Population Age 65 and over and Age 85 and over, Selected Years 1900–2014, and Projected 2020–2060," in *Older Americans 2016: Key Indicators of Well-Being*, Federal Interagency Forum on Aging-Related Statistics, August 2016, https://agingstats.gov/docs/LatestReport/Older-Americans-2016-Key-Indicators-of-WellBeing.pdf (accessed October 12, 2017)

OLDER ADULTS IN THE UNITED STATES

According to Census Bureau estimates, in 2020 there will be an estimated 56.4 million people aged 65 years and older living in the United States. (See Table 1.3.) The young-old (aged 65 to 74 years) will account for 59% (33.1 million) of the population aged 65 and older. The 16.6 million people aged 75 to 84 years will make up 29.5% of the older adult population, and 12% (6.7 million) will be the oldest-old (aged 85 years and older).

By 2030 the number of young-old is projected to rise to 39.2 million, the middle-old will be nearing 25.8 million, and the oldest-old will be 9.1 million. (See Table 1.3.) Older women are expected to outnumber older men. Longer female life expectancy, combined with the fact that men often marry younger women, contributes to a higher proportion of older women living alone (widowed or unmarried).

The Oldest-Old

The AoA states in *Profile of Older Americans: 2016* that adults who reached age 65 in 2015 had "an average life expectancy of an additional 19.4 years (20.6 years for females and 18 years for males)." The population aged 85 years and older is projected to grow from 6.3 million in 2015 to 7.5 million in 2025, a 19% increase in 10 years. (See Table 1.3.)

Some researchers believe death rates at older ages will decline more rapidly than is reflected in Census Bureau projections, which will result in even faster growth of this population segment. The Census Bureau reports that among the oldest-old, women dramatically outnumber men; in 2020 there will be nearly twice as many women aged 85 years and older than men. (See Table 1.3.)

Centenarians

During the first half of the 21st century the United States will experience a centenarian boom. Living to age 100 and older is no longer a rarity. The chances of living to age 100 have increased 40% since 1900. The centenarian population more than doubled during the 1980s. In 2020 there will be about 89,000 US residents aged 100 years and older. (See Table 1.3.) By 2060 that number is expected to increase to 604,000.

According to Guinness World Records (2018, http://www.guinnessworldrecords.com/records-5000/oldest-person), the oldest verified age attained by a human is 122 years and 164 days. Guinness World Records relies on data from the Gerontology Research Group (GRG), which tracks supercentenarians (people aged 110 years and older) throughout the world. The organization (http://www.grg.org/SC/WorldSCRankingsList.html) reports that, as of

TABLE 1.1

Estimated life expectancy at birth by country, 2016

Rank	Country	(Years)
1	Monaco	89.50
2	Singapore	85.00
3	Japan	85.00
4	Macau	84.50
5	San Marino	83.30
6	Iceland	83.00
7	Hong Kong	82.90
8	Andorra	82.80
9	Switzerland	82.60
10	Guernsey	82.50
11	Israel	82.40
12	Korea, South	82.40
13	Luxembourg	82.30
14	Italy	82.20
15	Australia	82.20
16	Sweden	82.10
17	Liechtenstein	81.90
18	Jersey	81.90
19	Canada	81.90
20	France	81.80
21	Norway	81.80
22	Spain	81.70
23	Austria	81.50
24	Anguilla	81.40
25	Netherlands	81.30
26	Bermuda	81.30
27	Isle of Man	81.20
28	New Zealand	81.20
29	Cayman Islands	81.20
30	Belgium	81.00
31	Finland	80.90
32	Ireland	80.80
33	United Kingdom	80.70
34	Germany	80.70
35	Greece	80.50
36	Saint Pierre and Miquelon	80.50
37	Malta	80.40
38	Faroe Islands	80.40
39	European Union	80.20
40	Taiwan	80.10
41	Virgin Islands	80.00
42	United States	79.80
43	Turks and Caicos Islands	79.80
44	Wallis Futuna	79.70
45	Saint Helena, Ascension, and Tristan da Cunha	79.50
46	Gibraltar	79.40
47	Denmark	79.40
48	Puerto Rico	79.40
49	Portugal	79.30
50	Guam	79.10

SOURCE: Adapted from "Country Comparison: Life Expectancy at Birth," in *The World Factbook*, Central Intelligence Agency, 2016, https://www.cia.gov/library/publications/the-world-factbook/rankorder/2102rank.html#us (accessed October 12, 2017)

TABLE 1.2

Countries with lowest estimated life expectancy at birth, 2016

195	Benin	61.90
196	Senegal	61.70
197	Malawi	61.20
198	Guinea	60.60
199	Burundi	60.50
200	Rwanda	60.10
201	Congo, Republic of the	59.30
202	Liberia	59.00
203	Cote d'Ivoire	58.70
204	Cameroon	58.50
205	Sierra Leone	58.20
206	Zimbabwe	58.00
207	Congo, Democratic Republic of the	57.30
208	Angola	56.00
209	Mali	55.80
210	Burkina Faso	55.50
211	Niger	55.50
212	Uganda	55.40
213	Botswana	54.50
214	Nigeria	53.40
215	Mozambique	53.30
216	Lesotho	53.00
217	Zambia	52.50
218	Somalia	52.40
219	Central African Republic	52.30
220	Gabon	52.10
221	Swaziland	51.60
222	Afghanistan	51.30
223	Guinea-Bissau	50.60
224	Chad	50.20

SOURCE: Adapted from "Country Comparison: Life Expectancy at Birth," in *The World Factbook*, Central Intelligence Agency, 2016, https://www.cia.gov/library/publications/the-world-factbook/rankorder/2102rank.html#us (accessed October 12, 2017)

Racial and Ethnic Diversity

The older population is becoming more ethnically and racially diverse, although at a slower pace than the overall population of the United States. In 2014 non-Hispanic whites made up 78% of the older population, with non-Hispanic African Americans (9%), Hispanics (8%), and non-Hispanic Asian Americans (4%) making up smaller segments. (See Figure 1.5.) By 2060 the composition of the older population is projected to be more racially and ethnically diverse: 55% will be non-Hispanic white, 22% Hispanic, 12% non-Hispanic African American, and 9% non-Hispanic Asian American. Although the older population is projected to increase among non-Hispanic African Americans, non-Hispanic Asian Americans, and Hispanics, the proportion of the older population that is Hispanic is projected to grow the most dramatically, from 8% in 2014 to 22% in 2060.

Marital Status

As in previous years, in 2016 older men were much more likely than older women to be married. Among people aged 65 years and older, 70% of men were married, compared with 45% of women. (See Figure 1.6.)

As older women outnumber older men in all age groups, it is not surprising that there are more widows

February 2018, it had validated 39 living supercentenarians: 38 women and one man. The Gerontology Research Group notes, however, that there are likely many additional unverified cases and estimates there may be as many as 300 to 450 living supercentenarians worldwide as of 2018. For the United States, the estimate is 60 to 75. In September 2017 Violet Brown, who was verified by Guinness World Records as the oldest person in the world, died in her native country of Jamaica at age 117 years and 189 days.

TABLE 1.3

Projections of the population by age and sex, 2020–60

[Resident population as of July 1. Numbers in thousands, except where noted.]

Sex and age	2020	2025	2030	2035	2040	2045	2050	2055	2060
Both sexes	**334,503**	**347,335**	**359,402**	**370,338**	**380,219**	**389,394**	**398,328**	**407,412**	**416,795**
Under 5 years	20,568	21,010	21,178	21,268	21,471	21,775	22,147	22,499	22,778
5 to 9 years	20,274	20,889	21,347	21,529	21,632	21,845	22,158	22,536	22,894
10 to 14 years	20,735	20,555	21,182	21,650	21,842	21,952	22,171	22,489	22,871
15 to 19 years	21,048	21,219	21,060	21,706	22,190	22,395	22,516	22,743	23,067
20 to 24 years	22,059	22,077	22,299	22,183	22,866	23,383	23,615	23,757	23,999
25 to 29 years	23,722	23,103	23,179	23,450	23,377	24,098	24,646	24,903	25,065
30 to 34 years	23,168	24,450	23,878	23,995	24,302	24,259	25,004	25,572	25,845
35 to 39 years	22,060	23,586	24,898	24,360	24,507	24,838	24,813	25,572	26,151
40 to 44 years	20,568	22,291	23,840	25,176	24,668	24,840	25,190	25,180	25,949
45 to 49 years	20,204	20,613	22,351	23,919	25,274	24,798	24,995	25,363	25,368
50 to 54 years	20,638	20,063	20,506	22,257	23,844	25,219	24,781	25,006	25,395
55 to 59 years	21,879	20,294	19,777	20,260	22,023	23,629	25,023	24,633	24,893
60 to 64 years	21,141	21,265	19,799	19,351	19,880	21,653	23,275	24,689	24,357
65 to 69 years	18,194	20,202	20,397	19,071	18,704	19,283	21,054	22,686	24,112
70 to 74 years	14,882	16,891	18,830	19,091	17,940	17,664	18,294	20,039	21,662
75 to 79 years	10,112	13,154	15,013	16,819	17,143	16,212	16,042	16,717	18,393
80 to 84 years	6,527	8,191	10,737	12,343	13,924	14,294	13,634	13,574	14,274
85 to 89 years	3,964	4,521	5,747	7,622	8,867	10,114	10,492	10,137	10,184
90 to 94 years	2,024	2,114	2,464	3,192	4,320	5,127	5,951	6,275	6,184
95 to 99 years	649	728	782	940	1,254	1,751	2,141	2,550	2,752
100 years and over	89	119	138	154	193	267	387	493	604
Median age (years)	38.5	39.3	40.1	41.0	41.6	42.0	42.4	42.7	43.0
Male	**165,036**	**171,489**	**177,528**	**183,030**	**188,093**	**192,919**	**197,727**	**202,671**	**207,764**
Under 5 years	10,520	10,747	10,833	10,879	10,983	11,138	11,329	11,509	11,652
5 to 9 years	10,360	10,676	10,910	11,003	11,055	11,164	11,325	11,519	11,702
10 to 14 years	10,584	10,500	10,821	11,061	11,158	11,215	11,327	11,490	11,685
15 to 19 years	10,749	10,835	10,762	11,093	11,341	11,446	11,508	11,624	11,790
20 to 24 years	11,300	11,290	11,404	11,354	11,706	11,972	12,091	12,165	12,289
25 to 29 years	12,161	11,818	11,841	11,982	11,956	12,327	12,609	12,742	12,825
30 to 34 years	11,781	12,510	12,194	12,241	12,402	12,392	12,776	13,069	13,210
35 to 39 years	11,099	11,979	12,725	12,430	12,494	12,669	12,670	13,062	13,361
40 to 44 years	10,272	11,193	12,086	12,845	12,569	12,648	12,834	12,843	13,241
45 to 49 years	10,010	10,266	11,194	12,097	12,869	12,612	12,706	12,903	12,921
50 to 54 years	10,182	9,889	10,165	11,100	12,013	12,796	12,564	12,675	12,885
55 to 59 years	10,651	9,929	9,672	9,969	10,911	11,833	12,627	12,426	12,560
60 to 64 years	10,147	10,229	9,578	9,362	9,685	10,631	11,559	12,364	12,201
65 to 69 years	8,567	9,556	9,676	9,105	8,936	9,285	10,227	11,157	11,967
70 to 74 years	6,900	7,804	8,747	8,901	8,426	8,309	8,683	9,604	10,523
75 to 79 years	4,538	5,938	6,760	7,623	7,808	7,447	7,388	7,780	8,655
80 to 84 years	2,783	3,529	4,660	5,351	6,087	6,289	6,062	6,060	6,454
85 to 89 years	1,545	1,808	2,327	3,115	3,626	4,181	4,374	4,284	4,330
90 to 94 years	686	749	897	1,178	1,612	1,919	2,258	2,407	2,414
95 to 99 years	181	216	243	299	405	572	703	851	931
100 years and over	20	29	35	41	52	73	106	137	170
Median age (years)	37.3	38.0	39.0	39.8	40.4	40.8	41.3	41.6	42.0
Female	**169,467**	**175,846**	**181,874**	**187,308**	**192,126**	**196,476**	**200,601**	**204,741**	**209,031**
Under 5 years	10,047	10,264	10,346	10,389	10,488	10,637	10,818	10,990	11,127
5 to 9 years	9,914	10,214	10,437	10,526	10,576	10,680	10,833	11,018	11,192
10 to 14 years	10,150	10,055	10,361	10,590	10,683	10,737	10,844	10,999	11,185
15 to 19 years	10,299	10,384	10,298	10,613	10,849	10,949	11,008	11,119	11,277
20 to 24 years	10,759	10,787	10,895	10,828	11,160	11,411	11,523	11,592	11,711
25 to 29 years	11,561	11,284	11,338	11,468	11,421	11,770	12,037	12,161	12,240
30 to 34 years	11,387	11,940	11,683	11,755	11,901	11,868	12,228	12,504	12,635
35 to 39 years	10,961	11,607	12,173	11,929	12,013	12,169	12,144	12,510	12,790
40 to 44 years	10,296	11,098	11,755	12,330	12,098	12,192	12,356	12,338	12,708
45 to 49 years	10,195	10,347	11,157	11,822	12,405	12,186	12,289	12,460	12,447
50 to 54 years	10,456	10,174	10,342	11,157	11,831	12,423	12,217	12,331	12,509
55 to 59 years	11,228	10,365	10,106	10,291	11,112	11,795	12,396	12,207	12,333
60 to 64 years	10,993	11,036	10,221	9,989	10,195	11,022	11,715	12,325	12,156
65 to 69 years	9,626	10,646	10,721	9,967	9,768	9,997	10,827	11,528	12,145
70 to 74 years	7,982	9,088	10,083	10,189	9,514	9,355	9,611	10,435	11,139
75 to 79 years	5,574	7,216	8,253	9,196	9,335	8,765	8,654	8,937	9,738
80 to 84 years	3,744	4,662	6,076	6,992	7,837	8,005	7,572	7,514	7,820
85 to 89 years	2,420	2,713	3,420	4,507	5,241	5,933	6,118	5,853	5,854
90 to 94 years	1,337	1,365	1,567	2,014	2,708	3,208	3,693	3,867	3,770
95 to 99 years	468	511	540	640	849	1,179	1,438	1,698	1,821
100 years and over	69	91	103	114	141	194	280	356	434
Median age (years)	39.8	40.6	41.4	42.3	42.9	43.3	43.6	43.8	44.1

TABLE 1.3

Projections of the population by age and sex, 2020–60 [CONTINUED]

[Resident population as of July 1. Numbers in thousands, except where noted.]

SOURCE: Adapted from "Table 9. Projections of the Population by Sex and Age for the United States: 2015 to 2060," in *2014 National Population Projections Summary Tables*, US Census Bureau, Population Division, December 2014, https://www.census.gov/data/tables/2014/demo/popproj/2014-summary-tables.html (accessed October 12, 2017)

FIGURE 1.5

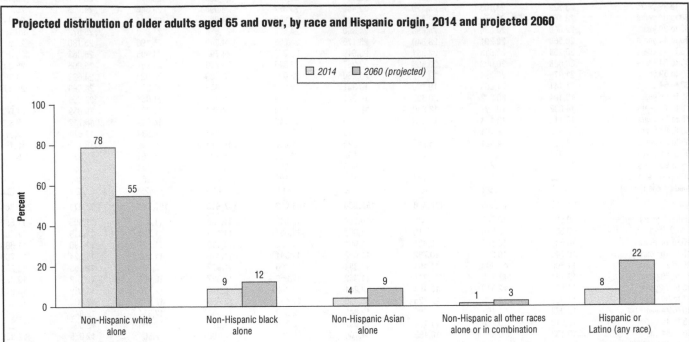

Projected distribution of older adults aged 65 and over, by race and Hispanic origin, 2014 and projected 2060

Note: Hispanics are not counted in any race group. The term "non-Hispanic white alone" is used to refer to people who reported being white and no other race and who are not Hispanic. The term "non-Hispanic black alone" is used to refer to people who reported being black or African American and no other race and who are not Hispanic, and the term "non-Hispanic Asian alone" is used to refer to people who reported only Asian as their race and who are not Hispanic. The use of single-race populations in this chart does not imply that this is the preferred method of presenting or analyzing data. The US Census Bureau uses a variety of approaches. The race group "non-Hispanic All other races alone or in combination" includes people who reported American Indian and Alaska Native alone who are not Hispanic; people who reported Native Hawaiian and Other Pacific Islander alone who are not Hispanic; and all people who reported tow or more races who are not Hispanic. "Hispanic" refers to an ethnic category; Hispanics may be of any race. Reference population: These data refer to the resident population.

SOURCE: "Population Age 65 and over, by Race and Hispanic Origin, 2014 and Projected 2060," in *Older Americans 2016: Key Indicators of Well-Being*, Federal Interagency Forum on Aging-Related Statistics, August 2016, https://agingstats.gov/docs/LatestReport/Older-Americans-2016-Key-Indicators-of-WellBeing.pdf (accessed October 13, 2017)

than widowers. In 2016 nearly three times as many women as men aged 65 years and older were widowed— 34% of women, compared with 12% of men. (See Figure 1.6.) Just 16% of older women and 13% of older men were divorced, and an even smaller proportion (5%) had never married.

Foreign-Born Older Adults

Gustavo López and Jynnah Radford of the Pew Research Center report in *Facts on U.S. Immigrants, 2015* (May 3, 2017, http://www.pewhispanic.org/2017/05/03/facts-on-u-s-immigrants-current-data/) that in 2015 the nation's foreign-born population numbered 43.2 million, accounting for an estimated 13.4% of the total US population. People aged 51 to 69 years, who are members of the baby boomer generation (born between 1946 and

1964), made up 25.9% of the immigrant population in 2015. People aged 70 years and older, members of the Greatest and Silent generations (born between 1910 and 1925 and 1925 and 1945, respectively), accounted for 9.7% of the immigrant population. Figure 1.1 shows the projected increase in the numbers of foreign-born and native-born US residents aged 65 years and older between 2015 and 2060.

In "The Painful Struggles of America's Older Immigrants" (Forbes.com, December 12, 2016), Chris Farrell notes that immigrants make up a larger proportion of the older adult population in "major gateway cities and states." For instance, in 2015, 46% of older adults in New York City were immigrants, and in California the proportion was nearly one in three. Farrell reports that

FIGURE 1.6

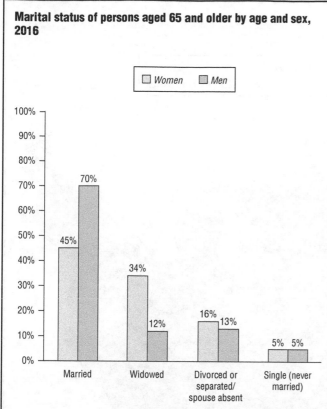

Marital status of persons aged 65 and older by age and sex, 2016

SOURCE: "Figure 2. Marital Status of Persons 65+, 2016," in *A Profile of Older Americans: 2016*, US Department of Health and Human Services, Administration for Community Living, Administration on Aging, April 2017, https://www.acl.gov/sites/default/files/Aging%20and%20Disability%20in%20America/2016-Profile.pdf (accessed October 13, 2017)

older immigrants tend to face greater financial difficulties than their native-born peers. About 40% of older immigrants in 2015 were in low-income families, compared with 30% of US-born older adults. Similarly, in 2015, 16% of foreign-born older adults were living below the poverty line, compared with 8% of their US-born cohorts.

WHERE OLDER AMERICANS LIVE

The AoA reports in *Profile of Older Americans: 2016* that the proportion of the population aged 65 years and older varies by state. In 2015 adults aged 65 years and older accounted for 18% or more of the population in three states. Florida had the largest proportion of older adults, with 19.4% of the total, followed by Maine (18.8%) and West Virginia (18.2%). Figure 1.7 shows people aged 65 years and older as a percentage of total population by state in 2015.

More than half of people aged 65 years and older lived in 10 states: California (5.2 million), Florida (3.9 million), Texas (3.2 million), New York (3 million), Pennsylvania (2.2 million), Ohio (1.8 million), Illinois (1.8 million), Michigan (1.6 million), North Carolina (1.5 million), and New Jersey (1.3 million). (See Table 1.4.)

Figure 1.8 shows growth in the older population by state between 2005 and 2015. In four states—Alaska (63%), Nevada (55.3%), Colorado (53.8%), and Georgia (50.2%)—the population aged 65 years and older increased by 50% or more.

According to the AoA, older adults relocate less often than any other age group. Of older adults who changed residence between 2015 and 2016, just 16% moved out of state; the majority (84%) remained in the same state (62% stayed in the same county, and 22% moved to a different county within the same state).

Older Americans Are More Religious

In *2014 U.S. Religious Landscape Study* (2018, http://www.pewforum.org/religious-landscape-study/age-distribution/), the Pew Research Center indicates that older Americans tend to be more religious than younger Americans. Consistent with this observation is the fact that older adults are also more likely to say they believe in God. Survey data reveal that 70% of people aged 65 years and older and 69% of those aged 50 to 64 years said they believe in God with absolute certainty, compared with 62% of people aged 30 to 49 years and 51% of young adults aged 18 to 29 years. Similarly, 65% of older Americans say religion is very important in their life, compared with 40% of people aged 18 to 29 years.

Lawrence T. White explains in "Why Are Old People So Religious?" (PsychologyToday.com, February 16, 2016) that data from 80 countries support the premise that people become more religious with advancing age. White observes that some psychologists and theologians believe that "religion—and spirituality more broadly—creates a sense of meaning and coherence in one's life that becomes especially important during the final stages of human development" and that "religion helps soothe fear and insecurity about one's own mortality."

ENJOYMENT OF OLDER AGE

Getting old isn't nearly as bad as people think it will be. Nor is it quite as good.

—Pew Research Center, "Growing Old in America: Expectations vs. Reality" (June 29, 2009)

In view of the myriad difficulties and challenges facing older adults, including ill health, inadequate financial resources, and the loss of friends and loved ones, it seems natural to assume that advancing age will be associated with less overall happiness and more worry. However, several studies refute this premise. Researchers find less worry among older adults than anticipated and note the ability of older adults to adapt to their changing life conditions.

In "The Real Roots of Midlife Crisis" (Atlantic.com, November 17, 2014), Jonathan Rauch explains that researchers have described happiness and age as a U-shaped

FIGURE 1.7

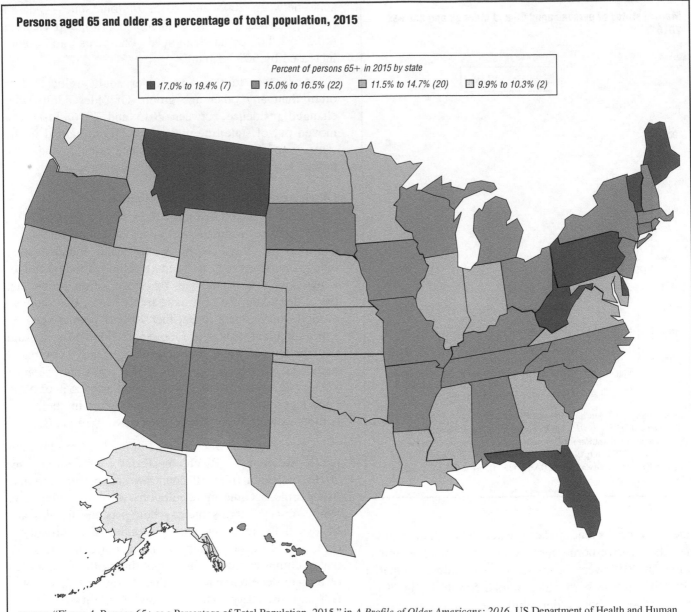

Persons aged 65 and older as a percentage of total population, 2015

Percent of persons 65+ in 2015 by state

■ 17.0% to 19.4% (7)   ■ 15.0% to 16.5% (22)   ■ 11.5% to 14.7% (20)   □ 9.9% to 10.3% (2)

SOURCE: "Figure 4. Persons 65+ as a Percentage of Total Population, 2015," in *A Profile of Older Americans: 2016*, US Department of Health and Human Services, Administration for Community Living, Administration on Aging, April 2017, https://www.acl.gov/sites/default/files/Aging%20and%20 Disability%20in%20America/2016-Profile.pdf (accessed October 13, 2017)

curve, with life satisfaction falling until it bottoms out during the late 40s or early 50s and then rising with age until the last years of life. The observed increase in happiness may be attributed to fewer responsibilities (child-rearing responsibilities are over, careers peak), and older adults tend to become more realistic in terms of their expectations of themselves and others.

Michael L. Thomas et al. report in "Paradoxical Trend for Improvement in Mental Health with Aging: A Community-Based Study of 1,546 Adults Aged 21–100 Years" (*Journal of Clinical Psychiatry*, vol. 77, no. 8, August 2016) on the results of a survey that looked at the mental health of more than 1,500 San Diego County, California, residents aged 21 to 99 years. The researchers

found that people in their 20s suffer the most stress and depression, while those in their 90s are the most content. Thomas et al. do not see the U-shaped curve observed by other researchers. Instead, they observe a direct linear relationship between age and mental health: the older people are, the less they experience stress, anxiety, and depression.

In "Why Elders Smile" (NYTimes.com, December 4, 2014), David Brooks suggests that older adults are more relaxed, in part because they do not have to worry about the future and are better able to enjoy the present. They are more adept at managing life's challenges and have mastered many life skills. Older adults also have perspective and recognize that "most setbacks are not the

TABLE 1.4

Population of persons aged 65 and older by state, 2015

State	Number of persons 65 and older[a]	Percent of all ages	Percent increase from 2005 to 2015	Percent below poverty 2015[b]
US total (50 states + DC)	47,760,852	14.9%	30.3%	8.8%
Alabama	764,162	15.7%	27.1%	9.9%
Alaska	72,837	9.9%	63.0%	4.5%
Arizona	1,120,054	16.4%	48.0%	9.0%
Arkansas	477,149	16.0%	24.2%	10.3%
California	5,188,754	13.3%	35.2%	9.9%
Colorado	711,625	13.0%	53.8%	7.0%
Connecticut	566,806	15.8%	19.3%	7.2%
Delaware	160,515	17.0%	43.2%	6.2%
District of Columbia	77,004	11.5%	15.8%	15.2%
Florida	3,942,468	19.4%	32.3%	10.3%
Georgia	1,304,924	12.8%	50.2%	9.7%
Hawaii	236,914	16.5%	35.4%	7.8%
Idaho	243,494	14.7%	47.8%	8.7%
Illinois	1,830,277	14.2%	20.6%	8.5%
Indiana	966,127	14.6%	24.4%	7.2%
Iowa	502,877	16.1%	15.1%	7.0%
Kansas	426,410	14.6%	19.6%	7.3%
Kentucky	672,765	15.2%	27.5%	11.2%
Louisiana	653,094	14.0%	22.7%	12.8%
Maine	250,536	18.8%	30.7%	8.8%
Maryland	849,571	14.1%	33.1%	7.3%
Massachusetts	1,045,222	15.4%	23.1%	9.2%
Michigan	1,570,671	15.8%	25.1%	7.8%
Minnesota	805,643	14.7%	29.7%	6.9%
Mississippi	439,701	14.7%	23.5%	12.5%
Missouri	954,922	15.7%	23.5%	8.5%
Montana	178,011	17.2%	37.3%	7.6%
Nebraska	278,711	14.7%	18.9%	7.4%
Nevada	422,118	14.6%	55.3%	8.4%
New Hampshire	218,942	16.5%	38.6%	6.1%
New Jersey	1,343,626	15.0%	20.0%	7.9%
New Mexico	330,405	15.8%	39.7%	11.1%
New York	2,964,315	15.0%	19.0%	11.2%
North Carolina	1,516,824	15.1%	43.2%	9.2%
North Dakota	107,281	14.2%	13.7%	8.9%
Ohio	1,842,952	15.9%	20.7%	7.6%
Oklahoma	576,250	14.7%	23.4%	8.4%
Oregon	660,876	16.4%	40.4%	7.3%
Pennsylvania	2,179,788	17.0%	15.5%	7.8%
Rhode Island	169,976	16.1%	14.5%	10.3%
South Carolina	794,795	16.2%	48.9%	9.3%
South Dakota	134,420	15.7%	22.6%	8.3%
Tennessee	1,016,552	15.4%	35.3%	9.8%
Texas	3,225,168	11.7%	42.9%	10.3%
Utah	307,867	10.3%	44.0%	6.8%
Vermont	109,893	17.6%	34.4%	6.6%
Virginia	1,188,393	14.2%	38.0%	7.3%
Washington	1,036,046	14.4%	45.0%	7.4%
West Virginia	336,288	18.2%	19.8%	8.5%
Wisconsin	902,134	15.6%	24.3%	7.1%
Wyoming	84,699	14.5%	36.1%	8.0%
Puerto Rico	626,962	18.0%	27.4%	41.0%

[a]Population estimates
[b]Poverty data for US are from the Current Population Survey, Poverty data for States and Puerto Rico are from the American Community Survey.

SOURCE: "Figure 6. The 65+ Population by State, 2015," in *A Profile of Older Americans: 2016*, US Department of Health and Human Services, Administration for Community Living, Administration on Aging, April 2017, https://www.acl.gov/sites/default/files/Aging%20and%20Disability%20in%20America/2016-Profile.pdf (accessed October 13, 2017)

end of the world," and their experience and empathy enable them to more accurately predict how events will unfold, closing the gap between expectations and reality.

Amit Bhattacharjee and Cassie Mogilner suggest in "Emotion Regulation in Older Age" (*Happiness from Ordinary and Extraordinary Experiences*, vol. 41, no. 1, June 2014) that older people seem better able than younger people to be happy with ordinary experiences such as seeing plants thriving in the garden or watching a movie. The researchers conclude, "young people actively looking to define themselves find it particularly rewarding to accumulate extraordinary experiences that mark their progression through life milestones. ... Once people grow older and have established a better sense of who they are, the experiences they view as self-defining are

FIGURE 1.8

Percentage increase in population aged 65 and older, 2005–15

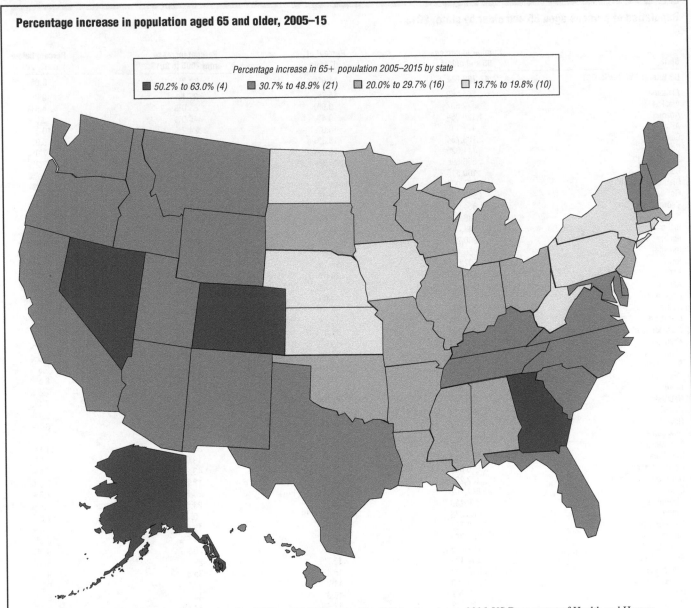

SOURCE: "Figure 5. Percent Increase in Population 65+, 2005 to 2015," in *A Profile of Older Americans: 2016*, US Department of Health and Human Services, Administration for Community Living, Administration on Aging, April 2017, https://www.acl.gov/sites/default/files/Aging%20and%20Disability%20in%20America/2016-Profile.pdf (accessed October 13, 2017)

just as likely to include the routine events that reveal how they like to spend their time."

Perceptions of Aging Influence Longevity and Happiness

In the landmark study "Longevity Increased by Positive Self-Perceptions of Aging" (*Journal of Personality and Social Psychology*, vol. 83, no. 2, August 2002), Becca R. Levy et al. report that older people with more positive self-perceptions of aging lived 7.5 years longer than those with less positive self-perceptions of aging, even after taking into account other factors, including age, gender, socioeconomic status, loneliness, and overall health. Analyzing data from the 660 participants aged 50 years and older in the Ohio Longitudinal Study of Aging and Retirement, the researchers compared mortality rates with responses made 23 years earlier by the participants. The responses included agreeing or disagreeing with statements such as "As you get older, you are less useful."

Levy et al. assert, "The effect of more positive self-perceptions of aging on survival is greater than the physiological measures of low systolic blood pressure and cholesterol, each of which is associated with a longer life span of 4 years or less. . . . [It] is also greater than the independent contribution of lower body mass index, no history of smoking, and a tendency to exercise; each of these factors has been found to contribute between 1 and 3 years of added life." They conclude that negative self-perceptions can diminish life expectancy, whereas positive self-perceptions can prolong it.

Andrew Steptoe and Jane Wardle of the University College London report in "Positive Affect Measured Using Ecological Momentary Assessment and Survival in Older Men and Women" (*Proceedings of the National Academy of Sciences*, vol. 108, no. 45, November 8, 2011), a study of more than 3,800 people aged 52 to 79 years, that those who said they were happiest had a 35% chance of living longer than those who said they felt least happy. The researchers conclude that their findings "provide further reason to target the positive well-being of older people. In addition to addressing the health status and material circumstances of older people, efforts to improve affective states may have beneficial health consequences."

Research conducted by Kerry A. Sargent-Cox, Kaarin J. Anstey, and Mary A. Luszcz and reported in "Longitudinal Change of Self-Perceptions of Aging and Mortality" (*Journals of Gerontology: Series B*, vol. 69, no. 2, February 18, 2013) confirms that how people view and interpret age-related changes influences their future health. Those who perceive age-related changes negatively are less likely to adapt well to these changes and, as a result, are more vulnerable to declining health.

In "Good Genes Are Nice, but Joy Is Better" (News.Harvard.edu, April 11, 2017), Liz Mineo reports on the results of an 80-year study of the health, well-being, and happiness of 268 Harvard University students who were sophomores at the university in 1938, when the study began. Over the years, the study grew to include the children of the original group. Researchers find that relationships, and how happy people are in their relationships, have a "powerful influence" on health. They also confirm that people who maintain close, warm relationships live longer than those who are isolated and lonely.

ATTITUDES ABOUT AGING

People of all ages hold beliefs and attitudes about aging and older adults. Even young children can distinguish age differences, and they display attitudes that appear to be characteristic of their generation. Because attitudes strongly influence behavior and because more Americans reach older ages than ever before, interaction with older people and deeply held beliefs about growing old are likely influenced by cultural and societal attitudes about aging and older adults. The availability, accessibility, adequacy, and acceptability of health care and other services intended to meet the needs of older people are similarly influenced by the attitudes of younger people. The prevailing attitudes and opinions of political leaders, decision makers, health and human services personnel, and taxpayers are particularly important in shaping policies, programs, services, and public sentiment.

In many countries and cultures, older people are held in high esteem. Their wisdom, experience, and contributions to the community are highly valued. Older adults are respected in some cases because they have endured and persevered in harsh living conditions and because they have accumulated wisdom and knowledge that younger generations need to survive and carry on the traditions of their culture. Examples outlined in "7 Cultures That Celebrate Aging and Respect Their Elders" (HuffingtonPost.com, February 25, 2014) include China, Greece, India, South Korea, and many Native American cultures.

In other cultures, older adults may be viewed as draining valuable or scarce resources. A person's worth may be measured in terms of income (the flow of money earned through employment, interest on investments, and other sources) and accumulated wealth. When older adults retire from full-time employment, they may lose status because they are no longer working, earning money, and "contributing" to society. When an individual's sense of self-worth and identity is closely bound to employment or occupation, retirement from the workforce can make him or her feel worthless. Anne Karpf discusses in "The Liberation of Growing Old" (NYTimes.com, January 3, 2015) such social attitudes and notes that, with many older adults remaining in the workforce or providing child care for working parents, "age can no longer be neatly correlated with economic activity."

Stereotypes Fuel Worries of Older Adults

Although people of all ages worry about the future, for older adults aging may signify a future threat to their health and well-being, diminished social status, a loss of power, and the possibility of a loss of control over their life. Researchers posit that social stereotypes, such as media portrayals of older adults as weak and helpless and of old age as a time of hardship, loss, and pain, have a powerful influence on attitudes and may be another source of worry for older adults. They contend that the image of a tragic old age can create worries about having a tragic old age. Worse still, the negative image of old age can become a self-fulfilling prophecy, thereby confirming negative stereotypes and promoting ageism (discrimination or unfair treatment based on age).

For example, in "Expectations about Memory Change across the Life Span Are Impacted by Aging Stereotypes" (*Psychology and Aging*, vol. 24, no. 1, March 2009), Tara T. Lineweaver, Andrea K. Berger, and Christopher Hertzog interviewed 373 people, in three different age groups, to assess their thoughts about memory throughout the adult life span. They were asked to rate the memory of different older adults, who were described as having positive or negative personality traits. Consistent with previous research, the study subjects believed that memory declines with advancing age. Furthermore, they rated adults described as having positive personality traits with having better memory ability and less age-related memory loss than those described as having negative personality traits. Another important finding was that the older subjects were more strongly influenced by the personality descriptions than the younger subjects.

Becca R. Levy et al. note in "Association between Positive Age Stereotypes and Recovery from Disability in Older Persons" (*Journal of the American Medical Association*, vol. 308, no. 19, November 21, 2012) that older adults who hold positive views of aging, such as associating it with wisdom, accomplishment, and satisfaction, are 44% more likely to fully recover from potentially disabling illnesses than those who hold negative stereotypes of aging. The researchers also report that older adults who view growing old as becoming helpless, useless, or unappreciated are less likely to seek preventive medical care and more likely to suffer from physical problems and memory loss.

Stereotypes about aging and older adults have become more negative over time. In "Increasing Negativity of Age Stereotypes across 200 Years: Evidence from a Database of 400 Million Words" (*PLOS One*, February 12, 2015), Reuben Ng et al. report that in 1880, age stereotypes reversed from positive to negative. The researchers attribute the medicalization of aging and the growing proportion of the population over the age of 65 as factors responsible for the rise in negative age stereotypes.

Bonnie Armstrong et al. report in "Stereotype Threat Effects on Older Adults' Episodic and Working Memory: A Meta-analysis" (*Gerontologist*, vol. 57, suppl. 2, August 1, 2017) that an analysis of 23 studies of older adults' memory performance found that exposure to negative age-based stereotypes can undermine older adults' memory test performance. Further, the investigators observed this negative effect on memory among older adults with varying levels of educational attainment.

Baby Boomers Challenge Stereotypes

Since their inception, baby boomers have left their mark on every US institution. As teenagers and young adults, they created and championed a unique blend of music, pop culture, and political activism. They have witnessed remarkable technological and medical advancements during their lifetime and have come to expect, and even loudly demand, solutions to health and social problems.

As the baby boomers join the ranks of older Americans, they are fomenting a cultural revolution. The boomers approaching age 65 are not content to be regarded as "old." Accustomed to freedom and independence, they want to be recognized and treated as individuals rather than as stereotypes. Overall, the aging boomers are better educated, healthier, and wealthier than any other older adult cohort in history. They are living longer, and many are redefining old age by reinventing retirement, continuing to pursue health, and challenging the public's perception of what it is to be old.

Although baby boomers are living longer than previous generations, they are not necessarily healthier in their 60s. Dana E. King et al. report in "The Status of Baby Boomers' Health in the United States: The Healthiest Generation?" (*JAMA Internal Medicine*, vol. 173, no. 5, March 11, 2013) that boomers suffer from more chronic diseases than past generations. They are more likely to be obese and to suffer from high blood pressure and high cholesterol (factors that are associated with increased risk of disease). Compared with their predecessors, they are more likely to be disabled, exercise less frequently, and consume more alcohol. According to King et al., one positive aspect is that fewer boomers have smoked cigarettes and, therefore, fewer suffer from smoking-related illnesses such as emphysema. Still, fewer describe themselves as in "excellent" health—just 13.2%, compared with 32% of the previous generation.

In "Sixty-Five Isn't What It Used to Be: Changes and Trends in the Perceptions of Older Adults" (*International Social Science Review*, vol. 88, no. 3, 2014), Mari Plikuhn, Ashlee Niehaus, and Rebecca D. Reeves report that perceptions of older adults have become less negative among both adults aged 18 to 64 years and adults aged 65 years and older. The researchers state that "a growing understanding of issues faced by older adults has led to a more realistic and positive view of the older years and a decline in negative stereotypes often associated with aging." Negative stereotypes associate aging with loneliness and poor health. Plikuhn, Niehaus, and Reeves credit the dramatic decline in negative perceptions and stereotypes of older adults in large part to the increasingly positive portrayal of older adults in the media and changing social attitudes about aging.

Baby boomers are redefining the meaning of aging and retirement. Tracy Carpenter-Aeby et al. note in "Exploring the Quality of Life for Baby Boomers Using a Systematic Literature Review" (*Medica Press*, vol. 1, no. 1, 2017) that boomers place a high value on their health and independence and that it will therefore be important for this generation to remain physically active and engaged in their communities. The researchers observe that providing aging boomers with a good quality of life will call for novel housing and community models and enhanced technology to deliver health care, transportation, and information services, along with improvements in mental health and substance abuse services and programs to prevent and treat chronic health conditions.

CHAPTER 2
THE ECONOMICS OF GROWING OLD IN THE UNITED STATES

Security was attained in the earlier days through the interdependence of members of families upon each other and of the families within a small community upon each other. The complexities of great communities and of organized industry make less real these simple means of security. Therefore, we are compelled to employ the active interest of the Nation as a whole through government in order to encourage a greater security for each individual who composes it. ... This seeking for a greater measure of welfare and happiness does not indicate a change in values. It is rather a return to values lost in the course of our economic development and expansion.

—Franklin D. Roosevelt, Message of the President to Congress, June 8, 1934

The economic status of older Americans (defined as those aged 65 years and older) is more varied than that of any other age group. Although some older adults are well off, most have limited resources. As a whole, the older US population has a lower economic status than the overall adult population. During retirement most people rely on Social Security (a program that provides retirement income and health care for older adults) and are supplemented by pensions and assets. Some must also depend on Supplemental Security Income (SSI), a federal assistance program administered by the Social Security Administration (SSA) that guarantees a minimum level of income for needy older, blind, and/or disabled individuals. It acts as a safety net for individuals who have little or no Social Security or other income and limited resources.

With fixed incomes and sharply limited potential to improve their incomes through employment, many older people become vulnerable to circumstances such as the loss of a spouse, prolonged illness, or even economic variations such as inflation or recession that further compromise their financial well-being, sometimes plunging them into poverty. One common scenario is a couple that has planned well for retirement but runs through all their assets to pay the health care costs of a long-term illness.

When the ill partner dies, the surviving spouse is left impoverished. Another example is retirees who discover, as many people did during the latter half of the first decade of the 21st century, that their retirement accounts had lost more than half of their value.

Some older adults may want to return to work, but their prospects are uncertain. The Great Recession (which lasted from late 2007 to mid-2009) resulted in historically high rates of unemployment across all age groups. Those rates declined after 2009. In 2010 employment growth resumed, and by December 2014 the labor force participation rate for Americans aged 55 years and older was higher than at the start of the recession. The labor force participation rate of this group has remained relatively stable since then. According to the US Bureau of Labor Statistics (BLS), in "Employment—Population Ratio and Labor Force Participation Rate by Age" (August 9, 2017, https://www.bls.gov/opub/ted/2017/employment-population-ratio-and-labor-force-participation-rate-by-age.htm), it was 38.8% in July 2017. Similarly, the unemployment rate among those aged 55 years and older remained low and stable from July 2016 to July 2017. In *The Employment Situation—July 2017* (August 4, 2017, https://www.bls.gov/news.release/archives/empsit_08042017.htm), the BLS indicates that it was just 3.2% in July 2017. By contrast, 11.6% of people aged 18 to 19 years and 7.4% of people aged 20 to 24 years were unemployed in July 2017.

In "Why Some Scars from the Recession May Never Vanish" (NYTimes.com, October 5, 2017), Ben Casselman observes that although the US economy created almost 16 million new jobs during the eight years after the Great Recession, many workers continued to suffer the effects of the recession. For example, parts of the country, such as Cleveland and Memphis, did not experience economic recovery during that period, and nearly 2 million more workers were receiving federal disability payments in 2017 than when the recession began in 2007. According to Casselman, some economists have attributed this uptick in disability claims to the fact that the US population is aging.

THE ECONOMIC WELL-BEING OF OLDER ADULTS

There are two important measures of an individual's or household's economic well-being. One is income, defined as the flow of money earned through employment, interest on investments, and other sources. The other is asset accumulation or wealth, the economic resources (property or other material possessions) owned by an individual or household.

Income Distribution

Jessica L. Semega, Kayla R. Fontenot, and Melissa A. Kollar of the US Census Bureau note in *Income and Poverty in the United States: 2016* (September 2017, https://www.census.gov/content/dam/Census/library/publications/2017/demo/P60-259.pdf) that from 2015 to 2016 the number of people living in poverty decreased for all age groups except people aged 65 years and older. Among these older adults, the poverty rate increased from 8.8% in 2015 to 9.3% in 2016.

The Census Bureau's official poverty measure does not take into account all the government programs designed to assist low-income families and individuals. The bureau introduced the Supplemental Poverty Measure (SPM) to account for many of these programs when assessing poverty levels. For example, the SPM considers the value of in-kind benefits, such as the Supplemental Nutrition Assistance Program (formerly known as the Food Stamp Program) and housing assistance. The overall SPM poverty rate decreased from 14.5% in 2015 to 14% in 2016. (See Figure 2.1.) It increased, however, among people aged 65 years and older, from 13.7% in 2015 to 14.5% in 2016.

According to the official poverty measure, an estimated 4.6 million older adults (9.3% of the older population) lived in poverty in 2016. (See Table 2.1.) By contrast, the SPM estimates that 7.2 million older adults (14.5% of the older population) were living in poverty.

In *A Profile of Older Americans: 2016* (April 2017, https://www.acl.gov/sites/default/files/Aging%20and%20Disability%20in%20America/2016-Profile.pdf), the Administration on Aging (AoA) indicates that the median reported income (the middle value; half of all people earn less and half earn more) for older adults in 2015 was $31,372 for males and $18,250 for females. Figure 2.2 shows the distribution of income among households headed by older adults. Households headed

FIGURE 2.1

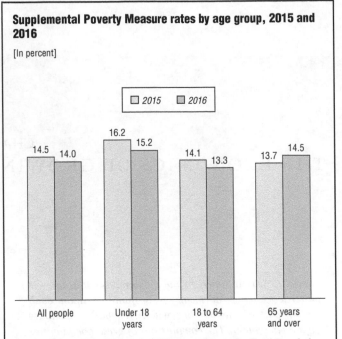

Supplemental Poverty Measure rates by age group, 2015 and 2016

[In percent]

SOURCE: Liana Fox, "Figure 1. SPM Poverty Rates for Total Population and by Age Group: 2015 and 2016," in *The Supplemental Poverty Measure: 2016*, US Census Bureau, September 2017, https://www.census.gov/content/dam/Census/library/publications/2017/demo/p60-261.pdf (accessed October 16, 2017)

by people aged 65 years and older had a median income of $57,360 in 2015, whereas the individual median income for older adults was $22,887. More than half (56%) of households headed by an older adult had an income of $50,000 or more, and 5% had an income less than $15,000. The AoA further reports that median household income for older adults in 2015 was highest for Asian Americans ($64,688), followed by non-Hispanic whites ($60,266), African Americans ($43,855), and Hispanics ($42,334).

Sources of Income

Unlike younger adults, who derive most of their income from employment, older adults rely on a variety of sources of income to meet their expenses. Since the 1960s Social Security has provided the largest share of income for older Americans. In 2014 Social Security benefits were a major source of income, providing at least 50% of total income reported for 61% of older beneficiaries. (See Figure 2.3.) For 33% of older beneficiaries, Social Security played an even bigger role, providing at least 90% of their total income.

The AoA explains in *Profile of Older Americans: 2016* that the income for most older adults comes from four main sources: Social Security, earnings, assets, and pensions. In 2014 Social Security accounted for 33%, earnings provided 32%, pensions (government employee

TABLE 2.1

Number and percentage of people in poverty by two poverty measures, 2016

[Numbers in thousands]

Characteristic	Number[a] (in thousands)	Official[a] Number Estimate	Official[a] Percent Estimate	SPM Number Estimate	SPM Percent Estimate	Difference Number	Difference Percent
All people	320,372	40,706	12.7	44,752	14.0	4,046	1.3
Sex							
Male	156,939	17,739	11.3	20,693	13.2	2,954	1.9
Female	163,433	22,967	14.1	24,059	14.7	1,092	0.7
Age							
Under 18 years	74,047	13,344	18.0	11,281	15.2	−2,062	−2.8
18 to 64 years	197,051	22,795	11.6	26,303	13.3	3,508	1.8
65 years and older	49,274	4,568	9.3	7,168	14.5	2,600	5.3
Type of unit							
Married couple	192,344	11,257	5.9	16,516	8.6	5,260	2.7
Cohabiting partners	24,994	6,576	26.3	3,261	13.0	−3,314	−13.3
Female reference person	42,758	11,647	27.2	11,655	27.3	7	Z
Male reference person	15,030	1,814	12.1	2,635	17.5	821	5.5
Unrelated individuals	45,246	9,413	20.8	10,685	23.6	1,272	2.8
Race[b] and Hispanic origin							
White	246,310	27,174	11.0	30,717	12.5	3,543	1.4
White, not Hispanic	195,453	17,304	8.9	19,446	9.9	2,142	1.1
Black	42,040	9,248	22.0	9,086	21.6	−162	−0.4
Asian	18,897	1,917	10.1	2,774	14.7	857	4.5
Hispanic (any race)	57,670	11,160	19.4	12,670	22.0	1,511	2.6
Nativity							
Native born	276,518	34,079	12.3	35,515	12.8	1,437	0.5
Foreign born	43,854	6,627	15.1	9,237	21.1	2,609	6.0
Naturalized citizen	20,409	2,045	10.0	3,205	15.7	1,160	5.7
Not a citizen	23,445	4,582	19.5	6,032	25.7	1,449	6.2
Educational attainment							
Total aged 25 and older	216,921	22,636	10.4	27,929	12.9	5,293	2.4
No high school diploma	22,541	5,599	24.8	6,356	28.2	757	3.4
High school, no college	62,512	8,309	13.3	10,139	16.2	1,830	2.9
Some college	57,765	5,430	9.4	6,615	11.5	1,184	2.1
Bachelor's degree or higher	74,103	3,299	4.5	4,819	6.5	1,521	2.1
Tenure							
Owner	210,698	14,761	7.0	19,149	9.1	4,388	2.1
Owner/mortgage	136,731	6,739	4.9	10,122	7.4	3,383	2.5
Owner/no mortgage/rent free	77,320	8,891	11.5	9,825	12.7	934	1.2
Renter	106,321	25,077	23.6	24,806	23.3	−271	−0.3
Residence							
Inside metropolitan statistical areas	276,816	33,808	12.2	39,125	14.1	5,317	1.9
Inside principal cities	104,295	16,598	15.9	18,057	17.3	1,459	1.4
Outside principal cities	172,521	17,211	10.0	21,068	12.2	3,858	2.2
Outside metropolitan statistical areas[c]	43,556	6,898	15.8	5,627	12.9	−1,271	−2.9
Region							
Northeast	55,558	5,982	10.8	6,874	12.4	892	1.6
Midwest	67,016	7,829	11.7	7,424	11.1	−406	−0.6
South	121,325	17,056	14.1	17,966	14.8	909	0.7
West	76,473	9,838	12.9	12,489	16.3	2,650	3.5
Health insurance coverage							
With private insurance	216,203	11,635	5.4	17,898	8.3	6,264	2.9
With public, no private insurance	76,117	22,446	29.5	19,646	25.8	−2,799	−3.7
Not insured	28,052	6,626	23.6	7,208	25.7	582	2.1
Work experience							
Total 18 to 64 years	197,051	22,795	11.6	26,303	13.3	3,508	1.8
All workers	150,904	8,743	5.8	12,111	8.0	3,368	2.2
Worked full-time, year-round	107,781	2,416	2.2	5,099	4.7	2,683	2.5
Less than full-time, year-round	43,123	6,327	14.7	7,012	16.3	685	1.6
Did not work at least 1 week	46,148	14,052	30.5	14,193	30.8	141	0.3

and private combined) contributed 21%, asset income accounted for 10%, and other sources added 4% of income for older adults. Figure 2.4 compares the sources of income for older adults in 1962 and 2014.

TABLE 2.1

Number and percentage of people in poverty by two poverty measures, 2016 [CONTINUED]

[Numbers in thousands]

Characteristic	Number[a] (in thousands)	Official[a] Number Estimate	Official[a] Percent Estimate	SPM Number Estimate	SPM Percent Estimate	Difference Number	Difference Percent
Disability status[d]							
Total 18 to 64 years	197,051	22,795	11.6	26,303	13.3	3,508	1.8
With a disability	15,405	4,123	26.8	3,905	25.4	−218	−1.4
With no disability	180,783	18,629	10.3	22,350	12.4	3,720	2.1

Z represents or rounds to zero.

[a]Includes unrelated individuals under the age of 15.

[b]Federal surveys give respondents the option of reporting more than one race. Therefore, two basic ways of defining a race group are possible. A group such as Asian may be defined as those who reported Asian and no other race (the race-alone or single-race concept) or as those who reported Asian regardless of whether they also reported another race (the race-alone-or-in-combination concept). This table shows data using the first approach (race alone). The use of the single-race population does not imply that it is the preferred method of presenting or analyzing data. The Census Bureau uses a variety of approaches. About 2.9 percent of people reported more than one race in the 2010 Census. Data for American Indians and Alaska Natives, Native Hawaiians and Other Pacific Islanders, and those reporting two or more races are not shown separately.

[c]The "Outside metropolitan statistical areas" category includes both micropolitan statistical areas and territory outside of metropolitan and micropolitan statistical areas.

[d]The sum of those with and without a disability does not equal the total because disability status is not defined for individuals in the US Armed Forces.

Note: Details may not sum to totals due to rounding. SPM = Supplemental Poverty Measure

SOURCE: Liana Fox, "Appendix Table A-2. Number and Percentage of People in Poverty by Different Poverty Measures: 2016," in *The Supplemental Poverty Measure: 2016*, US Census Bureau Current Population Reports, September 2017, https://www.census.gov/content/dam/Census/library/publications/2017/demo/p60-261.pdf (accessed October 16, 2017)

FIGURE 2.2

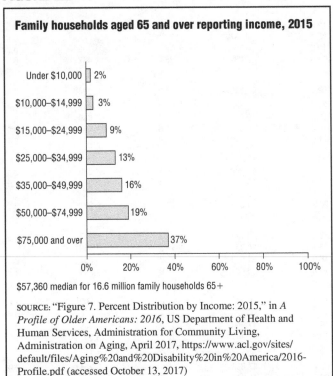

Family households aged 65 and over reporting income, 2015

$57,360 median for 16.6 million family households 65+

SOURCE: "Figure 7. Percent Distribution by Income: 2015," in *A Profile of Older Americans: 2016*, US Department of Health and Human Services, Administration for Community Living, Administration on Aging, April 2017, https://www.acl.gov/sites/default/files/Aging%20and%20Disability%20in%20America/2016-Profile.pdf (accessed October 13, 2017)

FIGURE 2.3

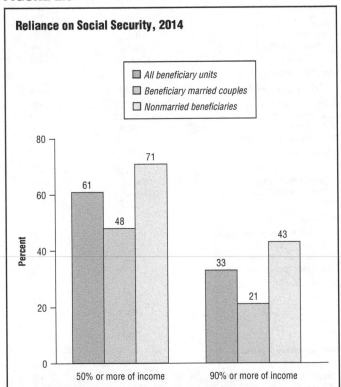

Reliance on Social Security, 2014

Note: A beneficiary unit is a married couple living together or a nonmarried person, which also includes persons who are separated or married but not living together.

SOURCE: "Percentage of Aged Units Receiving Social Security Benefits, by Relative Importance of Benefits to Total Income," in *Fast Facts and Figures about Social Security, 2016*, US Social Security Administration, Office of Retirement and Disability Policy, August 2016, https://www.ssa.gov/policy/docs/chartbooks/fast_facts/2016/fast_facts16.pdf (accessed October 16, 2017)

Pension Funds

Historically, many large employers, along with most local and state governments and the federal government, offered pension plans for retirement. In 1875 American Express Company established the first private pension plan (an employer-run retirement program) in the United States. General Motors Corporation provided the first modern plan during the 1940s.

Employers are not required to provide pensions, and pension plans do not have to include all workers; they

FIGURE 2.4

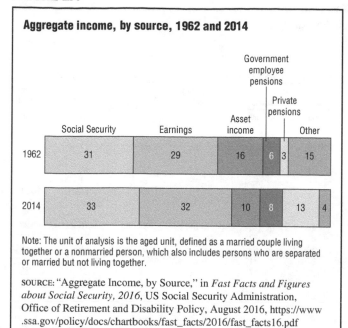

Aggregate income, by source, 1962 and 2014

	Social Security	Earnings	Asset income	Government employee pensions	Private pensions	Other
1962	31	29	16	6	3	15
2014	33	32	10	8	13	4

Note: The unit of analysis is the aged unit, defined as a married couple living together or a nonmarried person, which also includes persons who are separated or married but not living together.

SOURCE: "Aggregate Income, by Source," in *Fast Facts and Figures about Social Security, 2016*, US Social Security Administration, Office of Retirement and Disability Policy, August 2016, https://www.ssa.gov/policy/docs/chartbooks/fast_facts/2016/fast_facts16.pdf (accessed October 16, 2017)

may exclude certain jobs and/or individuals. Before 1976 pension plans could require an employee to work a lifetime for one company before becoming eligible for pension benefits. As required by the Employee Retirement Income Security Act (ERISA) of 1974, starting in 1976 an employee became eligible after 10 years of service. By 2000 most plans required five years of work before an employee became vested (eligible for benefits). In companies that offer pension plans, employees are eligible to begin receiving benefits when they retire or leave the company if they have worked for the requisite number of years and/or have reached the specified eligibility age.

DEFINED BENEFIT PLANS AND DEFINED CONTRIBUTION PLANS. There are two principal types of pension plans: defined benefit plans and defined contribution plans. As described earlier, defined benefit plans promise employees a specified monthly benefit at retirement. A defined benefit plan may stipulate the promised benefit as an exact dollar amount, such as $100 per month at retirement. More often, however, benefits are calculated using a plan formula that considers both salary and service—for example, 1% of the average salary for the last five years of employment multiplied by years of service with the employer.

A defined contribution plan does not promise employees a specific amount of benefits at retirement. Instead, the employee and/or employer contribute to a plan account, sometimes at a set rate, such as 5% of earnings annually. Generally, these contributions are invested on the employee's behalf, and the amount of future benefits varies depending on investment earnings.

An example of a defined contribution plan is the 401(k) plan. This plan allows employees to defer receiving a portion of their salary, which is contributed on their behalf to the plan. Income taxes are deferred until the money is withdrawn at retirement. In some instances employers match employee contributions. Created in 1978, these plans were named for section 401(k) of the Internal Revenue Code.

According to the Employee Benefit Research Institute, in "FAQs about Benefits—Retirement Issues" (2018, https://www.ebri.org/publications/benfaq/index.cfm?fa=retfaq14), in 2014 just 13% of US private-sector workers had a pension plan that provides a defined benefit, down from 28% in 1979. Although participation in defined benefit plans has declined, there has been increased participation in defined contribution plans that grow in response to employer and worker contributions. In 2017 access to retirement benefits ranged from 42% for workers in service occupations to 82% for professionals and those in management. (See Table 2.2.) Since the mid-1990s many employers have converted their defined benefit plans to hybrid plans that incorporate elements of both defined benefit and defined contribution plans. For example, cash balance plans are based on defined contributions of pay credits (based on an employee's compensation rate) and interest credits that are deposited annually by the employer into an account, the balance of which serves as the defined benefit.

PRIVATE AND PUBLIC PENSIONS. The SSA reports in *Fast Facts and Figures about Social Security, 2016* (August 2016, https://www.ssa.gov/policy/docs/chartbooks/fast_facts/2016/fast_facts16.pdf) that the proportion of older adults' income from pensions has grown markedly since the 1960s, with private pensions quadrupling by 2014. (See Figure 2.5.) During the same period the proportion of people receiving government employee pensions increased from 9% to 16%. The proportion of older adults with income from assets, the second-most-common source of income after Social Security, was slightly higher in 2014 (62%) than in 1962 (54%). The proportion of older adults with earned income declined from 36% in 1962 to 29% in 2014.

Unlike Social Security and many public plans, most private pension plans do not provide automatic cost-of-living adjustments. Without these adjustments, many retirees' incomes and purchasing power erode. Military, government, and Railroad Retirement pensioners are more likely to receive cost-of-living increases than are pensioners in the private sector.

FEDERAL PENSION LAWS. Pension plan funds are often invested in stocks and bonds, much as banks invest their depositors' money. When the investment choice is a good one, the company makes a profit on the money in the fund; bad investments result in losses.

TABLE 2.2

Percentage of private and public sector workers with retirement plan benefits, 2017

[All workers = 100 percent]

Characteristics	Civilian[a]			Private industry			State and local government		
	Access	Participation	Take-up rate	Access	Participation	Take-up rate	Access	Participation	Take-up rate
All workers	70	54	77	66	50	75	91	80	88
Worker characteristics									
Management, professional, and related	85	73	86	82	70	86	94	81	86
Management, business, and financial	88	77	88	87	76	88	—	—	—
Professional and related	84	71	85	79	67	84	93	80	86
Teachers	85	74	87	—	—	—	94	81	86
Primary, secondary, and special education school teachers	94	82	87	—	—	—	99	86	87
Registered nurses	89	74	84	—	—	—	—	—	—
Service	47	30	62	42	22	54	84	76	90
Protective service	79	63	80	61	32	52	92	86	94
Sales and office	72	53	74	70	51	72	91	80	88
Sales and related	67	41	62	67	41	61	—	—	—
Office and administrative support	75	60	80	72	57	79	92	81	88
Natural resources, construction, and maintenance	66	52	79	63	48	77	97	89	91
Construction, extraction, farming, fishing, and forestry	62	49	80	58	45	78	—	—	—
Installation, maintenance, and repair	69	54	78	67	51	76	—	—	—
Production, transportation, and material moving	71	54	76	71	53	75	90	80	89
Production	74	56	76	74	56	76	—	—	—
Transportation and material moving	69	52	75	68	50	74	—	—	—
Full time	81	65	80	77	60	78	99	87	88
Part time	38	22	59	38	21	56	46	39	84
Union	94	83	88	92	82	90	97	83	86
Nonunion	66	49	75	64	47	73	86	77	89
Average wage within the following categories:[b]									
Lowest 25 percent	45	25	55	42	21	51	78	68	87
Lowest 10 percent	34	15	44	33	14	41	67	58	87
Second 25 percent	70	52	74	66	46	70	94	83	88
Third 25 percent	82	68	83	78	64	81	98	86	88
Highest 25 percent	90	80	89	88	77	88	97	84	87
Highest 10 percent	91	81	89	89	81	90	96	82	85
Establishment characteristics									
Goods-producing industries	75	60	80	75	60	80	—	—	—
Service-providing industries	69	53	77	65	48	74	91	80	88
Education and health services	80	65	81	72	57	79	93	79	85
Educational services	88	76	86	72	64	89	93	79	86
Elementary and secondary schools	90	78	87	—	—	—	93	80	86
Junior colleges, colleges, and universities	91	77	85	88	78	89	92	76	83
Health care and social assistance	74	57	78	72	56	77	93	78	83
Hospitals	91	78	86	—	—	—	93	77	83
Public administration	91	84	92	—	—	—	91	84	92
1 to 99 workers	55	40	73	53	37	71	87	79	90
1 to 49 workers	50	36	72	49	34	71	85	78	91
50 to 99 workers	68	50	73	65	46	70	90	80	89
100 workers or more	85	68	80	83	65	78	93	80	87
100 to 499 workers	80	61	76	79	58	73	91	81	90
500 workers or more	91	77	85	89	76	85	93	80	86
Geographic areas									
Northeast	72	58	82	68	55	80	91	80	88
New England	73	57	78	71	55	78	86	68	80
Middle Atlantic	71	59	83	67	54	81	93	84	90
South	71	53	74	67	47	71	94	83	89
South Atlantic	71	54	76	68	50	74	92	79	87
East South Central	72	50	70	68	44	64	94	85	91
West South Central	70	52	74	65	45	69	97	87	90
Midwest	73	56	77	70	53	75	90	76	85
East North Central	72	55	76	70	52	75	88	74	84
West North Central	75	58	77	72	54	75	92	80	87
West	64	51	79	60	46	77	89	78	88
Mountain	66	52	78	63	47	75	86	78	91
Pacific	63	50	80	58	45	78	90	79	87

During the early 1970s several major plans were terminated before they accumulated sufficient assets to pay employees and their beneficiaries retirement benefits. These asset-poor plans were unable to make good on their promises, leaving retirees without benefits despite their years of service.

TABLE 2.2

Percentage of private and public sector workers with retirement plan benefits, 2017 [CONTINUED]

[All workers = 100 percent]

ªIncludes workers in private industry and state and local government.
ᵇSurveyed occupations are classified into wage categories based on the average wage for the occupation, which may include workers with earnings both above and below the threshold. The categories were formed using percentile estimates generated using wage data for March 2017.
Notes: Includes defined benefit pension plans and defined contribution retirement plans. Workers are considered as having access or as participating if they have access to or are participating in at least one of these plan types. The take-up rate is an estimate of the percentage of workers with access to a plan who participate in the plan, rounded for presentation. Dash indicates no workers in this category or data did not meet publication criteria.

SOURCE: "Table 1. Retirement Benefits: Access, Participation, and Take-Up Rates, March 2017," in *Employee Benefits in the United States—March 2017*, US Department of Labor, Bureau of Labor Statistics, July 21, 2017, https://www.bls.gov/news.release/pdf/ebs2.pdf (accessed October 16, 2017)

FIGURE 2.5

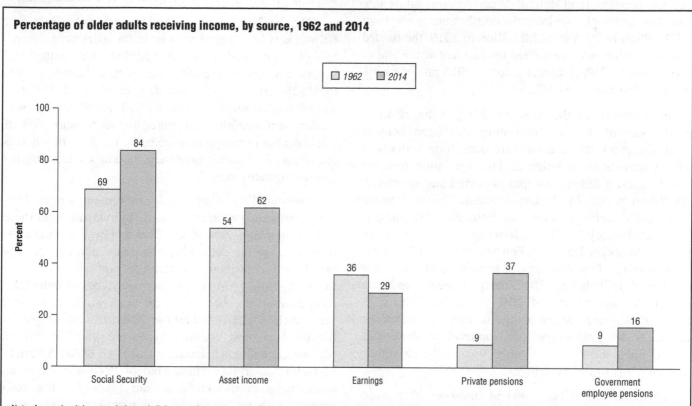

Percentage of older adults receiving income, by source, 1962 and 2014

Note: An aged unit is a married couple living together or a nonmarried person, which also includes persons who are separated or married but not living together.

SOURCE: "Percentage of Aged Units Receiving Income, by Source," in *Fast Facts and Figures about Social Security, 2016*, US Social Security Administration, Office of Retirement and Disability Policy, August 2016, https://www.ssa.gov/policy/docs/chartbooks/fast_facts/2016/fast_facts16.pdf (accessed October 16, 2017)

To protect retirement plan participants and their beneficiaries from these catastrophic losses, ERISA was passed in 1974. ERISA established a new set of rules for participation, added mandatory and quicker vesting schedules, fixed minimum funding standards, and set standards of conduct for administering plans and handling plan assets. It also required the disclosure of plan information, established a system for insuring the payment of pension benefits, and created Pension Benefit Guaranty Corporation, a federal corporation, to provide uninterrupted benefit payments when pension plans are terminated.

The Retirement Equity Act of 1984 requires pension plans to pay a survivor's benefit to the spouse of a deceased vested plan participant. Before 1984 some spouses received no benefits unless the employee was near retirement age at the time of death. Under the 1984 law, pension vesting begins at age 21, or after five years of being on the job, and employees who have a break in employment for reasons such as maternity leave do not lose any time already accumulated.

PENSION FUNDS DECLINE. Because both private and public pension funds are invested in the stock market, many pensions suffered serious losses in response to the Great Recession and its aftereffects. According to Zorast Wadia, Alan H. Perry, and Charles J. Clark, in *Milliman 2017 Corporate Pension Funding Study* (April 2017,

http://www.milliman.com/uploadedFiles/insight/2017/2017
-corporate-pension-funding-study.pdf), the 100 largest
corporate defined benefit pension plans suffered a $22
billion loss of funded status in fiscal year 2016, as even
robust stock market returns were unable to compensate for
past market downturns, unrealistic financial projections, a
spike in the number of retirees, and benefit increases made
during better times.

The losses in funding sustained during and after the
recession, along with the funding requirements of the
Pension Protection Act of 2006, which provides significant tax incentives to enhance and protect retirement
savings for millions of Americans, combined to create a
growing pension fund deficit. Wadia, Perry, and Clark
note that, although employers' contributions grew from
$31.1 billion in 2015 to $42.8 billion in 2016, the funded
ratio of pension plans remained unchanged; at the end of
2016 it was 81.2%, comparable to the 2015 rate of 81.9%
and the 2014 rate of 81.6%.

Furthermore, at the close of 2014, in an effort to
assist some of the country's most distressed pension
plans, Congress passed a measure permitting benefits of
current retirees to be reduced. The legislation reversed
four decades of federal law that protected already-earned
benefits from cuts. In "In Unprecedented Move, Pension
Plan Cuts Benefits Promised to Retirees" (Washington
Post.com, January 27, 2017), Jonnelle Marte reports that
the Iron Workers Local 17 Pension fund in Cleveland,
Ohio, was the first plan to cut benefits under the new
legislation. In February 2017 the plan began reducing
benefits by an average of 20% for about half of its
2,000 participants. Marte suggests that advocates for
retirement security worry that approval of these cuts
"could open the door for other financially struggling
pension plans to follow suit."

There have also been several instances of pension
fraud. For example, the article "Consultant Pleads Guilty
to Fraud, Pension Fund Theft" (Associated Press, September 15, 2017) indicates that in 2017 a consultant to a
Rhode Island medical firm pleaded guilty to embezzling
more than $700,000 from employees' retirement accounts
between 2007 and 2013.

Another recent instance of alleged pension fraud
involved former director of fixed income and head of
portfolio strategy at the New York State Common Retirement Fund, which is the investment arm of the New York
State and Local Employees' Retirement System and the
New York State and Local Police and Fire Retirement
System. In "N.Y. Pension Fund Manager Pleads Not
Guilty to Pay-to-Play Scheme" (Reuters, January 4,
2017), Nate Raymond reports that Navnoor Kang was
charged with steering $2 billion in trades to two broker-
ages in exchange for bribes that included vacations,
cocaine, and prostitutes.

Personal Savings

One of the most effective ways to prepare for retirement is to save for it. In the Employee Benefit Research
Institute issue brief *The 2017 Retirement Confidence Survey: Many Workers Lack Retirement Confidence and Feel
Stressed about Retirement Preparations* (March 21, 2017,
https://www.ebri.org/pdf/surveys/rcs/2017/IB.431.Mar17
.RCS17..21Mar17.pdf), Lisa Greenwald, Craig Cope-
land, and Jack VanDerhei present the results of the
2017 Retirement Confidence Survey. They report that
just 18% of Americans are very confident and 42% are
somewhat confident that they will have enough money
to live comfortably in retirement. The most confident
workers are those who participate in retirement plans.

The 2017 Retirement Confidence Survey finds that
US workers have saved very little for retirement. Nearly
half (47%) of workers reported having total savings and
investments, excluding the value of their homes, of less
than $25,000, and 24% said they have saved less than
$1,000 for retirement. Because this level of savings will
render them woefully unprepared for retirement, 57% of
workers plan to postpone retirement, and 50% of workers
are planning to supplement their income by working for
pay during retirement.

One popular way to save for retirement is to contribute to individual retirement plans. Individuals fund these
retirement plans themselves. The money that they contribute can be tax deductible, the plans' earnings are not
taxed, and contributors determine how the money is
invested. Since 1974 one of the major types of individual
retirement plans has been the individual retirement
account (IRA). IRAs fall into several different categories,
but the two most common types are traditional IRAs
(deductible and nondeductible) and Roth IRAs. A variety
of factors determine which kind of IRA best serves an
individual's needs. Profit-sharing plans for the self-
employed (formerly called Keogh plans) are another type
of individual retirement plan.

The 2017 Retirement Confidence Survey finds that
workers believe their retirement income will come from a
variety of sources. About three-quarters (78%) of US workers anticipate that their retirement income will primarily
come from an employer-sponsored retirement savings plan,
69% will rely on personal savings and investments, 64%
will rely on their IRAs as a source of income, 64% said
employment will be a source of income during retirement,
and 54% expect to receive a traditional pension.

NET WORTH

Because the economic well-being of households
depends on both income and wealth, assessment of
income alone is not the best measure of older adults'
financial health. To draw a more complete economic
profile of the older population, it is necessary to evaluate

older households in terms of measures of wealth, such as home equity, savings, and other assets and liabilities. For example, a household may be in the top one-fifth of income distribution but be saddled with a large amount of debt.

Net worth is a measure of economic valuation and an indicator of financial security that is obtained by subtracting total liabilities from total assets. Greater net worth enables individuals and households to weather financial challenges such as illness, disability, job loss, divorce, widowhood, or general economic downturns.

The Federal Reserve Board conducts a Survey of Consumer Finances every three years. The 2016 survey

(*Federal Reserve Bulletin*, vol. 103, no. 3, September 2017) reports that from 2013 to 2016 all age groups experienced increases in median family income. The median family income increased 10%, and the median net worth grew 16%. Adults aged 65 to 74 years did not, however, realize these gains. Between 2013 and 2016 their median income grew just 6% and their median net worth decreased 6%. (See Table 2.3 and Table 2.4.)

Older Adults Are Hard Hit by Low Interest Rates

According to Lauren Silva Laughlin, in "Here's the Bad News about Long-Term Interest Rates" (Fortune .com, April 5, 2016), low interest rates stimulate some sectors of the economy but actually harm retirees. Low

TABLE 2.3

Family income by age and other characteristics, 2013 and 2016

[Thousands of 2016 dollars, except as noted]

Family characteristic	Median income			Mean income		
	2013	2016	Percent change 2013–16	2013	2016	Percent change 2013–16
All families	48.1	52.7	10	89.9	102.7	14
Percentile of usual income						
Less than 20	15.7	16.2	3	15.7	17.1	9
20–39.9	31.4	33.1	5	31.4	34.2	9
40–59.9	50.2	54.1	8	51.1	54.8	7
60–79.9	80.3	86.1	7	82.5	94.1	14
80–89.9	125.5	135.3	8	127.3	139.4	10
90–100	230.1	251.5	9	409.9	487.5	19
Age of head (years)						
Less than 35	36.4	40.5	11	50.2	56.4	12
35–44	62.8	65.8	5	105.2	97.1	−8
45–54	62.8	69.5	11	107.1	131.4	23
55–64	56.8	61.0	7	113.5	141.3	24
65–74	47.4	50.1	6	101.9	106.6	5
75 or more	29.4	40.0	36	54.8	77.1	41
Education of head						
No high school diploma	23.1	26.5	15	31.0	38.8	25
High school diploma	38.1	40.5	6	52.3	57.2	9
Some college	45.0	47.7	6	67.2	67.4	0
College degree	90.2	92.1	2	165.1	189.7	15
Race or ethnicity of respondent						
White non-Hispanic	57.5	61.2	6	107.8	123.4	14
Black or African-American non-Hispanic	32.2	35.4	10	44.3	54.0	22
Hispanic or Latino	33.5	38.5	15	45.4	57.3	26
Other or multiple race	42.5	50.6	19	72.7	86.9	20
Housing status						
Owner	65.3	71.2	9	115.9	134.0	16
Renter or other	28.7	31.6	10	41.3	47.8	16
Urbanicity						
Metropolitan statistical area (MSA)	50.2	55.2	10	95.2	109.7	15
Non-MSA	37.8	38.7	2	54.3	54.1	0
Percentile of net worth						
Less than 25	24.5	25.3	3	32.4	34.2	6
25–49.9	39.8	42.0	6	48.3	50.9	5
50–74.9	57.5	64.8	13	67.9	74.9	10
75–89.9	90.2	90.8	1	103.1	113.4	10
90–100	189.1	215.9	14	372.4	456.9	23

Note: Income is measured for the year prior to the survey.

SOURCE: Jesse Bricker et al., "Table 1. Before-Tax Median and Mean Family Income, by Selected Characteristics of Families, 2013 and 2016 Surveys," in "Changes in US Family Finances from 2013 to 2016: Evidence from the Survey of Consumer Finances," *Federal Reserve Bulletin*, vol. 103, no. 3, September 2017, https://www.federalreserve.gov/publications/files/scf17.pdf (accessed October 16, 2017)

TABLE 2.4

Family net worth by age and other characteristics, 2013 and 2016

[Thousands of 2016 dollars, except as noted]

Family characteristic	Median net worth			Mean net worth		
	2013	2016	Percent change 2013–16	2013	2016	Percent change 2013–16
All families	83.7	97.3	16	551.3	692.1	26
Percentile of usual income						
Less than 20	6.6	7.0	6	66.6	77.5	16
20–39.9	28.8	30.0	4	116.7	120.5	3
40–59.9	57.1	88.6	55	169.9	227.8	34
60–79.9	166.3	170.6	3	361.8	370.7	2
80–89.9	296.9	396.5	34	651.1	800.5	23
90–100	1,161.0	1,629.0	40	3,430.7	4,526.6	32
Age of head (years)						
Less than 35	10.7	11.1	4	77.8	76.2	−2
35–44	48.2	59.8	24	358.0	288.7	−19
45–54	108.6	124.2	14	546.6	727.5	33
55–64	171.1	187.3	9	823.3	1,167.4	42
65–74	239.3	224.1	−6	1,089.8	1,066.0	−2
75 or more	200.8	264.8	32	665.3	1,067.0	60
Education of head						
No high school diploma	17.7	22.8	29	112.2	157.2	40
High school diploma	54.1	67.1	24	205.8	249.6	21
Some college	52.3	66.1	26	328.3	340.6	4
College degree	285.6	292.1	2	1,219.7	1,511.1	24
Race or ethnicity of respondent						
White non-Hispanic	146.4	171.0	17	727.8	933.7	28
Black or African-American non-Hispanic	13.6	17.6	29	102.1	138.2	35
Hispanic or Latino	14.2	20.7	46	111.0	191.2	72
Other or multiple race	42.5	64.8	52	383.6	457.8	19
Housing status						
Owner	201.5	231.4	15	807.3	1,034.2	28
Renter or other	5.5	5.2	−5	72.5	91.1	26
Urbanicity						
Metropolitan statistical area (MSA)	87.3	99.0	13	593.2	751.3	27
Non-MSA	70.1	87.9	25	269.4	276.3	3
Percentile of net worth						
Less than 25	†	0.2	—	−13.8	−12.1	12
25–49.9	32.3	39.8	23	37.0	44.7	21
50–74.9	173.3	192.0	11	183.2	204.1	11
75–89.9	521.6	605.0	16	563.2	659.3	17
90–100	1,930.0	2,387.5	24	4,150.0	5,336.0	29

† Less than 0.05 ($50).
— Not applicable.
Note: Net worth is the difference between families' gross assets and their liabilities.

SOURCE: Jesse Bricker et al., "Table 2. Family Median and Mean Net Worth, by Selected Characteristics of Families, 2013 and 2016 Surveys," in "Changes in US Family Finances from 2013 to 2016: Evidence from the Survey of Consumer Finances," *Federal Reserve Bulletin*, vol. 103, no. 3, September 2017, https://www.federalreserve.gov/publications/files/scf17.pdf (accessed October 16, 2017)

interest rates mean older adults are not earning the steady returns on savings they did just a decade ago. In 2006 the federal funds rate (the rate at which banks lend reserve balances to other banks on an overnight basis) was 5.25%; in October 2017 it was 1.41%.

Low interest rates also limit the use of annuities (investments designed to grow and ultimately pay its owner a specific amount for a fixed period or the owner's life) to generate income because the monthly income from a fixed annuity is based on the interest rate at the time of purchase. Similarly, they limit the growth of assets in pension funds, many of which are drastically underfunded. Low interest rates also have been blamed for rising premiums for long-term care insurance, which covers nursing home care, assisted living, and adult day care.

POVERTY

Poverty rates are measures of the economic viability of populations. Poverty standards were originally based on the "economy food plan," which the US Department of Agriculture (USDA) developed during the 1960s. The plan calculated the cost of a minimally adequate household food budget for different types of households by age of householder. Because USDA surveys showed that the average family spent one-third of its income on food, it was determined that a household with an income three times the amount needed for food was living fairly comfortably. In 1963 the poverty level was calculated by simply multiplying the cost of a minimally adequate food budget by three. Later, the Census Bureau began comparing family income before taxes with a set of poverty thresholds that vary based on family size and composition and are adjusted annually for inflation using the consumer price index (CPI; a measure of the average change in consumer prices over time in a fixed market basket of goods and services).

According to figures shown in Table 2.5, the poverty rate of adults aged 65 years and older in 2016 was 9.3%, representing 4.6 million older adults living in poverty. The rates recorded in 2016 for 18- to 64-year-olds (11.6%) and children under the age of 18 years (18%) both exceeded that of older adults. Census Bureau data reveal that in 1959 the poverty rate for people aged 65 years and older was 35%, well above the rates for the other age groups. (See Figure 2.6) The lowest level of poverty in the older population occurred in 2011, when the rate fell to 8.7%.

Poverty Thresholds Are Lower for Older Adults

The Census Bureau measures need for assistance using poverty thresholds (specific dollar amounts that determine poverty status). Each individual or family is assigned one of 48 possible poverty thresholds. Thresholds vary according to family size and the ages of the members. The thresholds do not vary geographically, and they are updated annually for inflation using the CPI.

One assumption used to determine poverty thresholds is that healthy older adults have lower nutritional requirements than younger people, so they require less money for food. This assumption has resulted in different poverty thresholds for the young and old. For example, in 2016 the poverty threshold for a single person under the age of 65 years was $12,486, as opposed to $11,511 for a person age 65 years or older. (See Table 2.6.) The 2016 poverty threshold for two adults including a householder under the age of 65 years was $16,072, compared with $14,507 for two adults including a householder aged 65 years or older.

This method of defining poverty fails to take into account the special financial and health challenges that older adults may face. For example, no household costs other than food are counted, although older adults spend a much greater percentage of their income on health care than younger people do. Also, the dollars allocated for food consider only the nutritional needs of healthy older adults; many are in poor health and may require costlier special diets or nutritional supplements.

WELL-OFF OLDER ADULTS

More older Americans live comfortably in the early 21st century than at any other time in history. Many of those in their 80s and 90s were born during the Great Depression (1929–1939). The enforced Depression-era frugality taught their families to economize and save. During the 1950s and 1960s, their peak earning years, they enjoyed a period of unprecedented economic expansion. Since then, many have raised their children, paid off their home mortgages, invested wisely, and collected Social Security payments.

Although these factors have contributed to a more favorable economic status for this cohort (a group of individuals that shares a common characteristic such as birth years and is studied over time) of older adults than they would have otherwise enjoyed, most older people are not wealthy. The AoA reports that in 2015, people aged 65 years and older reporting income had a median income of $22,887. Figure 2.7 shows the percent distribution by income of people aged 65 years and older. Only 21% of adults aged 65 years and older had incomes over $50,000 per year.

CONSUMER EXPENSES

On average, older households spend less than younger households because they generally have less money to spend, fewer dependents to support, and different needs and values. The BLS (April 2017, https://www.bls.gov/cex/22016/midyear/age.pdf) notes that in 2015–16 the mean (average) annual expenditure for people aged 65 to 74 years was $48,328, whereas those aged 75 years and older spent just $37,254. The greatest amounts were spent on housing (including utilities), food, transportation, and health care. Not surprisingly, older adults spend more on health care than any other age group, both in dollars and as a percentage of expenditures.

Per Capita Household Expenditures

Most older adult households contain fewer people than younger households. Although larger households, in general, cost more to feed, operate, and maintain, they are less expensive on a per capita basis. Home maintenance, such as replacing a roof or major appliance, costs the same for any household, but in larger households the per capita cost is lower. Purchasing small quantities of food for one or two people may be almost as costly as buying in bulk for a larger household. Because older adults often have limited transportation and mobility, they may be forced to buy food and other necessities at small neighborhood stores that generally charge more than supermarkets and warehouse stores. Larger households may also benefit from multiple incomes.

High energy costs also cause older adults physical and financial hardship, prompting some to suffer extreme heat and cold in their home. Programs such as the Low Income Home Energy Assistance Program (2018, https://www

TABLE 2.5

People in poverty, by selected characteristics, 2015 and 2016

[Numbers in thousands. People as of March of the following year.]

| | 2015 | | | 2016 | | | Change in poverty (2016 less 2015)[a] | |
| | | Below poverty | | | Below poverty | | | |
Characteristic	Total	Number	Percent	Total	Number	Percent	Number	Percent
People								
Total	318,454	43,123	13.5	319,911	40,616	12.7	−2,507	−0.8
Family status								
In families	258,121	29,893	11.6	259,863	27,762	10.7	−2,132	−0.9
Householder	82,199	8,589	10.4	82,854	8,081	9.8	−508	−0.7
Related children under age 18	72,558	13,962	19.2	72,674	12,803	17.6	−1,159	−1.6
Related children under age 6	23,459	4,923	21.0	23,531	4,586	19.5	−337	−1.5
In unrelated subfamilies	1,344	559	41.6	1,208	519	43.0	−40	1.4
Reference person	563	231	41.0	496	202	40.6	−29	−0.3
Children under age 18	701	321	45.9	622	298	48.0	−23	2.1
Unrelated individuals	58,988	12,671	21.5	58,839	12,336	21.0	−336	−0.5
Race[b] and Hispanic origin								
White	245,536	28,566	11.6	245,985	27,113	11.0	−1,453	−0.6
White, not Hispanic	195,450	17,786	9.1	195,221	17,263	8.8	−523	−0.3
Black	41,625	10,020	24.1	41,962	9,234	22.0	−786	−2.1
Asian	18,241	2,078	11.4	18,879	1,908	10.1	−170	−1.3
Hispanic (any race)	56,780	12,133	21.4	57,556	11,137	19.4	−996	−2.0
Sex								
Male	156,009	19,037	12.2	156,677	17,685	11.3	−1,351	−0.9
Female	162,445	24,086	14.8	163,234	22,931	14.0	−1,156	−0.8
Age								
Under age 18	73,647	14,509	19.7	73,586	13,253	18.0	−1,255	−1.7
Aged 18 to 64	197,260	24,414	12.4	197,051	22,795	11.6	−1,619	−0.8
Aged 65 and older	47,547	4,201	8.8	49,274	4,568	9.3	367	0.4
Nativity								
Native born	275,398	35,973	13.1	276,089	33,999	12.3	−1,974	−0.7
Foreign born	43,056	7,150	16.6	43,822	6,617	15.1	−534	−1.5
Naturalized citizen	20,084	2,255	11.2	20,409	2,045	10.0	−210	−1.2
Not a citizen	22,973	4,895	21.3	23,413	4,572	19.5	−324	−1.8
Region								
Northeast	55,779	6,891	12.4	55,470	5,969	10.8	−922	−1.6
Midwest	67,030	7,849	11.7	66,897	7,809	11.7	−40	Z
South	119,955	18,305	15.3	121,166	17,028	14.1	−1,276	−1.2
West	75,690	10,079	13.3	76,377	9,810	12.8	−269	−0.5
Residence								
Inside metropolitan statistical areas	274,046	35,718	13.0	276,430	33,741	12.2	−1,978	−0.8
Inside principal cities	103,617	17,368	16.8	104,182	16,572	15.9	−796	−0.9
Outside principal cities	170,429	18,350	10.8	172,248	17,169	10.0	−1,182	−0.8
Outside metropolitan statistical areas	44,408	7,405	16.7	43,481	6,875	15.8	−530	−0.9
Work experience								
Total, aged 18 to 64	197,260	24,414	12.4	197,051	22,795	11.6	−1,619	−0.8
All workers	150,229	9,457	6.3	150,904	8,743	5.8	−714	−0.5
Worked full-time, year-round	105,695	2,537	2.4	107,781	2,416	2.2	−120	−0.2
Less than full-time, year-round	44,534	6,920	15.5	43,123	6,327	14.7	−593	−0.9
Did not work at least 1 week	47,031	14,957	31.8	46,148	14,052	30.5	−905	−1.4
Disability status[c]								
Total, aged 18 to 64	197,260	24,414	12.4	197,051	22,795	11.6	−1,619	−0.8
With a disability	15,276	4,358	28.5	15,405	4,123	26.8	−235	−1.8
With no disability	181,069	20,000	11.0	180,783	18,629	10.3	−1,370	−0.7
Educational attainment								
Total, aged 25 and older	215,015	22,957	10.7	216,921	22,636	10.4	−321	−0.2
No high school diploma	23,453	6,171	26.3	22,541	5,599	24.8	−572	−1.5
High school, no college	62,002	8,016	12.9	62,512	8,309	13.3	293	0.4
Some college, no degree	57,660	5,550	9.6	57,765	5,430	9.4	−119	−0.2
Bachelor's degree or higher	71,900	3,221	4.5	74,103	3,299	4.5	78	Z

.acf.hhs.gov/ocs/programs/liheap), which is operated by the US Department of Health and Human Services' Administration for Children and Families, attempt to prevent older adults from suffering from a lack of heat in their home. The program helps eligible households meet their home energy needs.

TABLE 2.5

People in poverty, by selected characteristics, 2015 and 2016 [CONTINUED]

[Numbers in thousands. People as of March of the following year.]

aDetails may not sum to totals because of rounding.
bFederal surveys give respondents the option of reporting more than one race. Therefore, two basic ways of defining a race group are possible. A group such as Asian may be defined as those who reported Asian and no other race (the race-alone or single-race concept) or as those who reported Asian regardless of whether they also reported another race (the race-alone-or-in-combination concept). This table shows data using the first approach (race alone). The use of the single-race population does not imply that it is the preferred method of presenting or analyzing data. The Census Bureau uses a variety of approaches. About 2.9 percent of people reported more than one race in the 2010 Census. Data for American Indians and Alaska Natives, Native Hawaiians and Other Pacific Islanders, and those reporting two or more races are not shown separately.
cThe sum of those with and without a disability does not equal the total because disability status is not defined for individuals in the Armed Forces.

SOURCE: Jessica L. Semega, Kayla R. Fontenot, and Melissa A. Kollar, "Table 3. People in Poverty by Selected Characteristics: 2015 and 2016," in *Income and Poverty in the United States: 2016*, US Census Bureau, September 2017, https://www.census.gov/content/dam/Census/library/publications/2017/demo/P60-259.pdf (accessed October 16, 2017)

FIGURE 2.6

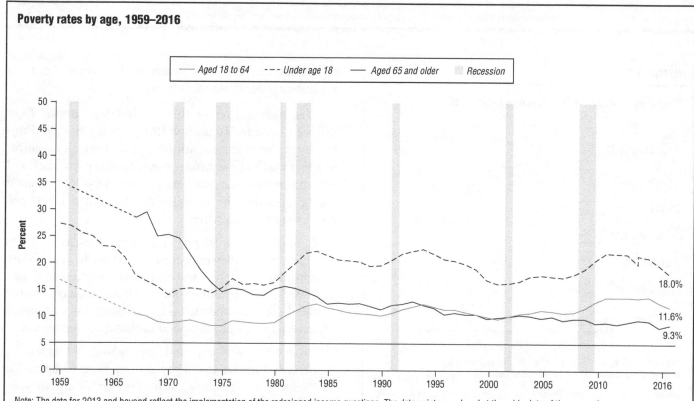

Poverty rates by age, 1959–2016

Note: The data for 2013 and beyond reflect the implementation of the redesigned income questions. The data points are placed at the midpoints of the respective years. Data for people aged 18 to 64 and aged 65 and older are not available from 1960 to 1965.

Jessica L. Semega, Kayla R. Fontenot, and Melissa A. Kollar, "Figure 5. Poverty Rates by Age: 1959 to 2016," in *Income and Poverty in the United States: 2016*, US Census Bureau, September 2017, https://www.census.gov/content/dam/Census/library/publications/2017/demo/P60-259.pdf (accessed October 16, 2017)

AGING CONSUMERS: A GROWING MARKET

Older adults have proven to be a lucrative market for many products. Many older adults are working beyond retirement, and these older workers may prove to be an untapped market for advertisers, affecting a number of consumer sectors. Older adults are redefining aging; only a minority of Americans expects to retire as their parents did. Older adults are now more likely to continue working, and working out, rather than retiring to the shuffleboard court or the rocking chair on the front porch. As a result, they are considered an important market for an expanding array of products, such as specialty foods, drinks, anti-aging cosmetics, and over-the-counter and prescription drugs, as well as products that are traditionally marketed to older adults, such as health and life insurance plans and burial plots.

Examples of other products and services marketed to older adults include devices that help them remain in their homes safely and comfortably, allowing them to "age in place." In "How to Profit from Aging Baby Boomers" (USNews.com, June 27, 2014), Dave Bernard

TABLE 2.6

Poverty thresholds, by size of family and number of related children under 18 years, 2016

Size of family unit	Weighted average thresholds	None	One	Two	Three	Four	Five	Six	Seven	Eight or more
One person (unrelated individual):	12,228									
Under age 65	12,486	12,486								
Aged 65 and older	11,511	11,511								
Two people:	15,569									
Householder under age 65	16,151	16,072	16,543							
Householder aged 65 and older	14,522	14,507	16,480							
Three people	19,105	18,774	19,318	19,337						
Four people	24,563	24,755	25,160	24,339	24,424					
Five people	29,111	29,854	30,288	29,360	28,643	28,205				
Six people	32,928	34,337	34,473	33,763	33,082	32,070	31,470			
Seven people	37,458	39,509	39,756	38,905	38,313	37,208	35,920	34,507		
Eight people	41,781	44,188	44,578	43,776	43,072	42,075	40,809	39,491	39,156	
Nine people or more	49,721	53,155	53,413	52,702	52,106	51,127	49,779	48,561	48,259	46,400

Related children under 18 years (column group header over None–Eight or more).

SOURCE: "Poverty Thresholds for 2016 by Size of Family and Number of Related Children under 18 Years," in *Poverty Thresholds*, US Census Bureau, 2017, https://www.census.gov/data/tables/time-series/demo/income-poverty/historical-poverty-thresholds.html (accessed October 16, 2017)

FIGURE 2.7

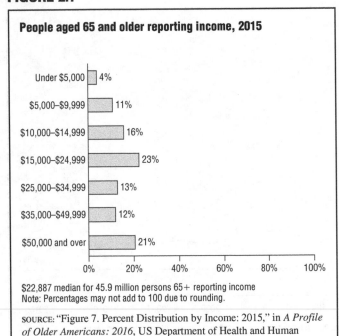

People aged 65 and older reporting income, 2015

- Under $5,000 — 4%
- $5,000–$9,999 — 11%
- $10,000–$14,999 — 16%
- $15,000–$24,999 — 23%
- $25,000–$34,999 — 13%
- $35,000–$49,999 — 12%
- $50,000 and over — 21%

$22,887 median for 45.9 million persons 65+ reporting income
Note: Percentages may not add to 100 due to rounding.

SOURCE: "Figure 7. Percent Distribution by Income: 2015," in *A Profile of Older Americans: 2016*, US Department of Health and Human Services, Administration for Community Living, Administration on Aging, April 2017, https://www.acl.gov/sites/default/files/Aging%20 and%20Disability%20in%20America/2016-Profile.pdf (accessed October 13, 2017)

power, ensure that this group will contain the most voracious older consumers ever.

The information in this section was drawn from SIR's Institute for Tomorrow (formerly the Boomer Project; https://www.institutefortomorrow.com), an organization that studies how different generations think, feel, and respond to marketing and advertising messages. Among the insights that the Institute for Tomorrow's research reveals are the following:

- Boomers at age 50 perceive themselves as 12 years younger, and they expect to live 35 more years. They consider themselves to be in early "middle age" and view 72 as the onset of old age. Boomers have created the "longevity climate"—by delaying retirement they have more money to spend during their longer lives.

- Boomers reject any and all age-related labels to describe themselves. They do not want to be called "seniors," "aged," or even "boomers," and they do not want to be compared with their parents' generation or any previous cohort of older adults.

- Boomers over the age of 50 do not want to reverse or stop the signs of aging, they simply want to postpone or slow the process. They are intent on seeking health rather than youth. Feeling younger is as important as looking younger for boomers eager to age "on their own terms." Boomers are avid participants in the growing number of health clubs, fitness centers, and wellness programs.

- Boomers want more time, which means that they value services that offer them free time to pursue work and leisure activities. Examples of these include cleaning, home maintenance, and gardening services.

- Boomers are becoming less interested in material possessions and more interested in gaining a variety of

explains that along with products and services to help older adults maintain their independence, companies that offer travel and recreation services, lifelong learning, and smart technology are targeting older adult consumers.

Baby Boomers: The Emerging "Silver" Market

The aging baby boomers (people born between 1946 and 1964) have been dubbed "zoomers" to reflect the generation's active lifestyle. Market researchers believe the sheer size of the boomer cohort and its history of self-indulgence, coupled with considerable purchasing

experiences. Rather than embracing the premise that "he who has the most toys wins," boomers believe that "he who chalks up the most experiences wins."

- Once dubbed the "me generation," boomers operate on the premise that they are entitled to special treatment, not because they have earned it by virtue of age, but simply because they deserve it. They want products and services that are relevant to them personally. Boomers also lead the "age of responsible consumerism" and are budget conscious, purchasing smaller homes and limiting holiday spending. They remain motivated to fulfill their own needs, whether these needs are for community, adventure, or a spiritual life.

- Boomers are lifelong learners and a "wired" generation—learning, connecting, and communicating online and via social networks. Continuing education classes and opportunities to learn and enrich their lives through travel are important to this generation.

- Boomers are still interested in promoting social change. The generation known for protesting the Vietnam War (1954–1975) and questioning authority and traditional American social mores continues to support global and local humanitarian and environmental action.

- Boomers do not want to relocate to traditional retirement enclaves and communities. Instead, they prefer to age in place, remaining in their own home. Having witnessed the institutionalization of their parents in nursing homes and other assisted living facilities, boomers are intent on remaining in their home, and in the community, for as long as they can.

Paul Davidson notes in "The Economy Is Still All about—Who Else?—Boomers" (USAToday.com, July 17, 2017), that boomers and older adults make a disproportionate contribution to consumer spending. Together, they account for about half of all consumption. Although they purchase fewer cars, clothing items, and televisions, they spend more on health care, travel, and entertainment. For example, in 2016 adults aged 50 years and older were responsible for more than half (57%) of credit card spending at hotels. By spending more on services than on goods, Davidson explains, boomers have helped boost US job growth, because most service jobs cannot be as easily automated or outsourced as manufacturing jobs.

In "Baby Boomers to Advertisers: Don't Forget about Us" (NYTimes.com, October 15, 2017), Janet Morrissey reports that some advertising industry observers feel that marketers have ignored boomers in favor of millennials (often defined as people born between 1981 and 1997), but this trend may be changing. Besides the medical products, life insurance, and reverse mortgages traditionally marketed to older consumers, some companies are actively seeking boomers' discretionary income. For example, in 2017 T-Mobile began promoting a phone plan for people

aged 55 years and older, and Mercedes-Benz created a Super Bowl ad that appealed to boomers by referencing the iconic 1969 movie *Easy Rider*.

SOCIAL SECURITY

We can never insure one hundred percent of the population against one hundred percent of the hazards and vicissitudes of life, but we have tried to frame a law which will give some measure of protection to the average citizen and to his family against the loss of a job and against poverty-ridden old age.

—President Franklin D. Roosevelt, on signing the Social Security Act, August 14, 1935

Social Security is a social insurance program that is funded through a dedicated payroll tax. It is also known as Old-Age, Survivors, and Disability Insurance (OASDI), which describes its three major classes of beneficiaries.

During the Great Depression poverty among the older population escalated. In 1934 more than half of older adults lacked sufficient income. Although 30 states had some form of an old-age pension program in place, by 1935 these programs were unable to meet the growing need. Just 3% of the older population received benefits under these state plans, and the average benefit amount was about $0.65 per day.

As advocated by President Franklin D. Roosevelt (1882–1945), social insurance would solve the problem of economic security for older adults by creating a work-related, contributory system in which workers would provide for their own future economic security through taxes paid while employed. By the time the Social Security Act was signed into law by President Roosevelt in August 1935, 34 nations were already operating some form of a social insurance program (government-sponsored efforts to provide for the economic well-being of a nation's citizens).

According to the SSA, in "Fact Sheet: Social Security" (September 14, 2017, https://www.ssa.gov/news/press/fact sheets/basicfact-alt.pdf), nearly nine out of 10 people aged 65 years and older received Social Security benefits in 2017. Retired workers and their dependents accounted for almost three-quarters (72%) of total benefits paid, while survivors of deceased workers accounted for 13% of the total, and disabled workers and their dependents accounted for 16% of benefits paid. An estimated 173 million US workers were covered by Social Security in 2017.

Although Social Security was not initially intended as a full pension, 21% of married older married couples and 43% of nonmarried older adults relied almost exclusively (for 90% or more of their income) on the program in 2014. (See Figure 2.3.) In "We Need to Expand the Most Effective Anti-poverty Program in America" (January 22, 2015, http://billmoyers.com/2015/01/22/need-expand-effective-anti-poverty-program-america), Alex Lawson of Moyers &

Company observes that programs such as Social Security were created to reduce the probability that Americans would fall into poverty during old age. Without it, 44% of older adults would be living in poverty, compared with the current 9%.

Social Security benefits are funded through the Federal Insurance Contributions Act (FICA), which provides that a mandatory tax be withheld from workers' earnings and be matched by their employers. (Self-employed workers pay both the employer and the employee shares of FICA taxes.) When covered workers retire (or are disabled), they draw benefits that are based on the amount they contributed to the fund. The amount of the benefit is directly related to the duration of employment and earnings; that is, people who have worked longer and earned higher wages receive larger benefits.

Workers can retire as early as age 62 and receive reduced Social Security benefits, or they can wait until full retirement age and receive full benefits. Until 2003 the full retirement age was 65, but beginning that year it began to increase gradually, such that for people born in 1960 or later, retirement age will be 67. A special credit is given to people who delay retirement beyond their full retirement age. This credit, which is a percentage added to the Social Security benefit, varies depending on the retiree's date of birth. Workers who reached full retirement age in 2008 or later can receive a credit of 8% per year.

Table 2.7 shows the relationship between earnings and Social Security benefits. It shows the average indexed monthly earnings (this is an amount that summarizes a worker's earnings) and the corresponding benefit amounts. Delaying retirement until age 70 yields

TABLE 2.7

Benefit amount for worker with maximum-taxable earnings, 2017

Retirement in Jan.	Retirement at age 62[a]			Retirement at age 65[b]			Retirement at age 66[c]			Retirement at age 70[d]		
		Monthly benefits			Monthly benefits			Monthly benefits			Monthly benefits	
	AIME	Initial	In 2018	AIME	Initial	In 2018	AIME	Initial	In 2018	AIME	Initial	In 2018
1987	$2,205	$666	$1,468	$2,009	$789	$1,738	$1,955	$806	$1,776	$1,725	$1,056	$2,328
1988	2,311	691	1,461	2,139	838	1,772	2,089	860	1,819	1,859	1,080	2,284
1989	2,490	739	1,502	2,287	899	1,828	2,217	911	1,853	2,000	1,063	2,162
1990	2,648	780	1,514	2,417	975	1,892	2,368	984	1,911	2,154	1,085	2,106
1991	2,792	815	1,502	2,531	1,022	1,884	2,502	1,079	1,988	2,332	1,163	2,144
1992	2,978	860	1,527	2,716	1,088	1,934	2,617	1,113	1,978	2,470	1,231	2,188
1993	3,154	899	1,552	2,878	1,128	1,947	2,801	1,181	2,038	2,605	1,289	2,223
1994	3,384	954	1,604	3,024	1,147	1,929	2,963	1,219	2,050	2,758	1,358	2,284
1995	3,493	972	1,590	3,219	1,199	1,961	3,112	1,248	2,041	2,896	1,474	2,410
1996	3,657	1,006	1,604	3,402	1,248	1,991	3,306	1,300	2,073	3,012	1,501	2,393
1997	3,877	1,056	1,636	3,634	1,326	2,055	3,490	1,364	2,114	3,189	1,609	2,494
1998	4,144	1,117	1,695	3,750	1,342	2,037	3,724	1,437	2,182	3,348	1,648	2,500
1999	4,463	1,191	1,785	3,926	1,373	2,057	3,847	1,451	2,174	3,496	1,684	2,523
2000	4,775	1,248	1,824	4,161	1,435	2,097	4,031	1,502	2,196	3,707	1,752	2,562
2001	5,126	1,314	1,856	4,440	1,538	2,172	4,272	1,593	2,250	3,912	1,879	2,653
2002	5,499	1,382	1,903	4,770	1,660	2,285	4,555	1,692	2,330	4,165	1,988	2,736
2003	5,729	1,412	1,916	5,099	1,721	2,337	4,890	1,814	2,462	4,321	2,045	2,776
2004	5,892	1,422	1,891	5,457	1,784	2,373	5,219	1,894	2,519	4,532	2,111	2,807
2005	6,137	1,452	1,881	5,827	1,874	2,426	5,574	1,982	2,566	4,786	2,252	2,916
2006	6,515	1,530	1,904	6,058	1,961	2,440	5,940	2,108	2,622	5,072	2,420	3,011
2007	6,852	1,598	1,924	6,229	1,998	2,406	6,177	2,194	2,642	5,406	2,672	3,218
2008	7,260	1,682	1,979	6,479	2,030	2,390	6,350	2,212	2,604	5,733	2,794	3,289
2009	7,685	1,769	1,968	6,861	2,172	2,416	6,606	2,323	2,585	6,090	3,054	3,398
2010	7,949	1,820	2,024	7,189	2,191	2,438	6,976	2,346	2,610	6,450	3,119	3,470
2011	7,928	1,803	2,006	7,579	2,249	2,502	7,299	2,366	2,632	6,683	3,193	3,552
2012	8,199	1,855	1,992	7,973	2,310	2,481	7,680	2,513	2,699	6,852	3,266	3,507
2013	8,539	1,923	2,030	8,230	2,414	2,549	8,074	2,533	2,675	7,095	3,350	3,538
2014	8,890	1,992	2,073	8,229	2,431	2,530	8,335	2,642	2,749	7,452	3,425	3,563
2015	9,066	2,025	2,071	8,479	2,452	2,508	8,314	2,663	2,725	7,747	3,501	3,581
2016	9,431	2,102	2,150	8,782	2,491	2,549	8,556	2,639	2,700	8,090	3,576	3,658
2017	9,784	2,153	2,197	9,076	2,542	2,593	8,843	2,687	2,741	8,426	3,538	3,609
2018	9,940	2,159	2,159	9,243	2,589	2,589	9,144	2,788	2,788	8,649	3,698	3,698

[a]Retirement at age 62 is assumed here to be at exact age 62 and 1 month. Such early retirement results in a reduced monthly benefit.
[b]Retirement at age 65 is assumed to be at exact age 65 and 0 months. For retirement in 2003 and later, the monthly benefit is reduced for early retirement. (For people born before 1938, age 65 is the normal retirement age. Normal retirement age will gradually increase to age 67.)
[c]Age 66 is the normal retirement age for people born in 1943–54. People who retired at age 66 and who were born before 1943 received delayed retirement credits; those born after 1954 will have their benefits reduced for early retirement.
[d]Retirement at age 70 maximizes the effect of delayed retirement credits.
Note: Initial monthly benefits paid at ages 65, 66, and 70 in 2000–2001 were slightly lower than the amounts shown above because such initial benefits were partially based on a cost-of-living adjustment (COLA) for December 1999 that was originally determined as 2.4 percent based on CPIs published by the Bureau of Labor Statistics. Pursuant to Public Law 106–554, however, this AIME = Average Indexed Monthly Earnings.

SOURCE: "Worker with Steady Earnings at the Maximum Level since Age 22," in *Workers with Maximum-Taxable Earnings*, US Social Security Administration, Office of the Chief Actuary, 2017, https://www.ssa.gov/oact/cola/examplemax.html (accessed October 16, 2017)

the highest ratio of retirement benefits to the average indexed monthly earnings.

Benefits and Beneficiaries

The SSA indicates in "Fact Sheet: Social Security" that the program paid benefits to nearly 62 million people in 2017. The majority (45 million) were retired workers and their dependents; the rest were disabled workers and their dependents (10.6 million) and survivors of deceased workers (6 million). In *Annual Statistical Supplement to the Social Security Bulletin, 2016* (May 2017, https://www.ssa.gov/policy/docs/statcomps/supplement/2016/supplement16.pdf), the SSA notes that 168.9 million people with earnings covered by Social Security paid payroll taxes in 2015. Social Security income in 2015 was an estimated $795 billion from workers and employers. Table 2.8 shows the number of beneficiaries of all the OASDI programs as well as the average monthly benefits that were paid in December 2015, the most recent month for which data were available as of February 2018.

Social Security Amendments of 1977

Ever since 1940, the year that Americans began receiving Social Security checks, monthly retirement benefits have steadily increased, but during the 1970s they soared. Legislation enacted in 1973 provided for automatic cost-of-living adjustments (COLAs) that were intended to prevent inflation from eroding Social Security benefits. The average benefit was indexed (annually adjusted) to keep pace with inflation as reflected by the CPI. COLAs were 9.9% in 1979 and peaked at 14.3% the following year. (See Table 2.9.) These increases threatened the continued financial viability of the entire system and prompted policy makers to reconsider the COLA formula.

Some legislators believed that indexing vastly overcompensated for inflation, causing relative benefit levels to rise higher than at any previous time in the history of the program. In an attempt to prevent future Social Security benefits from rising to what many considered excessive levels, Congress passed the Social Security Amendments of 1977 to restructure the benefit plan and design more realistic formulas for benefits. Along with redefining COLAs, the 1977 amendments raised the payroll tax slightly, increased the wage base, and reduced benefits.

There were no COLAs in 2010, 2011, and 2016. In 2017 it was just 0.3%, and in 2018 it was 2%. Table 2.9 shows how this COLA increase translated into SSI payments between 1975 and 2018.

The Earnings Test

Legislation enacted on January 1, 2000, changed the method of determining the amount that beneficiaries could earn while also receiving retirement or survivors' benefits. The retirement earnings test applies only to people younger than normal retirement age, which ranges from age 65 to 67, depending on year of birth. Social Security withholds benefits if annual retirement earnings exceed a certain level, called a retirement earnings test exempt amount, for people who have not yet attained normal retirement age. These exempt amounts generally increase annually with increases in the national average wage index.

TABLE 2.8

Number and average monthly benefit, by type of benefit and sex, December 2015

	All		Male		Female	
Type of benefit	Number	Average monthly benefit (dollars)	Number	Average monthly benefit (dollars)	Number	Average monthly benefit (dollars)
Total, OASDI	59,963,425	1,228.12	27,175,237	1,384.30	32,788,188	1,098.67
OASI	49,156,959	1,273.36	21,677,365	1,448.15	27,479,594	1,135.48
Retirement benefits	43,073,398	1,296.04	20,553,970	1,480.70	22,519,428	1,127.50
Retired workers	40,089,061	1,341.77	20,089,856	1,500.46	19,999,205	1,182.36
Spouses of retired workers	2,335,807	690.30	118,268	559.99	2,217,539	697.25
Children of retired workers	648,530	651.00	345,846	647.72	302,684	654.74
Survivor benefits	6,083,561	1,112.80	1,123,395	852.58	4,960,166	1,171.74
Children of deceased workers	1,892,885	832.14	994,658	831.44	898,227	832.91
Widowed mothers and fathers	139,719	939.94	11,267	810.23	128,452	951.32
Nondisabled widow(er)s	3,790,374	1,286.26	99,364	1,126.02	3,691,010	1,290.58
Disabled widow(er)s	259,331	719.11	17,941	534.44	241,390	732.84
Parents of deceased workers	1,252	1,133.46	165	1,050.83	1,087	1,146.00
DI	10,806,466	1,022.29	5,497,872	1,132.56	5,308,594	908.09
Disabled workers	8,909,430	1,165.79	4,581,300	1,288.71	4,328,130	1,035.67
Spouses of disabled workers	141,760	318.43	9,416	322.69	132,344	318.13
Children of disabled workers	1,755,276	350.77	907,156	352.36	848,120	349.08

Notes: OASDI = old age, survivor and disability insurance. OASI = old age and survivor insurance. DI = disability insurance.

SOURCE: "Table 5.A1. Number and Average Monthly Benefit, by Type of Benefit and Sex, December 2015," in *Annual Statistical Supplement to the Social Security Bulletin, 2016*, US Social Security Administration, May 2017, https://www.ssa.gov/policy/docs/statcomps/supplement/2016/supplement16.pdf (accessed October 16, 2017)

TABLE 2.9

Supplemental Security Income federal payment amounts, 1975–2018

Year	COLA[a]	Eligible individual	Eligible couple
1975	8.0%	$157.70	$236.60
1976	6.4%	167.80	251.80
1977	5.9%	177.80	266.70
1978	6.5%	189.40	284.10
1979	9.9%	208.20	312.30
1980	14.3%	238.00	357.00
1981	11.2%	264.70	397.00
1982	7.4%	284.30	426.40
1983	[b]7.0%	304.30	456.40
1984	3.5%	314.00	472.00
1985	3.5%	325.00	488.00
1986	3.1%	336.00	504.00
1987	1.3%	340.00	510.00
1988	4.2%	354.00	532.00
1989	4.0%	368.00	553.00
1990	4.7%	386.00	579.00
1991	5.4%	407.00	610.00
1992	3.7%	422.00	633.00
1993	3.0%	434.00	652.00
1994	2.6%	446.00	669.00
1995	2.8%	458.00	687.00
1996	2.6%	470.00	705.00
1997	2.9%	484.00	726.00
1998	2.1%	494.00	741.00
1999	1.3%	500.00	751.00
2000	[c]2.5%	513.00	769.00
2001	3.5%	531.00	796.00
2002	2.6%	545.00	817.00
2003	1.4%	552.00	829.00
2004	2.1%	564.00	846.00
2005	2.7%	579.00	869.00
2006	4.1%	603.00	904.00
2007	3.3%	623.00	934.00
2008	2.3%	637.00	956.00
2009	5.8%	674.00	1,011.00
2010	0.0%	674.00	1,011.00
2011	0.0%	674.00	1,011.00
2012	3.6%	698.00	1,048.00
2013	1.7%	710.00	1,066.00
2014	1.5%	721.00	1,082.00
2015	1.7%	733.00	1,100.00
2016	0.0%	733.00	1,100.00
2017	0.3%	735.00	1,103.00
2018	2.0%	750.00	1,125.00

[a]Cost-of-living adjustment.
[b]The increase effective for July 1983 was a legislated increase.
[c]Originally determined as 2.4 percent based on consumer price index published by the Bureau of Labor Statistics. Pursuant to Public Law 106–554, however, the COLA is effectively now 2.5 percent.

SOURCE: "SSI Monthly Payment Amounts, 1975–2018," in *SSI Federal Payment Amounts*, US Social Security Administration, Office of the Chief Actuary, 2017, https://www.ssa.gov/oact/cola/SSIamts.html (accessed October 16, 2017)

TABLE 2.10

Annual retirement earnings test exempt amounts, 2000–18

Year	Lower amount[a]	Higher amount[b]
2000	$10,080	$17,000
2001	10,680	25,000
2002	11,280	30,000
2003	11,520	30,720
2004	11,640	31,080
2005	12,000	31,800
2006	12,480	33,240
2007	12,960	34,440
2008	13,560	36,120
2009	14,160	37,680
2010	14,160	37,680
2011	14,160	37,680
2012	14,640	38,880
2013	15,120	40,080
2014	15,480	41,400
2015	15,720	41,880
2016	15,720	41,880
2017	16,920	44,880
2018	17,040	45,360

[a]Applies in years before the year of attaining NRA (normal retirement age).
[b]Applies in the year of attaining NRA, for months prior to such attainment.

SOURCE: "Annual Retirement Earnings Test Exempt Amounts," in *Exempt Amounts under the Earnings Test*, US Social Security Administration, Office of the Chief Actuary, 2017, https://www.ssa.gov/oact/cola/rtea.html (accessed October 16, 2017)

prior work, and the funds come from general tax revenues rather than from Social Security taxes.

In 1972 Congress passed the legislation establishing SSI to replace several state-administered programs and to provide a uniform federal benefit based on uniform eligibility standards. Although SSI is a federal program, some states provide a supplement to the federal benefit.

According to the SSA (July 2017, https://www.ssa.gov/policy/docs/statcomps/ssi_monthly/2017-08/table02.pdf), of the nearly 8.3 million people receiving SSI benefits in August 2017, more than 2.2 million were aged 65 years and older. (See Table 2.11.) Although payments vary by age group, the average monthly benefit received by older adults in July 2017 was $438.72. (See Table 2.12.)

WHAT LIES AHEAD FOR SOCIAL SECURITY?

The Social Security program faces long-range financing challenges that, if unresolved, threaten its solvency (the ability to meet financial obligations on time) in the coming decades. Historically, the program collected more money than it had to pay out. However, according to the program's trustees, in *The 2017 Annual Report of the Board of Trustees of the Federal Old-Age and Survivors Insurance and Federal Disability Insurance Trust Funds* (July 13, 2017, https://www.ssa.gov/OACT/TR/2017/tr2017.pdf), since 2010 Social Security expenditures have exceeded the noninterest income of its combined trust funds.

According to the trustees, the OASDI trust funds will be depleted in 2034, leaving Social Security unable to

Table 2.10 shows the exempt amounts between 2000 and 2018. One dollar in Social Security benefits is withheld for every $2 of earnings more than the lower exempt amount. Similarly, $1 in benefits is withheld for every $3 of earnings more than the higher exempt amount.

SUPPLEMENTAL SECURITY INCOME

SSI is designed to provide monthly cash payments to older, blind, and/or disabled people who have low incomes. SSI is administered by the SSA, but unlike Social Security benefits, SSI benefits are not based on

TABLE 2.11

Supplemental Security Income recipients by eligibility category and age, August 2016–August 2017

| Month | Total | Eligibility category | | Age | | |
		Aged	Blind and disabled	Under 18	18–64	65 or older
2016						
August	8,319,067	1,168,067	7,151,000	1,238,448	4,893,019	2,187,600
September	8,286,748	1,167,505	7,119,243	1,222,611	4,875,434	2,188,703
October	8,293,919	1,169,223	7,124,696	1,226,872	4,873,569	2,193,478
November	8,290,184	1,170,911	7,119,273	1,222,700	4,869,395	2,198,089
December	8,251,161	1,164,589	7,086,572	1,213,079	4,845,735	2,192,347
2017						
January	8,285,732	1,168,990	7,116,742	1,221,000	4,862,868	2,201,864
February	8,276,218	1,167,300	7,108,918	1,218,688	4,856,212	2,201,318
March	8,257,636	1,166,837	7,090,799	1,206,786	4,847,358	2,203,492
April	8,260,837	1,167,516	7,093,321	1,211,101	4,843,661	2,206,075
May	8,269,186	1,168,088	7,101,098	1,210,258	4,849,886	2,209,042
June	8,234,017	1,166,333	7,067,684	1,196,505	4,828,826	2,208,686
July	8,241,556	1,167,656	7,073,900	1,201,510	4,825,767	2,214,279
August	8,258,549	1,170,424	7,088,125	1,199,480	4,837,135	2,221,934

Note: Data are for the end of the specified month.

SOURCE: "Table 2. Recipients, by Eligibility Category and Age, August 2016–August 2017," in *SSI Monthly Statistics, August 2017*, US Social Security Administration, Office of the Chief Actuary, August 2017, https://www.ssa.gov-/policy/docs/statcomps/ssi_monthly/2017-08/table02.pdf (accessed October 16, 2017)

pay scheduled benefits in full to older adult retirees and their beneficiaries. The trustees urge immediate action, observing that solvency of the combined OASDI trust funds for the next 75 years could be restored if policy makers increase the combined payroll tax rate and reduce scheduled benefits.

To a large extent, demographic changes precipitated this crisis. Social Security is a "pay-as-you-go" program, with the contributions of active workers paying the retirement benefits of those currently retired. The program is solvent at this time because the number of employees contributing to the system is sufficient. Although about 10,000 baby boomers head into retirement each day, many still remain in the workforce. This still relatively large cohort of boomers is funding the smaller cohort of retirees born during the low birth-rate cycle of the Great Depression. As a result, there are still fewer retirees depleting funds than there are workers contributing. The trustees note that when monthly Social Security benefits began in 1940, a man aged 65 could expect to live an average of about 12.7 additional years; by 2030 a typical 65-year-old man is likely to live on average another 20 years. (See Table 2.13.)

Saving Social Security

There are three basic ways to resolve Social Security's financial problems: raise taxes, cut benefits, or make Social Security taxes earn more by investing the money. It is most likely that restoring Social Security's long-term financial balance will require a combination of increased revenues and reduced expenditures. The ways to increase revenues include:

- Increasing Social Security payroll taxes
- Investing trust funds in securities with potentially higher yields than the government bonds in which they are currently invested
- Increasing income taxes on Social Security benefits

The ways to reduce expenditures include:

- Reducing initial benefits to retirees
- Raising the retirement age (already slated to rise from 65 to 67 by 2027)
- Lowering COLAs
- Limiting benefits based on beneficiaries' other income and assets

Other possible ways to reform Social Security include means testing, which would reduce benefits to workers if their wealth exceeded a predetermined threshold, permitting the federal government to invest a portion of the funds that enter the Social Security system in an effort to grow these funds, and helping people to save money in other ways such that they do not rely as heavily on Social Security in retirement.

Ensuring the Long-Term Solvency of Social Security

Protecting Social Security is vitally important to the nation's retirees and aging baby boomers who will soon retire, but attempts to reform the program have not gained much support in Congress. In June 2017 the US representatives Sam Johnson (1930–; R-TX) and Adrian Smith (1970–; R-NE) introduced the Providing Choice for Social Security Retirees Act (H.R. 3112). The law would provide workers who delay retirement the option of claiming their

TABLE 2.12

Average monthly Supplemental Security Income payment, by eligibility category, age, and source of payment, July 2016–July 2017

[In dollars]

Month	Total	Eligibility category		Age		
		Aged	Blind and disabled	Under 18	18–64	65 or older
2016			*All sources*			
July	540.99	427.59	559.57	649.51	560.99	435.29
August	540.16	427.84	558.54	645.09	560.58	435.44
September	540.09	427.90	558.54	644.32	561.11	435.53
October	540.66	428.23	559.11	645.63	561.45	435.79
November	539.02	427.98	557.30	639.22	560.63	435.58
December	542.38	429.37	560.98	649.58	563.49	436.76
2017						
January	542.46	430.82	560.81	647.58	563.34	438.26
February	540.18	429.69	558.33	638.81	562.08	437.41
March	543.51	431.29	562.01	650.78	564.63	438.72
April	542.75	431.13	561.15	648.29	563.90	438.63
May	540.97	430.97	559.09	639.76	563.09	438.57
June	543.27	431.36	561.77	651.16	564.47	438.90
July	542.00	431.17	560.33	645.89	563.68	438.72
			Federal payments			
2016						
July	525.37	393.66	546.26	643.16	547.25	406.38
August	524.53	393.87	545.23	638.74	546.84	406.51
September	524.39	393.88	545.17	637.97	547.34	406.54
October	525.00	394.24	545.78	639.27	547.71	406.85
November	523.33	394.02	543.95	632.87	546.89	406.66
December	526.74	395.65	547.62	643.24	549.72	408.01
2017						
January	526.08	395.34	546.89	641.03	549.02	408.08
February	523.77	394.20	544.39	632.23	547.78	407.24
March	527.12	395.82	548.09	644.26	550.33	408.57
April	526.38	395.64	547.25	641.77	549.63	408.50
May	524.57	395.53	545.17	633.24	548.81	408.48
June	526.89	395.91	547.88	644.66	550.22	408.82
July	525.64	395.70	546.47	639.41	549.47	408.65
			State supplementation			
2016						
July	141.81	147.22	139.78	61.67	150.10	149.25
August	141.77	147.25	139.72	61.61	150.02	149.28
September	142.04	147.46	140.00	61.59	150.25	149.52
October	141.82	147.25	139.78	61.55	150.08	149.29
November	141.78	147.25	139.72	61.48	149.97	149.29
December	141.99	147.42	139.94	61.59	150.21	149.44
2017						
January	146.01	151.74	143.85	63.24	154.36	153.82
February	145.94	151.62	143.80	63.30	154.28	153.74
March	146.17	151.81	144.05	63.28	154.49	153.91
April	146.07	151.79	143.91	63.22	154.38	153.86
May	146.07	151.74	143.93	63.24	154.40	153.83
June	146.13	151.71	144.01	63.28	154.39	153.81
July	146.01	151.61	143.88	63.18	154.23	153.73

SSI = Supplemental Security Income.
Note: Data are for the end of the specified month and exclude retroactive payments.

SOURCE: "Table 7. Average Monthly Payment, by Eligibility Category, Age, and Source of Payment, July 2016–July 2017," in *SSI Monthly Statistics, July 2017*, US Social Security Administration, Office of Policy, July 2017, https://www.ssa.gov/policy/docs/statcomps/ssi_monthly/2017-07/table07.pdf (accessed October 16, 2017)

delayed retirement credit as a "partial lump sum," starting with those who become initially entitled for retired worker benefits after 2018. The amount of the lump sum would be calculated by birth year and age of initial benefit entitlement. The bill was referred to the House Committee on Ways and Means' Subcommittee on Social Security in July 2017, where it remained as of February 2018.

In March 2017 the US representative Charlie Crist (1956–; D-FL) introduced the Save Social Security Act of 2017 (H.R. 1631). This bill aims to increase the amount of money that high earners pay into the Social Security program by, for instance, expanding the portion of wages and self-employment income that are subject to Social Security payroll taxes. The proposed law would

TABLE 2.13

Life expectancy at birth and age 65, selected years 1940–2095

Calendar year	Intermediate				Low-cost				High-cost			
	At birth[a]		At age 65[b]		At birth[a]		At age 65[b]		At birth[a]		At age 65[b]	
	Male	Female	Male	Female	Male	Female	Male	Female	Male	Female	Male	Female
1940	70.4	76.6	12.7	14.7	70.3	76.4	12.7	14.7	70.6	76.9	12.7	14.7
1945	72.3	78.3	13.0	15.4	72.0	78.0	13.0	15.4	72.6	78.8	13.0	15.4
1950	73.5	79.7	13.1	16.2	73.0	79.2	13.1	16.2	74.0	80.2	13.1	16.2
1955	74.1	80.2	13.1	16.7	73.5	79.6	13.1	16.7	74.8	81.0	13.1	16.7
1960	74.8	80.7	13.2	17.4	74.0	79.9	13.2	17.4	75.8	81.6	13.2	17.4
1965	75.8	81.2	13.5	18.0	74.8	80.3	13.5	18.0	77.0	82.4	13.5	18.0
1970	77.0	82.1	13.8	18.5	75.8	80.9	13.8	18.5	78.4	83.5	13.8	18.5
1975	77.9	82.8	14.2	18.7	76.5	81.5	14.2	18.7	79.6	84.4	14.2	18.7
1980	78.8	83.5	14.7	18.8	77.2	82.0	14.7	18.8	80.7	85.3	14.7	18.8
1985	79.5	84.1	15.4	19.1	77.7	82.4	15.4	19.1	81.7	86.0	15.4	19.1
1990	80.2	84.6	16.1	19.4	78.2	82.8	16.1	19.4	82.6	86.7	16.1	19.5
1995	81.0	85.2	16.8	19.8	78.7	83.1	16.7	19.7	83.6	87.4	16.8	19.9
2000	81.5	85.6	17.5	20.2	79.1	83.4	17.4	20.1	84.3	88.0	17.7	20.4
2005	82.0	86.0	18.2	20.7	79.4	83.7	17.9	20.5	84.9	88.5	18.4	21.1
2006	82.1	86.0	18.3	20.8	79.4	83.7	18.0	20.5	85.1	88.6	18.6	21.2
2007	82.2	86.1	18.4	20.9	79.5	83.8	18.1	20.6	85.2	88.7	18.7	21.3
2008	82.3	86.2	18.4	21.0	79.5	83.8	18.1	20.6	85.3	88.8	18.8	21.4
2009	82.4	86.3	18.5	21.1	79.6	83.9	18.2	20.7	85.5	88.9	19.0	21.5
2010	82.5	86.4	18.6	21.1	79.7	83.9	18.2	20.7	85.6	89.1	19.1	21.6
2011	82.6	86.4	18.7	21.2	79.7	84.0	18.3	20.8	85.7	89.1	19.2	21.7
2012	82.7	86.5	18.8	21.3	79.8	84.0	18.3	20.8	85.9	89.2	19.3	21.9
2013	82.8	86.6	18.9	21.4	79.9	84.1	18.4	20.8	86.0	89.3	19.5	22.0
2014	82.9	86.7	18.9	21.4	79.9	84.1	18.4	20.9	86.1	89.4	19.6	22.1
2015	83.0	86.7	19.0	21.5	80.0	84.2	18.5	20.9	86.2	89.5	19.7	22.2
2016	83.1	86.8	19.1	21.6	80.0	84.2	18.5	21.0	86.4	89.7	19.8	22.3
2020	83.4	87.1	19.4	21.8	80.2	84.4	18.6	21.1	86.8	90.0	20.3	22.7
2025	83.9	87.5	19.7	22.1	80.5	84.6	18.8	21.2	87.4	90.5	20.8	23.2
2030	84.3	87.8	20.0	22.4	80.8	84.8	19.0	21.4	87.9	90.9	21.3	23.6
2035	84.7	88.1	20.4	22.7	81.0	85.0	19.2	21.5	88.5	91.4	21.8	24.0
2040	85.0	88.4	20.7	22.9	81.3	85.2	19.3	21.7	88.9	91.8	22.3	24.4
2045	85.4	88.7	21.0	23.2	81.5	85.4	19.5	21.8	89.4	92.1	22.7	24.8
2050	85.8	89.0	21.2	23.5	81.7	85.6	19.6	22.0	89.9	92.5	23.1	25.2
2055	86.1	89.3	21.5	23.7	82.0	85.8	19.8	22.1	90.3	92.9	23.5	25.5
2060	86.4	89.6	21.8	23.9	82.2	86.0	20.0	22.3	90.7	93.2	23.9	25.9
2065	86.8	89.8	22.0	24.2	82.4	86.2	20.1	22.4	91.1	93.5	24.2	26.2
2070	87.1	90.1	22.3	24.4	82.6	86.3	20.3	22.5	91.5	93.8	24.6	26.5
2075	87.4	90.3	22.5	24.6	82.8	86.5	20.4	22.7	91.8	94.2	24.9	26.8
2080	87.7	90.6	22.8	24.8	83.1	86.7	20.5	22.8	92.2	94.4	25.2	27.1
2085	88.0	90.8	23.0	25.1	83.3	86.9	20.7	22.9	92.5	94.7	25.6	27.4
2090	88.2	91.1	23.2	25.3	83.5	87.0	20.8	23.1	92.9	95.0	25.9	27.7
2095	88.5	91.3	23.5	25.5	83.7	87.2	21.0	23.2	93.2	95.3	26.2	28.0

Notes: The cohort life expectancy at a given age for a given year is the average remaining number of years expected prior to death for a person at that exact age, born on January 1, using the mortality rates for the series of years in which the individual will actually reach each succeeding age if he or she survives.

[a]Cohort life expectancy at birth for those born in the calendar year is based on a combination of actual, estimated, and projected death rates for birth years 1940 through 2014. For birth years after 2014, these values depend on estimated and projected death rates.

[b]Age 65 cohort life expectancy for those attaining age 65 in calendar years 1940 though 2013 depends on actual death rates or on a combination of actual, estimated, and projected death rates. After 2013, these values depend on estimated and projected death rates.

SOURCE: "Table V.A5. Cohort Life Expectancy," in *The 2017 Annual Report of the Board of Trustees of the Federal Old-Age and Survivors Insurance and Federal Disability Insurance Trust Funds*, US Social Security Administration, Office of the Chief Actuary, July 2017, https://www.ssa.gov/OACT/TR/2017/tr2017.pdf (accessed October 16, 2017).

apply the payroll taxes to earnings over $300,000 (under current law they only apply to the first $127,200 of income in 2017). This bill also was referred to committee, where it remained as of February 2018.

AMERICANS ARE CONCERNED ABOUT CHANGES TO SOCIAL SECURITY. Frank Newport of Gallup, Inc., reports in "Young, Old in U.S. Plan on Relying More on Social Security" (May 25, 2017, http://news.gallup.com/poll/211085/nonretirees-rely-social-security.aspx) that a Gallup survey in April 2017 found that 25% of Americans aged 18 to 29 years, 28% of those aged 30 to 49 years,

and 43% of those aged 50 to 64 years expect Social Security to be a major source of their retirement funds. The survey also found that 58% of retirees said Social Security is a major source of their retirement income.

Nevertheless, Americans are not completely confident that they will receive Social Security benefits when they retire. In *Many Americans Doubt They Will Get Social Security Benefits* (August 13, 2015, http://news.gallup.com/poll/184580/americans-doubt-social-security-benefits.aspx), Newport reports that more than half (51%) of non-retirees are doubtful that they will receive Social

Security benefits when they retire. Nearly half (43%) of current retirees are concerned about eventual cuts in benefits, and two-thirds of Americans think that the Social Security system has major problems (45%) or is in a state of crisis (21%). When given a choice between raising taxes or cutting benefits to ensure the continuing solvency of the system, more Americans favor raising taxes (51%) than curbing benefits (37%).

CHAPTER 3

LIVING ARRANGEMENTS OF THE OLDER POPULATION

The vast majority of older Americans live independently in the community. They are not institutionalized in facilities such as nursing homes or retirement homes. The Administration on Aging (AoA) notes in *A Profile of Older Americans: 2016* (April 2017, https://www.acl.gov/sites/default/files/Aging%20and%20Disability%20in%20America/2016-Profile.pdf) that although the overall number of older Americans living in nursing homes was small—nearly 1.5 million (3.1%) people who were 65 years and older in 2015—the percentage of older adults in nursing homes increased significantly with advancing age, from 1% of 65- to 74-year-olds, to 3% of 75- to 84-year-olds, and to 9% of those aged 85 years and older.

The living arrangements of older adults are important because they are closely associated with their health, well-being, and economic status. For example, older adults who live alone are more likely to live in poverty than those who live with their spouse or other family members. Older adults living alone may also be socially isolated, and their health may suffer because there are no family members or others nearby to serve as caregivers.

LIVING WITH A SPOUSE, OTHER RELATIVES, OR ALONE

Table 3.1 shows that 31 million (25%) out of 125.8 million households were headed by a person aged 65 years or older in 2016. It also shows that the median age (the middle value; half of all householders are younger and half are older) of householders has consistently increased over the past three decades. Figure 3.1 shows the steady rise in the number of households headed by householders aged 65 years and older between 1980 and 2016, compared with the relatively unchanged number of households headed by people under the age of 30 years.

According to the AoA in *Profile of Older Americans: 2016*, more than half (59%) of community-dwelling, civilian (noninstitutionalized—people who are not in the US military, school, jail, or mental health facilities) older adults lived with their spouse in 2016. Significantly more older men than women—73% (15.5 million) of older men, compared with 47% (12 million) of older women—lived with their spouse. (See Figure 3.2.) This disparity occurs because women usually live longer than men, are generally younger than the men they marry, and are far less likely to remarry after the death of a spouse, largely because there are relatively few available older men.

In addition, the proportion of older adults living with their spouse decreased with age. US Census Bureau data reveal that in 2016, 17.6 million adults aged 65 to 74 years lived with their spouse, compared with 7.4 million adults aged 75 to 84 years and 1.7 million aged 85 years and older. (See Table 3.2.)

Multigenerational Households

The Census Bureau in its American Community Survey finds that 7.3 million grandparents were living in the same household as their grandchildren under the age of 18 years in 2016 and that 2.5 million (35%) of these grandparents were responsible for their grandchildren. (See Table 3.3.) Of the grandparents living with grandchildren, more than 1 million had an income below the poverty level. (See Table 3.4.)

Until recently, multigenerational living often occurred when older adults exhausted their resources. The Great Recession (which lasted from late 2007 to mid-2009), job losses, and foreclosures, however, prompted many younger adults to move in with parents and/or grandparents. In "A Record 60.6 Million Americans Live in Multigenerational Households" (August 11, 2016, http://www.pewresearch.org/fact-tank/2016/08/11/a-record-60-6-million-americans-live-in-multigenerational-households/), D'Vera Cohn and Jeffrey S. Passel of the Pew Research Center report that 60.6 million people in the United States (19% of the population) lived in

TABLE 3.1

Households by age of householder, 1960–2016

[Numbers in thousands, except for medians]

Year	All households	Under 25	25 to 29 years	30 to 34 years	35 to 44 years	45 to 54 years	55 to 64 years	65 to 74 years	75 years and older	Median age
					Age of householder					
2016	125,819	6,361	9,453	10,594	21,222	23,295	23,896	17,551	13,448	51.9
2015	124,587	6,370	9,350	10,725	21,121	23,566	23,509	16,886	13,061	51.6
2014[a]	123,229	6,404	9,300	10,677	21,123	23,733	23,205	15,981	12,806	51.2
2013	122,459	6,314	9,251	10,767	21,334	24,068	22,802	15,349	12,575	50.9
2012	121,084	6,180	9,208	10,638	21,240	24,196	22,779	14,517	12,326	50.6
2011[b]	119,927	6,231	9,283	10,204	21,458	24,768	22,246	13,587	12,151	50.2
2011	118,682	6,140	9,331	10,241	21,251	24,530	21,828	13,348	12,015	50.1
2010	117,538	6,233	9,446	9,811	21,519	24,872	20,387	13,164	12,106	49.7
2009	117,181	6,357	9,463	9,839	22,171	24,633	19,883	12,842	11,992	49.3
2008	116,783	6,553	9,400	9,825	22,448	24,536	19,909	12,284	11,829	49.0
2007	116,011	6,662	9,667	9,767	22,779	24,141	19,266	11,926	11,803	48.6
2006	114,384	6,795	9,223	9,896	23,016	23,732	18,264	11,687	11,772	48.3
2005	113,343	6,734	9,173	10,141	23,248	23,392	17,503	11,528	11,623	48.0
2004	112,000	6,609	8,738	10,421	23,221	23,138	16,824	11,499	11,550	47.8
2003	111,278	6,611	8,535	10,521	24,069	22,623	16,261	11,361	11,299	47.5
2002	109,297	6,391	8,412	10,576	24,031	22,208	15,203	11,472	11,004	47.2
2001	108,209	6,409	8,521	10,510	24,054	21,969	14,277	11,490	10,979	47.0
2000	104,705	5,860	8,520	10,107	23,955	20,927	13,592	11,325	10,419	46.8
1999	103,874	5,770	8,519	10,300	23,969	20,158	13,571	11,373	10,216	46.6
1998	102,528	5,435	8,463	10,570	23,943	19,547	13,072	11,272	10,225	46.3
1997	101,018	5,160	8,647	10,667	23,823	18,843	12,469	11,679	9,729	46.1
1996	99,627	5,282	8,354	10,871	23,227	18,007	12,401	11,908	9,578	46.0
1995	98,990	5,444	8,400	11,052	22,914	17,590	12,224	11,803	9,562	45.9
1994	97,107	5,265	8,472	11,245	22,293	16,837	12,188	11,639	9,168	45.7
1993[b]	96,426	5,257	8,859	11,198	21,862	16,413	12,154	11,668	9,014	45.6
1993	96,391	5,022	8,614	11,127	21,718	16,576	12,438	11,834	9,061	45.9
1992	95,669	4,859	8,810	11,197	21,774	15,547	12,559	12,043	8,878	45.7
1991	94,312	4,882	9,246	11,077	21,304	14,751	12,524	12,001	8,526	45.4
1990	93,347	5,121	9,423	11,049	20,555	14,514	12,529	11,733	8,423	45.3
1989	92,830	5,415	9,624	11,300	19,952	14,018	12,805	11,590	8,127	45.1
1988	91,066	5,228	9,614	10,969	19,323	13,630	12,846	11,410	8,045	45.3
1987	89,479	5,197	9,652	10,850	18,703	13,211	12,868	11,250	7,748	45.3
1986	88,458	5,503	9,781	10,629	17,997	13,099	12,852	11,157	7,439	45.2
1985	86,789	5,438	9,637	10,377	17,481	12,628	13,073	10,851	7,305	45.4
1984	85,407	5,510	9,848	9,960	16,596	12,471	13,121	10,700	7,201	45.6
1983	83,918	5,695	9,465	9,639	16,020	12,354	13,074	10,603	7,067	45.9
1982	83,527	6,109	9,525	9,802	15,326	12,505	12,947	10,379	6,933	45.8
1981	82,368	6,443	9,514	9,639	14,463	12,694	12,704	10,226	6,685	45.9
1980	80,776	6,569	9,252	9,252	13,980	12,654	12,525	10,112	6,432	46.1
1979	77,330	6,342	8,679	8,317	13,328	12,585	12,284	9,753	6,042	46.6
1978	76,030	6,220	8,598	8,233	12,969	12,602	12,183	9,383	5,842	46.6
1977	74,142	5,991	8,385	7,782	12,482	12,905	11,780	9,210	5,606	46.9
1976	72,867	5,877	8,298	7,212	12,227	12,820	11,631	9,258	5,544	47.2
1975	71,120	5,834	7,810	7,137	11,861	12,916	11,301	8,910	5,350	47.3
1974	69,859	5,857	7,527	6,804	11,703	12,939	11,149	8,716	5,162	47.3
1973	68,251	5,476	7,116	6,447	11,721	12,805	11,212	8,369	5,104	47.6
1972	66,676	5,194	6,794	6,009	11,529	12,758	11,138	8,165	5,090	48.0
1971	64,778	4,737	6,239	5,682	11,813	12,588	11,021	7,793	4,909	48.1
1970	63,401	4,359	6,101	5,593	11,810	12,216	10,824	7,744	4,756	48.1
1969	62,214	4,094	5,910	5,447	11,817	12,230	10,622	7,540	4,554	48.1
1968	60,813	3,852	5,336	5,325	12,003	12,038	10,394	7,536	4,327	48.2
1967	59,236	3,587	5,288	5,099	11,998	11,892	9,909	7,321	4,143	48.1
1966	58,406	3,571	4,991	5,086	11,944	11,806	9,745	7,224	4,038	48.1
1965	57,436	3,413	4,808	5,119	12,009	11,523	9,600	7,173	3,790	47.9
1964	56,149	3,110	4,546	5,167	12,176	11,192	9,327	6,998	3,630	47.7
1963	55,270	2,889	4,386	5,314	12,005	11,072	9,103	6,909	3,592	47.7
1962	54,764	2,909	4,349	5,435	11,802	10,906	9,057	6,960	3,346	47.6
1961	53,557	2,628	4,341	5,387	11,596	11,047	9,026	6,355	3,179	47.6
1960	52,799	2,559	4,317	5,407	11,614	10,878	8,599	6,380	3,045	47.3

multigenerational households in 2014, compared with 51.5 million (17% of the population) in 2009. Multigenerational living increased across all racial, ethnic, and age groups. In 2014 more than one-fifth of older Americans lived in multigenerational households: 23% of those aged 55 to 64 years and 21% of adults aged 65 years and older. Nearly 27 million people lived in three-generation households, and 3.2 million were in households that consisted of skipped generations (such as just grandparents and grandchildren).

Multigenerational households often form in response to financial difficulties or working parents' need for help

TABLE 3.1

Households by age of householder, 1960–2016 [CONTINUED]

[Numbers in thousands, except for medians]

[a]The 2014 Current Population Survey Annual Social and Economic Supplement (CPS ASEC) included redesigned questions for income and health insurance coverage. All of the approximately 98,000 addresses were selected to receive the improved set of health insurance coverage items. The improved income questions were implemented using a split panel design. Approximately 68,000 addresses were selected to receive a set of income questions similar to those used in the 2013 CPS ASEC. The remaining 30,000 addresses were selected to receive the redesigned income questions. The source of data for this table is the CPS ASEC sample of 98,000 addresses.
[b]Revised based on population from the most recent decennial census.
Note: This table uses the householder's person weight to describe characteristics of people living in households. As a result, estimates of the number of households do not match estimates of housing units from the Housing Vacancy Survey (HVS). The HVS is weighted to housing units, rather than the population, in order to more accurately estimate the number of occupied and vacant housing units.

SOURCE: "Table HH-3. Households, by Age of Householder: 1960 to Present," in *Historical Household Tables*, US Census Bureau, 2016, https://www.census .gov/data/tables/time-series/demo/families/households.html, April 2017 (accessed October 17, 2017)

FIGURE 3.1

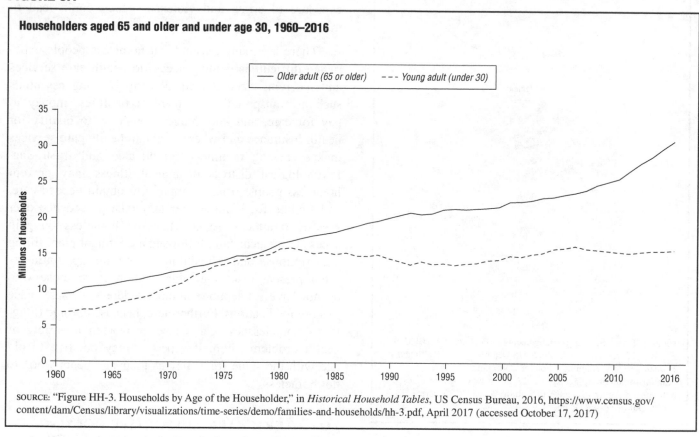

Householders aged 65 and older and under age 30, 1960–2016

Legend: —— Older adult (65 or older)　- - - Young adult (under 30)

SOURCE: "Figure HH-3. Households by Age of the Householder," in *Historical Household Tables*, US Census Bureau, 2016, https://www.census.gov/ content/dam/Census/library/visualizations/time-series/demo/families-and-households/hh-3.pdf, April 2017 (accessed October 17, 2017)

with child care. Other circumstances, such as parents unable to care for their children because of incarceration, mental health issues, or substance abuse, may also prompt grandparents to assume responsibility for their grandchildren.

HOMELESSNESS

The National Coalition on Homelessness notes in "Elder Homelessness" (2018, http://nationalhomeless .org/issues/elderly) that multiple studies reveal an increase in the proportion of older adults between the ages of 50 and 64 in the homeless population. The organization notes that older Americans may be less likely than

younger Americans to be homeless because safety-net programs such as Social Security, Supplemental Security Income (SSI), Medicare (a medical insurance program for older adults and people with disabilities), and senior housing help prevent homelessness.

There are reports of a growing population of homeless older adults. Adam Nagourney reports in "Old and on the Street: The Graying of America's Homeless" (NYTimes.com, May 31, 2016), that in 2014 more than 306,000 people over the age of 50 were homeless and that these older adults accounted for 31% of the US homeless population. More detailed information is available about people in homeless shelters. According to the

FIGURE 3.2

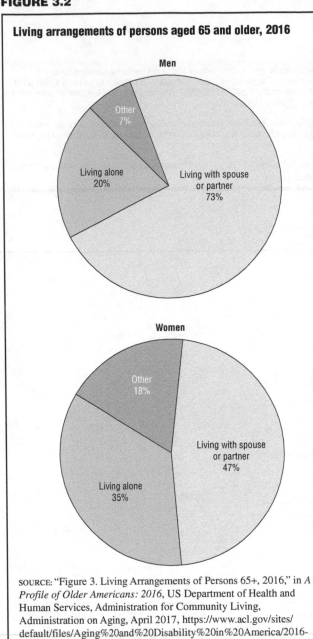

Living arrangements of persons aged 65 and older, 2016

Men

Other
7%

Living alone
20%

Living with spouse
or partner
73%

Women

Other
18%

Living with spouse
or partner
47%

Living alone
35%

SOURCE: "Figure 3. Living Arrangements of Persons 65+, 2016," in *A Profile of Older Americans: 2016*, US Department of Health and Human Services, Administration for Community Living, Administration on Aging, April 2017, https://www.acl.gov/sites/default/files/Aging%20and%20Disability%20in%20America/2016-Profile.pdf (accessed October 13, 2017)

US Department of Housing and Urban Development (HUD), 16.5% of all people in shelters in 2007 were aged 51 years and older; by 2015 this group accounted for 21.4% of sheltered homeless people. (See Figure 3.3.)

The aging of the large population of baby boomers (people born between 1946 and 1964) is primarily responsible for the 20% increase in older homeless people since 2007. Nagourney reports that many of these older adults have been homeless for decades, having lost their homes during the late 1970s and 1980s when federal housing cutbacks and epidemic drug use forced them onto the streets. Others have spent time in various institutions, such as prisons and mental or rehabilitation health facilities, and

the more recently homeless include those who lost their jobs or simply cannot afford to pay rent.

Among the concerns about homelessness are the inherent health-related issues. The relationship between homelessness, health, and illness is complex. Some health problems precede homelessness and contribute to it, whereas others are consequences of homelessness. In addition, homelessness often complicates access and adherence to treatment. For example, mental illness or substance abuse (dependency on alcohol or drugs) may limit a person's ability to work, leading to poverty and homelessness. Without protection from the cold, rain, and snow, exposure to weather may result in illnesses such as bronchitis or pneumonia. Homelessness also increases exposure to crime and violence, which could lead to trauma and injuries.

There are many reasons that homeless people experience difficulties gaining access to health care services and receiving needed medical care. Lacking essentials such as transportation to medical facilities, money to pay for care, and knowledge about how to qualify for health insurance and where to obtain health care services makes seeking treatment complicated and frustrating. Psychological distress or mental illness may prevent homeless people from attempting to obtain needed care, and finding food and shelter may take precedence over seeking treatment. Even when the homeless do gain access to medical care, following a treatment plan, filling prescriptions, and scheduling follow-up appointments often present insurmountable challenges to those who do not have a telephone number, address, or safe place to store medications. Furthermore, because chronic (long-term) homelessness can cause or worsen a variety of health problems, homeless people may not live to old age with the same frequency as their age peers who are not homeless.

LONG-TERM CARE, SUPPORTIVE HOUSING, AND OTHER RESIDENTIAL ALTERNATIVES

Spouses and other relatives are still the major caretakers of older, dependent members of American society. However, the number of people aged 65 years and older living in long-term care facilities such as nursing homes is rising because the older population is increasing rapidly. Although many older adults now live longer, healthier lives, the increase in overall length of life has amplified the need for long-term care facilities and supportive housing.

Growth of the home health care industry during the early 1990s only slightly slowed the increase in the numbers of Americans entering nursing homes. Supportive housing (assisted living, congregate housing, and continuing care retirement communities) offers alternatives

TABLE 3.2

Marital status by age and sex, 2016

[Numbers in thousands, except for percentages]

	Total Number	Married spouse present Number	Married spouse absent Number	Widowed Number	Divorced Number	Separated Number	Never married Number	Total Percent	Married spouse present Percent	Married spouse absent Percent	Widowed Percent	Divorced Percent	Separated Percent	Never married Percent
Both sexes														
Total 15+	257,615	125,256	3,613	14,856	25,539	5,276	83,074	100.0	48.6	1.4	5.8	9.9	2.0	32.2
15–17 years	13,071	36	69	17	28	64	12,856	100.0	0.3	0.5	0.1	0.2	0.5	98.4
18–19 years	7,750	100	42	—	24	49	7,533	100.0	1.3	0.5	—	0.3	0.6	97.2
20–24 years	21,919	1,993	133	26	198	273	19,296	100.0	9.1	0.6	0.1	0.9	1.2	88.0
25–29 years	22,429	6,988	380	48	626	432	13,955	100.0	31.2	1.7	0.2	2.8	1.9	62.2
30–34 years	21,321	10,787	387	84	1,282	540	8,241	100.0	50.6	1.8	0.4	6.0	2.5	38.6
35–39 years	20,383	12,497	408	150	1,856	568	4,903	100.0	61.3	2.0	0.7	9.1	2.8	24.1
40–44 years	19,613	12,529	320	204	2,432	706	3,423	100.0	63.9	1.6	1.0	12.4	3.6	17.5
45–49 years	20,677	13,162	352	356	3,085	618	3,103	100.0	63.7	1.7	1.7	14.9	3.0	15.0
50–54 years	21,875	13,929	348	588	3,526	633	2,852	100.0	63.7	1.6	2.7	16.1	2.9	13.0
55–64 years	41,115	26,421	555	1,992	6,786	903	4,459	100.0	64.3	1.3	4.8	16.5	2.2	10.8
65–74 years	27,917	17,635	343	3,872	4,062	345	1,659	100.0	63.2	1.2	13.9	14.5	1.2	5.9
75–84 years	14,050	7,437	181	4,339	1,378	124	590	100.0	52.9	1.3	30.9	9.8	0.9	4.2
85+ years	5,496	1,740	96	3,178	255	23	205	100.0	31.7	1.7	57.8	4.6	0.4	3.7
15–17 years	13,071	36	69	17	28	64	12,856	100.0	0.3	0.5	0.1	0.2	0.5	98.4
18+ years	244,544	125,220	3,544	14,839	25,511	5,212	70,218	100.0	51.2	1.4	6.1	10.4	2.1	28.7
15–64 years	210,152	98,444	2,993	3,467	19,844	4,785	80,620	100.0	46.8	1.4	1.6	9.4	2.3	38.4
65+ years	47,463	26,813	620	11,389	5,695	492	2,454	100.0	56.5	1.3	24.0	12.0	1.0	5.2
Male														
Total 15+	124,953	62,628	1,860	3,469	10,708	2,207	44,079	100.0	50.1	1.5	2.8	8.6	1.8	35.3
15–17 years	6,603	22	33	7	16	38	6,487	100.0	0.3	0.5	0.1	0.2	0.6	98.2
18–19 years	3,968	32	23	—	9	29	3,875	100.0	0.8	0.6	—	0.2	0.7	97.7
20–24 years	11,055	732	57	13	89	108	10,056	100.0	6.6	0.5	0.1	0.8	1.0	91.0
25–29 years	11,283	2,980	185	19	249	139	7,711	100.0	26.4	1.6	0.2	2.2	1.2	68.3
30–34 years	10,556	4,948	225	23	555	188	4,616	100.0	46.9	2.1	0.2	5.3	1.8	43.7
35–39 years	10,054	6,058	213	31	829	207	2,716	100.0	60.3	2.1	0.3	8.2	2.1	27.0
40–44 years	9,640	6,341	157	50	987	298	1,807	100.0	65.8	1.6	0.5	10.2	3.1	18.7
45–49 years	10,125	6,319	177	124	1,420	286	1,799	100.0	62.4	1.7	1.2	14.0	2.8	17.8
50–54 years	10,708	6,914	186	178	1,546	272	1,613	100.0	64.6	1.7	1.7	14.4	2.5	15.1
55–64 years	19,768	13,353	283	464	2,914	412	2,342	100.0	67.5	1.4	2.3	14.7	2.1	11.8
65–74 years	12,952	9,427	156	916	1,516	153	784	100.0	72.8	1.2	7.1	11.7	1.2	6.1
75–84 years	6,254	4,383	106	974	517	66	209	100.0	70.1	1.7	15.6	8.3	1.0	3.3
85+ years	1,988	1,119	59	673	61	12	63	100.0	56.3	3.0	33.8	3.1	0.6	3.2
15–17 years	6,603	22	33	7	16	38	6,487	100.0	0.3	0.5	0.1	0.2	0.6	98.2
18+ years	118,349	62,606	1,827	3,462	10,692	2,169	37,592	100.0	52.9	1.5	2.9	9.0	1.8	31.8
15–64 years	103,759	47,699	1,539	907	8,614	1,977	43,023	100.0	46.0	1.5	0.9	8.3	1.9	41.5
65+ years	21,194	14,929	321	2,563	2,094	231	1,057	100.0	70.4	1.5	12.1	9.9	1.1	5.0
Female														
Total 15+	132,662	62,628	1,753	11,387	14,831	3,069	38,995	100.0	47.2	1.3	8.6	11.2	2.3	29.4
15–17 years	6,468	14	37	10	12	26	6,368	100.0	0.2	0.6	0.2	0.2	0.4	98.5
18–19 years	3,782	68	19	—	15	20	3,658	100.0	1.8	0.5	—	0.4	0.5	96.7
20–24 years	10,864	1,261	75	14	109	165	9,240	100.0	11.6	0.7	0.1	1.0	1.5	85.1
25–29 years	11,146	4,008	195	29	378	293	6,244	100.0	36.0	1.7	0.3	3.4	2.6	56.0
30–34 years	10,766	5,839	162	62	727	351	3,624	100.0	54.2	1.5	0.6	6.8	3.3	33.7
35–39 years	10,329	6,439	195	119	1,027	362	2,187	100.0	62.3	1.9	1.2	9.9	3.5	21.2
40–44 years	9,973	6,187	163	154	1,446	407	1,615	100.0	62.0	1.6	1.5	14.5	4.1	16.2
45–49 years	10,552	6,843	175	233	1,665	332	1,304	100.0	64.9	1.7	2.2	15.8	3.1	12.4
50–54 years	11,167	7,015	162	410	1,980	361	1,239	100.0	62.8	1.4	3.7	17.7	3.2	11.1
55–64 years	21,347	13,068	271	1,528	3,872	491	2,117	100.0	61.2	1.3	7.2	18.1	2.3	9.9
65–74 years	14,964	8,208	187	2,956	2,545	192	875	100.0	54.9	1.3	19.8	17.0	1.3	5.8
75–84 years	7,796	3,054	76	3,365	861	58	381	100.0	39.2	1.0	43.2	11.0	0.7	4.9
85+ years	3,509	621	36	2,506	194	10	141	100.0	17.7	1.0	71.4	5.5	0.3	4.0
15–17 years	6,468	14	37	10	12	26	6,368	100.0	0.2	0.6	0.2	0.2	0.4	98.5
18+ years	126,194	62,614	1,717	11,376	14,819	3,043	32,626	100.0	49.6	1.4	9.0	11.7	2.4	25.9
15–64 years	106,393	50,745	1,454	2,560	11,230	2,808	37,597	100.0	47.7	1.4	2.4	10.6	2.6	35.3
65+ years	26,269	11,884	299	8,827	3,601	261	1,397	100.0	45.2	1.1	33.6	13.7	1.0	5.3

Dash ("—") represents or rounds to zero.
Note: Prior to 2001, this table included group quarters people.

SOURCE: Adapted from "Table A1. Marital Status of People 15 Years and over, by Age, Sex, and Personal Earnings: 2016," in *America's Families and Living Arrangements: 2016*, US Census Bureau, April 2017, https://www.census.gov/data/tables/2016/demo/families/cps-2016.html (accessed October 17, 2017)

to nursing home care. The overarching goal of supportive housing is to enable older adults to receive needed assistance while retaining as much independence as possible.

TABLE 3.3

Grandparents living with grandchildren, 2016

	United States Estimate
Total	**195,787,513**
Living with own grandchildren under 18 years	7,271,261
Grandparent responsible for own grandchildren under 18 years	2,519,737
Grandparent responsible less than 6 months	248,814
Grandparent responsible 6 to 11 months	234,919
Grandparent responsible 1 or 2 years	548,114
Grandparent responsible 3 or 4 years	403,942
Grandparent responsible 5 years or more	1,083,948
Grandparent not responsible for own grandchildren under 18 years	4,751,524
Not living with own grandchildren under 18 years	188,516,252

SOURCE: "B10050. Grandparents Living with Own Grandchildren under 18 Years by Responsibility for Own Grandchildren by Length of Time Responsible for Own Grandchildren for the Population 30 Years and Over," in *American Community Survey*, US Census Bureau, 2017, https://factfinder.census.gov/bkmk/table/1.0/en/ACS/16_1YR/B10050 (accessed October 17, 2017)

TABLE 3.4

Grandparents living with grandchildren, by poverty status, 2016

	United States Estimate
Total	**7,271,071**
Income in the past 12 months below poverty level	**1,027,572**
Grandparent responsible for own grandchildren under 18 years	482,121
30 to 59 years	303,667
60 years and over	178,454
Grandparent not responsible for own grandchildren under 18 years	545,451
Income in the past 12 months at or above poverty level	**6,243,499**
Grandparent responsible for own grandchildren under 18 years	2,037,535
30 to 59 years	1,172,811
60 years and over	864,724
Grandparent not responsible for own grandchildren under 18 years	4,205,964

SOURCE: "B10059. Poverty Status in the Past 12 Months of Grandparents Living with Own Grandchildren under 18 Years by Responsibility for Own Grandchildren and Age of Grandparent," in *American Community Survey*, US Census Bureau, 2017, https://factfinder.census.gov/bkmk/table/1.0/en/ACS/16_1YR/B10059 (accessed October 17, 2017)

There are three broad classes of supportive housing for older adults. The smallest and most affordable options usually house 10 or fewer older adults and are often in homes in residential neighborhoods. Residents share bathrooms, bedrooms, and living areas. These largely unregulated facilities are alternately known as board-and-care facilities, domiciliary care, personal care homes, adult foster care, senior group homes, and sheltered housing.

Residential care facilities, assisted living residences, and adult congregate living facilities tend to be larger, more expensive, and offer more independence and privacy than board-and-care facilities. Most offer private rooms or apartments as well as large common areas for activities and meals.

Continuing care retirement communities and life care communities are usually large complexes that offer a comprehensive range of services from independent living to skilled nursing home care. These facilities are specifically designed to provide nearly all needed care, except hospital care, within one community. Facilities in this group tend to be the costliest.

Nursing Homes

Nursing homes fall into three categories: residential care facilities, intermediate care facilities, and skilled nursing facilities. Each provides a different range and intensity of services:

- A residential care facility provides meals and housekeeping for its residents, plus some basic medical monitoring, such as administering medications. This type of home is for people who are fairly independent and do not need constant medical attention but need help with tasks such as laundry and cleaning. Many residential care facilities also provide social activities and recreational programs for their residents.

FIGURE 3.3

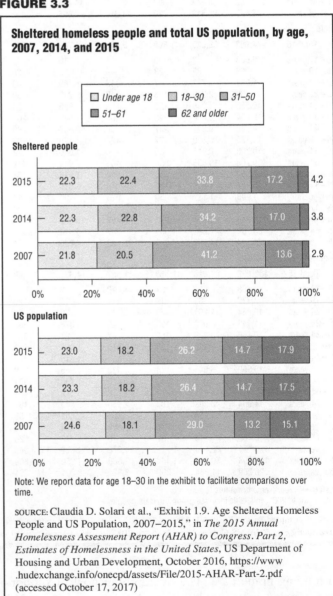

Sheltered homeless people and total US population, by age, 2007, 2014, and 2015

Note: We report data for age 18–30 in the exhibit to facilitate comparisons over time.

SOURCE: Claudia D. Solari et al., "Exhibit 1.9. Age Sheltered Homeless People and US Population, 2007–2015," in *The 2015 Annual Homelessness Assessment Report (AHAR) to Congress. Part 2, Estimates of Homelessness in the United States*, US Department of Housing and Urban Development, October 2016, https://www.hudexchange.info/onecpd/assets/File/2015-AHAR-Part-2.pdf (accessed October 17, 2017)

• An intermediate care facility offers room and board and nursing care as necessary for people who can no longer live independently. Much like residential care facilities, intermediate care facilities provide exercise and social programs, and some offer physical therapy and rehabilitation programs.

• A skilled nursing facility provides around-the-clock nursing care, plus on-call physician coverage. Skilled nursing facilities are for patients who need intensive nursing care, as well as services such as occupational, physical, or respiratory therapies.

NURSING HOME RESIDENTS. The National Center for Health Statistics reports in *2016: With Chartbook on Long-Term Trends in Health* (May 2017, https://www.cdc.gov/nchs/data/hus/2016/092.pdf) that there were 15,656 certified nursing homes in 2015. These facilities had an occupancy rate of 80.3% and housed 1.4 million residents. (See Table 3.5.) The highest occupancy

TABLE 3.5

Nursing homes and occupancy rates, by state, selected years 1995–2015

[Data are based on a census of certified nursing facilities]

State	Nursing homes				Beds			
	1995	2000	2014	2015	1995	2000	2014	2015
					Number			
United States	**16,389**	**16,886**	**15,643**	**15,656**	**1,751,302**	**1,795,388**	**1,693,943**	**1,694,777**
Alabama	221	225	226	227	23,353	25,248	26,388	26,506
Alaska	15	15	18	18	814	821	693	693
Arizona	152	150	147	145	16,162	17,458	16,605	16,523
Arkansas	256	255	229	228	29,952	25,715	24,558	24,463
California	1,382	1,369	1,217	1,213	140,203	131,762	119,866	119,046
Colorado	219	225	214	217	19,912	20,240	20,431	20,560
Connecticut	267	259	229	229	32,827	32,433	27,673	27,608
Delaware	42	43	46	45	4,739	4,906	4,876	4,791
District of Columbia	19	20	19	19	3,206	3,078	2,766	2,766
Florida	627	732	689	689	72,656	83,365	83,545	83,668
Georgia	352	363	357	358	38,097	39,817	39,975	39,857
Hawaii	34	45	46	46	2,513	4,006	4,213	4,313
Idaho	76	84	78	79	5,747	6,181	5,951	5,977
Illinois	827	869	761	762	103,230	110,766	98,348	98,489
Indiana	556	564	528	541	59,538	56,762	59,555	61,048
Iowa	419	467	443	442	39,959	37,034	31,950	31,843
Kansas	429	392	345	344	30,016	27,067	25,730	25,756
Kentucky	288	307	287	289	23,221	25,341	26,300	27,060
Louisiana	337	337	280	279	37,769	39,430	35,066	34,537
Maine	132	126	105	103	9,243	8,248	6,953	6,904
Maryland	218	255	228	228	28,394	31,495	28,115	28,013
Massachusetts	550	526	416	413	54,532	56,030	48,320	47,990
Michigan	432	439	433	437	49,473	50,696	46,521	46,669
Minnesota	432	433	377	377	43,865	42,149	30,319	29,934
Mississippi	183	190	205	204	16,059	17,068	18,434	18,426
Missouri	546	551	512	512	52,679	54,829	55,273	55,245
Montana	100	104	83	80	7,210	7,667	6,732	6,693
Nebraska	231	236	219	217	18,169	17,877	16,005	15,961
Nevada	42	51	52	54	3,998	5,547	6,040	6,256
New Hampshire	74	83	76	76	7,412	7,837	7,501	7,525
New Jersey	300	361	361	365	43,967	52,195	52,051	52,538
New Mexico	83	80	71	73	6,969	7,289	6,869	7,070
New York	624	665	628	626	107,750	120,514	117,131	116,666
North Carolina	391	410	422	423	38,322	41,376	45,088	45,221
North Dakota	87	88	81	80	7,125	6,954	6,131	6,009
Ohio	943	1,009	954	959	106,884	105,038	90,653	90,667
Oklahoma	405	392	309	305	33,918	33,903	28,962	28,580
Oregon	161	150	137	137	13,885	13,500	12,210	12,274
Pennsylvania	726	770	699	699	92,625	95,063	88,236	88,133
Rhode Island	94	99	84	84	9,612	10,271	8,720	8,720
South Carolina	166	178	188	187	16,682	18,102	19,631	19,758
South Dakota	114	114	111	111	8,296	7,844	6,945	6,893
Tennessee	322	349	321	319	37,074	38,593	37,268	36,719
Texas	1,266	1,215	1,212	1,222	123,056	125,052	136,000	137,396
Utah	91	93	99	100	7,101	7,651	8,577	8,639
Vermont	23	44	37	37	1,862	3,743	3,174	3,174
Virginia	271	278	288	286	30,070	30,595	32,497	32,447
Washington	285	277	221	220	28,464	25,905	21,286	21,145
West Virginia	129	139	127	126	10,903	11,413	10,888	10,858
Wisconsin	413	420	389	388	48,754	46,395	33,959	33,800
Wyoming	37	40	39	38	3,035	3,119	2,965	2,950

TABLE 3.5

Nursing homes and occupancy rates, by state, selected years 1995–2015 [CONTINUED]

[Data are based on a census of certified nursing facilities]

State	Residents				Occupancy rate*			
	1995	2000	2014	2015	1995	2000	2014	2015
	Number							
United States	1,479,550	1,480,076	1,368,667	1,360,970	84.5	82.4	80.8	80.3
Alabama	21,691	23,089	22,731	22,721	92.9	91.4	86.1	85.7
Alaska	634	595	612	626	77.9	72.5	88.3	90.3
Arizona	12,382	13,253	11,428	11,588	76.6	75.9	68.8	70.1
Arkansas	20,823	19,317	17,688	17,655	69.5	75.1	72.0	72.2
California	109,805	106,460	102,245	102,674	78.3	80.8	85.3	86.2
Colorado	17,055	17,045	16,309	16,290	85.7	84.2	79.8	79.2
Connecticut	29,948	29,657	24,250	24,018	91.2	91.4	87.6	87.0
Delaware	3,819	3,900	4,314	4,253	80.6	79.5	88.5	88.8
District of Columbia	2,576	2,858	2,539	2,540	80.3	92.9	91.8	91.8
Florida	61,845	69,050	73,487	73,492	85.1	82.8	88.0	87.8
Georgia	35,933	36,559	33,930	33,399	94.3	91.8	84.9	83.8
Hawaii	2,413	3,558	3,663	3,568	96.0	88.8	86.9	82.7
Idaho	4,697	4,640	3,841	3,881	81.7	75.1	64.5	64.9
Illinois	83,696	83,604	72,563	71,952	81.1	75.5	73.8	73.1
Indiana	44,328	42,328	38,893	39,267	74.5	74.6	65.3	64.3
Iowa	27,506	29,204	24,859	24,585	68.8	78.9	77.8	77.2
Kansas	25,140	22,230	18,337	18,204	83.8	82.1	71.3	70.7
Kentucky	20,696	22,730	23,008	23,453	89.1	89.7	87.5	86.7
Louisiana	32,493	30,735	25,854	25,722	86.0	77.9	73.7	74.5
Maine	8,587	7,298	6,239	6,199	92.9	88.5	89.7	89.8
Maryland	24,716	25,629	24,430	24,572	87.0	81.4	86.9	87.7
Massachusetts	49,765	49,805	41,255	40,794	91.3	88.9	85.4	85.0
Michigan	43,271	42,615	39,374	39,275	87.5	84.1	84.6	84.2
Minnesota	41,163	38,813	26,695	25,725	93.8	92.1	88.0	85.9
Mississippi	15,247	15,815	16,129	16,026	94.9	92.7	87.5	87.0
Missouri	39,891	38,586	38,326	38,418	75.7	70.4	69.3	69.5
Montana	6,415	5,973	4,619	4,466	89.0	77.9	68.6	66.7
Nebraska	16,166	14,989	12,043	11,938	89.0	83.8	75.2	74.8
Nevada	3,645	3,657	4,821	4,827	91.2	65.9	79.8	77.2
New Hampshire	6,877	7,158	6,767	6,706	92.8	91.3	90.2	89.1
New Jersey	40,397	45,837	45,185	44,998	91.9	87.8	86.8	85.6
New Mexico	6,051	6,503	5,439	5,502	86.8	89.2	79.2	77.8
New York	103,409	112,957	105,390	104,684	96.0	93.7	90.0	89.7
North Carolina	35,511	36,658	37,058	36,612	92.7	88.6	82.2	81.0
North Dakota	6,868	6,343	5,664	5,571	96.4	91.2	92.4	92.7
Ohio	79,026	81,946	76,325	75,523	73.9	78.0	84.2	83.3
Oklahoma	26,377	23,833	19,108	18,854	77.8	70.3	66.0	66.0
Oregon	11,673	9,990	7,343	7,379	84.1	74.0	60.1	60.1
Pennsylvania	84,843	83,880	79,598	78,822	91.6	88.2	90.2	89.4
Rhode Island	8,823	9,041	8,011	7,966	91.8	88.0	91.9	91.4
South Carolina	14,568	15,739	16,773	16,830	87.3	86.9	85.4	85.2
South Dakota	7,926	7,059	6,381	6,301	95.5	90.0	91.9	91.4
Tennessee	33,929	34,714	28,897	28,246	91.5	89.9	77.5	76.9
Texas	89,354	85,275	93,170	93,316	72.6	68.2	68.5	67.9
Utah	5,832	5,703	5,515	5,518	82.1	74.5	64.3	63.9
Vermont	1,792	3,349	2,686	2,628	96.2	89.5	84.6	82.8
Virginia	28,119	27,091	28,486	27,874	93.5	88.5	87.7	85.9
Washington	24,954	21,158	17,005	16,969	87.7	81.7	79.9	80.3
West Virginia	10,216	10,334	9,535	9,471	93.7	90.5	87.6	87.2
Wisconsin	43,998	38,911	27,485	26,804	90.2	83.9	80.9	79.3
Wyoming	2,661	2,605	2,364	2,268	87.7	83.5	79.7	76.9

*Percentage of beds occupied (number of nursing home residents per 100 nursing home beds).

Notes: Annual numbers of nursing homes, beds, and residents are based on the Centers for Medicare & Medicaid Services' reporting cycle. Starting with 2013 data, a new editing rule was used for number of beds. For the US, the number of beds decreased by less than 1%. For most states, this caused little or no change in the data. The change in the number of beds also caused a change in some occupancy rates. Because of the methodology change, trends should be interpreted with caution. Data for additional years are available.

SOURCE: "Table 92. Nursing Homes, Beds, Residents, and Occupancy Rates, by State: United States, Selected Years 1995–2015," in *Health, United States, 2016: With Chartbook on Long-Term Trends in Health*, National Center for Health Statistics, May 2017, https://www.cdc.gov/nchs/data/hus/2016/092.pdf (accessed October 17, 2017)

rates were in North Dakota (92.7%), the District of Columbia (91.8%), Rhode Island (91.4%), South Dakota (91.4%), and Alaska (90.3%). The lowest occupancy rates were in Oregon (60.1%), Utah (63.9%), Indiana (64.3%), and Idaho (64.9%).

DIVERSIFICATION OF NURSING HOMES. To remain competitive with home health care and the increasing array of alternative living arrangements for older adults, many nursing homes have begun offering specialized services. In *Long-Term Care Providers and Services*

FIGURE 3.4

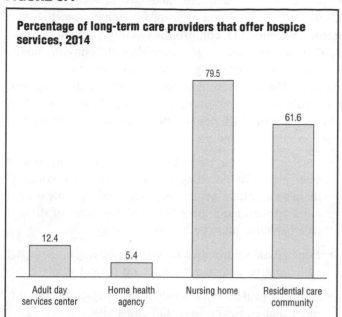

Percentage of long-term care providers that offer hospice services, 2014

SOURCE: Lauren Harris-Kojetin et al., "Figure 17. Percentage of Long-Term Care Services Providers That Provide Hospice Services, by Sector: United States, 2014," in "Long-Term Care Providers and Services Users in the United States: Data from the National Study of Long-Term Care Providers, 2013–2014," *Vital and Health Statistics*, series 3, no. 38, February 2016, https://www.cdc.gov/nchs/data/series/sr_03/sr03_038.pdf (accessed October 18, 2017)

FIGURE 3.5

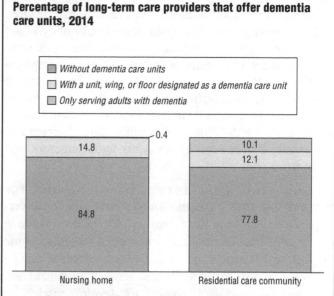

Percentage of long-term care providers that offer dementia care units, 2014

SOURCE: Lauren Harris-Kojetin et al., "Figure 20. Percent Distribution of Long-Term Care Service Providers, by Sector and Dementia Care Unit: United States, 2014," in "Long-Term Care Providers and Services Users in the United States: Data from the National Study of Long-Term Care Providers, 2013–2014," *Vital and Health Statistics*, series 3, no. 38, February 2016, https://www.cdc.gov/nchs/data/series/sr_03/sr03_038.pdf (accessed October 18, 2017)

Users in the United States: Data from the National Study of Long-Term Care Providers, 2013–2014 (February 2016, https://www.cdc.gov/nchs/data/series/sr_03/sr03_038 .pdf), Lauren Harris-Kojetin et al. of the Centers for Disease Control and Prevention report that in 2014 more than three-quarters (79.5%) of all nursing homes offered hospice (end-of-life) care. (See Figure 3.4.) In 2014, 14.8% of nursing homes had a designated dementia care unit for residents suffering from loss of intellectual functioning, memory loss, and personality changes. (See Figure 3.5.)

Collaborating with other providers of health care services or on their own, many nursing homes also offer services such as adult day care and visiting nurse services for people who still live at home. Other programs include respite plans that allow caregivers who need to travel for business or vacation to leave an older relative in the nursing home temporarily.

THE PIONEER NETWORK. In response to concerns about quality of life and quality of care issues in nursing homes, a group of nursing home reform advocates from throughout the United States established the Pioneer Network in 1997 as a forum for changing the culture of eldercare. The Pioneer Network calls for a focus on person-directed values that affirm and support each person's individuality and abilities; these values apply to elders as well as those who work with them. In "Our Vision and Mission" (2018, https://www.pioneernetwork

.net/about-us/mission-vision-values/), the Pioneer Network describes its vision as "a culture of aging that is life-affirming, satisfying, humane and meaningful." It is committed to the following values and principles:

- Know each person
- Each person can and does make a difference
- Relationship is the fundamental building block of a transformed culture
- Respond to spirit, as well as mind and body
- Risk taking is a normal part of life
- Put person before task
- All elders are entitled to self-determination wherever they live
- Community is the antidote to institutionalization
- Do unto others as you would have them do unto you
- Promote the growth and development of all
- Shape and use the potential of the environment in all its aspects: physical, organizational, psycho/social/spiritual
- Practice self-examination, searching for new creativity and opportunities for doing better
- Recognize that culture change and transformation are not destinations but a journey, always a work in progress

To catalyze and support change, the Pioneer Network creates opportunities for learning and networking for providers and caregivers. For example, it offers in-person and online continuing education and training programs for supervisors and midlevel staff and nurse leaders. Besides keeping providers up-to-date about policy issues and culture change, the Pioneer Network focuses on ways to better meet the needs of residents. For example, a December 2017 online course, "Leaders Can Influence Clinical Care: Successful Pain Management for Elders Living with Dementia," offered leaders guidance about how to improve the clinical outcomes (how patients fare as a result of treatment) of residents with dementia who suffer from pain.

INNOVATION AND CULTURE CHANGE IMPROVE THE QUALITY OF LIFE FOR RESIDENTS. Industry observers frequently decry the care that is provided in nursing homes. The media publicizes instances of elder abuse (neglect, exploitation, or mistreatment of older adults) and other quality of care issues. Several organizations, however, have actively sought to develop models of health service delivery that improve the clinical care and quality of life for nursing home residents.

The Innovations Exchange program (https://innovations.ahrq.gov) of the Agency for Healthcare Research and Quality (AHRQ), part of the US Department of Health and Human Services, offers profiles of nursing home innovations and assessments of the effectiveness of these innovations in terms of improving residents' quality of life and satisfaction. The program also examines nursing homes' ability to attract and retain staff and their financial performance. By sharing and publicizing these innovations, the AHRQ aims to improve the quality of nursing home care.

For example, the AHRQ describes in "Messaging System Enables Nursing Home Residents to E-mail Loved Ones without a Computer, Leading to Enhanced Quality of Life" (August 27, 2014, https://innovations.ahrq.gov/profiles/messaging-system-enables-nursing-home-residents-e-mail-loved-ones-without-computer-leading) the use of a messaging system that enables residents to send and receive email from family and friends without using a computer. Residents read incoming email on printouts and respond by writing handwritten notes that are digitized and emailed. The AHRQ reports that improving residents' ability to communicate with others outside of the facility has "enhanced residents' quality of life."

In "Program to Promote Adherence to Standards of Professional Conduct Improves Staff Perceptions of Patient Safety Culture and Reduces Disruptive Clinician Behavior" (August 22, 2016, https://innovations.ahrq.gov/profiles/program-promote-adherence-standards-professional-conduct-improves-staff-perceptions-patient), the AHRQ reports on innovations by the Ohio-based Catholic Healthcare Partners (now Mercy Health Partners) that

improve service delivery and professional conduct. Examples of common disruptive behaviors that can harm residents and compromise safety include the use of disrespectful language, intimidating behavior, angry outbursts, and throwing instruments, charts, or other objects. The innovative action to combat this problem consisted of distribution of a toolkit to help ensure that clinicians and staff behave professionally. The toolkit contained the following:

- Letters from the chief executive officer and senior vice president detailing the organization's commitment to a culture of patient safety and to professional behavior and the expectation that instances of disruptive behavior must be reported

- Educational information describing the negative impact of disruptive clinician behavior on patient safety

- Code of professional conduct and personal commitment that clinicians and staff must sign

- A video showing examples of acceptable and unacceptable professional conduct, with commentary from national experts in the field

- A survey form detailing the type, frequency, and source of disruptive behavior witnessed and/or experienced by staff, along with their impressions of the effectiveness of the organization's response

- Additional resources such as *Team Strategies and Tools to Enhance Performance and Patient Safety (TeamSTEPPS) Pocket Guide*, developed by the US Department of Defense and the AHRQ, which presents strategies for improving communication and teamwork with the goal of improving patient safety

The AHRQ reports that this initiative "enhanced staff perceptions of the culture of patient safety and improved professional conduct, including reducing incidents of disruptive behavior." AHRQ patient safety scores improved, and staff reported fewer instances of disruptive behavior.

THE EDEN ALTERNATIVE. Developed in 1991 by William Thomas, the Eden Alternative (http://www.edenalt.org) is an international nonprofit organization that, like the Pioneer Network, seeks to transform nursing homes. The Eden Alternative states that it is "dedicated to creating quality of life for Elders and their care partners, wherever they may live." It strives to create nursing homes that are rich and vibrant human habitats where plants, children, and animals bring life-enriching energy to residents. The philosophy of the Eden Alternative is that providing a stimulant-rich environment will help minimize the hopelessness that nursing home residents often feel.

The Eden Alternative offers a variety of training programs aimed at sharpening leadership skills, strengthening interpersonal relationships, growing strong teams, and emphasizing person-directed practices in care. An example is the 10-month-long online training program "Less Is More: Well-Being before the Med Cart," which teaches about the risks of overuse of medication and the need to weigh the risks and benefits of medications for each individual. The program is offered to teams of providers consisting of nurses, nurse practitioners, social workers, physicians, pharmacists, and physical therapists. The training produces measurable benefits. Following the pilot program, there was a 16% reduction in the average number of daily scheduled medications per individual, a 39% reduction in the average amount of time spent administering medications, and a 40% reduction in the number of people receiving mood-altering medications.

The Eden Alternative also works with facility leaders to help them identify opportunities to improve and take the necessary steps to create and maintain a person-directed culture of care. Nursing homes based on its model, or adopting it, are operating throughout the United States. These facilities may apply to join the Eden Registry, which in 2017 included hundreds of member organizations.

By providing gardenlike settings filled with plants and encouraging relationships with children and pets, the Eden Alternative hopes to improve the human spirit and dispel loneliness. The principles of an Eden Alternative nursing home are:

1. The three plagues of loneliness, helplessness, and boredom account for the bulk of suffering among our Elders.

2. An Elder-centered community commits to creating a human habitat where life revolves around close and continuing contact with plants, animals, and children. It is these relationships that provide the young and old alike with a pathway to a life worth living.

3. Loving companionship is the antidote to loneliness. Elders deserve easy access to human and animal companionship.

4. An Elder-centered community creates opportunity to give as well as receive care. This is the antidote to helplessness.

5. An Elder-centered community imbues daily life with variety and spontaneity by creating an environment in which unexpected and unpredictable interactions and happenings can take place. This is the antidote to boredom.

6. Meaningless activity corrodes the human spirit. The opportunity to do things that we find meaningful is essential to human health.

7. Medical treatment should be the servant of genuine human caring, never its master.

8. An Elder-centered community honors its Elders by de-emphasizing top-down bureaucratic authority, seeking instead to place the maximum possible decision-making authority into the hands of the Elders or into the hands of those closest to them.

9. Creating an Elder-centered community is a never-ending process. Human growth must never be separated from human life.

10. Wise leadership is the lifeblood of any struggle against the three plagues. For it, there can be no substitute.

Thomas's initiatives also include the Green House Project (http://www.thegreenhouseproject.org/), small group homes for older adults, built to a residential scale that situates necessary clinical care within a social model in which primacy is given to the older adults' quality of life. The goal of this social model is to provide frail older adults with an environment that promotes autonomy, dignity, privacy, and choice.

Green Houses are designed to feel more like homes than typical long-term care institutions and to blend easily into their community or surroundings. The first Green House in the nation opened in May 2003 in Tupelo, Mississippi, developed by United Methodist Senior Services of Mississippi. The Robert Wood Johnson Foundation (https://www.rwjf.org/en/how-we-work/grants-explorer/featured-programs/the-green-house-project.html) reports that in 2018 more than 260 Green Houses were operating or being developed in 32 states.

Characteristics of People Receiving Long-Term Care

Harris-Kojetin et al. report that in 2014 there were 282,200 people enrolled in adult day services centers, 835,200 people living in residential care communities, and 1.4 million residents in nursing homes. In 2013 more than 4.9 million patients received home health services, and 1.3 million received hospice services. Together, these long-term care service providers served nearly 8.8 million people annually. Figure 3.6 shows the distribution of long-term care recipients by type of provider and age. Users of all types of long-term care services are overwhelmingly female and non-Hispanic white. (See Figure 3.7 and Figure 3.8.)

Many users of long-term care services received help with the activities of daily living. For example, 96.4% of nursing home residents needed help with bathing, 91.8% needed help dressing, 87.9% required assistance with toileting, and 58% needed help eating. (See Figure 3.9.)

Assisted Living

Assisted living, also called residential care, arose to bridge a gap in long-term care. It is intended to meet the needs of older adults who wish to live independently but require some of the services (e.g., housekeeping, meals,

FIGURE 3.6

Long-term care providers by type of provider and age group of recipients, 2013 and 2014

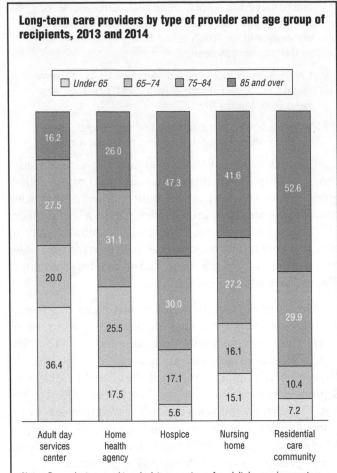

Notes: Denominators used to calculate percentages for adult day services centers, nursing homes, and residential care communities were the number of current participants enrolled in adult day services centers, the number of current residents in nursing homes, and the number of current residents in residential care communities in 2014, respectively. Denominators used to calculate percentages for home health agencies and hospices were the number of patients who received care from Medicare-certified home health agencies at any time in 2013 and the number of patients who received care from Medicare-certified hospices at any time in 2013, respectively. Percentages may not add to 100 because of rounding. Percentages are based on the unrounded numbers.

SOURCE: Lauren Harris-Kojetin et al., "Figure 22. Percent Distribution of Long-Term Care Services Users, by Sector and Age Group: United States, 2013 and 2014," in "Long-Term Care Providers and Services Users in the United States: Data from the National Study of Long-Term Care Providers, 2013–2014," *Vital and Health Statistics*, series 3, no. 38, February 2016, https://www.cdc.gov/nchs/data/series/sr_03/sr03_038.pdf (accessed October 18, 2017)

FIGURE 3.7

Long-term care providers by type of provider and sex of service users, 2013 and 2014

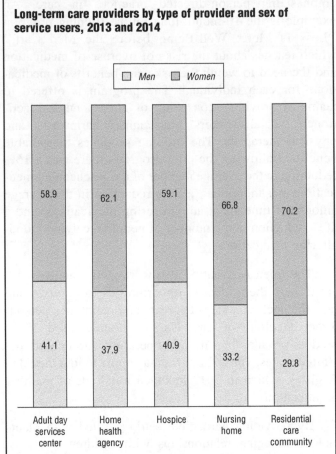

Notes: Denominators used to calculate percentages for adult day services centers, nursing homes, and residential care communities were the number of current participants enrolled in adult day services centers, the number of current residents in nursing homes, and the number of current residents in residential care communities in 2014, respectively. Denominators used to calculate percentages for home health agencies and hospices were the number of patients whose episode of care ended at any time in 2013 and the number of patients who received care from Medicare-certified hospices at any time in 2013, respectively. Percentages may not add to 100 because of rounding. Percentages are based on the unrounded numbers.

SOURCE: Lauren Harris-Kojetin et al., "Figure 23. Percent Distribution of Long-Term Care Services Users, by Sector and Sex: United States, 2013 and 2014," in "Long-Term Care Providers and Services Users in the United States: Data from the National Study of Long-Term Care Providers, 2013–2014," *Vital and Health Statistics*, series 3, no. 38, February 2016, https://www.cdc.gov/nchs/data/series/sr_03/sr03_038.pdf (accessed October 18, 2017)

transportation, and assistance with other activities of daily living) provided by a nursing home. Assisted living offers a flexible array of services that enable older adults to maintain as much independence as they can, for as long as possible.

Because assisted living refers to a concept and philosophy as opposed to a regulated provider of health services such as a hospital or skilled nursing facility, there is no uniform description of the services an assisted living residence must offer, and as a result there is considerable variation among assisted living facilities. These residences are regulated at the state level, and each state has its own

definition of what constitutes an assisted living facility and its own set of rules that govern them.

Assisted living residences may be located on the grounds of retirement communities or in nursing homes, or they may be freestanding residential facilities. They vary in size, location, and services. Some are high-rise apartment complexes, whereas others are converted private homes. Most contain between four and 100 units, which vary in size from one room to a full apartment. Table 3.6 shows the estimated numbers and size of residential care communities in 2010, 2012, and 2014.

FIGURE 3.8

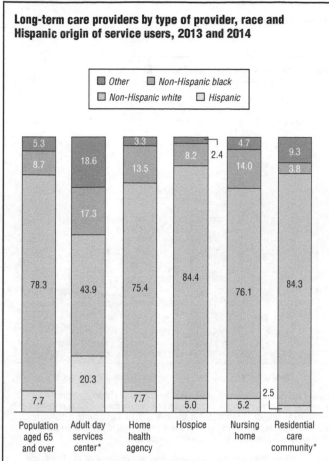

Long-term care providers by type of provider, race and Hispanic origin of service users, 2013 and 2014

Legend:
- Other
- Non-Hispanic black
- Non-Hispanic white
- Hispanic

Population aged 65 and over: 5.3 / 8.7 / 78.3 / 7.7
Adult day services center*: 18.6 / 17.3 / 43.9 / 20.3
Home health agency: 3.3 / 13.5 / 75.4 / 7.7
Hospice: 8.2 / 2.4 / 84.4 / 5.0
Nursing home: 4.7 / 14.0 / 76.1 / 5.2
Residential care community*: 9.3 / 3.8 / 84.3 / 2.5

*Includes non-Hispanic American Indian or Alaska Native, non-Hispanic Asian, non-Hispanic Native Hawaiian or other Pacific Islander, non-Hispanic of two or more races, and unknown race and ethnicity.
Notes: Denominators used to calculate percentages for adult day services centers, nursing homes, and residential care communities were the number of current participants enrolled in adult day services centers, the number of current residents in nursing homes, and the number of current residents in residential care communities in 2014, respectively. Denominators used to calculate percentages for home health agencies and hospices were the number of patients who received care from Medicare-certified home health agencies at any time in 2013 and the number of patients who received care from Medicare-certified hospices at any time in 2013, respectively. Percentages may not add to 100 because of rounding. Percentages are based on the unrounded numbers.

SOURCE: Lauren Harris-Kojetin et al., "Figure 24. Percent Distribution of Long-Term Care Services Users, by Sector and Race and Hispanic Origin: United States, 2013 and 2014," in "Long-Term Care Providers and Services Users in the United States: Data from the National Study of Long-Term Care Providers, 2013–2014," *Vital and Health Statistics*, series 3, no. 38, February 2016, https://www.cdc.gov/nchs/data/series/sr_03/sr03_038.pdf (accessed October 18, 2017)

Assisted living licensing regulations vary from state to state. Most states require staff certification and training, and all assisted living facilities must comply with local building codes and fire safety regulations.

BOARD-AND-CARE FACILITIES. Board-and-care facilities were the earliest form of assisted living. In *Licensed Board and Care Homes: Preliminary Findings from the 1991 National Health Provider Inventory* (April 11, 1994, https://aspe.hhs.gov/basic-report/licensed-board-and-care-homes-preliminary-findings-1991-national-health-provider-inventory), Robert F. Clark et al. define the term

board-and-care homes as "non-medical community-based facilities that provide protective oversight and/or personal care in addition to meals and lodging to one or more residents with functional or cognitive limitations." Typically, board-and-care residents have their own bedrooms and bathrooms or share them with one other person, whereas other living areas are shared.

Although many board-and-care facilities offer residents safe, homelike environments and attentive caregivers, there have been many well-publicized instances of fraud and abuse. Observers attribute the variability in quality of these facilities to the fact that they are unregulated in many states and as a result receive little oversight.

In an attempt to stem abuses, the federal government passed the Keys Amendment in 1978. Under the terms of this legislation, residents living in board-and-care facilities that fail to provide adequate care are subject to reduced SSI payments. This move was intended to penalize substandard board-and-care operators, but advocates for older adults contend that it actually penalizes the SSI recipients and has not reduced reports of abuse. With the 1992 reauthorization of the Older Americans Act of 1965, Congress provided for long-term care ombudsman programs that are designed to help prevent the abuse, exploitation, and neglect of residents in long-term care facilities such as board-and-care residences and nursing homes. Paid and volunteer ombudsmen monitor facilities and act as advocates for residents.

The AoA reports in "Long-Term Care Ombudsman Program" (September 5, 2017, https://www.acl.gov/programs/protecting-rights-and-preventing-abuse/long-term-care-ombudsman-program) that in fiscal year 2015, 1,300 full-time long-term care staff members and 7,734 trained volunteers provided ombudsman services to long-term care residents throughout the United States. They investigated and resolved 74% of a total of 199,238 complaints. The most frequent complaints leveled against nursing facilities in 2015 related to:

- Inadequate discharge/planning
- Unanswered requests for help
- Disrespectful treatment of residents, poor staff attitudes
- Resident/roommate conflict
- Administration of medications

The most frequent concerns at board-and-care facilities were:

- Quality and choice of food
- Disrespectful treatment of residents and poor staff attitudes
- Administration of medications
- Improper eviction or inadequate discharge/planning
- Hazardous conditions or equipment in disrepair

FIGURE 3.9

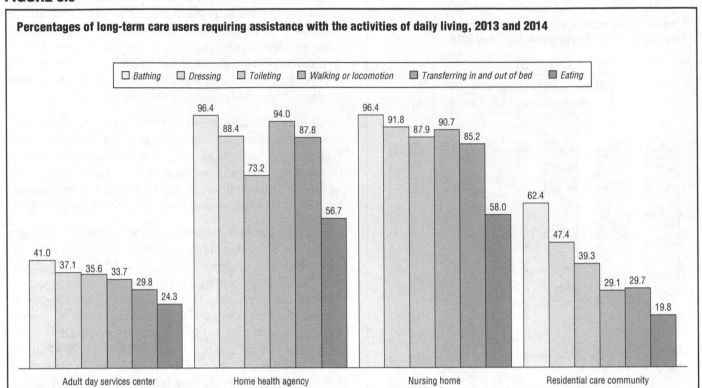

Percentages of long-term care users requiring assistance with the activities of daily living, 2013 and 2014

□ Bathing   □ Dressing   □ Toileting   □ Walking or locomotion   ■ Transferring in and out of bed   ■ Eating

Adult day services center: 41.0, 37.1, 35.6, 33.7, 29.8, 24.3
Home health agency: 96.4, 88.4, 73.2, 94.0, 87.8, 56.7
Nursing home: 96.4, 91.8, 87.9, 90.7, 85.2, 58.0
Residential care community: 62.4, 47.4, 39.3, 29.1, 29.7, 19.8

Notes: Denominators used to calculate percentages for adult day services centers, nursing homes, and residential care communities were the number of current participants enrolled in adult day services centers, the number of current residents in nursing homes, and the number of current residents in residential care communities in 2014, respectively. The denominator used to calculate percentages for home health agencies was the number of patients whose episode of care ended at any time in 2013. Participants, patients, or residents were considered needing any assistance with a given activity if they needed help or supervision from another person or used special equipment to perform the activity. Data on need for assistance with activities of daily living were not available for hospice patients. Percentages are based on the unrounded numbers.

SOURCE: Lauren Harris-Kojetin et al., "Figure 27. Percentage of Long-Term Care Services Users Needing Any Assistance with Activities of Daily Living, by Sector and Activity: United States, 2013 and 2014," in "Long-Term Care Providers and Services Users in the United States: Data from the National Study of Long-Term Care Providers, 2013–2014," *Vital and Health Statistics*, series 3, no. 38, February 2016, https://www.cdc.gov/nchs/data/series/sr_03/sr03_038.pdf (accessed October 18, 2017).

TABLE 3.6

Residential care communities, by bed size, 2010, 2012, and 2014

Characteristic	2014 national study of long-term care providers		2012 national study of long-term care providers		2010 national survey of residential care facilities	
	Weighted number	Weighted percent	Weighted number	Weighted percent	Weighted number	Weighted percent
Number of residential care communities	**30,200**	**100.0**	**22,200**	**100.0**	**31,100**	**100.0**
Small (4–10 beds)	14,500	47.9	9,300	41.7	15,400	50.0
Medium (11–25 beds)	4,500	14.9	3,700	16.8	4,900	16.0
Large (26–100 beds)	9,100	30.1	7,300	32.7	8,700	28.0
Extra large (more than 100 beds)	2,100	7.0	1,900	8.7	2,100	7.0
Number of beds	**1,000,000**	**100.0**	**851,400**	**100.0**	**971,900**	**100.0**
Small (4–10 beds)	89,600	9.0	64,700	7.6	96,700	9.9
Medium (11–25 beds)	76,900	7.7	86,900	10.2	86,800	8.9
Large (26–100 beds)	522,600	52.3	434,800	51.1	493,800	50.8
Extra large (more than 100 beds)	310,900	31.1	265,000	31.1	294,600	30.3

SOURCE: Lauren Harris-Kojetin et al., "Table 4.4. Residential Care Communities and Beds, by Bed Size and Survey Year," in "Long-Term Care Providers and Services Users in the United States: Data from the National Study of Long-Term Care Providers, 2013–2014," *Vital and Health Statistics*, series 3, no. 38, February 2016, https://www.cdc.gov/nchs/data/series/sr_03/sr03_038.pdf (accessed October 18, 2017).

In *A Few States Fell Short in Timely Investigation of the Most Serious Nursing Home Complaints: 2011–2015* (September 2017, https://oig.hhs.gov/oei/reports/oei-01-16-00330.pdf), the Department of Health and Human

FIGURE 3.10

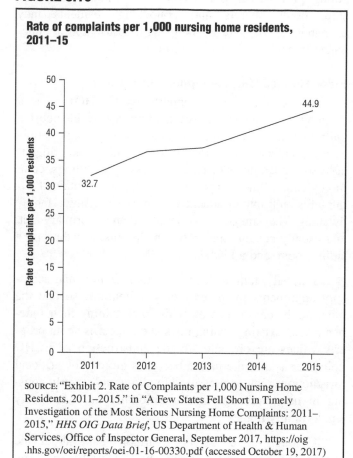

Rate of complaints per 1,000 nursing home residents, 2011–15

SOURCE: "Exhibit 2. Rate of Complaints per 1,000 Nursing Home Residents, 2011–2015," in "A Few States Fell Short in Timely Investigation of the Most Serious Nursing Home Complaints: 2011–2015," *HHS OIG Data Brief*, US Department of Health & Human Services, Office of Inspector General, September 2017, https://oig.hhs.gov/oei/reports/oei-01-16-00330.pdf (accessed October 19, 2017)

FIGURE 3.11

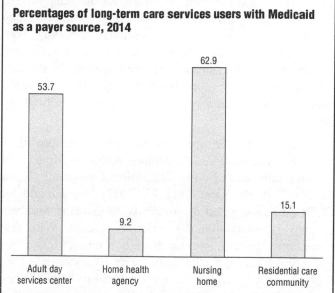

Percentages of long-term care services users with Medicaid as a payer source, 2014

Notes: Denominators used to calculate percentages for adult day services centers, nursing homes, and residential care communities were the number of current participants enrolled in adult day services centers, the number of current residents in nursing homes, and the number of current residents in residential care communities in 2014, respectively. The denominator used to calculate percentages for home health agencies was the number of patients whose episode of care ended at any time in 2013. Data on Medicaid as payer source were not available for hospice patients.

SOURCE: Lauren Harris-Kojetin et al., "Figure 25. Percentage of Long-Term Care Services Users with Medicaid as Payer Source, by Sector: United States, 2013 and 2014," in "Long-Term Care Providers and Services Users in the United States: Data from the National Study of Long-Term Care Providers, 2013–2014," *Vital and Health Statistics*, series 3, no. 38, February 2016, https://www.cdc.gov/nchs/data/series/sr_03/sr03_038.pdf (accessed October 18, 2017)

Services, Office of Inspector General, reports that the rate of complaints about nursing homes rose significantly between 2011 and 2015, from 32.7 complaints per 1,000 residents to 44.9 complaints per 1,000 residents (See Figure 3.10.) Although most complaints are investigated promptly, some states, such as Tennessee and Georgia, did not complete their investigations within required timeframes of two working days for critical (immediate jeopardy) complaints or 10 working days for all other complaints.

COSTS OF ASSISTED LIVING. The cost of assisted living varies based on geography, unit size, and the services needed. Most assisted living facilities charge monthly rates, and some require long-term leases. The Genworth 2017 Cost of Care Survey (August 2017, https://www.genworth.com/about-us/industry-expertise/cost-of-care.html) reports that the national median monthly rate for assisted living in 2017 was $3,750, representing an increase of 3.4% over 2016.

Residents or their families generally pay for assisted living using their own financial resources. Some health insurance programs or long-term care insurance policies reimburse for specific health-related care that is provided, and some state and local governments offer subsidies for rent or services for low-income older adults. Others may

provide subsidies in the form of an additional payment for those who receive SSI or Medicaid. Figure 3.11 shows that just 15.1% of people in residential care communities used Medicaid as a payer source, compared with 62.9% of nursing home residents.

Continuing Care Retirement Communities

Continuing care retirement communities (CCRCs), also known as life care communities, offer a continuum of care (independent living, assisted living, and nursing home care) in a single facility or on common grounds. The goal of CCRCs is to enable residents to age in place (remaining in their own home rather than relocating to an assisted living facility or other supportive housing). When residents become ill or disabled, for example, they do not have to relocate to a nursing home, because medical care is available on the CCRC campus.

Like assisted living facilities, CCRCs vary in location, design, and amenities. They range from urban high rises to semirural campuses and from 100 to more than 1,000 residents. Most include common dining rooms, activity and exercise areas, indoor and outdoor recreation areas, and swimming pools.

Typically, residents are required to pay an entrance fee and a fixed monthly fee in return for housing, meals, personal care, recreation, and nursing services. Many CCRCs offer other payment options, including both entrance fee and fee-for-service (paid for each visit, procedure, or treatment delivered) arrangements. In the past entrance fees were nonrefundable; by 2015, however, many CCRCs offered refundable or partially refundable entrance fees.

CCRCs may be operated by private, nonprofit, or religious organizations. According to Sarah Mouser, in "Is an Independent Living Retirement Community Right for Me?" (Forbes.com, July 25, 2017), the demand for CCRCs has increased dramatically as growing numbers of baby boomers join the ranks of retirees. With few exceptions, government or private insurance does not cover the costs of CCRCs. In "The Everything-in-One Promise of a Continuing Care Community" (NYTimes.com, February 26, 2016), John F. Wasik reports that there were about 2,000 CCRCs in the United States in 2016 and notes that entrance fees average about $250,000 and may be as high as $1 million.

Shared Housing and Cohousing

Older adults may share living quarters to reduce expenses, share household and home maintenance responsibilities, and gain companionship. Many choose to share the same homes in which they raised their families because these houses are often large enough to accommodate more than one or two people. Shared housing is often called cohousing, but the terms are not exactly the same.

Most shared housing consists of a single homeowner taking a roommate to share living space and expenses. Shared housing can also include households with three or more roommates and family-like cooperatives in which large groups of people live together. In contrast, cohousing usually refers to planned or intentional communities of private dwellings with shared common areas that include dining rooms, meeting rooms, and recreation facilities. Shared housing and cohousing are cost-effective alternatives for those who wish to remain in their own home and for older adults who cannot afford assisted living or CCRCs.

The cohousing concept originated in Denmark during the 1960s and spread to the United States during the 1980s. According to the Cohousing Association of the United States (http://www.cohousing.org/directory), in 2017 there were more than 300 cohousing communities operating or in development in 37 states and the District of Columbia. Cohousing participants are involved in planning the community and maintaining it, and most cohousing groups make their decisions by consensus.

Shared housing or intergenerational cohousing may also meet the needs of younger as well as older people.

Along with the benefits of cost-sharing and companionship, home sharers and cohousing residents may exchange services (e.g., help with household maintenance in exchange for babysitting).

Elder Cottage Housing Opportunity Units

Elder cottage housing opportunity (ECHO) units, or "granny flats," are small, freestanding, removable housing units that are located on the same lot as a single-family house. Another name used by local zoning authorities is accessory apartments or units. Accessory dwellings, commonly called "in-law apartments," are self-contained living units built into or attached to an existing single-family dwelling. They are generally smaller than the primary unit, and usually contain one or two bedrooms, a bathroom, a sitting room, and a kitchen.

Generally, families construct ECHO units and accessory apartments for parents or grandparents so that the older adults can be nearby while maintaining their independence. Existing zoning laws and concerns about property values are obstacles to the construction of ECHO units, but as this alternative becomes more popular, local jurisdictions may be pressured to allow multifamily housing in neighborhoods that traditionally have had only single-family homes.

Although there are no available data about the number of new and existing ECHO units, in "The Hottest Home Amenity: In-Law Apartments" (WSJ.com, November 6, 2014), Katy McLaughlin reports that homes with accessory dwelling units typically sell for 60% more than similar single-family homes and have become "the hottest amenity in real estate these days." She notes that a 2012 building industry survey of homebuyers indicated that nearly one-third (32%) of those with living parents "expected to have an aging relative live with them in the future." McLaughlin states, "While the adult children get the peace of mind of having mom and dad nearby, real-estate agents say the in-law accommodations are adding value to their homes."

Retirement Communities

Developers such as the industry leader Del Webb (a division of PulteGroup) have constructed communities and even entire small "cities" exclusively for older adults. Examples include the Sun City communities in Arizona, Florida, and Texas. The Arizona and Florida communities opened during the 1960s and the Texas community in 1996.

In 2018 Del Webb (https://www.delwebb.com) boasted more than 50 communities in 17 states. Homes in most of these properties were available only to those families in which at least one member was 55 years or older, and no one under the age of 19 years was allowed to reside permanently. Many communities offer clubs, golf courses, social organizations, fitness clubs, organized travel, and recreational complexes. Medical facilities are located nearby.

OWNING AND RENTING A HOME

In the press release "Quarterly Residential Vacancies and Homeownership, Second Quarter 2017" (July 27, 2017, https://www.census.gov/housing/hvs/files/qtr217/Q217press.pdf), the Census Bureau notes that the overall homeownership rate during the second quarter of 2017 was 63.7%, down from the highest rate of 69.2% during the fourth quarter of 2004. (See Figure 3.12.) During the second quarter of 2017, 75.4% of adults aged 55 to 64 years and 78.2% of adults aged 65 years and older owned their own homes. (See Table 3.7.)

The AoA reports in *Profile of Older Americans: 2016* that 44% of older adults (36% of homeowners and 78% of renters) in 2015 devoted more than a third of their income to housing costs. In 2015 the median value of homes owned by older adults was $150,000, but because the median purchase price of these homes was just $53,000, 78% of older homeowners had no mortgage debt; they owned their homes free and clear.

Renters generally pay a higher percentage of their income for housing than do homeowners. Unlike most homeowners, who pay fixed monthly mortgage payments, renters often face annual rent increases. Many older adult renters living on fixed incomes are unprepared to pay these increases. Homeowners also benefit from their home equity and can borrow against it in times of financial need. In contrast, renters do not build equity and do not get a return on their investment. Also, mortgage payments are tax deductible, whereas rent payments are not.

Reverse Mortgages

To supplement their retirement income or to pay for health care, many older Americans turn to reverse mortgages. Reverse mortgages allow homeowners to convert some of their home equity into cash, making it possible for them to avoid selling their home.

In a traditional mortgage, homeowners make monthly payments to the lender. In a reverse mortgage the lender pays the homeowner in monthly installments and in most cases no repayment is due until the homeowner dies, sells the house, or moves. Reverse mortgages help homeowners who have considerable equity in their home to stay in their home and still meet their financial obligations.

A key disadvantage of a reverse mortgage is that when the home is no longer used as the primary residence of the borrower, the cash, interest, and finance charges must be repaid. This is generally accomplished by selling the home, and the spouse or heirs only receive any funds in excess of this obligation.

In an effort to prevent loan defaults, the requirements for obtaining a reverse mortgage became more stringent in 2015. The new rules, which apply to reverse mortgage loans under the Home Equity Conversion Mortgage program, require borrowers to pass a financial assessment. Borrowers must show that they can pay property taxes and insurance premiums on the property. Historically, reverse mortgages were based on the borrower's age, the value of the home, and prevailing interest rates.

FIGURE 3.12

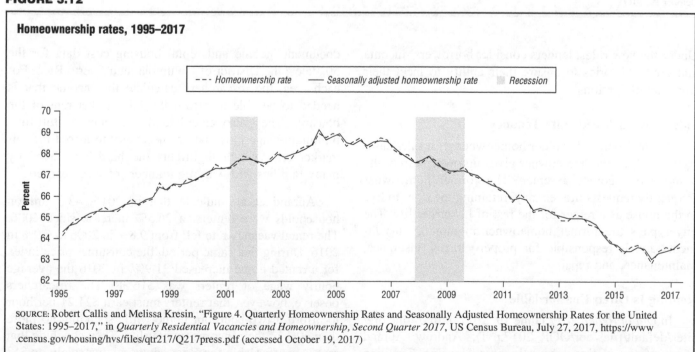

Homeownership rates, 1995–2017

SOURCE: Robert Callis and Melissa Kresin, "Figure 4. Quarterly Homeownership Rates and Seasonally Adjusted Homeownership Rates for the United States: 1995–2017," in *Quarterly Residential Vacancies and Homeownership, Second Quarter 2017*, US Census Bureau, July 27, 2017, https://www.census.gov/housing/hvs/files/qtr217/Q217press.pdf (accessed October 19, 2017).

TABLE 3.7

Homeownership rates, by age of householder, 2011–17

	Homeownership rates (percent)					
Year/quarter	United States Rate	Under 35 years Rate	35 to 44 years Rate	45 to 54 years Rate	55 to 64 years Rate	65 years and over Rate
2017						
Second quarter	63.7	35.3	58.8	69.3	75.4	78.2
First quarter	63.6	34.3	59.0	69.4	75.6	78.6
2016						
Fourth quarter	63.7	34.7	58.7	69.8	74.8	79.5
Third quarter	63.5	35.2	58.4	69.1	74.9	79.0
Second quarter	62.9	34.1	58.3	69.1	74.7	77.9
First quarter	63.5	34.2	58.9	69.2	75.7	78.8
2015						
Fourth quarter	63.8	34.7	59.3	70.1	75.2	79.3
Third quarter	63.7	35.8	58.1	69.9	75.3	78.7
Second quarter	63.4	34.8	58.0	69.9	75.4	78.5
First quarter	63.7	34.6	58.4	70.1	75.8	79.0
2014						
Fourth quarter	64.0	35.3	58.8	70.5	75.8	79.5
Third quarter	64.4	36.0	59.1	70.1	76.6	80.0
Second quarter	64.7	35.9	60.2	70.7	76.4	80.1
First quarter	64.8	36.2	60.7	71.4	76.4	79.9
2013						
Fourth quarter	65.2	36.8	60.9	71.4	76.5	80.7
Third quarter	65.3	36.8	61.1	71.3	76.2	81.2
Second quarter	65.0	36.7	60.3	70.9	76.7	80.9
First quarter	65.0	36.8	60.1	71.3	77.0	80.4
2012						
Fourth quarter	65.4	37.1	60.4	72.1	77.6	80.7
Third quarter	65.5	36.3	61.8	72.0	76.9	81.4
Second quarter	65.5	36.5	62.2	71.4	77.1	81.6
First quarter	65.4	36.8	61.4	71.3	77.8	80.9
2011						
Fourth quarter	66.0	37.6	62.3	72.7	79.0	80.9
Third quarter	66.3	38.0	63.4	72.7	78.6	81.1
Second quarter	65.9	37.5	63.8	72.3	77.8	80.8
First quarter	66.4	37.9	64.4	73.1	78.6	81.0

SOURCE: Robert Callis and Melissa Kresin, "Table 6. Homeownership Rates by Age of Householder: 2011 to 2017," in *Quarterly Residential Vacancies and Homeownership, Second Quarter 2017*, US Census Bureau, July 27, 2017, https://www.census.gov/housing/hvs/files/qtr217/Q217press.pdf (accessed October 19, 2017)

Under the new rules, lenders consider borrowers' income and credit histories to ensure their ability to meet their financial obligations.

Sale/Leaseback with Life Tenancy

Another option for older homeowners is a sale/lease-back in which the homeowner gives up ownership of the home and becomes a renter. The former homeowner frequently requests life tenancy, retaining the right to live in the house as a renter for the rest of his or her life. The buyer pays the former homeowner in monthly installments and is responsible for property taxes, insurance, maintenance, and repairs.

Renting Is Often Unaffordable

In *Out of Reach 2017* (June 19, 2017, http://nlihc.org/sites/default/files/oor/OOR_2017.pdf), Andrew Aurand et al. of the National Low Income Housing Coalition document income and rental housing cost data for the 50 states, the District of Columbia, and Puerto Rico. For each area, the researchers calculate the income that is needed to be able to afford the fair market rent of the housing. They also calculate the number of full-time minimum-wage jobs that are necessary to afford the fair market rent, which highlights the hardships faced by many families with varying numbers of wage earners.

Aurand et al. indicate that in 2016, 43.3 million households were renters, a 26.5% increase since 2006. The rental vacancy rate fell from 9.8% in 2006 to 6.9% in 2016. During that same period, the consumer price index for a rented home increased 31.9%. In 2016 the average hourly wage of renters was $16.38. The researchers observe, however, that renters must earn $21.21 per hour to afford a two-bedroom home while spending no more than 30% of their income on housing. They conclude that rent is unaffordable for older adults relying solely on SSI payments. Aurand et al. report that the maximum federal SSI payment for individuals in 2017 was $735 per month, which would not allow an older adult to rent even a modest efficiency apartment anywhere in the United States.

HOUSING CHALLENGES FOR OLDER ADULTS
Physical Hazards and Accommodations

Home characteristics that are considered desirable by younger householders may present challenges to older adults. For example, the staircase in a two-story house may become a formidable obstacle to an older adult suffering from arthritis, heart disease, or other disabling conditions. Narrow halls and doorways cannot accommodate walkers and wheelchairs. High cabinets and shelves may be beyond the reach of an arthritis sufferer. Although houses can be modified to meet the physical needs of older or disabled people, some older houses cannot be remodeled as easily, and retrofitting them may be quite costly. Owners of condominiums in Florida, whose young-old (aged 65 to 74 years) residents once prized second- and third-floor units for their breezes and golf course views, are now considering installing elevators for residents in their 80s and 90s who find climbing stairs more difficult.

Older adults, as well as advocates on their behalf, express a strong preference for aging in place. Much research confirms that most people over the age of 55 years want to remain in familiar surroundings rather than move to alternative housing. To live more comfortably, those older adults who have the means can redesign and reequip their home to accommodate the physical changes that are associated with aging.

Simple adaptations include replacing doorknobs with levers that can be pushed downward with a fist or elbow, requiring no gripping or twisting; replacing light switches with flat "touch" switches; placing closet rods at adjustable heights; installing stoves with front- or side-mounted controls; and marking steps with bright colors. More complex renovations include replacing a bathroom with a wet room (a tiled space that is large enough to accommodate a wheelchair and equipped with a showerhead, waterproof chair, and sloping floor for a drain), placing electrical outlets higher than usual, and widening passageways and doorways for walkers, wheelchairs, or scooters.

Anticipating the increase in the older population, some real estate developers are manufacturing houses that are designed to meet the needs of older adults and prolong their ability to live independently. These houses feature accommodations such as nonskid flooring, walls strong enough to support grab bars, outlets at convenient heights, levers instead of knobs on doors and plumbing fixtures, and doorways and hallways wide enough for wheelchair access.

More technologically advanced homes, called smart homes, feature an array of adaptive technologies, such as embedded computers, sensors that detect motion and falls, and automated blood pressure monitoring, that aim to help older adults remain in their homes and age in place. Jacqueline Howard reports in "Using Technology to Help Older Adults Keep Their Independence" (CNN.com, September 25, 2017) that, in the foreseeable future, in-home technologies will include stoves and ovens with blinking light systems to alert users that they have been left unattended and gait-sensing technology that will "learn" an individual's walking patterns and alert a caregiver should they change. Clocks will broadcast personalized reminders about appointments and visitors, and automatic medication dispensers will remind older adults to take their medications. Robotic caregivers will perform household chores, provide companionship, and connect with home security systems.

PUBLIC HOUSING

Congress passed the US Housing Act of 1937 to create low-income public housing, but according to the Milbank Memorial Fund and the Council of Large Public Housing Authorities, in *Public Housing and Supportive Services for the Frail Elderly: A Guide for Housing Authorities and Their Collaborators* (September 2006, https://www.milbank.org/wp-content/files/documents/0609 publichousing/0609publichousing.pdf), by 1952 only a small percentage of available housing was occupied by older adults. After 1956, when Congress authorized the development of dedicated public housing for the elderly and specifically made low-income older adults eligible for such housing, the situation improved. During the 1960s and 1970s many developments for low-income older adults were constructed. These apartments were sufficient for most residents, but they were not designed to enable residents to age in place. They lacked the flexibility and the range of housing options necessary to meet the needs of frail older adults. Residents who entered public housing as young-old aged in place and are now the older-old (aged 75 years and older) and are in need of more supportive and health services than they were two decades ago.

Public housing itself has also aged. Most of it is more than 40 years old. Many developments are badly rundown and in need of renovation. Most are unequipped to offer the range of supportive services that are required by increasingly frail and dependent residents. Absent supportive services, the bleak alternative may be moving older people into costly, isolated institutions. Older adults may suffer unnecessary institutionalization, and nursing home care is far costlier than community-based services.

The Section 202 Supportive Housing for the Elderly Act was passed in 2010. The act supports the development and maintenance of housing options for older adults with very low incomes. It encourages the enhancement of existing units and expanding access to assisted living facilities and programs that enable older adults to remain in the community. It also supports HUD's creation of an information clearinghouse of affordable housing projects for older adults.

In "HUD's Public Housing Program" (2018, https://www.hud.gov/topics/rental_assistance/phprog), HUD reports that in 2018 approximately 1.2 million households lived in public housing units, which were managed by 3,300 housing authorities. Eligibility for public housing is based on income (the limits vary by location), age, disability, family status, and US citizenship or eligible immigration status.

Jeremy Harper describes the challenges of meeting the needs of an aging population with sharply limited budgets in "Facing the Challenges of Affordable Senior Housing" (UrbanLand.uli.org, September 20, 2017). He reports that attendees at the Urban Land Institute's Housing Opportunity 2017 Conference (https://housingconference.uli.org) in September 2017 presented a variety of potential public- and private-sector initiatives to provide affordable housing for older adults. For example, HUD reported that having an on-site service coordinator at senior housing centers reduced residents' hospitalization rates by 20%. A nonprofit real estate developer described an effort in Richmond, Virginia, that integrates housing for low-income older adults into mixed-use developments that include market-rate units as well as retail space. Another developer presented plans for a mixed-use redevelopment project in Washington, D.C., that will contain 1,800 residential units of various types, along with 181,000 square feet of retail space. The project will include a building containing 200 government-subsidized units for older adults equipped with a food pantry, computer labs, a business center, walking paths, and an outdoor courtyard with a koi pond.

CHAPTER 4

WORKING AND RETIREMENT: NEW OPTIONS FOR OLDER ADULTS

Americans head off to their jobs each day as much for daily meaning as for daily bread.

—Studs Terkel, *Working: People Talk about What They Do All Day and How They Feel about What They Do* (1974)

Historically, Americans aged 65 years and older have made substantial contributions to society. Examples of accomplished older adults include:

- Benjamin Franklin (1706–1790)—writer, scientist, inventor, and statesman—helped draft the Declaration of Independence at age 70.

- Thomas Alva Edison (1847–1931) worked on inventions, including the light bulb, the microphone, and the phonograph, until his death at the age of 84.

- Rear Admiral Grace Murray Hopper (1906–1992), one of the early computer scientists and a coauthor of the computer language COBOL, maintained an active speaking and consulting schedule until her death at age 85.

- Margaret Mead (1901–1978), the noted anthropologist, returned to New Guinea when she was 72 and exhausted a much younger television film crew as they tried to keep up with her.

- Albert Einstein (1879–1955), who formulated the theory of relativity, was working on a unifying theory of the universe when he died at age 76.

- Georgia O'Keeffe (1887–1986) created masterful paintings when she was more than 80 years of age.

Older adults continue to play vital roles in industry, government, and the arts. Notable examples include:

- Betty White (1922–), a popular actress, author, producer, radio host, singer, and philanthropist, won a primetime Emmy Award at age 88 in 2010 and a Grammy Award at age 90 in 2012.

- Warren Buffett (1930–) is the most successful investor of the 21st century and was the wealthiest person in the world in 2008 at age 78. With a fortune estimated at $67 billion in 2015, he has pledged to give nearly all of his fortune to charity after his death.

- US Senator John McCain (1936–; R-AZ) was 76 years old when he was elected in 2012 to a 14th term as senator. He was the Republican presidential candidate during the 2008 election.

- Madeleine Albright (1937–), the US secretary of state from 1997 to 2001, is the president of the Harry S. Truman Scholarship Foundation and chair of the National Democratic Institute for International Affairs.

- Nancy Pelosi (1940–; D-CA) served as the Speaker of the US House of Representatives from January 2007 to January 2011. She was the first woman to hold that position.

- James Hansen (1941–), the former head of the National Aeronautics and Space Administration's Goddard Institute for Space Studies and an adjunct professor in Columbia University's Earth Institute and director of the Program on Climate Science, Awareness, and Solutions, is known for increasing public awareness of global warming and its effects on climate change.

- Hillary Rodham Clinton (1947–) was the 67th US secretary of state from 2009 to 2013 and was the Democratic candidate during the 2016 presidential election. She was also the First Lady of the United States from 1993 to 2001 and a US senator for New York from 2001 to 2009.

DEFINING AND REDEFINING RETIREMENT

Retirement in the United States is usually defined by withdrawal from the paid labor force and receipt of income from pension plans, Social Security, or other retirement plans. There are, however, many people who may be viewed as being retired, although they do not fulfill the criteria of the generally accepted definition of retirement. For example, workers who retire from the military or other federal employment, which provide pension benefits after 20 years of service, may choose to continue to work and remain in the labor force for years, collecting both a salary and a pension. Other workers retire from full-time employment but continue to work part time to supplement their pension, Social Security, or retirement benefits. As a result, not all workers collecting pensions are retired, and some workers collecting salaries are retired.

Besides expanding the definition of the term *retirement*, an increasing number of older Americans are not subscribing to the traditional timing and lifestyle of retirement. Retirement is no longer an event, it is a process, and work and retirement are no longer mutually exclusive. Although many older adults still choose to retire from full-time employment at age 65, they remain active by exploring new careers, working part time, volunteering, and engaging in a variety of leisure activities. An increasing proportion of older adults work well beyond age 65, and some choose not to retire at all.

In 2018 prospective retirees included the baby boom generation (people born between 1946 and 1964). This generation faces unique difficulties when contemplating retirement, including low interest rates and a postrecession economy. In "Baby Boomers Delaying Retirement: Generational Shifts at Work" (Forbes.com, June 2, 2017), Ben Eubanks reports that during the first quarter of 2017 workers aged 55 years and older had 4.8% job growth, surpassing any other age group. The Employee Benefit Research Institute finds that 26% of workers intend to work until age 70 and that another 6% feel they will never be able to retire. By comparison, in 1991 about half of workers surveyed anticipated retiring by age 65.

Art Swift of Gallup, Inc., notes in *Most U.S. Employed Adults Plan to Work Past Retirement Age* (May 8, 2017, http://news.gallup.com/poll/210044/employed-adults-plan-work-past-retirement-age.aspx) that a survey conducted in April 2017 found that 63% of employed US adults plan to work part time after age 65. Eleven percent plan to continue to work full time after age 65 and 25% plan to stop working altogether at age 65.

RECASTING WORK AND RETIREMENT

Throughout much of human history the average length of life was relatively short. According to Elizabeth Arias, Melonie Heron, and Jiaquan Xu of the Centers for Disease Control and Prevention, in *United States Life Tables, 2012* (November 28, 2016, https://www.cdc.gov/nchs/data/nvsr/nvsr65/nvsr65_08.pdf), in 1900 life expectancy in the United States was just 47.3 years. In a world where most people did not expect to live beyond age 50, it was essential that personal, educational, and professional milestones be attained by certain ages. Obtaining an education, job training, marriage, parenthood, and retirement not only were designated to particular periods of life but also were expected generally to occur only once in a lifetime.

This regimented pattern of life was maintained by tradition and reinforced by laws and regulations. In the United States, government regulations and institutional rules prescribed the ages at which education began, work life ended, and pension and Social Security benefits commenced. This timetable was based on the assumptions that these activities were to be performed "on time" and in sequence and that most growth and development occurred during the first half of life, whereas the second half was, in general, characterized by decline and disinvestment.

Social and demographic trends (including increased longevity and improved health), technological advances, and economic realities have transformed the size and composition of the labor force as well as the nature of family and work. Examples of these changes include:

- Marriage and childbearing are often postponed in favor of pursuing education and careers. Advances in reproductive technology have enabled women to delay having children by 20 years. Figure 4.1 shows that the rate of women aged 40 to 44 years giving birth rose from 5.5 births per 1,000 women in 1990 to 11 births per 1,000 women in 2015.

- Formal learning was once the exclusive province of the young. Nonetheless, middle-aged and older adults are increasingly returning to school. According to the US Census Bureau, in "Back to School: 2016–2017" (July 26, 2016, https://www.census.gov/content/dam/Census/newsroom/facts-for-features/2016/cb16-ff.15.pdf), 14.7% of all college students were aged 35 years and older in 2014, and 34.5% of part-time students were aged 35 years and older. Distance learning programs and classes offered online have created opportunities for older adults who wish to continue their education.

- Career changes and retraining have become the norm rather than the exception. Americans once pursued a single career during their lifetime. Many workers now change jobs and even careers several times. According to the American Council on Education (2017, http://www.acenet.edu), an increasing number of adults, from military veterans to people aged 50 years and older, are returning to work in second, third, or even fourth careers.

- Age-based mandatory retirement no longer exists in most private-sector industries. Amendments in 1976 and 1986 to the Age Discrimination in Employment Act (ADEA) of 1967 prohibit employment discrimination against people aged 40 years and older. The

FIGURE 4.1

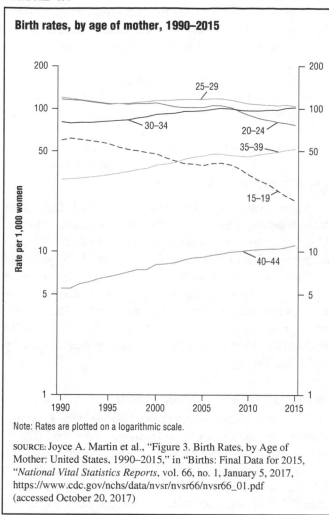

Birth rates, by age of mother, 1990–2015

Note: Rates are plotted on a logarithmic scale.

SOURCE: Joyce A. Martin et al., "Figure 3. Birth Rates, by Age of Mother: United States, 1990–2015," in "Births: Final Data for 2015, "*National Vital Statistics Reports*, vol. 66, no. 1, January 5, 2017, https://www.cdc.gov/nchs/data/nvsr/nvsr66/nvsr66_01.pdf (accessed October 20, 2017)

Older Workers Benefit Protection Act of 1990 amended ADEA by making it illegal for employers to discriminate in the provision of benefits, such as life insurance, health insurance, disability benefits, pensions, and retirement benefits for older workers. Historically, mandatory retirement ages were justified by the argument that some occupations were either too dangerous for older workers or required high levels of physical and mental acuity. Retirement is still compulsory for federal law officers (age 57), correctional officers and firefighters (ages 55 to 60), air traffic controllers (age 56), and commercial airline pilots (raised from age 60 in 1959 to 65 in 2007). National park rangers must retire at age 57 and lighthouse service workers at age 55. Many states, including Alabama, Alaska, Arizona, Connecticut, Florida, Louisiana, Maryland, Massachusetts, Michigan, Minnesota, Missouri, New Hampshire, New Jersey, New York, Ohio, South Dakota, Virginia, Wisconsin, and Wyoming, require judges to retire. Nevertheless, mandatory retirement ages have been faulted because they are arbitrary and are not based on actual physical evaluations of individual workers. As a result, some

detractors view the practice of age-based mandatory retirement as a form of age discrimination.

Although a conventional American life generally included education, work, and retirement, in that order, the current cohort (a group of individuals that shares a common characteristic such as birth years and is studied over time) of workers and retirees has the opportunity to blend, reorder, and repeat these activities as desired. Many gerontologists (professionals who study the social, psychological, and biological aspects of aging) and other aging researchers posit that there is a "third age," a stage of working life when older workers can actively renegotiate their relationship with the labor force. Their choices may include remaining in the workforce, retiring, or returning to work for periods of part-time, full-time, or seasonal employment. Not all workers and retirees will choose to stray from the conventional course, but increasingly they have the option to do so.

A CHANGING ECONOMY AND CHANGING ROLES

The Agrarian Culture

When the US economy was predominantly agricultural, children were put to work as soon as they were able to contribute to the family upkeep. Similarly, workers who lived beyond age 65 did not retire; they worked as long as they were physically able. When older adults were no longer able to work, younger family members cared for them. Older people were valued and respected for their accumulated knowledge and experience and were integral members of the interconnected family and labor systems.

Industrial Society

The Industrial Revolution shifted workers from the farm to manufacturing jobs. The work was physically demanding, the hours long, and the tasks rigidly structured. Women labored in factories and at home caring for the family. Older people found themselves displaced. Their skills and experience were not relevant to new technologies, and they could not physically compete with the large number of young workers eager to exploit new economic opportunities.

As industrial workers matured, some were promoted to positions as supervisors and managers. For older workers who had been with the same company for many years, labor unions provided a measure of job security through the seniority system ("first hired, last fired"). In an increasingly youth-oriented society, however, older workers were often rejected in favor of younger laborers. Frequent reports of age discrimination prompted Congress to pass ADEA. The act made it illegal for employers or unions to discharge, refuse to hire, or otherwise discriminate on the basis of age. Victims are eligible for lost wages (the amount is doubled in the most blatant cases) and workers wrongfully terminated may also seek reinstatement.

The Information Age

The US economy continued its dramatic shift away from smokestack industries such as mining and manufacturing to an economy in which service occupations and the production and dissemination of information predominate. As a result, the demand for highly educated workers has grown, and the demand for workers who perform physical labor has decreased. Many information-age careers such as those in the fields of health, law, information technology, and communications are ideally suited for older workers because they do not require physical labor, and employers benefit from the cumulative experience of older workers.

THE AGING LABOR FORCE

As the baby boom generation approaches retirement age, the proportion of the US population aged 65 years and older will increase significantly. However, the US labor force is already undergoing a shift toward a greater number of older workers and a relative scarcity of new entrants.

According to the US Bureau of Labor Statistics (BLS), the median age (the middle value; half are younger and half are older) of the US labor force is increasing, from 37.7 years in 1994, to 41.9 years in 2014, to a projected 42.4 years in 2024. (See Table 4.1.)

Older Adults in the Labor Force

The BLS (2018, https://www.bls.gov/cps/cpsaat03 .pdf) reports that in 2017 older workers accounted for 18.6% of the entire US labor force. In *Older Workers* (July 2008, https://www.bls.gov/spotlight/2008/older_workers/ pdf/older_workers_bls_spotlight.pdf), the BLS notes that between 1948 and 2007 the labor force participation of men aged 65 years and older generally declined until the

late 1990s, when rates leveled off or even rose slightly. The observed decline in older adults' participation in the labor force during the 1970s and into the 1980s has been attributed to widespread mandatory retirement practices in many industries that forced workers to retire at age 65. In addition, the eligibility age for Social Security benefits was reduced from 65 to 62 years of age during the 1960s, enabling workers to retire earlier. The labor force participation rate for older workers was at record lows during the 1980s and early 1990s, but has been increasing since the late 1990s as a larger share of older workers are remaining in or returning to the labor force.

Mitra Toossi and Elka Torpey of the BLS indicate in *Older Workers: Labor Force Trends and Career Options* (May 2017, https://www.bls.gov/careeroutlook/2017/article/ older-workers.htm) that 40% of people aged 55 years and older were working or seeking work in 2014. They observe that older workers are the only group in which the labor participation rate has been rising substantially. The 55-and-older age group accounted for 12.4% of the labor force in 1998 and 22.4% in 2016, and is projected to reach 24.8% by 2024. (See Table 4.2.)

Unemployment among Older Adults

The BLS reports in "Record Unemployment among Older Workers Does Not Keep Them out of the Job Market" (March 2010, https://www.bls.gov/opub/ils/pdf/opbils81 .pdf) that the unemployment rate for workers aged 55 years and older significantly increased between 2007 and 2010, when 7.1% of older adults in the labor force were unemployed. By July 2017 the unemployment rate among workers aged 55 years and older had decreased to 3.2%, the lowest of any age group (except for workers aged 45 to 54 years, which also had a rate of 3.2%). (See Table 4.3.)

Older Women Opt to Work Rather than Retire

Between 1994 and 2014 labor force participation rates generally rose among women aged 55 years and older, from 24% in 1994 to 30.5% in 2004 to 34.9% in 2014. (See Table 4.4.) The BLS projects that the participation rate of women aged 55 years and older will increase to 35.4% by 2024. Between 1994 and 2014 the participation rate for women aged 55 to 64 years rose from 48.9% to 58.8%, and among women aged 65 to 74 years the rate increased from 13.6% to 22.4%. Likewise, the labor force participation of women aged 70 to 74 years grew from 8.7% in 1994 to 15.6% in 2014, and among women aged 75 years and older from 3.5% to 5.9%. These increases have narrowed the gap in labor force participation rates between men and women.

Most older women in the 21st century spent some time in the labor force when they were younger. The older the woman, however, the less likely she is to have ever worked outside the home. In the United States the

TABLE 4.1

Median age of the labor force, 1994, 2004, 2014, and projected 2024

Group	1994	2004	2014	2024
Total	37.7	40.3	41.9	42.4
Men	37.7	40.1	41.8	42.0
Women	37.7	40.5	42.0	42.8
White	37.7	40.8	42.6	43.0
Black	36.0	38.6	39.6	40.0
Asian	37.5	39.3	41.2	42.8
Hispanic origin	33.7	35.0	37.3	38.9
White non-Hispanic	38.5	41.8	44.1	44.4

SOURCE: Mitra Toossi, "Table 6. Median Age of the Labor Force, by Sex, Race and Ethnicity, 1994, 2004, 2014, and Projected 2024," in "Labor Force Projections to 2024: the Labor Force Is Growing, but Slowly," *Monthly Labor Review*, December 2015, https://www.bls.gov/opub/mlr/2015/ article/labor-force-projections-to-2024.htm (accessed October 20, 2017)

TABLE 4.2

Labor force shares by age, 1970–2014 and projected 2014–24

Year	Labor force 16 to 24	Projected labor force 16 to 24	Labor force 25 to 54	Projected labor force 25 to 54	Labor force 55⁺	Projected labor force 55⁺
1970	21.6%		60.9%		17.5%	
1971	22.3%		60.5%		17.2%	
1972	23.2%		60.1%		16.7%	
1973	23.9%		60.2%		15.9%	
1974	24.1%		60.4%		15.5%	
1975	24.1%		60.6%		15.3%	
1976	24.3%		60.8%		14.9%	
1977	24.4%		60.9%		14.7%	
1978	24.5%		61.0%		14.5%	
1979	24.2%		61.5%		14.3%	
1980	23.7%		62.3%		14.1%	
1981	23.1%		63.1%		13.8%	
1982	22.3%		64.0%		13.7%	
1983	21.7%		64.8%		13.5%	
1984	21.1%		65.8%		13.1%	
1985	20.5%		66.6%		12.9%	
1986	19.8%		67.5%		12.6%	
1987	19.2%		68.3%		12.5%	
1988	18.5%		69.1%		12.4%	
1989	17.9%		69.8%		12.4%	
1990	17.9%		70.2%		11.9%	
1991	17.3%		71.0%		11.8%	
1992	16.9%		71.4%		11.8%	
1993	16.7%		71.7%		11.6%	
1994	16.5%		71.6%		11.9%	
1995	16.2%		71.9%		11.9%	
1996	15.8%		72.3%		11.9%	
1997	15.7%		72.1%		12.1%	
1998	15.9%		71.7%		12.4%	
1999	16.0%		71.3%		12.7%	
2000	15.8%		71.1%		13.1%	
2001	15.6%		70.8%		13.6%	
2002	15.4%		70.2%		14.3%	
2003	15.1%		69.8%		15.1%	
2004	15.1%		69.3%		15.6%	
2005	14.9%		68.8%		16.2%	
2006	14.8%		68.4%		16.8%	
2007	14.5%		68.1%		17.3%	
2008	14.3%		67.7%		18.1%	
2009	13.9%		67.3%		18.8%	
2010	13.6%		66.9%		19.5%	
2011	13.7%		66.2%		20.1%	
2012	13.7%		65.3%		20.9%	
2013	13.8%		64.9%		21.4%	
2014	13.7%		64.6%		21.7%	
2015	13.5%		64.4%		22.1%	
2016	13.3%	13.3%	64.2%	64.2%	22.4%	22.4%
2017		12.7%		64.1%		23.1%
2018		12.5%		64.0%		23.6%
2019		12.3%		64.0%		24.0%
2020		12.1%		63.8%		24.3%
2021		12.0%		63.8%		24.5%
2022		11.8%		63.9%		24.6%
2023		11.6%		63.9%		24.7%
2024		11.5%		63.9%		24.8%

SOURCE: Mitra Toossi and Elka Torpey, "Chart 1. US Labor Force Shares by Age, 1970 to 2014 and Projected 2014–24 (Percent)," in *Older Workers: Labor Force Trends and Career Options*, US Department of Labor, Bureau of Labor Statistics, May 2017, https://www.bls.gov/careeroutlook/2017/article/older-workers.htm (accessed October 20, 2017)

group of women in their late 50s and early 60s in 2017 was the first to work outside the home in large numbers and is approaching retirement. Women in this cohort who are single, widowed, or divorced often continue to work to support themselves because they do not have sufficient Social Security credits to retire.

Married older women are increasingly choosing to keep working after their husband retires, breaking with the practice of joining their husband in retirement. In 1977 about one-third of employed women aged 65 years and older were married, but the BLS reports in *Women in the Labor Force: A Databook* (December 2015, https://www.bls.gov/opub/reports/womens-databook/archive/women-in-the-labor-force-a-databook-2015.pdf) that in 2014 more than half (58.4%) of married women were employed. Historically, some of the reasons cited for the growing

TABLE 4.3

Unemployment by age groups, July 2016–July 2017

Characteristic	Number of unemployed persons (in thousands)			Unemployment rates					
	July 2016	June 2017	July 2017	July 2016	Mar. 2017	Apr. 2017	May 2017	June 2017	July 2017
Age									
Total, 16 years and over	7,749	6,977	6,981	4.9	4.5	4.4	4.3	4.4	4.3
16 to 19 years	920	801	775	15.6	13.7	14.7	14.3	13.3	13.2
16 to 17 years	326	312	332	15.3	17.4	16.8	13.1	13.9	15.5
18 to 19 years	590	498	428	15.7	11.2	12.5	14.6	13.2	11.6
20 years and over	6,829	6,175	6,205	4.5	4.1	4.0	3.9	4.0	4.0
20 to 24 years	1,347	1,130	1,133	8.9	7.3	7.3	6.7	7.5	7.4
25 years and over	5,472	5,078	5,078	4.0	3.8	3.6	3.6	3.7	3.6
25 to 54 years	4,140	3,902	3,914	4.1	3.9	3.8	3.8	3.8	3.8
25 to 34 years	1,789	1,575	1,652	5.0	4.5	4.4	4.9	4.4	4.6
35 to 44 years	1,151	1,113	1,184	3.5	3.9	3.6	3.3	3.4	3.6
45 to 54 years	1,200	1,214	1,078	3.5	3.2	3.4	3.2	3.6	3.2
55 years and over	1,324	1,160	1,162	3.7	3.4	3.2	3.1	3.2	3.2

Note: Detail for the seasonally adjusted data shown in this table will not necessarily add to totals because of the independent seasonal adjustment of the various series. Updated population controls are introduced annually with the release of January data.

SOURCE: Adapted from "Table A-10. Selected Unemployment Indicators, Seasonally Adjusted," in *The Employment Situation—July 2017* US Department of Labor, Bureau of Labor Statistics, August 4, 2017, https://www.bls.gov/news.release/archives/empsit_08042017.pdf (accessed October 20, 2017)

proportion of older married women in the workforce are:

- Older women have careers they find personally satisfying as well as financially rewarding.

- They need to secure their retirement to prevent the poverty that has historically afflicted widows.

- Their income helps maintain the family standard of living and may be vital when their husband has been pressured to retire by his employer or suffers failing health.

- They enjoy social interactions at the workplace. Women value relationships with coworkers more than men do, and as a result women often find retirement more isolating.

Part-Time versus Full-Time Work

Older workers may find increasing opportunities for flexible employment and alternative work arrangements, such as working as independent contractors or on-call workers rather than as employees or daily workers. For employers, hiring older part-time workers is often an attractive alternative to hiring younger full-time workers. Some employers value older workers' maturity, dependability, and experience. Others hire older workers to reduce payroll expenses. This reduction is achieved when part-time workers are hired as independent contractors and do not receive benefits.

Employers Favor Older Workers

In "10 Jobs Hiring Older Workers" (USnews.com, May 12, 2017), Emily Brandon observes that some fields actively seek older workers because they have special skills or can more readily connect with prospective customers. Brandon reports that a study conducted by Boston College's Center for Retirement Research finds that older workers, especially those embarking on second careers, may be well suited for jobs such as sales demonstrators in stores; messengers who deliver documents and packages; tailors, dressmakers and seamstresses; security guard supervisors, public transportation attendants, bridge tenders, and crossing guards; taxi drivers and chauffeurs; and guides in museums and historical sites.

DISPELLING MYTHS AND STEREOTYPES ABOUT OLDER WORKERS

Older workers are often stereotyped by the mistaken belief that performance declines with age. However, performance studies reveal that older workers perform intellectually as well as or better than workers 30 years younger by maintaining their problem solving, communication, and creative skills. In "The Demands of Work in the 21st Century" (Lisa Finkelstein et al., editors, *Facing the Challenges of a Multi-age Workforce: A Use-Inspired Approach*, 2015), Margaret E. Beier concludes, "There is no evidence to suggest that older workers will be at a disadvantage in the 21st-century workplace."

Myth: Older Workers Have Overly Increased Absenteeism

Because aging is associated with declining health, older workers are often assumed to have markedly higher rates of illnesses and absences from work. Somewhat surprisingly, the chronic (long-term) health conditions that older adults may suffer tend to be manageable and do not affect attendance records. In fact, absence rates for

TABLE 4.4

Labor force participation rate, by age, sex, race, and ethnicity, 1994, 2004, 2014, and projected 2024

[In percent]

Group	Participation rate				Percentage-point change			Annual growth rate		
	1994	2004	2014	2024	1994–2004	2004–2014	2014–2024	1994–2004	2004–2014	2014–2024
Total, 16 years and older	**66.6**	**66.0**	**62.9**	**60.9**	**−0.6**	**−3.1**	**−2.0**	**−0.1**	**−0.5**	**−0.3**
16 to 24	66.4	61.1	55.0	49.7	−5.3	−6.1	−5.3	−0.8	−1.0	−1.0
16 to 19	52.7	43.9	34.0	26.4	−8.8	−9.9	−7.6	−1.8	−2.5	−2.5
20 to 24	77.0	75.0	70.8	68.2	−2.0	−4.2	−2.6	−0.3	−0.6	−0.4
25 to 54	83.4	82.8	80.9	81.2	−0.6	−1.9	0.3	−0.1	−0.2	0
25 to 34	83.2	82.7	81.2	81.3	−0.5	−1.5	0.1	−0.1	−0.2	0
35 to 44	84.8	83.6	82.2	81.7	−1.2	−1.4	−0.5	−0.1	−0.2	−0.1
45 to 54	81.7	81.8	79.6	81.0	0.1	−2.2	1.4	0	−0.3	0.2
55 and older	30.1	36.2	40.0	39.4	6.1	3.8	−0.6	1.9	1.0	−0.2
55 to 64	56.8	62.3	64.1	66.3	5.5	1.8	2.2	0.9	0.3	0.3
55 to 59	67.7	71.1	71.4	74.2	3.4	0.3	2.8	0.5	0.0	0.4
60 to 64	44.9	50.9	55.8	58.8	6.0	4.9	3.0	1.3	0.9	0.5
60 to 61	54.5	59.2	63.4	67.1	4.7	4.2	3.7	0.8	0.7	0.6
62 to 64	38.7	44.4	50.2	53.2	5.7	5.8	3.0	1.4	1.2	0.6
65 and older	12.4	14.4	18.6	21.7	2.0	4.2	3.1	1.5	2.6	1.6
65 to 74	17.2	21.9	26.2	29.9	4.7	4.3	3.7	2.4	1.8	1.3
65 to 69	21.9	27.7	31.6	36.2	5.8	3.9	4.6	2.4	1.3	1.4
70 to 74	11.8	15.3	18.9	22.8	3.5	3.6	3.9	2.6	2.1	1.9
75 to 79	6.6	8.8	11.3	14.4	2.2	2.5	3.1	2.9	2.5	2.5
75 and older	5.4	6.1	8.0	10.6	0.7	1.9	2.6	1.2	2.7	2.9
Men, 16 years and older	**75.1**	**73.3**	**69.2**	**66.2**	**−1.8**	**−4.1**	**−3.0**	**−0.2**	**−0.6**	**−0.4**
16 to 24	70.3	63.9	56.4	50.2	−6.4	−7.5	−6.2	−0.9	−1.2	−1.2
16 to 19	54.1	43.9	33.5	27.5	−10.2	−10.4	−6.0	−2.1	−2.7	−2.0
20 to 24	83.1	79.6	73.9	68.3	−3.5	−5.7	−5.6	−0.4	−0.7	−0.8
25 to 54	91.7	90.5	88.2	87.3	−1.2	−2.3	−0.9	−0.1	−0.3	−0.1
25 to 34	92.6	91.9	88.7	87.0	−0.7	−3.2	−1.7	−0.1	−0.4	−0.2
35 to 44	92.8	91.9	90.5	90.1	−0.9	−1.4	−0.4	−0.1	−0.2	0
45 to 54	89.1	87.5	85.6	84.4	−1.6	−1.9	−1.2	−0.2	−0.2	−0.1
55 and older	37.8	43.2	45.9	44.0	5.4	2.7	−1.9	1.3	0.6	−0.4
55 to 64	65.5	68.7	69.9	69.9	3.2	1.2	0	0.5	0.2	0
55 to 59	76.9	77.6	76.8	76.3	0.7	−0.8	−0.5	0.1	−0.1	−0.1
60 to 64	52.8	57.0	61.9	63.8	4.2	4.9	1.9	0.8	0.8	0.3
60 to 61	64.8	64.9	69.7	69.7	0.1	4.8	0	0	0.7	0
62 to 64	45.1	50.8	56.2	59.9	5.7	5.4	3.7	1.2	1.0	0.6
65 and older	16.9	19.0	23.0	25.7	2.1	4.0	2.7	1.2	1.9	1.1
65 to 74	21.7	26.7	30.6	34.0	5.0	3.9	3.4	2.1	1.4	1.1
65 to 69	26.8	32.6	36.1	40.0	5.8	3.5	3.9	2.0	1.0	1.0
70 to 74	15.8	19.4	22.8	26.6	3.6	3.4	3.8	2.1	1.6	1.6
75 to 79	9.8	12.4	14.5	17.3	2.6	2.1	2.8	2.4	1.6	1.8
75 and older	8.6	9.0	11.0	13.5	0.4	2.0	2.5	.5	2.0	2.1
Women, 16 years and older	**58.8**	**59.2**	**57.0**	**55.8**	**0.4**	**−2.2**	**−1.2**	**0.1**	**−0.4**	**−0.2**
16 to 24	62.5	58.7	53.6	48.6	−3.8	−5.1	−5.0	−0.6	−0.9	−1.0
16 to 19	51.3	43.8	34.5	25.9	−7.5	−9.3	−8.6	−1.6	−2.4	−2.8
20 to 24	71.0	70.5	67.7	66.5	−0.5	−2.8	−1.2	−0.1	−0.4	−0.2
25 to 54	75.3	75.3	73.9	75.2	0.0	−1.4	1.3	0	−0.2	0.2
25 to 34	74.0	73.6	73.8	74.9	−0.4	0.2	1.1	−0.1	0	0.1
35 to 44	77.1	75.6	74.1	73.9	−1.5	−1.5	−0.2	−0.2	−0.2	0
45 to 54	74.6	76.5	73.8	77.0	1.9	−2.7	3.2	0.3	−0.4	0.4
55 and older	24.0	30.5	34.9	35.4	6.5	4.4	0.5	2.4	1.4	0.1
55 to 64	48.9	56.3	58.8	62.9	7.4	2.5	4.1	1.4	0.4	0.7
55 to 59	59.2	65.0	66.4	72.2	5.8	1.4	5.8	0.9	0.2	0.8
60 to 64	37.8	45.4	50.2	54.2	7.6	4.8	4.0	1.8	1.0	0.8
60 to 61	45.3	54.0	57.6	64.8	8.7	3.6	7.2	1.8	0.6	1.2
62 to 64	33.1	38.7	44.7	47.1	5.6	6.0	2.4	1.6	1.5	0.5
65 and older	9.2	11.1	15.1	18.4	1.9	4.0	3.3	1.9	3.1	2.0
65 to 74	13.6	18.0	22.4	26.2	4.4	4.4	3.8	2.8	2.2	1.6
65 to 69	17.9	23.3	27.5	32.8	5.4	4.2	5.3	2.7	1.7	1.8
70 to 74	8.7	12.0	15.6	18.5	3.3	3.6	2.9	3.3	2.7	1.7
75 to 79	4.4	6.3	8.9	12.0	1.9	2.6	3.1	3.7	3.5	3.0
75 and older	3.5	4.3	5.9	8.4	0.8	1.6	2.5	2.1	3.2	3.6

older full-time wage and salary workers are only slightly higher than those of younger workers. According to the BLS, in 2016 the absence rate for workers aged 55 years and older was 3.3%, the same rate reported for those aged 16 to 19 years. (See Table 4.5.)

Myth: It Costs More to Hire Older Workers

One widely accepted myth is that hiring and training older workers is not a sound investment because they will not remain on the job long. The BLS, however, indicates that in January 2016 workers aged 55 to

[In percent]

Group	Participation rate				Percentage-point change			Annual growth rate		
	1994	2004	2014	2024	1994–2004	2004–2014	2014–2024	1994–2004	2004–2014	2014–2024
Race										
White	67.1	66.3	63.1	60.8	−0.8	−3.2	−2.3	−0.1	−0.5	−0.4
Men	75.9	74.1	69.8	66.5	−1.8	−4.3	−3.3	−0.2	−0.6	−0.5
Women	58.9	58.9	56.7	55.2	0	−2.2	−1.5	0	−0.4	−0.3
Black	63.4	63.8	61.2	59.7	0.4	−2.6	−1.5	0.1	−0.4	−0.2
Men	69.1	66.7	63.6	60.7	−2.4	−3.1	−2.9	−0.4	−0.5	−0.5
Women	58.7	61.5	59.2	58.9	2.8	−2.3	−0.3	0.5	−0.4	−0.1
Asian	65.3	65.9	63.6	63.0	0.6	−2.3	−0.6	0.1	−0.4	−0.1
Men	74.3	75.0	72.4	71.3	0.7	−2.6	−1.1	0.1	−0.4	−0.2
Women	56.9	57.6	55.8	55.7	0.7	−1.8	−0.1	0.1	−0.3	0.0
All other race groups*	—	66.4	67.6	63.1	—	1.2	−4.5	—	0.2	−0.7
Men	—	73.2	72.0	68.3	—	−1.3	−3.7	—	−0.2	−0.5
Women	—	60.0	63.3	57.8	—	3.3	−5.5	—	0.5	−0.9
Ethnicity:										
Hispanic origin	66.1	68.6	66.1	65.9	2.5	−2.5	−0.2	0.4	−0.4	0
Men	79.2	80.4	76.1	74.3	1.2	−4.3	−1.8	0.2	−0.5	−0.2
Women	52.9	56.1	56.0	57.4	3.2	−0.1	1.4	0.6	0	0.2
Other than Hispanic origin	66.6	65.6	62.3	59.7	−1.0	−3.3	−2.6	−0.2	−0.5	−0.4
Men	74.6	72.2	67.9	64.3	−2.4	−4.3	−3.6	−0.3	−0.6	−0.5
Women	59.4	59.6	57.2	55.5	0.2	−2.4	−2.1	0	−0.4	−0.4
White non-Hispanic	67.2	65.9	62.4	60.7	−1.3	−3.5	−1.7	−0.2	−0.5	−0.3
Men	75.5	73.0	68.4	66.0	−2.5	−4.6	−2.4	−0.3	−0.6	−0.4
Women	60.1	59.3	56.9	55.7	−0.8	−2.4	−1.2	−0.1	−0.4	−0.2
Age of baby boomers	30 to 48	40 to 58	50 to 68	60 to 78						

Notes: *The "all other groups" category includes (1) those classified as being of multiple racial origin and (2) the racial categories of (2a) American Indian and Alaska Native and (2b) Native Hawaiian and Other Pacific Islanders.
Dash indicates no data collected for category. Details may not sum to totals because of rounding.

SOURCE: Mitra Toossi, "Table 3. Civilian Labor Force, Participation Rate, by Age, Gender, Race, and Ethnicity, 1994, 2004, 2014, and Projected 2024 (in Percent)," in "Labor Force Projections to 2024: the Labor Force Is Growing, but Slowly," *Monthly Labor Review*, December 2015, https://www.bls.gov/opub/mlr/2015/article/pdf/labor-force-projections-to-2024.pdf (accessed October 20, 2017)

64 years had a median job tenure of 10.1 years, which was more than three times longer than the 2.8 years for workers aged 25 to 34 years. (See Table 4.6.) Research conducted by the AARP repeatedly demonstrates that workers aged 50 to 60 years work for an average of 15 years. Furthermore, the Mature Workers Employment Alliance, an organization that assists older workers to transition to new positions, asserts that the future work life of employees over the age of 50 generally exceeds the life of the technology for which they are trained.

The AARP indicates that although older workers' health, disability, and life insurance costs are higher than those of younger workers, they are offset by lower costs because of fewer dependents. Older workers have generally earned more vacation time and have higher pension costs, and they take fewer risks, which means they have lower accident rates. Workers over the age of 50 years file fewer workers' compensation claims than younger workers; the largest numbers of claims are filed by workers between the ages of 30 and 34 years. Fringe benefit costs for workers of all ages are about the same overall. Finally, retaining experienced older workers actually reduces employer costs that are associated with recruiting, hiring, and training new, younger workers.

Myth: Older Workers Are Technophobes

There is a pervasive myth that older adults are unable to learn or use new information technology. David Z. Morris dispels this myth in "Survey: Older Workers Are Actually More Comfortable with Technology" (Fortune.com, August 7, 2016), observing that a 2016 survey found that workers aged 55 years "adopted technology as quickly as their younger peers—and felt less anxiety about it." Older workers used about five forms of technology per week, slightly more than workers aged 18 to 34 years, and were just as likely as younger workers to use laptops, tablets, and smartphones. Furthermore, older workers reported fewer problems working across multiple devices than did younger workers.

Myth: Older Workers Are Not Innovators

The stereotype of older workers as slow to learn new skills, unwilling to take risks, and unable to adapt to change is fading as older entrepreneurs and innovators gain recognition. In *The Demographics of Innovation in the United States* (February 2016, http://www2.itif.org/2016-demographics-of-innovation.pdf), Adams Nager et al. of the Information Technology & Innovation Foundation report that a 2016 survey of 900 innovators aged 18 to 80 years in technology finds that contrary to popular belief, innovators are not young adults. Just 5.8% of innovators

TABLE 4.5

Absences from work, by age and sex, 2016

[Numbers in thousands]

Characteristic	Full-time wage and salary workers[a]	2016 Absence rate[a]			2016 Lost worktime rate[b]		
		Total	Illness or injury	Other reasons	Total	Illness or injury	Other reasons
Age and sex							
Total, 16 years and over	110,922	2.9	2.0	0.9	1.5	1.0	0.5
16 to 19 years	1,295	3.3	2.1	1.2	1.3	0.8	0.5
20 to 24 years	8,786	2.7	1.8	0.9	1.2	0.7	0.5
25 years and over	100,842	2.9	2.0	0.9	1.5	1.0	0.5
25 to 54 years	78,243	2.8	1.8	1.0	1.4	0.9	0.5
55 years and over	22,599	3.3	2.6	0.7	1.7	1.4	0.3
Men, 16 years and over	61,841	2.2	1.6	0.6	1.1	0.8	0.3
16 to 19 years	765	3.1	1.8	1.3	1.2	0.7	0.5
20 to 24 years	4,901	2.3	1.7	0.6	0.9	0.7	0.2
25 years and over	56,175	2.2	1.6	0.6	1.1	0.9	0.3
25 to 54 years	43,869	2.1	1.5	0.6	1.0	0.8	0.3
55 years and over	12,306	2.8	2.3	0.6	1.5	1.3	0.3
Women, 16 years and over	49,081	3.7	2.4	1.3	1.9	1.2	0.8
16 to 19 years	530	3.5	2.6	0.9	1.5	1.1	0.5
20 to 24 years	3,884	3.2	1.9	1.3	1.5	0.7	0.8
25 years and over	44,667	3.7	2.4	1.3	2.0	1.2	0.8
25 to 54 years	34,374	3.7	2.2	1.4	2.0	1.1	0.9
55 years and over	10,293	3.9	3.0	0.9	2.0	1.6	0.4
Race and Hispanic or Latino Ethnicity							
White	86,366	2.8	1.9	0.9	1.5	1.0	0.5
Black or African American	13,974	3.3	2.3	1.0	1.8	1.3	0.5
Asian	7,004	2.1	1.3	0.8	1.0	0.6	0.5
Hispanic or Latino	19,022	2.7	1.8	0.9	1.4	0.9	0.5

[a]Absences are defined as instances when persons who usually work 35 or more hours per week (full time) worked less than 35 hours during the reference week for one of the following reasons: own illness, injury, or medical problems; child care problems; other family or personal obligations; civic or military duty; and maternity or paternity leave. Excluded are situations in which work was missed due to vacation or personal days, holiday, labor dispute, and other reasons. For multiple jobholders, absence data refer only to work missed at their main jobs. The absence rate is the ratio of workers with absences to total full-time wage and salary employment.

[b]Hours absent as a percent of hours usually worked.

Note: Estimates for the above race groups (white, black or African American, and Asian) do not sum to totals because data are not presented for all races. Persons whose ethnicity is identified as Hispanic or Latino may be of any race. All self-employed workers are excluded, both those with incorporated businesses and those with unincorporated businesses. The estimates of full-time wage and salary employment shown in this table do not match those in other tables because the estimates in this table are based on the full CPS sample and those in the other tables are based on a quarter of the sample only. Updated population controls are introduced annually with the release of January data.

CPS = Current Population Survey

SOURCE: "46. Absences from Work of Employed Full-Time Wage and Salary Workers by Age, Sex, Race, and Hispanic or Latino Ethnicity," in *Labor Force Statistics from the Current Population Survey*, US Department of Labor, Bureau of Labor Statistics, February 8, 2017, https://www.bls.gov/cps/cpsaat46.htm (accessed October 20, 2017)

were aged 30 years and younger. The rate of innovation was highest among those aged 46 to 55 years, a fact that points to innovation being concentrated in older populations.

AGE DISCRIMINATION

Although the 1967 ADEA and its amendments were enacted to ban discrimination against workers based on their age, the act was also intended to promote the employment of older workers based on their abilities. Besides making it illegal for employers to discriminate based on age in hiring, discharging, and compensating employees, the act also prohibited companies from coercing older workers into accepting incentives to early retirement. In 1990 ADEA was strengthened with the passing of the Older Workers Benefit Protection Act. Besides prohibiting discrimination in employee benefits based on age, it provides that an employee's waiver of

the right to sue for age discrimination, a clause sometimes included in severance packages, is invalid unless it is "voluntary and knowing."

Nevertheless, age bias and discrimination persist, even though age discrimination in the workplace is against the law. More than 15,000 claims of age discrimination are filed with the Equal Employment Opportunity Commission (EEOC) every year. Most cases involve older workers who believe they were terminated unfairly, but a number of the cases involve workers who believe they have experienced age discrimination in hiring practices.

The number of claims received by the EEOC rose from 15,785 during fiscal year (FY) 1997 to 18,376 during FY 2017. (See Table 4.7.) Agency data reveal that most claimants do not win. Of the claims that were resolved in FY 2017, the EEOC found "reasonable cause" that age

TABLE 4.6

Median years of tenure with current employer for employed workers, by age and sex, selected years 2006–16

Age and sex	January 2006	January 2008	January 2010	January 2012	January 2014	January 2016
Total						
16 years and over	4.0	4.1	4.4	4.6	4.6	4.2
16 to 17 years	0.6	0.7	0.7	0.7	0.7	0.6
18 to 19 years	0.7	0.8	1.0	0.8	0.8	0.8
20 to 24 years	1.3	1.3	1.5	1.3	1.3	1.3
25 years and over	4.9	5.1	5.2	5.4	5.5	5.1
25 to 34 years	2.9	2.7	3.1	3.2	3.0	2.8
35 to 44 years	4.9	4.9	5.1	5.3	5.2	4.9
45 to 54 years	7.3	7.6	7.8	7.8	7.9	7.9
55 to 64 years	9.3	9.9	10.0	10.3	10.4	10.1
65 years and over	8.8	10.2	9.9	10.3	10.3	10.3
Men						
16 years and over	4.1	4.2	4.6	4.7	4.7	4.3
16 to 17 years	0.7	0.7	0.7	0.6	0.7	0.6
18 to 19 years	0.7	0.8	1.0	0.8	0.9	0.8
20 to 24 years	1.4	1.4	1.6	1.4	1.4	1.3
25 years and over	5.0	5.2	5.3	5.5	5.5	5.2
25 to 34 years	2.9	2.8	3.2	3.2	3.1	2.9
35 to 44 years	5.1	5.2	5.3	5.4	5.4	5.0
45 to 54 years	8.1	8.2	8.5	8.5	8.2	8.4
55 to 64 years	9.5	10.1	10.4	10.7	10.7	10.2
65 years and over	8.3	10.4	9.7	10.2	10.0	10.2
Women						
16 years and over	3.9	3.9	4.2	4.6	4.5	4.0
16 to 17 years	0.6	0.6	0.7	0.7	0.7	0.6
18 to 19 years	0.7	0.8	1.0	0.8	0.8	0.8
20 to 24 years	1.2	1.3	1.5	1.3	1.3	1.2
25 years and over	4.8	4.9	5.1	5.4	5.4	5.0
25 to 34 years	2.8	2.6	3.0	3.1	2.9	2.6
35 to 44 years	4.6	4.7	4.9	5.2	5.1	4.8
45 to 54 years	6.7	7.0	7.1	7.3	7.6	7.5
55 to 64 years	9.2	9.8	9.7	10.0	10.2	10.0
65 years and over	9.5	9.9	10.1	10.5	10.5	10.4

SOURCE: "Table 1. Median Years of Tenure with Current Employer for Employed Wage and Salary Workers by Age and Sex, Selected Years, 2006–2016," in *Economic News Release*, US Department of Labor, Bureau of Labor Statistics, September 22, 2016, https://www.bls.gov/news.release/tenure.t01.htm (accessed October 20, 2017)

discrimination may have occurred in just 485 cases and found "no reasonable cause" in 15,880 cases.

Pressure to Retire

There are many forms of subtle discrimination against older workers as well as ways that employers can directly or indirectly exert pressure on older employees to resign or retire. This form of discrimination is "under the radar" and in many instances violates the spirit, if not the letter, of ADEA.

From an employer's standpoint, age discrimination is simply the consequence of efforts to reduce payroll expenses. Employment decisions are not only based on how much an employee contributes to the company but also on the salary and benefits the company must provide the employee, relative to the cost of other employees. Because salary tends to increase with longevity on the job, older workers usually receive higher wages than younger workers. Thus, if two employees are equally productive and the older one has a higher salary, a company has an economic incentive to lay off the older worker or strongly encourage early retirement.

For many workers, early retirement is untenable. Early retirement benefits are usually less than regular retirement benefits and may be insufficient to allow a retiree to live comfortably without working. Finding a new job is more challenging for older workers, particularly during periods of high unemployment, and they are frequently unemployed for longer periods than are younger job seekers. Furthermore, workers who refuse to accept early retirement may find themselves without jobs at all, perhaps with no pension and no severance pay.

Some labor economists contend that early retirements, whether voluntary or coerced, deprive the nation of skilled workers needed for robust growth and divest the government of the revenue that these workers would have contributed in payroll taxes.

Filing ADEA Claims: Suing the Company

The costs involved in filing an age discrimination suit are high. Besides the financial outlay for legal representation, workers who sue their employers may be stigmatized and face further discrimination. Future

TABLE 4.7

Age Discrimination in Employment Act charges, fiscal years 1997–2017

	Fiscal year 1997	Fiscal year 1998	Fiscal year 1999	Fiscal year 2000	Fiscal year 2001	Fiscal year 2002	Fiscal year 2003	Fiscal year 2004	Fiscal year 2005	Fiscal year 2006	Fiscal year 2007	Fiscal year 2008	Fiscal year 2009	Fiscal year 2010	Fiscal year 2011	Fiscal year 2012	Fiscal year 2013	Fiscal year 2014	Fiscal year 2015	Fiscal year 2016	Fiscal year 2017
Receipts	15,785	15,191	14,141	16,008	17,405	19,921	19,124	17,837	16,585	16,548	19,103	24,582	22,778	23,264	23,465	22,857	21,396	20,588	20,144	20,857	18,376
Resolutions	18,279	15,995	15,448	14,672	15,155	18,673	17,352	15,792	14,076	14,146	16,134	21,415	20,529	24,800	26,080	27,335	22,371	20,148	21,273	22,594	22,430
Resolutions by type																					
Settlements	642 / 3.5%	755 / 4.7%	816 / 5.3%	1,156 / 7.9%	1,006 / 6.6%	1,222 / 6.5%	1,285 / 7.4%	1,377 / 8.7%	1,326 / 9.4%	1,417 / 10.0%	1,795 / 11.1%	1,974 / 9.2%	1,935 / 9.4%	2,250 / 9.1%	2,231 / 8.6%	2,001 / 7.3%	1,781 / 8.0%	1,567 / 7.8%	1,703 / 8.0%	1,445 / 6.4%	1,288 / 5.7%
Withdrawals w/benefits	762 / 4.2%	580 / 3.6%	578 / 3.7%	560 / 3.8%	551 / 3.6%	671 / 3.6%	710 / 4.1%	787 / 5.0%	764 / 5.4%	767 / 5.4%	958 / 5.9%	1,252 / 5.8%	1,161 / 5.7%	1,322 / 5.3%	1,369 / 5.2%	1,280 / 4.7%	1,296 / 5.8%	1,251 / 6.2%	1,279 / 6.0%	1,252 / 5.5%	1,181 / 5.3%
Administrative closures	4,986 / 27.3%	4,175 / 26.1%	3,601 / 23.3%	3,232 / 22.0%	3,963 / 26.1%	6,254 / 33.5%	2,824 / 16.3%	3,550 / 22.5%	2,537 / 18.0%	2,639 / 18.7%	2,754 / 17.1%	6,387 / 29.8%	4,031 / 19.6%	4,167 / 16.8%	4,230 / 16.2%	4,045 / 14.8%	3,642 / 16.3%	3,619 / 18.0%	3,700 / 17.4%	3,729 / 16.5%	3,596 / 16.0%
No reasonable cause	11,163 / 61.1%	9,863 / 61.7%	9,172 / 59.4%	8,517 / 58.0%	8,388 / 55.3%	9,725 / 52.1%	11,976 / 69.0%	9,563 / 60.6%	8,866 / 63.0%	8,746 / 61.8%	10,002 / 62.0%	11,124 / 51.9%	12,788 / 62.3%	16,308 / 65.8%	17,454 / 66.9%	19,239 / 70.4%	15,113 / 67.6%	13,159 / 65.3%	13,980 / 65.7%	15,548 / 68.8%	15,880 / 70.8%
Reasonable cause	726 / 4.0%	622 / 3.9%	1,281 / 8.3%	1,207 / 8.2%	1,247 / 8.2%	801 / 4.3%	557 / 3.2%	515 / 3.3%	583 / 4.1%	612 / 4.3%	625 / 3.9%	678 / 3.2%	614 / 3.0%	753 / 3.0%	796 / 3.1%	770 / 2.8%	539 / 2.4%	552 / 2.7%	611 / 2.9%	620 / 2.7%	485 / 2.2%
Successful conciliations	74 / 0.4%	119 / 0.7%	184 / 1.2%	241 / 1.6%	409 / 2.7%	208 / 1.1%	166 / 1.0%	139 / 0.9%	169 / 1.2%	177 / 1.3%	186 / 1.2%	220 / 1.0%	202 / 1.0%	252 / 1.0%	273 / 1.0%	343 / 1.3%	221 / 1.0%	232 / 1.2%	321 / 1.5%	339 / 1.5%	202 / 0.9%
Unsuccessful conciliations	652 / 3.6%	503 / 3.1%	1,097 / 7.1%	966 / 6.6%	838 / 5.5%	593 / 3.2%	391 / 2.3%	376 / 2.4%	414 / 2.9%	435 / 3.1%	439 / 2.7%	458 / 2.1%	412 / 2.0%	501 / 2.0%	523 / 2.0%	427 / 1.6%	318 / 1.4%	320 / 1.6%	290 / 1.4%	281 / 1.2%	283 / 1.3%
Merit resolutions	2,130 / 11.7%	1,957 / 12.2%	2,675 / 17.3%	2,923 / 19.9%	2,804 / 18.5%	2,694 / 14.4%	2,552 / 14.7%	2,679 / 17.0%	2,673 / 19.0%	2,796 / 19.8%	3,378 / 20.9%	3,904 / 18.2%	3,710 / 18.1%	4,325 / 17.4%	4,396 / 16.9%	4,051 / 14.8%	3,616 / 16.2%	3,370 / 16.7%	3,593 / 16.9%	3,317 / 14.7%	2,954 / 13.2%
Monetary benefits (millions)*	$44.3	$34.7	$38.6	$45.2	$53.7	$55.7	$48.9	$69.0	$77.7	$51.5	$66.8	$82.8	$72.1	$93.6	$95.2	$91.6	$97.9	$77.7	$99.1	$88.2	$90.1

FY = fiscal year.

EEOC = Equal Employment Opportunity Commission.

*Does not include monetary benefits obtained through litigation.

Notes: The total of individual percentages may not always sum to 100% due to rounding. EEOC total workload includes charges carried over from previous fiscal years, new charge receipts and charges transferred to EEOC from Fair Employment Practice Agencies (FEPAs). Resolution of charges each year may therefore exceed receipts for that year because workload being resolved is drawn from a combination of pending, new receipts and FEPA transfer charges rather than from new charges only.

SOURCE: "Age Discrimination in Employment Act FY 1997–FY 2017," in *Enforcement and Litigation Statistics*, US Equal Opportunity Commission, 2018, http://www.eeoc.gov/eeoc/statistics/enforcement/adea.cfm (accessed February 16, 2018)

employers may be reluctant to hire a worker who has filed a discrimination suit against a former employer. Workers caught in this scenario can suffer emotional and financial damage that may adversely affect them for the rest of their life. Nonetheless, many workers do choose to sue their employers.

US Supreme Court Decisions Augment ADEA

In response to the Great Recession, which lasted from late 2007 to mid-2009, and the continuing economic uncertainty, in 2017 some companies instituted layoffs and reductions in force in an effort to reduce costs and remain viable. Because reductions in force aim to reduce payroll, some target higher-paid workers, who are often older adults with longer tenures. ADEA is violated if an employment policy that seems neutral, such as the criteria for workers to be laid off, actually exerts a statistically significant adverse or "disparate impact" when applied to workers aged 40 years and older versus younger workers.

Protections for older workers were strengthened in 2005 by the US Supreme Court decision in *Smith v. City of Jackson* (544 US 228) that workers aged 40 years and older may prove discrimination under ADEA using a disparate impact theory. The court stated that plaintiffs in age discrimination lawsuits do not have to prove that employers intended to discriminate, only that layoffs had a disparate impact on older workers. This ruling is significant because claimants are not required to show that an employer deliberately targeted a single employee or group of employees. Instead, claimants can prevail if they are able to demonstrate that an employer used a neutral business practice (with no intent to discriminate) that had an adverse impact on people aged 40 years and older.

In 2008 the Supreme Court ruled in *Meacham et al. v. Knolls Atomic Power Laboratory* (554 US 84) that an employer defending against a disparate impact age bias claim, and not the employee making the charge, bears the burden of proving that the adverse action (in this case a reduction in workforce plan) was based on a reasonable factor other than age. The disparate impact theory is based on the principle that a policy that appears neutral may still have an adverse impact on a protected class, in this case, older workers.

The Supreme Court ruling in *Gross v. FBL Financial Services, Inc.* (557 US 167 [2009]) essentially reversed its earlier position, making it more difficult for older workers to prevail in age discrimination suits. The ruling eliminated the requirement that employers prove they had a legitimate reason other than age for laying off older workers. Instead, the burden of proof now falls to older workers, who must prove that age was the key factor. The ruling reversed a jury verdict in favor of an insurance adjuster in Iowa who filed a claim because his company demoted him and gave his job to a younger worker.

According to David G. Savage, in "Supreme Court Makes Age Bias Suits Harder to Win" (LATimes.com, June 19, 2009), the high court determined that "the judge had erred by allowing the plaintiff to win without proving he had been demoted because of his age." In "Reductions in Force: The Supreme Court Escalates the Legal Risks" (July 26, 2008, https://www.ebglaw.com/news/reductions-in-force-the-supreme-court-escalates-the-legal-risks/), Frank C. Morris Jr. of Epstein Becker & Green P.C. states that "precisely at a time when the economy may force employers to make more [reductions in force] decisions, the Supreme Court has made defending such decisions decidedly harder for employers."

RECENT AGE DISCRIMINATION CASES AND COURT DECISIONS. Ethan Baron reports in "Google Age-Discrimination Lawsuit: Nearly 300 People Have Signed onto Class Action" (Siliconbeat.com, July 31, 2017) that a ruling by Judge Howard R. Lloyd of the US District Court of the Northern District of California revealed that 269 people have filed a class action, claiming that Google discriminated against them in hiring on the basis of their age.

In "Amid Drive for Tech-Savvy Workforce, AT&T Faces Suit for Age Bias" (*New Jersey Law Journal*, vol. 222, no. 28, July 10, 2017), Charles Toutant reports that a suit filed by Stephen Console and Laura Mattiacci of Console Mattiacci Law, LLC, accused AT&T of age discrimination. The suit alleges that the dismissal of older workers was part of the company's effort to improve workers' technology skills and that the dismissals reflected age-based stereotyping. Toutant notes that Console Mattiacci "has had a string of victories in age discrimination suits recently, including a $370,000 verdict on behalf of another AT&T employee in the Eastern District of Pennsylvania in January 2016 and a $51.5 million verdict in a suit by an engineer for Lockheed Martin in the District of New Jersey in January 2017."

BABY BOOMERS AND RETIREES WANT TO DO GOOD WORK

Baby Boomers Will Transform Retirement

Large numbers of boomers are crafting their encores and helping to create a movement for personal renewal and social good.

—Marci Alboher, in *The Encore Career Handbook: How to Make a Living and a Difference in the Second Half of Life* (2013)

In *Encore Careers: The Persistence of Purpose* (2014, https://encore.org/wp-content/uploads/files/2014Encore ResearchOverview.pdf), Encore.org, an organization aiming to use older adults' skills and expertise to improve communities worldwide, and Penn Schoen Berland, a market research firm, indicate that about 25 million Americans aged 50 to 70 years are interested in launching so-called encore careers to address social needs. The following are the key findings of the survey:

- More than half (55%) of Americans feel that using their skills and expertise to help others is a crucial part of what they want to do after their primary careers.

- In 2014 there were fewer financial barriers to starting encore careers than there were in 2011. Just one out of eight (12%) of those interested in encore careers expressed concern about earning enough income in a social-impact encore.

- About one-third (34%) of those in encore careers have worked for more than a decade in their encores; just half (50%) have less than five years' experience.

- The majority (86%) of those in encore careers consider their encores as or more enjoyable than their prior careers.

- Nearly three-fifths (57%) of those in encores have household incomes of less than $45,000. Only about one in seven (14%) reported household incomes greater than $90,000.

The survey concludes that the option of pursuing an encore career is considered desirable by a large number of older adults. The researchers assert, "More likely to involve new kinds of work, including entrepreneurships, as extensions of familiar roles, social-impact encore careers offer millions of midlife Americans the means to apply their life skills and knowledge to contribute to the greater good, no matter their academic credentials or economic status."

Volunteerism in Retirement

Volunteerism among older adults is a relatively new phenomenon. Historically, older adults were seen as the segment of society most in need of care and support. As medical technology enables people to live longer, healthier lives, and as stereotypes about aging shatter, the older population is being recognized as a valuable resource for volunteer organizations.

Every day millions of older Americans perform volunteer work in their communities. With free time as well as the wisdom and experience derived from years of living, they make ideal volunteers. Older adult volunteers are educated and skilled and can offer volunteer organizations many of the professional services they would otherwise have to purchase, such as legal, accounting, public relations, information systems support, and human resource management. Perhaps more important, they have empathy and compassion because they have encountered many of the same problems that are faced by those they seek to help.

According to the BLS, in *Volunteering in the United States—2015* (February 25, 2016, https://www.bls.gov/news.release/pdf/volun.pdf), volunteer rates in September 2015 were the lowest for young adults aged 16 to 24 years (21.8% of the population), adults aged 25 to 34 years (22.3%), and adults aged 65 years and older (23.5%). (See Table 4.8.) Volunteers aged 65 years and older did, however, devote the most time (a median of 94 hours during the year) to volunteer activities. (See Table 4.9.) Older volunteers were more likely to work for religious organizations than younger volunteers. The BLS notes that 42.7% of volunteers aged 65 years and older volunteered primarily for religious organizations, compared with 22% of volunteers aged 20 to 24 years. (See Table 4.10.)

NATIONAL SERVICE ORGANIZATIONS. Efforts to establish a national senior service during the administration of President John F. Kennedy (1917–1963) are described by Peter Shapiro in *A History of National Service in America* (1994). In 1963 Kennedy proposed the National Service Corps "to provide opportunities for service for those aged persons who can assume active roles in community volunteer efforts." When the National Service Corps was proposed, a scant 11% of the older population was involved in any kind of volunteerism. The plan to engage older adults in full-time, intensive service, with a minimum one-year commitment, to combat urban and rural poverty was viewed as revolutionary. Although the National Service Corps proposal was championed by the Kennedy administration and widely supported in the public and private sectors, it was defeated in Congress, where reactionary lawmakers linked it to efforts aimed at promoting racial integration in the South.

Despite the defeat of the National Service Corps, the idea of harnessing the volunteer power of older adults caught on. The Economic Opportunity Act of 1964 gave rise to the Volunteers in Service to America (VISTA) and eventually led to the launch of service programs involving low-income older adults, such as the Foster Grandparent, Senior Companion, and Senior Community Service Employment programs. The Foster Grandparent program matched 1,000 adults aged 60 years and older with 2,500 children living in orphanages and other institutions. The older adults would spend four hours a day, five days a week, feeding, cuddling, rocking, and exercising disabled children.

The success of the Foster Grandparent program exceeded all expectations. In 1971 the program was incorporated into the newly created ACTION agency, along with the Peace Corps, VISTA, the Service Corps of Retired Executives (SCORE), and the Active Corps of Executives. The Foster Grandparent program has since become part of the Senior Corps, a network of programs that tap the experience, skills, and talents of older adults to meet community challenges. Through its three programs (Foster Grandparent, Senior Companion, and Retired and Senior Volunteer), more than 360,000 Americans aged 55 years and older assisted local nonprofits, public agencies, and faith-based organizations in 2014. The Corporation for National and

TABLE 4.8

Volunteers by age groups and other selected characteristics, September 2015

[Numbers in thousands]

Characteristics in September 2015	Total, both sexes Civilian noninstitutional population	Total, both sexes Volunteers Number	Total, both sexes Volunteers Percent of population	Men Civilian noninstitutional population	Men Volunteers Number	Men Volunteers Percent of population	Women Civilian noninstitutional population	Women Volunteers Number	Women Volunteers Percent of population
Age									
Total, 16 years and over	251,325	62,623	24.9	121,365	26,498	21.8	129,960	36,126	27.8
16 to 24 years	38,525	8,415	21.8	19,409	3,702	19.1	19,115	4,714	24.7
16 to 19 years	16,612	4,382	26.4	8,425	2,089	24.8	8,187	2,293	28.0
20 to 24 years	21,913	4,033	18.4	10,984	1,613	14.7	10,928	2,421	22.2
25 years and over	212,801	54,208	25.5	101,956	22,796	22.4	110,844	31,412	28.3
25 to 34 years	42,901	9,548	22.3	21,211	3,836	18.1	21,690	5,712	26.3
35 to 44 years	39,719	11,490	28.9	19,454	4,768	24.5	20,265	6,723	33.2
45 to 54 years	42,588	11,933	28.0	20,816	5,127	24.6	21,772	6,806	31.3
55 to 64 years	40,763	10,213	25.1	19,602	4,384	22.4	21,161	5,829	27.5
65 years and over	46,830	11,024	23.5	20,872	4,681	22.4	25,957	6,343	24.4
Race and Hispanic or Latino ethnicity									
White	197,152	51,986	26.4	96,294	22,222	23.1	100,858	29,764	29.5
Black or African American	31,479	6,086	19.3	14,315	2,378	16.6	17,164	3,708	21.6
Asian	14,466	2,596	17.9	6,734	1,037	15.4	7,732	1,558	20.2
Hispanic or Latino ethnicity	39,828	6,165	15.5	19,849	2,583	13.0	19,979	3,582	17.9
Educational attainment[a]									
Less than a high school diploma	23,528	1,900	8.1	11,802	781	6.6	11,726	1,120	9.5
High school graduates, no college[b]	61,199	9,576	15.6	30,074	4,097	13.6	31,125	5,479	17.6
Some college or associate degree	56,948	15,102	26.5	26,155	6,043	23.1	30,793	9,059	29.4
Bachelor's degree and higher[c]	71,126	27,629	38.8	33,925	11,875	35.0	37,201	15,755	42.4
Marital status									
Single, never married	76,268	15,143	19.9	40,226	6,672	16.6	36,042	8,471	23.5
Married, spouse present	124,783	37,348	29.9	62,869	16,825	26.8	61,914	20,523	33.1
Other marital status[d]	50,274	10,132	20.2	18,270	3,000	16.4	32,005	7,132	22.3
Presence of own children under 18 years[e]									
Without own children under 18	184,577	41,738	22.6	91,802	18,263	19.9	92,775	23,475	25.3
With own children under 18	66,748	20,885	31.3	29,563	8,235	27.9	37,185	12,651	34.0
Employment status									
Civilian labor force	157,627	42,563	27.0	83,920	19,700	23.5	73,708	22,862	31.0
Employed	149,639	40,701	27.2	79,812	18,934	23.7	69,826	21,767	31.2
Full time[f]	121,914	32,085	26.3	69,954	16,535	23.6	51,959	15,549	29.9
Part time[g]	27,725	8,616	31.1	9,858	2,399	24.3	17,867	6,218	34.8
Unemployed	7,989	1,861	23.3	4,107	766	18.7	3,882	1,095	28.2
Not in the labor force	93,698	20,060	21.4	37,446	6,797	18.2	56,252	13,263	23.6

[a]Data refer to persons 25 years and over.
[b]Includes persons with a high school diploma or equivalent.
[c]Includes persons with bachelor's, professional, and doctoral degrees.
[d]Includes divorced, separated, and widowed persons.
[e]Own children include sons, daughters, stepchildren, and adopted children. Not included are nieces, nephews, grandchildren, and other related and unrelated children.
[f]Usually work 35 hours or more a week at all jobs.
[g]Usually work less than 35 hours a week at all jobs.
Note: Data on volunteers relate to persons who performed unpaid volunteer activities for an organization at any point from September 1, 2014, through the survey period in September 2015. Estimates for the above race groups (white, black or African American, and Asian) do not sum to totals because data are not presented for all races. Persons whose ethnicity is identified as Hispanic or Latino may be of any race.

SOURCE: "Table 1. Volunteers by Selected Characteristics, September 2015," in *Volunteering in the United States—2015*, US Department of Labor, Bureau of Labor Statistics, February 25, 2016, https://www.bls.gov/news.release/pdf/volun.pdf (accessed October 23, 2017)

Community Service notes in "Current Volunteers" (2018, https://www.nationalservice.gov/programs/senior-corps/current-volunteers) that in 2017, 245,000 volunteers delivered services at 28,100 unique sites in their communities.

Another successful national volunteer program involving older adults is SCORE, which uses retired business executives as counselors and consultants to small businesses. Established by the Small Business Administration (SBA) in 1964, the program works with recipients of SBA loans and others, assisting them to draft business plans, evaluate profitability, and develop marketing strategies. One objective of the program is to reduce default rates on these loans. SCORE mentors business owners and provides one-on-one counseling, consultation via email, and training sessions.

Points of Light (2018, http://www.pointsoflight.org/facts) is another organization that offers people of all ages opportunities to volunteer in their communities.

TABLE 4.9

Volunteers by annual hours volunteered and other selected characteristics, September 2015

Characteristics in September 2015	Total volunteers (thousands)	Total	Percent distribution of total annual hours spent volunteering at all organizations					Not reporting annual hours	Median annual hours[a]
			1 to 14 hour(s)	15 to 49 hours	50 to 99 hours	100 to 499 hours	500 hours and over		
Sex									
Total, both sexes	62,623	100.0	21.1	24.7	15.1	27.4	5.9	5.9	52
Men	26,498	100.0	20.4	24.1	15.2	28.2	6.4	5.8	52
Women	36,126	100.0	21.7	25.1	15.0	26.9	5.5	5.9	50
Age									
Total, 16 years and over	62,623	100.0	21.1	24.7	15.1	27.4	5.9	5.9	52
16 to 24 years	8,415	100.0	24.9	29.0	14.6	20.3	3.7	7.6	36
16 to 19 years	4,382	100.0	23.9	30.1	16.2	20.3	2.5	7.1	36
20 to 24 years	4,033	100.0	26.0	27.7	12.9	20.2	5.0	8.2	36
25 years and over	54,208	100.0	20.5	24.0	15.1	28.5	6.2	5.6	52
25 to 34 years	9,548	100.0	27.7	25.8	14.2	21.2	4.6	6.4	36
35 to 44 years	11,490	100.0	23.0	26.3	15.8	25.9	4.5	4.4	48
45 to 54 years	11,933	100.0	20.5	24.5	15.7	28.4	5.6	5.4	52
55 to 64 years	10,213	100.0	18.7	24.3	14.8	29.9	6.8	5.4	56
65 years and over	11,024	100.0	13.5	19.2	14.9	36.5	9.4	6.5	94
Race and Hispanic or Latino ethnicity									
White	51,986	100.0	20.8	24.9	15.4	27.5	5.8	5.5	52
Black or African American	6,086	100.0	20.7	22.0	14.1	28.6	6.4	8.4	52
Asian	2,596	100.0	25.8	26.5	11.7	24.6	4.5	6.9	40
Hispanic or Latino ethnicity	6,165	100.0	22.4	24.6	12.8	27.6	5.8	6.8	48
Educational attainment[b]									
Less than a high school diploma	1,900	100.0	22.4	22.0	13.3	28.4	5.5	8.4	52
High school graduates, no college[c]	9,576	100.0	21.5	23.2	13.9	27.2	7.1	7.1	52
Some college or associate degree	15,102	100.0	21.8	23.4	14.0	29.1	6.4	5.4	52
Bachelor's degree and higher[d]	27,629	100.0	19.4	24.8	16.3	28.7	5.8	5.0	52
Marital status									
Single, never married	15,143	100.0	25.5	27.0	14.3	20.9	4.5	7.7	36
Married, spouse present	37,348	100.0	19.5	24.2	15.4	29.8	6.1	5.0	52
Other marital status[e]	10,132	100.0	20.8	22.7	14.8	28.4	6.8	6.5	52
Presence of own children under 18 years[f]									
Men:									
No own children under 18 years old	18,263	100.0	19.4	23.9	15.2	27.5	7.1	6.8	52
With own children under 18 years old	8,235	100.0	22.6	24.5	15.1	29.7	4.6	3.5	50
Women:									
No own children under 18 years old	23,475	100.0	20.0	24.0	14.9	28.0	6.3	6.8	52
With own children under 18 years old	12,651	100.0	24.8	27.2	15.1	24.7	3.9	4.4	40
Employment status									
Civilian labor force	42,563	100.0	22.9	26.0	15.2	25.9	4.5	5.5	48
Employed	40,701	100.0	22.9	26.2	15.2	25.8	4.3	5.5	48
Full time[g]	32,085	100.0	23.3	26.4	15.4	25.4	4.1	5.4	48
Part time[h]	8,616	100.0	21.4	25.7	14.5	27.5	5.0	5.8	49
Unemployed	1,861	100.0	23.4	21.7	14.2	26.6	8.1	6.0	52
Not in the labor force	20,060	100.0	17.3	21.8	14.8	30.7	8.8	6.6	66

The organization is involved in 250,000 service projects per year, and the 20 million hours of service its volunteers contribute annually is valued at $482 million.

Other volunteer service organizations that offer opportunities for older adults to contribute their time, energy, and talents include the AARP-sponsored Create the Good (http://createthegood.org), which connects people to volunteer programs and projects, and the Experience Corps (http://www.aarp.org/experience-corps), in which volunteers tutor and mentor students, providing literacy coaching and homework help, while serving as consistent role models.

TABLE 4.9

Volunteers by annual hours volunteered and other selected characteristics, September 2015 [CONTINUED]

aFor those reporting annual hours.
bData refer to persons 25 years and over.
cIncludes persons with a high school diploma or equivalent.
dIncludes persons with bachelor's, professional, and doctoral degrees.
eIncludes divorced, separated, and widowed persons.
fOwn children include sons, daughters, stepchildren, and adopted children. Not included are nieces, nephews, grandchildren, and other related and unrelated children.
gUsually work 35 hours or more a week at all jobs.
hUsually work less than 35 hours a week at all jobs.
Note: Data on volunteers relate to persons who performed unpaid volunteer activities for an organization at any point from September 1, 2014, through the survey period in September 2015. Estimates for the above race groups (white, black or African American, and Asian) do not sum to totals because data are not presented for all races. Persons whose ethnicity is identified as Hispanic or Latino may be of any race.

SOURCE: "Table 2. Volunteers by Annual Hours of Volunteer Activities and Selected Characteristics, September 2015," in *Volunteering in the United States— 2015*, US Department of Labor, Bureau of Labor Statistics, February 25, 2016, https://www.bls.gov/news.release/pdf/volun.pdf (accessed October 23, 2017)

TABLE 4.10

Volunteers by type of organization and other selected characteristics, September 2015

Characteristics in September 2015	Total volunteers (thousands)	Total	Civic, political, professional, or international	Educational or youth service	Environmental or animal care	Hospital or other health	Public safety	Religious	Social or community service	Sport, hobby, cultural, or arts	Other	Not determined
Sex												
Total, both sexes	62,623	100.0	4.8	25.2	2.9	6.6	1.1	33.1	14.6	3.7	5.2	2.8
Men	26,498	100.0	5.9	23.9	2.7	5.3	1.7	32.6	15.6	4.0	5.6	2.8
Women	36,126	100.0	4.0	26.2	3.0	7.6	0.6	33.5	14.0	3.4	4.8	2.8
Age												
Total, 16 years and over	62,623	100.0	4.8	25.2	2.9	6.6	1.1	33.1	14.6	3.7	5.2	2.8
16 to 24 years	8,415	100.0	3.8	30.6	3.9	8.5	1.2	25.4	14.4	3.3	4.9	4.0
16 to 19 years	4,382	100.0	3.8	33.6	4.1	7.2	0.8	28.6	11.9	2.8	4.1	3.1
20 to 24 years	4,033	100.0	3.7	27.3	3.6	9.9	1.7	22.0	17.1	3.7	5.9	5.0
25 years and over	54,208	100.0	5.0	24.4	2.7	6.3	1.0	34.3	14.7	3.7	5.2	2.6
25 to 34 years	9,548	100.0	4.0	28.6	3.6	8.0	1.7	28.2	14.7	2.5	5.8	2.9
35 to 44 years	11,490	100.0	4.4	37.6	1.8	5.1	1.0	27.7	11.7	4.0	4.4	2.5
45 to 54 years	11,933	100.0	4.6	29.4	2.6	5.4	0.9	33.4	13.7	3.4	3.6	2.9
55 to 64 years	10,213	100.0	5.3	16.2	3.4	6.3	0.9	39.5	16.2	4.0	5.7	2.5
65 years and over	11,024	100.0	6.6	9.3	2.4	7.3	0.9	42.7	17.3	4.5	6.8	2.3
Race and Hispanic or Latino ethnicity												
White	51,986	100.0	5.0	24.8	3.1	6.7	1.2	32.6	14.7	3.8	5.4	2.7
Black or African American	6,086	100.0	3.4	25.6	1.0	5.9	0.6	41.2	12.7	1.8	3.8	4.0
Asian	2,596	100.0	3.9	32.1	1.2	8.3	0.6	29.1	13.4	3.1	4.7	3.5
Hispanic or Latino ethnicity	6,165	100.0	4.2	31.3	1.6	5.6	0.7	37.3	10.5	2.3	3.4	3.2
Educational attainment[b]												
Less than a high school diploma	1,900	100.0	2.3	19.9	1.0	2.7	1.1	52.7	12.1	1.6	3.7	2.9
High school graduates, no college[c]	9,576	100.0	4.5	21.7	2.1	5.1	2.2	40.3	13.8	3.4	4.8	2.2
Some college or associate degree	15,102	100.0	5.1	23.3	2.4	5.9	1.2	36.3	15.3	3.1	4.9	2.4
Bachelor's degree and higher[d]	27,629	100.0	5.3	26.3	3.2	7.2	0.6	29.9	14.8	4.3	5.6	2.9
Marital status												
Single, never married	15,143	100.0	4.7	27.0	4.6	8.2	1.2	23.5	16.4	4.3	5.9	4.2
Married, spouse present	37,348	100.0	4.7	26.2	2.2	5.7	1.1	37.6	12.6	3.4	4.2	2.3
Other marital status[e]	10,132	100.0	5.4	18.9	2.8	7.8	0.8	31.2	19.5	3.5	7.4	2.8
Presence of own children under 18 years[f]												
Men:												
No own children under 18 years old	18,263	100.0	6.3	18.1	3.4	6.0	1.5	33.7	17.4	4.2	6.4	3.1
With own children under 18 years old	8,235	100.0	5.0	36.8	1.1	3.7	2.2	30.3	11.4	3.5	3.8	2.2
Women:												
No own children under 18 years old	23,475	100.0	4.7	16.1	3.9	9.0	0.7	36.1	16.7	4.1	5.6	3.3
With own children under 18 years old	12,651	100.0	2.9	45.1	1.4	5.1	0.4	28.8	9.0	2.2	3.4	1.9
Employment status												
Civilian labor force	42,563	100.0	5.0	27.3	2.9	6.5	1.2	30.8	14.8	3.7	5.1	2.8
Employed	40,701	100.0	5.0	27.0	2.9	6.6	1.3	30.8	14.8	3.8	5.1	2.8
Full time[g]	32,085	100.0	5.2	27.0	2.9	6.6	1.4	30.2	15.3	3.7	5.0	2.9
Part time[h]	8,616	100.0	4.6	27.1	2.9	6.3	0.9	33.1	12.8	4.1	5.6	2.4
Unemployed	1,861	100.0	3.2	32.2	4.2	4.1	0.2	29.3	15.1	2.8	5.7	3.4
Not in the labor force	20,060	100.0	4.6	21.0	2.7	7.0	0.7	38.1	14.3	3.5	5.2	2.9

TABLE 4.10

Volunteers by type of organization and other selected characteristics, September 2015 [CONTINUED]

aMain organization is defined as the organization for which the volunteer worked the most hours during the year.
bData refer to persons 25 years and over.
cIncludes persons with a high school diploma or equivalent.
dIncludes persons with bachelor's, professional, and doctoral degrees.
eIncludes divorced, separated, and widowed persons.
fOwn children include sons, daughters, stepchildren, and adopted children. Not included are nieces, nephews, grandchildren, and other related and unrelated children.
gUsually work 35 hours or more a week at all jobs.
hUsually work less than 35 hours a week at all jobs.
Note: Data on volunteers relate to persons who performed unpaid volunteer activities for an organization at any point from September 1, 2014, through the survey period in September 2015. Estimates for the above race groups (white, black or African American, and Asian) do not sum to totals because data are not presented for all races. Persons whose ethnicity is identified as Hispanic or Latino may be of any race.

SOURCE: "Table 4. Volunteers by Type of Main Organization for Which Volunteer Activities Were Performed and Selected Characteristics, September 2015," in *Volunteering in the United States—2015*, US Department of Labor, Bureau of Labor Statistics, February 25, 2016, https://www.bls.gov/news.release/pdf/volun.pdf (accessed October 23, 2017)

CHAPTER 5
EDUCATION, VOTING, AND POLITICAL BEHAVIOR

EDUCATIONAL ATTAINMENT OF OLDER AMERICANS

Educational attainment influences employment and socioeconomic status, which in turn affect the quality of life of older adults. Higher levels of education are often associated with greater earning capacity, higher standards of living, and better overall health status.

In 2016, 29.4% of adults aged 55 years and older had earned a high school diploma, and 17.4% had obtained an undergraduate college (bachelor's) degree. (See Table 5.1.) Table 5.2 shows that among both women and men the number of those aged 55 years and older that had completed high school and college grew steadily between 1940 and 2016, yet even in 2016 slightly more men than women had completed four or more years of college.

In *A Profile of Older Americans: 2016* (April 2017, https://www.acl.gov/sites/default/files/Aging%20and%20 Disability%20in%20America/2016-Profile.pdf), the Administration on Aging (AoA) reports that between 1970 and 2016 the percentage of adults aged 65 years and older that had completed high school grew from 28% to 85%. In 2016 more than a quarter (28%) had earned a bachelor's degree or higher. The percentage who had completed high school varied considerably by race and ethnic origin in 2016: 90% of non-Hispanic whites, 80% of non-Hispanic Asian Americans, 77% of non-Hispanic African Americans, 71% of Native Americans/Alaskan Natives, and 54% of Hispanics.

Lifelong Learning

Live as if you were to die tomorrow. Learn as if you were to live forever.

—Mohandas Gandhi

Campuses are graying as a growing number of older people head back to school. Older adults are major participants in programs once called adult education (college courses that do not lead to a formal degree). They are also attending two- and four-year colleges to pursue undergraduate and graduate

degrees, as well as taking personal enrichment classes and courses that are sponsored by community senior centers and parks and recreation facilities. For example, in "AACC Fast Facts 2017" (January 2017, https://www .aacc.nche.edu/wp-content/uploads/2017/09/AACCFact Sheet2017.pdf), the American Association of Community Colleges indicates that as of 2016, 10% of community college students were aged 40 years and older. In 2016 an estimated 4 million (18%) students in degree-granting programs were aged 35 years and older. (See Table 5.3.) By 2021 this number is anticipated to increase to 4.5 million (19%).

The American Association of Community Colleges reports in "About 50 Plus Initiative" (2018, http://plus 50.aacc.nche.edu/aboutplus50/Pages/default.aspx) that the Plus 50 Initiative was established in 2008 to help a pilot group of 13 community colleges expand their offerings for students aged 50 years and older. By 2015 the number of students had increased to nearly 37,500, and about 12,200 older adults had completed a degree or certificate. Another ambitious initiative, the Plus 50 Encore Completion Program, helps older adults earn certificates in high-demand occupations that "give back" in areas such as education, health care, and social services.

Older adults' motivations for returning to school have changed over time. Although they once may have taken courses primarily for pleasure, older students in the 21st century are as likely to return to school for work-related education. They are learning new skills, retraining for new careers, or enhancing their existing skills to remain competitive. Homemakers displaced by divorce or widowhood are often seeking training to enable them to reenter the workforce.

ROAD SCHOLAR MEETS OLDER ADULTS' NEEDS FOR EDUCATION AND ADVENTURE. Founded in 1975, Road Scholar (formerly known as Elderhostel) is a nonprofit organization that offers learning adventures for people

TABLE 5.1

Educational attainment by selected characteristics, 2016

[Numbers in thousands. Civilian noninstitutionalized population[a].]

Detailed years of school	All races		Males		Females		25 to 34 years old		35 to 54 years old		55 years and older	
	Number	Percent	Number	Percent	Number	Percent	Number	Percent	Number	Percent	Number	Percent
	215,015	100	103,372	100	111,643	100	43,763	100	82,571	100	88,682	100
Elementary or high school, no diploma												
Less than 1 year, no diploma	763	0.4	347	0.3	417	0.4	57	0.1	263	0.3	443	0.5
1st–4th grade, no diploma	1,651	0.8	837	0.8	814	0.7	152	0.4	536	0.7	963	1.1
5th–6th grade, no diploma	3,380	1.6	1,686	1.6	1,694	1.5	401	0.9	1,437	1.7	1,542	1.7
7th–8th grade, no diploma	3,698	1.7	1,827	1.8	1,871	1.7	457	1.1	1,199	1.5	2,042	2.3
9th grade, no diploma	3,376	1.6	1,702	1.7	1,674	1.5	588	1.3	1,369	1.7	1,418	1.6
10th grade, no diploma	3,706	1.7	1,874	1.8	1,832	1.6	643	1.5	1,294	1.6	1,769	2.0
11th grade, no diploma	4,062	1.9	2,064	2.0	1,998	1.8	861	2.0	1,523	1.8	1,677	1.9
12th grade, no diploma	2,817	1.3	1,504	1.5	1,313	1.2	564	1.3	1,109	1.3	1,145	1.3
Elementary or high school, GED												
Less than 1 year, GED	55	—	28	—	27	—	22	0.1	13	—	20	—
1st–4th grade, GED	139	0.1	65	0.1	74	0.1	29	0.1	54	0.1	55	0.1
5th–6th grade, GED	55	—	27	—	28	—	7	—	14	—	34	—
7th–8th grade, GED	435	0.2	238	0.2	197	0.2	63	0.1	118	0.1	254	0.3
9th grade, GED	634	0.3	324	0.3	310	0.3	99	0.2	285	0.4	250	0.3
10th grade, GED	1,444	0.7	817	0.8	627	0.6	302	0.7	539	0.7	604	0.7
11th grade, GED	2,006	0.9	1,134	1.1	873	0.8	482	1.1	783	1.0	742	0.8
12th grade, GED	1,337	0.6	741	0.7	596	0.5	296	0.7	551	0.7	490	0.6
High school diploma	55,896	26.0	27,407	26.5	28,490	25.5	9,924	22.7	19,941	24.2	26,032	29.4
College, no degree												
Less than 1 year college, no degree	5,045	2.4	2,360	2.3	2,685	2.4	1,079	2.5	1,871	2.3	2,096	2.4
One year of college, no degree	11,715	5.5	5,383	5.2	6,332	5.7	2,585	5.9	4,347	5.3	4,784	5.4
Two years of college, no degree	13,841	6.4	6,644	6.4	7,197	6.5	2,849	6.5	4,969	6.0	6,023	6.8
Three years of college, no degree	3,674	1.7	1,730	1.7	1,944	1.7	983	2.3	1,286	1.6	1,405	1.6
Four or more years of college, no degree	1,728	0.8	894	0.9	834	0.8	524	1.2	632	0.8	572	0.7
Associate's degree, vocational												
Less than 1 year college, vocational/associates	497	0.2	197	0.2	300	0.3	81	0.2	204	0.3	212	0.2
One year of college, vocational/associates	1,150	0.5	451	0.4	698	0.6	241	0.6	447	0.5	461	0.5
Two years of college, vocational/associates	5,857	2.7	2,921	2.8	2,936	2.6	1,185	2.7	2,409	2.9	2,263	2.6
Three years of college, vocational/associates	852	0.4	389	0.4	463	0.4	181	0.4	350	0.4	320	0.4
Four or more years of college, vocational/associates	898	0.4	448	0.4	450	0.4	173	0.4	403	0.5	322	0.4
Associate's degree, academic												
Less than 1 year college, academic/associates	114	0.1	35	—	79	0.1	29	0.1	38	0.1	48	0.1
One year of college, academic/associates	746	0.4	289	0.3	456	0.4	169	0.4	317	0.4	260	0.3
Two years of college, academic/associates	8,169	3.8	3,334	3.2	4,834	4.3	1,638	3.7	3,394	4.1	3,137	3.5
Three years of college, academic/associates	1,746	0.8	684	0.7	1,063	1.0	457	1.1	738	0.9	551	0.6
Four or more years of college, academic/associates	1,628	0.8	708	0.7	920	0.8	437	1.0	664	0.8	527	0.6
Bachelors degree	44,778	20.8	21,281	20.6	23,497	21.1	11,131	25.4	18,177	22.0	15,470	17.4
Master's degree[b]	19,958	9.3	8,829	8.5	11,129	10.0	3,863	8.8	8,418	10.2	7,676	8.7
Professional degree	3,178	1.5	1,841	1.8	1,337	1.2	549	1.3	1,288	1.6	1,341	1.5
Doctorate degree	3,986	1.9	2,332	2.3	1,654	1.5	664	1.5	1,589	1.9	1,733	2.0

[a]Excluding members of the armed forces living in barracks.
[b]Detail on graduate school attendance and length of master's degree program, available in previous years, discontinued due to questionnaire changes in 2015.
Notes: A dash (—) represents zero or rounds to zero. GED = General Equivalency Diploma.

SOURCE: Adapted from "Table 3. Detailed Years of School Completed by People 25 Years and over by Sex, Age Groups, Race and Hispanic Origin: 2016," in *Educational Attainment in the United States: 2016—Detailed Tables*, US Census Bureau, March 2017, https://www.census.gov/data/tables/2016/demo/education-attainment/cps-detailed-tables.html (accessed October 23, 2017)

TABLE 5.2

Educational attainment of adults aged 55 and older, 1940–2016

[Numbers in thousands. Noninstitutionalized population except where otherwise specified.]

Age, sex, and years	Total	Elementary		High school		College		Median
		0 to 4 years	5 to 8 years	1 to 3 years	4 years	1 to 3 years	4 years or more	
55 years and older								
Both sexes								
2016	88,682	1,406	3,584	6,009	28,481	22,981	26,221	NA
2015	86,411	1,447	3,690	6,276	28,457	21,785	24,756	NA
2014	84,134	1,365	3,829	6,094	27,962	21,059	23,825	NA
2013	81,778	1,306	3,931	6,043	27,046	20,387	23,066	NA
2012	79,478	1,348	3,974	6,344	26,531	19,343	21,937	NA
2011	76,163	1,372	4,073	5,983	25,622	18,408	20,705	NA
2010	74,008	1,440	4,118	6,051	25,125	17,354	19,920	NA
2009	72,077	1,555	4,101	6,338	24,154	16,877	19,051	NA
2008	70,092	1,411	4,294	6,338	23,779	16,378	17,892	NA
2007	68,226	1,576	4,458	6,680	23,408	15,505	16,599	NA
2006	66,485	1,628	4,610	6,508	22,961	14,824	15,956	NA
2005	64,745	1,614	4,803	6,784	22,392	14,083	15,069	NA
2004	63,034	1,465	4,907	6,821	21,918	13,434	14,488	NA
2003	61,633	1,589	5,372	6,876	21,554	12,884	13,358	NA
2002	59,644	1,528	5,639	7,258	20,728	12,117	12,374	NA
2001	58,238	1,544	5,589	7,178	20,622	11,864	11,440	NA
2000	56,008	1,524	5,780	6,921	20,059	11,126	10,598	NA
1999	55,303	1,589	5,978	7,096	19,742	10,722	10,174	NA
1998	54,337	1,624	6,126	7,385	19,526	10,022	9,654	NA
1997	53,352	1,628	6,622	7,543	18,823	9,565	9,169	NA
1996	52,742	1,642	6,716	7,520	18,549	9,642	8,677	NA
1995	52,022	1,755	7,048	7,232	18,320	9,662	8,005	NA
1994	51,516	1,802	7,382	7,454	18,228	8,890	7,761	NA
1993	52,117	2,058	8,038	7,637	18,626	8,106	7,652	NA
1992	51,740	2,118	8,133	7,756	18,397	8,005	7,332	NA
1991	51,439	2,341	8,668	7,675	18,954	6,540	7,258	12.6
1990	50,798	2,349	9,239	7,893	18,050	6,202	7,064	12.3
1989	50,421	2,412	9,395	7,907	18,102	5,914	6,693	12.3
1988	50,128	2,325	9,969	7,860	18,004	5,705	6,263	12.3
1987	49,858	2,408	10,544	7,766	17,310	5,799	6,033	12.2
1986	49,383	2,611	10,699	7,917	16,876	5,515	5,767	12.2
1985	48,969	2,612	11,052	7,872	16,516	5,208	5,708	12.2
1984	48,324	2,584	11,131	7,636	16,353	5,026	5,593	12.2
1983	47,723	2,769	11,348	7,703	15,470	4,915	5,514	12.1
1982	47,102	2,818	11,541	7,751	15,091	4,807	5,095	12.1
1981	46,391	2,983	11,909	7,600	14,464	4,721	4,711	12.0
1980	45,670	2,994	12,326	7,451	13,869	4,494	4,535	12.0
1979	43,806	2,924	12,230	6,999	13,088	4,321	4,245	12.0
1978	42,977	3,013	12,593	7,069	12,376	4,086	3,843	11.6
1977	42,176	3,047	12,740	6,823	11,977	3,835	3,754	11.3
1976	41,429	3,107	12,674	6,915	11,346	3,709	3,677	11.1
1975	40,613	3,303	13,045	6,730	10,798	3,442	3,295	10.8
1974	39,817	3,461	13,302	6,615	10,060	3,233	3,145	10.4
1973	39,163	3,424	13,467	6,504	9,604	3,060	3,105	10.2
1972	38,659	3,471	13,706	6,351	9,136	2,952	3,042	10.0
1971	38,787	3,808	14,430	6,225	8,463	2,878	2,982	9.6
1970	38,126	3,957	14,647	5,877	8,005	2,797	2,843	9.2
1969	37,424	4,012	14,576	5,801	7,768	2,615	2,653	9.1
1968	36,789	4,244	14,522	5,760	7,085	2,624	2,558	8.9
1967	36,155	4,310	14,849	5,495	6,622	2,443	2,434	8.7
1966	35,540	4,438	14,742	5,392	6,240	2,358	2,370	8.6
1965	34,969	4,612	14,814	5,293	5,844	2,194	2,215	8.5
1964	34,335	4,888	14,701	4,954	5,598	2,159	2,033	8.3
1962	33,247	5,048	14,707	4,442	4,994	2,166	1,890	8.1
1960	31,902	5,169	14,944	4,503	3,757	2,051	1,479	8.5
1959	30,567	4,752	13,485	4,060	3,996	1,775	1,545	8.1
1957	29,548	5,153	12,996	3,602	3,864	1,462	1,461	8.0
1952	26,206	4,554	12,638	2,982	3,080	1,346	1,264	7.7
1950	25,427	4,940	11,947	2,791	2,704	1,170	1,005	8.3
1947	23,234	4,393	11,601	2,179	2,581	1,003	825	7.5
1940	19,592	4,178	10,467	1,656	1,633	685	579	8.2

aged 55 years and older. In *2016 Annual Report* (November 2016, https://www.roadscholar.org/globalassets/development/rs_annualreport_nov16_web.pdf), Road Scholar explains that it provided educational opportunities to more than 100,000 older adults in fiscal year 2016. Road Scholar programs are conducted in every state and in

TABLE 5.2

Educational attainment of adults aged 55 and older, 1940–2016 [CONTINUED]

[Numbers in thousands. Noninstitutionalized population except where otherwise specified.]

Age, sex, and years	Total	Elementary		High school		College		Median
		0 to 4 years	5 to 8 years	1 to 3 years	4 years	1 to 3 years	4 years or more	
Male								
2016	40,988	624	1,708	2,814	12,374	10,236	13,231	NA
2015	39,895	608	1,765	2,707	12,398	9,863	12,556	NA
2014	38,850	544	1,790	2,800	12,150	9,320	12,246	NA
2013	37,621	557	1,790	2,605	11,539	9,060	12,070	NA
2012	36,489	614	1,775	2,754	11,220	8,574	11,552	NA
2011	35,027	597	1,934	2,625	10,676	8,230	10,966	NA
2010	33,778	647	1,923	2,611	10,399	7,672	10,525	NA
2009	32,814	689	1,874	2,669	9,886	7,456	10,241	NA
2008	31,841	631	1,932	2,751	9,510	7,259	9,759	NA
2007	30,920	721	2,060	2,884	9,505	6,723	9,026	NA
2006	30,060	705	2,090	2,784	9,488	6,193	8,837	NA
2005	29,198	717	2,157	2,896	8,918	6,167	8,341	NA
2004	28,347	639	2,192	2,885	8,631	5,841	8,159	NA
2003	27,694	729	2,423	2,912	8,425	5,694	7,510	NA
2002	26,608	664	2,601	3,048	8,063	5,257	6,975	NA
2001	25,908	697	2,558	2,964	8,073	5,131	6,485	NA
2000	25,023	706	2,696	2,817	7,816	4,906	6,079	NA
1999	24,694	712	2,746	2,911	7,712	4,756	5,856	NA
1998	24,197	755	2,740	3,000	7,745	4,461	5,496	NA
1997	23,668	773	3,026	3,060	7,417	4,139	5,255	NA
1996	23,352	795	3,058	2,998	7,198	4,254	5,055	NA
1995	22,881	839	3,153	2,980	6,980	4,254	4,675	NA
1994	22,669	894	3,327	3,037	6,987	3,962	4,462	NA
1993	23,038	992	3,595	3,174	7,178	3,587	4,508	NA
1992	22,836	1,033	3,676	3,277	6,991	3,549	4,312	NA
1991	22,708	1,217	3,980	3,183	7,287	2,850	4,193	12.4
1990	22,337	1,182	4,141	3,274	6,986	2,707	4,046	12.4
1989	22,167	1,202	4,198	3,317	7,003	2,616	3,829	12.3
1988	21,989	1,117	4,471	3,366	6,968	2,455	3,609	12.3
1987	21,855	1,160	4,762	3,261	6,673	2,504	3,496	12.3
1986	21,622	1,275	4,813	3,286	6,509	2,355	3,385	12.2
1985	21,391	1,252	5,001	3,234	6,387	2,229	3,289	12.2
1984	21,014	1,209	4,951	3,270	6,265	2,185	3,132	12.2
1983	20,769	1,343	4,986	3,282	5,906	2,141	3,117	12.1
1982	20,508	1,362	5,026	3,313	5,759	2,102	2,946	12.1
1981	20,237	1,394	5,165	3,292	5,597	2,032	2,758	12.0
1980	19,967	1,424	5,436	3,206	5,409	1,986	2,506	11.9
1979	19,292	1,446	5,479	2,964	5,167	1,935	2,301	11.8
1978	18,939	1,467	5,701	2,919	4,919	1,824	2,110	11.4
1977	18,608	1,502	5,770	2,787	4,835	1,700	2,011	11.2
1976	18,233	1,507	5,733	2,884	4,473	1,646	1,989	11.0
1975	17,903	1,628	5,845	2,871	4,308	1,480	1,768	10.5
1974	17,579	1,693	6,042	2,817	3,993	1,356	1,682	10.1
1973	17,263	1,678	6,111	2,774	3,811	1,245	1,645	9.9
1972	17,120	1,728	6,252	2,698	3,612	1,215	1,614	9.6
1971	17,288	1,913	6,629	2,668	3,285	1,214	1,579	9.1
1970	17,074	2,011	6,655	2,583	3,127	1,182	1,516	9.0
1969	16,822	2,003	6,701	2,536	3,099	1,086	1,397	8.8
1968	16,609	2,137	6,728	2,523	2,816	1,078	1,328	8.7
1967	16,398	2,247	6,827	2,379	2,685	989	1,271	8.5
1966	16,201	2,288	6,944	2,317	2,491	939	1,223	8.3
1965	16,015	2,368	6,992	2,265	2,331	893	1,164	8.2
1964	15,789	2,504	6,897	2,159	2,237	876	1,113	8.1
1962	15,440	2,644	6,813	2,032	2,030	864	1,057	8.0
1960	14,895	2,704	7,121	1,969	1,453	853	796	8.4
1959	14,304	2,491	6,436	1,759	1,584	718	857	7.9
1957	13,967	2,696	6,244	1,570	1,493	608	831	7.7
1952	12,544	2,428	6,162	1,318	1,262	528	636	7.5
1950	12,277	2,609	5,808	1,209	1,111	500	569	8.2
1947	11,424	2,393	5,656	939	1,109	464	482	7.3
1940	9,815	2,293	5,249	724	660	313	361	8.1
Female								
2016	47,694	782	1,875	3,195	16,107	12,745	12,990	NA
2015	46,516	839	1,925	3,570	16,059	11,922	12,201	NA
2014	45,284	821	2,039	3,295	15,812	11,739	11,578	NA
2013	44,158	749	2,141	3,438	15,507	11,327	10,996	NA

TABLE 5.2

Educational attainment of adults aged 55 and older, 1940–2016 [CONTINUED]

[Numbers in thousands. Noninstitutionalized population except where otherwise specified.]

Age, sex, and years	Total	Years of school completed						Median
		Elementary		High school		College		
		0 to 4 years	5 to 8 years	1 to 3 years	4 years	1 to 3 years	4 years or more	
2012	42,989	734	2,199	3,590	15,311	10,769	10,384	NA
2011	41,136	775	2,140	3,358	14,946	10,178	9,739	NA
2010	40,230	793	2,195	3,440	14,725	9,682	9,395	NA
2009	39,263	867	2,228	3,669	14,268	9,421	8,810	NA
2008	38,251	780	2,362	3,588	14,269	9,119	8,133	NA
2007	37,306	855	2,398	3,796	13,902	8,781	7,573	NA
2006	36,425	922	2,521	3,761	13,472	8,630	7,119	NA
2005	35,547	897	2,645	3,887	13,474	7,916	6,728	NA
2004	34,687	826	2,715	3,936	13,287	7,593	6,329	NA
2003	33,939	860	2,949	3,964	13,129	7,190	5,848	NA
2002	33,035	864	3,038	4,210	12,664	6,860	5,399	NA
2001	32,329	847	3,032	4,213	12,549	6,733	4,956	NA
2000	30,985	817	3,085	4,105	12,243	6,218	4,517	NA
1999	30,609	879	3,232	4,186	12,031	5,965	4,319	NA
1998	30,140	868	3,386	4,386	11,780	5,560	4,160	NA
1997	29,684	855	3,596	4,483	11,407	5,427	3,916	NA
1996	29,390	848	3,659	4,523	11,350	5,387	3,623	NA
1995	29,142	915	3,894	4,255	11,340	5,410	3,330	NA
1994	28,848	909	4,054	4,419	11,242	4,926	3,298	NA
1993	29,080	1,066	4,442	4,462	11,447	4,519	3,149	NA
1992	28,904	1,084	4,456	4,478	11,409	4,455	3,021	NA
1991	28,729	1,125	4,687	4,495	11,667	3,690	3,066	12.3
1990	28,461	1,167	5,098	4,619	11,063	3,495	3,019	12.3
1989	28,255	1,211	5,195	4,587	11,099	3,300	2,863	12.3
1988	28,139	1,208	5,498	4,495	11,034	3,250	2,655	12.3
1987	28,004	1,248	5,782	4,504	10,637	3,294	2,539	12.2
1986	27,762	1,336	5,886	4,630	10,367	3,160	2,382	12.2
1985	27,578	1,360	6,052	4,638	10,129	2,979	2,420	12.2
1984	27,309	1,377	6,183	4,363	10,086	2,843	2,459	12.2
1983	26,954	1,428	6,364	4,423	9,567	2,774	2,398	12.1
1982	26,593	1,458	6,511	4,435	9,330	2,705	2,150	12.1
1981	26,152	1,589	6,742	4,308	8,868	2,690	1,954	12.0
1980	25,703	1,571	6,889	4,245	8,460	2,509	2,030	12.0
1979	24,514	1,474	6,750	4,034	7,920	2,389	1,944	12.0
1978	24,038	1,545	6,889	4,149	7,457	2,263	1,733	11.6
1977	23,568	1,546	6,972	4,034	7,141	2,135	1,742	11.0
1976	23,196	1,602	6,942	4,029	6,871	2,063	1,690	11.0
1975	22,710	1,675	7,198	3,858	6,490	1,962	1,527	10.9
1974	22,238	1,762	7,261	3,799	6,068	1,880	1,463	10.7
1973	21,900	1,746	7,359	3,729	5,790	1,814	1,461	10.5
1972	21,539	1,743	7,455	3,654	5,526	1,737	1,425	10.3
1971	21,500	1,896	7,805	3,556	5,179	1,665	1,402	9.9
1970	21,052	1,946	7,993	3,292	4,879	1,615	1,327	9.5
1969	20,601	2,009	7,878	3,264	4,669	1,526	1,255	9.4
1968	20,180	2,106	7,795	3,237	4,269	1,544	1,229	9.2
1967	19,756	2,063	8,021	3,117	3,937	1,454	1,164	8.9
1966	19,339	2,152	7,797	3,074	3,749	1,419	1,147	8.9
1965	18,955	2,243	7,821	3,026	3,514	1,300	1,048	8.7
1964	18,546	2,383	7,805	2,794	3,360	1,282	920	8.5
1962	17,807	2,404	7,894	2,410	2,964	1,302	833	8.3
1960	17,007	2,465	7,823	2,534	2,304	1,198	683	8.6
1959	16,263	2,261	7,049	2,301	2,412	1,057	688	8.3
1957	15,581	2,457	6,752	2,032	2,371	854	630	8.2
1952	13,662	2,126	6,476	1,664	1,818	818	628	7.9
1950	13,150	2,331	6,139	1,582	1,593	670	436	8.4
1947	11,810	2,000	5,945	1,240	1,472	539	343	7.6
1940	9,777	1,886	5,217	932	973	372	219	8.3

150 countries around the world. Programs include three- to five-day classes, field trips, and cultural excursions. They provide older adults with opportunities to study diverse cultures, explore ancient histories, study literature and art, and learn about modern people and issues. Some participants attend programs that are held on local college or university campuses, whereas others embark on programs that involve transcontinental or international travel.

Adventure programs combine learning with outdoor sports such as walking, hiking, camping, kayaking, and biking. For example, a bicycle tour of the Netherlands also includes instruction about the country's history, art, and people. Shipboard programs explore history, art, ecology, and culture aboard a floating classroom.

Service-learning programs involve both education and hands-on work to serve the needs of a community.

TABLE 5.2

Educational attainment of adults aged 55 and older, 1940–2016 [CONTINUED]

[Numbers in thousands. Noninstitutionalized population except where otherwise specified.]

Notes:
Starting in 2012, data were created using population controls based on 2010 Census data.
Starting in 2001, data were created using population controls based on Census 2000 data.
Starting in 2001, data are from the expanded CPS sample.
Begining with data for 1992, a new question results in different categories than for earlier years.
Data shown as 'High school, 4 years' are now collected in the category 'High school graduate.'
Data shown as 'College 1 to 3 years' are now collected in the 'Some college' and the two 'Associate degree' categories.
Data shown as 'College 4 years or more,' are now collected in the categories, 'Bachelor's degree,' 'Master's degree,' 'Doctorate degree,' and 'Professional degree.'
Due to the change in question format, median years of schooling cannot be derived.
For the years 1959 and earlier, total includes persons who did not report on years of school completed.

SOURCE: Adapted from, "Table A-1. Years of School Completed by People 25 Years and over, by Age and Sex: Selected Years 1940 to 2016," in *Educational Attainment in the United States: 2016–Detailed Tables*, US Census Bureau, March 2017, https://www.census.gov/data/tables/2016/demo/education-attainment/cps-detailed-tables.html (accessed October 23, 2017)

Older adults conduct wildlife or marine research, tutor children, or build affordable housing. The organization also offers a series of intergenerational programs in which older adults and their grandchildren explore subjects that appeal to both young and old, including dinosaurs, hot-air ballooning, and space travel.

OLDER ADULTS ARE TECH-SAVVY AND ONLINE. Rapid technological change has intensified the need for information management skills and ongoing technology training. The growing importance of knowledge- and information-based jobs has created a workforce that is rapidly becoming accustomed to continuous education, training, and retraining throughout one's work life.

Computer technology, especially use of the internet, has also gained importance in Americans' lives outside of work, facilitating communication via email and enabling interactions and transactions that once required travel to now occur in their home. Examples include online banking and shopping, email communication with physicians and other health care providers, and participation in online support groups.

Monica Anderson and Andrew Perrin of the Pew Research Center report in *Tech Adoption Climbs among Older Adults* (May 17, 2017, http://www.pewinternet.org/2017/05/17/tech-adoption-climbs-among-older-adults/) high internet use by older adults. In 2016, 67% of adults aged 65 years and older were using the internet, and half had a high-speed broadband connection at home. Of older adults who used the internet, three-quarters went online every day and 8% were online constantly.

According to Anderson and Perrin, more than half (58%) of adults aged 65 years and older said technology has had a largely positive impact on society. As noted in previous studies, younger, more educated, and more affluent older adults own and use technologies at rates similar to adults under the age of 65 years, while those who are older, less affluent, and less educated are less tech savvy and less likely to embrace new technologies.

Younger (aged 65 to 69 years), higher-income (annual household income of $75,000 or more), and more educated older adults used the internet and broadband at rates comparable to younger adults in 2016. Anderson and Perrin report that 82% of adults aged 65 to 69 years used the internet in 2016, and 66% in that age group had broadband access. Eighty-seven percent of older adults with incomes in excess of $75,000 had broadband access in their home.

More than four out of 10 (42%) adults aged 65 years and older owned a smartphone in 2016, twice as many as did in 2013. Anderson and Perrin report that 42% of older adults who owned a cellphone had a smartphone; in 2013, just 23% owned a smartphone. About one-third (32%) of older adults owned a tablet, and about one out of five (19%) owned an e-reader. Tablet ownership was higher among older adults with more education and those living in higher-income households. Roughly two-thirds (62%) of older adults with an annual income of $75,000 or more owned a tablet in 2016, as did more than half (56%) of those with a college degree. By contrast, just 16% of older adults with a household income of less than $30,000 a year and 18% of those with a high school diploma or less owned a tablet.

OLDER ADULTS USE SOCIAL MEDIA. Anderson and Perrin find that although young people are still much more likely than older internet users to use social media, about one-third (34%) of older adults used social media such as Facebook and Twitter in 2016, up seven percentage points from 2013, when just 27% did so. Almost half (45%) of adults under the age of 75 years accessed social networking sites, while just 20% of those aged 80 years and older did so. Among older adults who use social media, many are active users. For example, among those who used Facebook in 2016, 70% logged in every day. Furthermore, older adults who received their news from social media did so at the same rate as users aged 18 to 29 years.

THEY ALSO TEXT, BLOG, AND TWEET. There are few reliable statistics about the numbers of older adults who

TABLE 5.3

Enrollment in degree-granting institutions, by sex and age, selected years 1970–2021

[In thousands]

| Attendance status, sex, and age | 1970 | 1980 | 1990 | 2000 | 2003 | 2004 | 2005 | 2006 | 2007 | 2008 | 2009 | 2010 | 2011 | 2012 | 2013 | 2016 | 2021 |
| | | | | | | | | | | | | Projected | | | | | |
1	2	3	4	5	6	7	8	9	10	11	12	13	14	15	16	17	18
All students	**8,581**	**12,097**	**13,819**	**15,312**	**16,911**	**17,272**	**17,487**	**17,759**	**18,248**	**19,103**	**20,428**	**21,016**	**20,994**	**21,253**	**21,485**	**22,194**	**23,755**
14 to 17 years old	263	257	153	131	169	166	187	184	200	195	217	202	202	207	208	219	244
18 and 19 years old	2,579	2,852	2,777	3,258	3,355	3,367	3,444	3,561	3,690	3,813	4,041	4,056	4,025	4,343	4,331	4,358	4,765
20 and 21 years old	1,885	2,395	2,593	3,005	3,391	3,516	3,563	3,573	3,570	3,649	3,945	4,101	4,174	4,386	4,368	4,361	4,603
22 to 24 years old	1,469	1,947	2,202	2,600	3,086	3,166	3,114	3,185	3,280	3,443	3,594	3,758	3,708	3,823	3,922	3,996	4,037
25 to 29 years old	1,091	1,843	2,083	2,044	2,311	2,418	2,469	2,506	2,651	2,840	3,096	3,253	3,319	3,057	3,116	3,389	3,545
30 to 34 years old	527	1,227	1,384	1,333	1,418	1,440	1,438	1,472	1,519	1,609	1,741	1,805	1,807	1,678	1,726	1,833	2,037
35 years old and over	767	1,577	2,627	2,942	3,181	3,199	3,272	3,277	3,339	3,554	3,794	3,840	3,758	3,759	3,812	4,038	4,524
Males	**5,044**	**5,874**	**6,284**	**6,722**	**7,260**	**7,387**	**7,456**	**7,575**	**7,816**	**8,189**	**8,770**	**9,045**	**9,026**	**9,107**	**9,160**	**9,261**	**9,741**
14 to 17 years old	125	106	66	58	67	62	68	69	88	93	103	94	95	90	90	92	101
18 and 19 years old	1,355	1,368	1,298	1,464	1,474	1,475	1,523	1,604	1,669	1,704	1,806	1,820	1,819	1,896	1,886	1,876	2,040
20 and 21 years old	1,064	1,219	1,259	1,411	1,541	1,608	1,658	1,628	1,634	1,695	1,876	1,948	1,973	2,102	2,088	2,060	2,154
22 to 24 years old	1,004	1,075	1,129	1,222	1,411	1,437	1,410	1,445	1,480	1,555	1,606	1,723	1,682	1,760	1,798	1,799	1,792
25 to 29 years old	796	983	1,024	908	1,007	1,039	1,057	1,040	1,148	1,222	1,382	1,410	1,442	1,354	1,370	1,452	1,491
30 to 34 years old	333	564	605	581	602	619	591	628	638	691	709	731	715	691	707	729	792
35 years old and over	366	559	902	1,077	1,158	1,147	1,149	1,160	1,159	1,228	1,287	1,320	1,300	1,215	1,223	1,252	1,372
Females	**3,537**	**6,223**	**7,535**	**8,591**	**9,651**	**9,885**	**10,032**	**10,184**	**10,432**	**10,914**	**11,658**	**11,971**	**11,968**	**12,146**	**12,325**	**12,933**	**14,014**
14 to 17 years old	137	151	87	73	102	104	119	115	112	102	114	108	108	118	119	127	143
18 and 19 years old	1,224	1,484	1,479	1,794	1,880	1,892	1,920	1,956	2,021	2,109	2,236	2,236	2,206	2,447	2,446	2,482	2,725
20 and 21 years old	821	1,177	1,334	1,593	1,851	1,908	1,905	1,945	1,936	1,954	2,069	2,154	2,201	2,284	2,280	2,301	2,449
22 to 24 years old	464	871	1,073	1,378	1,675	1,729	1,704	1,740	1,800	1,888	1,987	2,036	2,027	2,063	2,125	2,197	2,245
25 to 29 years old	296	859	1,059	1,136	1,304	1,379	1,413	1,466	1,502	1,618	1,713	1,844	1,877	1,703	1,746	1,937	2,055
30 to 34 years old	194	663	779	752	816	821	847	844	881	918	1,032	1,074	1,092	987	1,020	1,103	1,246
35 years old and over	401	1,018	1,725	1,865	2,023	2,052	2,123	2,117	2,180	2,326	2,507	2,520	2,458	2,544	2,590	2,786	3,152
Full-time	**5,816**	**7,098**	**7,821**	**9,010**	**10,326**	**10,610**	**10,797**	**10,957**	**11,270**	**11,748**	**12,723**	**13,082**	**13,001**	**13,146**	**13,262**	**13,586**	**14,497**
14 to 17 years old	246	231	134	121	146	138	152	148	169	168	181	170	171	163	164	174	194
18 and 19 years old	2,374	2,544	2,471	2,823	2,934	2,960	3,026	3,120	3,244	3,359	3,513	3,495	3,413	3,644	3,637	3,665	4,014
20 and 21 years old	1,649	2,007	2,137	2,452	2,841	2,926	2,976	2,972	2,985	3,043	3,271	3,363	3,392	3,438	3,427	3,426	3,623
22 to 24 years old	904	1,181	1,405	1,714	2,083	2,143	2,122	2,127	2,205	2,347	2,535	2,584	2,504	2,689	2,758	2,808	2,846
25 to 29 years old	426	641	791	886	1,086	1,132	1,174	1,225	1,299	1,369	1,520	1,605	1,628	1,477	1,507	1,641	1,723
30 to 34 years old	113	272	383	418	489	517	547	571	556	571	663	744	759	646	665	705	785
35 years old and over	104	221	500	596	747	795	800	794	812	890	1,041	1,121	1,135	1,088	1,104	1,168	1,312
Males	**3,504**	**3,689**	**3,808**	**4,111**	**4,638**	**4,739**	**4,803**	**4,879**	**5,029**	**5,234**	**5,671**	**5,837**	**5,793**	**5,843**	**5,873**	**5,931**	**6,263**
14 to 17 years old	121	95	55	51	58	49	53	52	74	73	78	71	75	58	58	60	67
18 and 19 years old	1,261	1,219	1,171	1,252	1,291	1,297	1,339	1,404	1,465	1,516	1,580	1,574	1,532	1,588	1,581	1,578	1,722
20 and 21 years old	955	1,046	1,035	1,156	1,305	1,360	1,398	1,372	1,366	1,407	1,547	1,586	1,591	1,642	1,632	1,617	1,698
22 to 24 years old	686	717	768	834	995	1,001	982	992	1,043	1,105	1,177	1,214	1,171	1,269	1,296	1,301	1,305
25 to 29 years old	346	391	433	410	503	498	506	533	578	597	665	714	736	640	649	693	719
30 to 34 years old	77	142	171	186	209	231	225	235	231	249	281	301	296	291	298	310	341
35 years old and over	58	80	174	222	277	302	300	291	273	287	343	376	392	355	359	371	412

TABLE 5.3

Enrollment in degree-granting institutions, by sex and age, selected years 1970–2021 [CONTINUED]

[In thousands]

| Attendance status, sex, and age | 1970 | 1980 | 1990 | 2000 | 2003 | 2004 | 2005 | 2006 | 2007 | 2008 | 2009 | 2010 | 2011 | 2012 | Projected | | |
| | | | | | | | | | | | | | | | 2013 | 2016 | 2021 |
1	2	3	4	5	6	7	8	9	10	11	12	13	14	15	16	17	18
Females	2,312	3,409	4,013	4,899	5,688	5,871	5,994	6,078	6,240	6,513	7,052	7,245	7,208	7,303	7,388	7,655	8,234
14 to 17 years old	125	136	78	70	88	89	98	95	95	95	103	99	96	104	105	113	127
18 and 19 years old	1,113	1,325	1,300	1,571	1,643	1,662	1,687	1,716	1,779	1,843	1,933	1,921	1,880	2,057	2,056	2,087	2,292
20 and 21 years old	693	961	1,101	1,296	1,536	1,566	1,578	1,601	1,619	1,636	1,724	1,777	1,801	1,797	1,794	1,808	1,925
22 to 24 years old	218	464	638	880	1,088	1,142	1,140	1,135	1,163	1,242	1,358	1,370	1,333	1,421	1,462	1,507	1,540
25 to 29 years old	80	250	358	476	583	634	668	692	721	772	855	890	892	837	858	948	1,004
30 to 34 years old	37	130	212	232	280	286	322	336	324	322	382	444	463	355	367	395	445
35 years old and over	46	141	326	374	471	493	500	503	539	603	697	745	743	733	745	797	900
Part-time	2,765	4,999	5,998	6,303	6,585	6,662	6,690	6,802	6,978	7,355	7,705	7,934	7,993	8,107	8,224	8,608	9,258
14 to 17 years old	16	26	19	10	23	28	36	36	31	27	36	32	31	45	44	46	50
18 and 19 years old	205	308	306	435	421	407	417	440	446	453	528	561	612	699	694	693	751
20 and 21 years old	236	388	456	553	551	590	586	601	585	606	674	739	782	947	942	936	980
22 to 24 years old	564	765	796	886	1,003	1,023	992	1,058	1,074	1,096	1,059	1,174	1,204	1,134	1,164	1,188	1,192
25 to 29 years old	665	1,202	1,291	1,158	1,224	1,286	1,296	1,282	1,352	1,471	1,576	1,649	1,692	1,580	1,609	1,748	1,823
30 to 34 years old	414	954	1,001	915	929	923	891	901	963	1,037	1,078	1,060	1,047	1,032	1,061	1,128	1,252
35 years old and over	663	1,356	2,127	2,345	2,434	2,404	2,472	2,483	2,527	2,664	2,753	2,719	2,624	2,671	2,708	2,870	3,212
Males	1,540	2,185	2,476	2,611	2,622	2,648	2,653	2,696	2,786	2,955	3,099	3,208	3,233	3,264	3,287	3,329	3,478
14 to 17 years old	4	12	11	7	9	13	15	17	14	20	25	23	20	31	31	32	34
18 and 19 years old	94	149	127	212	183	178	184	200	204	188	226	245	287	308	305	298	318
20 and 21 years old	108	172	224	255	236	248	260	257	269	289	329	362	382	460	456	443	456
22 to 24 years old	318	359	361	388	416	436	428	452	438	450	430	508	510	491	502	498	487
25 to 29 years old	450	592	591	498	504	540	551	507	570	625	717	695	706	714	721	759	772
30 to 34 years old	257	422	435	395	392	388	365	393	406	442	428	430	419	400	408	419	451
35 years old and over	309	479	728	855	882	845	850	869	886	941	944	944	908	859	864	881	960
Females	1,225	2,814	3,521	3,692	3,963	4,014	4,038	4,106	4,192	4,401	4,606	4,726	4,760	4,843	4,936	5,279	5,780
14 to 17 years old	12	14	9	3	14	15	21	20	17	7	11	9	12	13	13	14	15
18 and 19 years old	112	159	179	223	238	230	233	240	242	265	303	316	325	390	389	395	433
20 and 21 years old	128	216	233	298	315	342	327	344	317	318	345	377	400	487	486	492	524
22 to 24 years old	246	407	435	497	587	588	564	605	637	646	629	666	694	643	663	690	705
25 to 29 years old	216	609	700	660	721	746	745	774	781	846	858	953	985	866	888	989	1,050
30 to 34 years old	158	532	567	520	537	535	526	508	557	595	651	630	629	632	653	709	801
35 years old and over	354	876	1,399	1,491	1,552	1,560	1,623	1,614	1,640	1,723	1,810	1,775	1,716	1,812	1,844	1,989	2,252

Note: Distributions by age are estimates based on samples of the civilian noninstitutional population from the US Census Bureau's Current Population Survey. Data through 1995 are for institutions of higher education, while later data are for degree-granting institutions. Degree-granting institutions grant associate's or higher degrees and participate in Title IV federal financial aid programs. The degree-granting classification is very similar to the earlier higher education classification, but it includes more 2-year colleges and excludes a few higher education institutions that did not grant degrees. Detail may not sum to totals because of rounding.

SOURCE: "Table 224. Total Fall Enrollment in Degree-Granting Institutions, by Attendance Status, Sex, and Age: Selected Years, 1970 through 2021," in *2012 Tables and Figures*, National Center for Education Statistics, December 2012, https://nces.ed.gov/programs/digest/d12/tables/dt12_224.asp (accessed October 23, 2017)

create and maintain blogs or send text messages. In *Social Media Update 2016* (November 11, 2016, http://www.pewinternet.org/2016/11/11/social-media-update-2016/), Shannon Greenwood, Andrew Perrin, and Maeve Duggan of Pew report that in 2016, 18% of adults aged 50 to 64 years and 8% of those aged 65 years and older used Instagram, and 21% of adults aged 50 to 64 years and 10% of those aged 65 years and older used Twitter.

OLDER ADULTS PLAY VIDEO GAMES. Video games are popular among older adults. According to Anna Brown of Pew, in "Younger Men Play Video Games, but So Do a Diverse Group of Other Americans" (September 11, 2017, http://www.pewresearch.org/fact-tank/2017/09/11/younger-men-play-video-games-but-so-do-a-diverse-group-of-other-americans/), a 2017 survey found that 27% of men aged 50 years and older and 30% of women in the same age group played online video games. Twenty-four percent of adults aged 65 years and older played video games. For some, console game versions of their once-favorite sports help them to stay "in the game," even when an injury, disability, or illness prevents them from actually participating in tennis, bowling, or golf. Others feel that playing video games helps them to exercise their brains, eye-hand coordination, and reflexes. Still others simply find video games as diverting and entertaining as do younger players.

Playing video games improves a number of cognitive functions. In "Video Game Training Enhances Cognition of Older Adults: A Meta-analytic Study" (*Psychology and Aging*, vol. 29, no. 3, September 2014), Pilar Toril, José M. Reales, and Soledad Ballesteros reviewed 20 studies published between 1986 and 2013 to determine if video game training enhances cognitive functions. They find that video game training in older adults produces positive effects on several cognitive functions that decline with aging, including reaction time, attention, and memory.

In particular, physically active videogames ("exergames") benefit older adults. Emma Stanmore et al. report in "The Effect of Active Video Games on Cognitive Functioning in Clinical and Non-clinical Populations: A Meta-analysis of Randomized Controlled Trials" (*Neuroscience and Biobehavioral Reviews*, vol. 78, July 2017) an analysis of the results of 17 studies, which shows that exergames help improve older adults' overall cognitive function and may even prevent cognitive decline. The effects of exergames were greater than other physical activity, such as using a stationary bicycle or stretch and balance training. The reason for this may be that combining aerobic exercise with cognitive-demanding activities stimulates and preserves new neurons (nerve cells) in the brain.

THE POLITICS OF OLDER ADULTS

Older adults are vitally interested in politics and government, and they are especially interested in the issues that directly influence their life, including eligibility for and reform to Social Security as well as benefits and coverage by Medicare (a federal health insurance program for people aged 65 years and older and people with disabilities). Historically, they are more likely to vote than adults in other age groups, and because many have retired from the workforce they have time to advocate for the policies and candidates they favor.

In *A Wider Partisan and Ideological Gap between Younger, Older Generations* (March 20, 2017, http://www.pewresearch.org/fact-tank/2017/03/20/a-wider-partisan-and-ideological-gap-between-younger-older-generations/), Shiva Maniam and Samantha Smith of Pew indicate that the Silent Generation (people born between 1929 and 1946) who were aged 71 to 88 years in 2017 leaned Republican. The Silent Generation is the most Republican of all the age cohorts (a group of individuals that shares a common characteristic such as birth years and is studied over time). More than one-third (36%) of the Silent Generation identified as conservative Republican or Republican leaning as did 31% of baby boomers (people born between 1946 and 1964).

Older Adults' Views on US Morals and Major Social Issues

Jim Norman of Gallup, Inc., observes in *Views of U.S. Moral Values Slip to Seven-Year Lows* (May 22, 2017, http://news.gallup.com/poll/210917/views-moral-values-slip-seven-year-lows.aspx) that younger and older Americans differ in terms of their views about the nation's moral values and the moral acceptability of a wide range of social and political issues. Norman notes that in 2017, 51% of adults aged 65 years and older felt that moral values are in a poor state, compared with 33% of adults aged 34 years and younger.

Interestingly, in recent years an increasing proportion of Democrats aged 55 years and older say they are social liberals. In *Social Liberals Nearly Tie Social Conservatives in U.S.* (July 28, 2017, http://news.gallup.com/poll/214598/social-liberals-nearly-tie-social-conservatives.aspx), Lydia Saad of Gallup notes that social liberalism has grown among college-educated older Democrats. The percentage identifying themselves as liberal grew from 26% in 2001–05 to 50% in 2015–17. This increase has resulted in roughly the same proportion of Americans describing themselves as socially liberal (30%) and socially conservative (34%).

US Politicians Are Growing Older

Kevin King reports in "The 115th Congress Is among the Oldest in History" (Quorum.us, November 9, 2017) that in 2017 Congress was the oldest it has ever been. The average age of a US senator was 61 and of a member of the US House of Representatives was 57. In 2017 the oldest senator in the 115th Congress was Dianne

Feinstein (1933–; D-CA), and the oldest representative was John Conyers Jr. (1929–; D-MI).

King observes that "the average American is 20 years younger than their representative in Congress." He also notes that in 2017 Democratic leaders in the House of Representatives were on average 24 years older than their Republican counterparts and that one-third of representatives over the age of 60 years represented districts with a median age (the middle value; half of all people are younger and half are older) of 35 years or younger. For example, Representative Donald Young (1933–; R-AK) was 83 and the median age of his constituents was 33. King also reports that more than half of the senators up for reelection in 2018 were over age 65.

"GRAY POWER": A POLITICAL BLOC

AARP believes strongly in the principles of collective purpose, collective voice and the collective power of the 50+ population to change the market based on their needs. These principles guide our efforts.

—AARP, "About AARP: Social Impact" (2018)

A higher proportion of adults aged 55 to 74 years vote than any other age group, and it is inevitable that the increasing number of Americans in this cohort will wield an enormous political impact. With nearly 38 million members, the AARP (2017, https://www.aarp.org/about-aarp/?intcmp=AE-HP-FTR-ABOUT) exercises considerable influence when lobbying political leaders about the issues that concern older Americans.

As part of its mission, the AARP advocates on behalf of older adults. It is known as a powerful advocate on a range of legislative, consumer, and legal issues. To this end, the organization monitors issues that are pertinent to the lives of older Americans, assesses public opinion on such issues, and keeps policy makers apprised of these opinions. Advocacy efforts include becoming involved in litigation when the decision could have a significant effect on the lives of older Americans. In cases regarding age discrimination, pensions, health care, economic security, and consumer issues, AARP lawyers file amicus briefs (legal documents filed by individuals or groups that are not actual parties to a lawsuit but that are interested in influencing the outcome of the lawsuit) and support third-party lawsuits to promote the interests of older people.

The AARP responds to political and policy issues of concern to its constituency. For example, it asserts in the press release "AARP Delivers 2 Million Petitions to Senate Urging Rejection of Cuts to Social Security, Medicare" (October 19, 2017, https://press.aarp.org/2017-10-19-AARP-Delivers-2-Million-Petitions-Senate-Urging-Reject-Cuts-Social-Security-Medicare) that it presented to the Senate a petition signed by more than 2 million AARP members exhorting the Senate to reject measures that would slash Social Security and Medicare benefits. Nancy LeaMond, an executive vice president of AARP, asserts, "Tens of millions of Americans of all ages depend on Social Security and Medicare, and the proposed Senate budget would impose deep cuts to these lifeline programs. We hope to see you support solutions that address the needs of the people you represent."

The AARP also offered its enthusiastic support for the Seniors Tax Hike Prevention Act of 2017, bipartisan legislation introduced by the US senators Rob Portman (1955–; R-OH) and Sherrod Brown (1952–; D-OH). In the press release "AARP Backs Bipartisan Bill to Protect Seniors from Looming Tax Hike" (October 18, 2017, https://press.aarp.org/2017-10-18-AARP-Backs-Bipartisan-Bill-to-Protect-Seniors-from-Looming-Tax-Hike), Jo Ann Jenkins, the chief executive officer of AARP, explains that if this legislation is not passed, older taxpayers with high health costs will have higher taxes because the threshold for medical expense deductions will increase from 7.5% of income to 10%.

CHAPTER 6
ON THE ROAD: OLDER ADULT DRIVERS

Readily available transportation is a vital factor in the quality of life of older adults. Transportation is essential for accessing health care, establishing and maintaining social and family relationships, obtaining food and other necessities, and preserving independence and self-esteem.

The ability to drive often determines whether an older adult is able to live independently. Driving is the primary mode of transportation in the United States, and personal vehicles remain the transportation mode of choice for almost all Americans, including older people. Surveys conducted by the AARP repeatedly confirm that people over the age of 65 years make nearly all their trips in private vehicles, either as drivers or passengers. Even in urban areas where public transit is readily available, private vehicles are still used by most older people, and nondrivers rely on family members or friends for transport.

The National Highway Traffic Safety Administration (NHTSA) confirms in "Alternative Transportation—It Could Work for You" (2017, https://one.nhtsa.gov/people/ injury/olddrive/Driving%20Safely%20Aging%20Web/page6 .html) that older adult nondrivers rely on alternative forms of transportation, such as rides from family or friends, public transportation, walking, senior vans, or taxicabs.

The national Eldercare Locator (https://eldercare .acl.gov/Public/index.aspx), an information and referral service for older adults operated by the US Department of Health and Human Services (HHS), reports that nearly one in five calls it receives are about transportation issues. In "Transportation Is Top Need for Seniors Calling for Help" (USAToday.com, June 23, 2015), Paul Singer reports that the majority of callers are women. Many callers are frustrated because they do not have transportation to get to medical appointments, to the grocery store, or to socialize. Sandy Markwood, CEO of the National Association of Area Agencies on Aging, observes that transportation is a vital link to needed services for older adults. "You can have the best services in the world in the community," she notes, "but if people can't get to them, they have no value."

The NHTSA states in *Older Drivers* (2017, https:// www.nhtsa.gov/road-safety/older-drivers) that drivers aged 65 years and older, who numbered 47.8 million in 2015, are a significant and growing segment of the driving population. In "Older Drivers: Q&As" (September 2017, http://www.iihs.org/iihs/topics/t/older-drivers/qanda), the Insurance Institute for Highway Safety (IIHS) reports that in 2015 there were 25.3 million licensed drivers aged 70 years and older, which is more than three-quarters (80%) of the population aged 70 years and older and about 12% of drivers of all ages.

Federal Highway Administration data show that in 2015 more than 40 million licensed drivers were aged 65 years and older, with a similar percentage of drivers among older men and older women. (See Table 6.1.) Projections suggest that as younger members of the baby boom generation (those born between 1946 and 1964) reach retirement age, the number of drivers aged 65 years and older will continue to grow.

Donald H. Camph observes in *A New Vision of America's Highways: Long-Distance Travel, Recreation, Tourism, and Rural Travel* (March 2007) that, although many older adults drive (and many more are expected to do so in the future), driving is not a viable alternative for a significant number of older people. Many older adults choose to stop or limit their driving for health or safety reasons. Others do not have access to a vehicle. Camph also asserts that "more than 50 percent of nondrivers aged years 65 and older—or 3.6 million Americans—stay home on any given day at least partially because they lack transportation options."

Limited income also restricts many older adults' use of automobiles. According to the US Bureau of Labor

TABLE 6.1

Licensed drivers, by sex and percentage in each age group and relation to population, 2015

	Male drivers			Female drivers			Total drivers		
Age	Number	Percent of total drivers	Drivers as percent of age group*	Number	Percent of total drivers	Drivers as percent of age group*	Number	Percent of total drivers	Drivers as percent of age group*
Under 16	32,495	0.0	1.5	32,620	0.0	1.6	65,115	0.0	1.5
16	527,382	0.5	24.7	537,502	0.5	26.3	1,064,884	0.5	25.4
17	966,677	0.9	45.1	953,781	0.9	46.5	1,920,458	0.9	45.8
18	1,304,619	1.2	60.5	1,245,801	1.1	60.4	2,550,420	1.2	60.5
19	1,530,017	1.4	70.0	1,459,755	1.3	70.2	2,989,772	1.4	70.1
(19 and under)	4,361,190	4.1	40.4	4,229,459	3.8	41.0	8,590,649	3.9	40.7
20	1,645,437	1.5	73.4	1,578,873	1.4	74.4	3,224,310	1.5	73.9
21	1,707,768	1.6	74.6	1,660,552	1.5	76.6	3,368,320	1.5	75.6
22	1,791,158	1.7	76.8	1,740,421	1.6	79.2	3,531,579	1.6	78.0
23	1,857,286	1.7	77.8	1,831,076	1.7	80.9	3,688,362	1.7	79.3
24	1,912,171	1.8	79.1	1,905,706	1.7	82.2	3,817,877	1.8	80.6
(20–24)	8,913,820	8.3	76.4	8,716,628	7.9	78.7	17,630,448	8.1	77.5
25–29	9,599,910	8.9	84.1	9,665,917	8.8	87.5	19,265,827	8.8	85.8
30–34	9,483,821	8.8	87.1	9,635,915	8.7	89.3	19,119,736	8.8	88.2
35–39	8,948,342	8.3	88.0	9,139,345	8.3	89.6	18,087,687	8.3	88.8
40–44	8,976,495	8.3	89.5	9,130,641	8.3	89.6	18,107,136	8.3	89.6
45–49	9,439,868	8.8	91.3	9,547,861	8.6	90.8	18,987,729	8.7	91.1
50–54	10,129,724	9.4	92.4	10,358,348	9.4	91.1	20,488,072	9.4	91.7
55–59	9,858,801	9.2	93.0	10,209,251	9.2	91.1	20,068,052	9.2	92.0
60–64	8,621,325	8.0	94.6	9,025,845	8.2	90.7	17,647,170	8.1	92.5
65–69	7,217,544	6.7	95.0	7,570,860	6.9	89.4	14,788,404	6.8	92.0
70–74	4,974,735	4.6	93.9	5,257,499	4.8	85.0	10,232,234	4.7	89.1
75–79	3,267,202	3.0	90.5	3,566,555	3.2	79.0	6,833,757	3.1	84.1
80–84	2,157,345	2.0	89.4	2,364,088	2.1	69.8	4,521,433	2.1	78.0
85 and over	1,699,564	1.6	94.4	2,016,567	1.8	57.1	3,716,131	1.7	69.7
Total	107,649,686	100.0	85.0	110,434,779	100.0	83.2	218,084,465	100.0	84.1

*These percentages are computed using population estimates of the Bureau of the Census. Under-16 age group is compared to 14 and 15-year-old population estimates; the other age brackets coincide with those from the Bureau of the Census.

SOURCE: "Distribution of Licensed Drivers—2015 by Sex and Percentage in Each Age Group and Relation to Population," in *Highway Statistics 2015*, US Department of Transportation, Federal Highway Administration, September 2016, https://www.fhwa.dot.gov/policyinformation/statistics/2015/pdf/dl20.pdf (accessed October 23, 2017)

Statistics, car ownership costs are the second-largest household expense in the United States, and the average household spends nearly as much to own and operate a car as it does on food and health care combined. Table 6.2 shows that the percentage of the total annual expenditures for transportation remained close to 17% from 2012 through 2015.

Although lower gasoline prices can have a favorable impact on consumer spending for gasoline (see Figure 6.1), the cost of owning and operating an automobile may be prohibitive for older adults living on fixed incomes. As a result, an ever-increasing proportion of the older population depends on alternative forms of transportation in those areas where such transport is available. Some older adults, however, remain isolated and immobilized by the absence of accessible, affordable transportation in their communities.

According to the US Government Accountability Office (GAO), in *Transportation for Older Adults: Measuring Results Could Help Determine if Coordination Efforts Improve Mobility* (December 10, 2014, https://www.gao.gov/assets/670/667375.pdf), state and local transportation agencies and aging organizations use a variety of approaches to coordinate transportation services for older adults. For example, travel-training programs help older adults identify and gain access to transportation resources. Other programs offer transportation services directly. For example, Ride Connection (https://rideconnection.org/), a nonprofit organization in Oregon that draws on volunteer drivers and community transportation partners, provided 559,444 rides to older adults and others in 2016.

TRANSPORTATION INITIATIVES ADDRESS NEEDS OF OLDER ADULTS

Because ensuring access to transportation is key to older adults' independence and quality of life, several federal agencies and initiatives aim to address this need. The Administration on Aging (AoA) funds state and local agencies that provide transportation services for older adults. Within the US Department of Transportation (DOT), the Federal Transit Administration's Enhanced Mobility of Seniors and Individuals with Disabilities program also serves older adults. Other federal agency programs, including some within the US Department of Veterans Affairs (VA), fund access to transportation services for older adult beneficiaries. The Interagency

TABLE 6.2

Percentage distribution of total annual expenditures by major category, 2012–15

Spending category	2012	2013	2014	2015
Average annual expenditures	100.0	100.0	100.0	100.0
Food	12.8	12.9	12.6	12.5
Food at home	7.6	7.8	7.4	7.2
Food away from home	5.2	5.1	5.2	5.4
Alcoholic beverages	0.9	0.9	0.9	0.9
Housing	32.8	33.6	33.3	32.9
Shelter	19.2	19.7	19.6	19.2
Utilities, fuels, and public services	7.1	7.3	7.3	6.9
Household operations	2.3	2.2	2.2	2.3
Housekeeping supplies	1.2	1.3	1.2	1.2
Household furnishings and equipment	3.1	3.0	3.0	3.2
Apparel and services	3.4	3.1	3.3	3.3
Transportation	17.5	17.6	17.0	17.0
Vehicle purchases (net outlay)	6.2	6.4	6.2	7.1
Gasoline and motor oil	5.4	5.1	4.6	3.7
Other vehicle expenses	4.8	5.1	5.1	4.9
Public and other transportation	1.1	1.1	1.1	1.2
Healthcare	6.9	7.1	8.0	7.8
Entertainment	5.1	4.9	5.1	5.1
Personal care products and services	1.2	1.2	1.2	1.2
Reading	0.2	0.2	0.2	0.2
Education	2.3	2.2	2.3	2.3
Tobacco products and smoking supplies	0.6	0.6	0.6	0.6
Miscellaneous	1.6	1.3	1.5	1.6
Cash contributions	3.7	3.6	3.3	3.2
Personal insurance and pensions	10.9	10.8	10.7	11.3
Life and other personal insurance	0.7	0.6	0.6	0.6
Pensions and Social Security	10.2	10.2	10.1	10.7

SOURCE: "Table B. Percent Distribution of Total Annual Expenditures by Major Category for All Consumer Units, Consumer Expenditure Survey, 2012–2015," in "Consumer Expenditures in 2015," *BLS Reports*, US Department of Labor, Bureau of Labor Statistics, April 2017, https://www.bls.gov/opub/reports/consumer-expenditures/2015/home.htm (accessed October 23, 2017)

Coordinating Council on Access and Mobility (Coordinating Council) leads federal efforts to improve the efficiency and effectiveness of transportation services.

The Coordinating Council sponsors United We Ride, a national interagency initiative that supports states and their localities to develop coordinated human service delivery systems. The National Center on Senior Transportation (NCST) aims to assist older adults to remain active, vital members of their communities by offering a range of transportation options and alternatives. The NCST-sponsored Senior Transportation program is a collaborative effort that coordinates research and services intended to develop new transportation solutions, especially for rural areas. The program also champions the creative use of technology to connect volunteers, older drivers, and older adults in need of transportation services. The NCST is overseen by Easter Seals Inc. and receives funding via the DOT's Federal Transit Administration.

MOTOR VEHICLE ACCIDENTS

The IIHS, a nonprofit organization dedicated to reducing losses from motor vehicle accidents, reports that apart from the youngest drivers, older drivers have the highest rates of fatal crashes per mile driven. Although older drivers tend to limit their number of miles driven as they age and they drive at the safest times (in daylight and avoiding rush-hour traffic), their rate of accidents per mile is high. In "Older Drivers: Fatality Facts" (December 2017, http://www.iihs.org/iihs/topics/t/older-drivers/fatalityfacts/older-people), the IIHS observes that in 2015, motor vehicle crashes accounted for less than 1% of fatalities among people aged 70 years and older and that fatal crash rates increase markedly at ages 70 to 74 years and are highest among drivers 85 years and older.

The oldest and youngest drivers have the highest fatality rates on a per-mile-driven basis, but a key difference between the two age groups is that older drivers involved in crashes are less likely than younger drivers to hurt others; older drivers pose more of a danger to themselves. Drivers under the age of 35 years are also more likely to be speeding and are responsible for far more of the speeding-related fatal crashes than are older adult drivers. (See Figure 6.2.)

Table 6.3 shows that in 2015 the death rate (the number of deaths per 100,000 population) for motor vehicle–related injuries for adults aged 65 years and older was 15.3 per 100,000, compared with 12.8 per 100,000 for adults aged 45 to 64 years. The higher fatality rates of adults aged 75 to 84 years (17.5 per 100,000) and 85 years and older (21.7) who were involved in crashes are attributable to older adults' fragility as opposed to the likelihood of being involved in an accident. Older people are more susceptible to injury, especially chest injuries, and are more likely to die as a result of those injuries.

The IIHS reports in "Older Drivers: Fatality Facts" that in 2016, 74% of motor vehicle crash fatalities among people aged 70 years and older involved occupants in passenger vehicles, and 17% were pedestrians. Between 1997 and 2016, deaths of older adult passengers in motor vehicle crashes declined 25%, and deaths of older pedestrians declined 14%.

The IIHS further reports that 42% of fatalities involving drivers aged 80 years and older in 2016 were multiple-vehicle crashes that occurred at intersections. By contrast, multiple-vehicle crashes at intersections accounted for 20% of fatal crashes among drivers aged 16 to 59 that year.

Older adults also suffer nonfatal injuries when they are the drivers or passengers in motor vehicle crashes. In 2015 the National Center for Injury Prevention and Control recorded 265,668 nonfatal motor vehicle injuries in adults aged 65 to 85 years. (See Table 6.4; this figure shows the 210,848 injuries to occupants of vehicles and the 95,170 injuries attributable to other transport.) Motor vehicle accidents (called "Unintentional MV-occupant" in Table 6.4) were the fourth-leading cause of nonfatal injuries among adults aged 65 to 85 years in the United States in 2015.

FIGURE 6.1

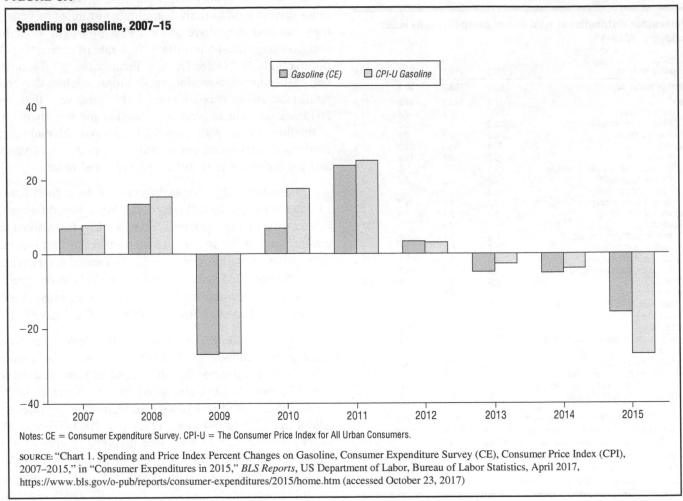

Spending on gasoline, 2007–15

Notes: CE = Consumer Expenditure Survey. CPI-U = The Consumer Price Index for All Urban Consumers.

SOURCE: "Chart 1. Spending and Price Index Percent Changes on Gasoline, Consumer Expenditure Survey (CE), Consumer Price Index (CPI), 2007–2015," in "Consumer Expenditures in 2015," *BLS Reports*, US Department of Labor, Bureau of Labor Statistics, April 2017, https://www.bls.gov/o-pub/reports/consumer-expenditures/2015/home.htm (accessed October 23, 2017)

The data about older drivers are not all bad. According to the Centers for Disease Control and Prevention (CDC), in "Older Adult Drivers" (November 30, 2017, https://www.cdc.gov/motorvehiclesafety/older_adult_drivers/index.html), older drivers take fewer risks than younger drivers by limiting their driving on high-speed roads, during bad weather, at night, and in heavy traffic. Figure 6.3 shows the percentages of older adult drivers who tend to avoid driving under certain conditions.

AGE-RELATED CHANGES MAY IMPAIR OLDER DRIVERS' SKILLS

Most older adults retain their driving skills, but some age-related changes in vision, hearing, cognitive functions (attention, memory, and reaction times), reflexes, and flexibility of the head and neck may impair the skills that are critical for safe driving. For example, reaction time becomes slower and more variable with advancing age, and arthritis (inflammation that causes pain and loss of movement of the joints) in the neck or shoulder may limit sufferers' ability to turn their necks well enough to merge into traffic, see when backing up, and navigate intersections where the angle of intersecting roads is less than perpendicular.

Changes such as reduced muscle mass and the resultant reduction in strength, as well as decreases in the efficiency of the circulatory, cardiac, and respiratory systems, are strictly related to aging. Others are attributable to the fact that certain diseases, such as arthritis and glaucoma (a disease in which fluid pressure inside the eyes slowly rises, leading to vision loss or blindness), tend to strike at later ages. The functional losses that are associated with these conditions are usually gradual, and many afflicted older drivers are able to adapt to them. Most older adults do not experience declines until very old age, and most learn to adjust to the limitations imposed by age-related changes. Still, a substantial proportion of older adults do stop driving in response to age-related changes. In "New Data on Older Drivers" (April 27, 2015), the CDC reports that of older adults who reduced their driving, 40% said they did so because of vision problems.

Two publications, the *Clinician's Guide to Assessing and Counseling Older Drivers* (2015, https://geriatricscareonline.org/ProductAbstract/clinician%27s-guide-to-assessing-and-counseling-older-drivers/B022), published by the American Geriatrics Society, and the *Physician's*

FIGURE 6.2

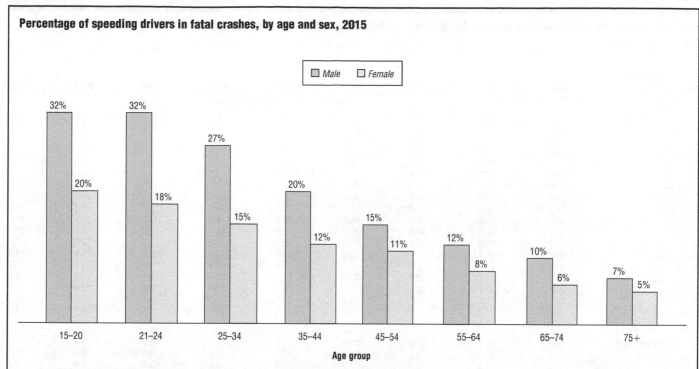

Percentage of speeding drivers in fatal crashes, by age and sex, 2015

☐ Male ☐ Female

SOURCE: "Figure 1. Percentage of Speeding Drivers in Fatal Crashes, by Age and Gender, 2015," in "Speeding," *Traffic Safety Facts 2015 Data* National Highway Traffic Safety Administration, National Center for Statistics and Analysis, July 2017, https://crashstats.nhtsa.dot.gov/Api/Public/ViewPublication/812409 (accessed October 23, 2017)

Guide to Assessing and Counseling Older Drivers (2010, https://one.nhtsa.gov/people/injury/olddrive/OlderDrivers Book/pages/Contents.html), published by the American Medical Association (AMA) and the NHTSA, detail medical conditions and medications and their potential effects on driving and highlight treatment methods and counseling measures that can minimize these effects. These measures include screening and assessing older adults' functional abilities for driving and advising older drivers about transitioning from driving to other forms of transportation. The guides also discuss legal and ethical issues related to the safety of older drivers and state licensing and reporting laws.

Acute and Chronic Medical Problems

Examples of acute (short-term) medical problems that can impair driving performance include:

- Acute myocardial infarction (heart attack)

- Stroke (sudden death of a portion of the brain cells due to a lack of blood flow and oxygen) and other traumatic brain injury

- Syncope (fainting) and vertigo (dizziness)

- Seizures (sudden attacks or convulsions characterized by generalized muscle spasms and loss of consciousness)

- Surgery

- Delirium (altered mental state characterized by wild, irregular, and incoherent thoughts and actions) from any cause

The AMA and the NHTSA note that a variety of chronic (long-term) medical conditions can also compromise driving function, including:

- Visual disorders such as cataracts, diabetic retinopathy (damage to the blood vessels that supply the retina that can result in blindness), macular degeneration (a degenerative condition that can cause blurred vision), glaucoma, retinitis pigmentosa (an inherited condition that causes night blindness and tunnel vision), and low visual acuity (the inability to distinguish fine details) even after correction with lenses. Along with visual acuity, other visual functions decline with advancing age. For example, sensitivity to glare increases and may be exacerbated by cataracts. Because driving is largely a visual task, impaired vision can significantly compromise the ability to read signs, see lane lines, and identify pedestrians in the dark or during inclement weather.

- Cardiovascular disorders such as angina (chest pain from a blockage in a coronary artery that prevents oxygen-rich blood from reaching part of the heart) or syncope pose dangers to drivers because acute pain or even transient loss of consciousness increases the risk of accidents.

TABLE 6.3

Death rates for motor vehicle-related injuries, by selected characteristics, selected years 1950–2015

[Data are based on death certificates]

Sex, race, Hispanic origin, and age	1950[a]	1960[b]	1970	1980	1990	2000	2010	2014	2015
All persons				Deaths per 100,000 resident population					
All ages, age-adjusted[b]	24.6	23.1	27.6	22.3	18.5	15.4	11.3	10.8	11.4
All ages, crude	23.1	21.3	26.9	23.5	18.8	15.4	11.4	11.1	11.7
Under 1 year	8.4	8.1	9.8	7.0	4.9	4.4	2.0	1.7	1.8
1–14 years	9.8	8.6	10.5	8.2	6.0	4.3	2.3	2.2	2.2
1–4 years	11.5	10.0	11.5	9.2	6.3	4.2	2.8	2.5	2.6
5–14 years	8.8	7.9	10.2	7.9	5.9	4.3	2.2	2.0	2.1
15–24 years	34.4	38.0	47.2	44.8	34.1	26.9	16.6	15.3	15.9
15–19 years	29.6	33.9	43.6	43.0	33.1	26.0	13.6	11.9	12.4
20–24 years	38.8	42.9	51.3	46.6	35.0	28.0	19.7	18.3	19.2
25–34 years	24.6	24.3	30.9	29.1	23.6	17.3	14.0	13.9	14.7
35–44 years	20.3	19.3	24.9	20.9	16.9	15.3	11.6	11.1	11.9
45–64 years	25.2	23.0	26.5	18.0	15.7	14.3	11.9	12.0	12.8
45–54 years	22.2	21.4	25.5	18.6	15.6	14.2	12.0	12.1	12.8
55–64 years	29.0	25.1	27.9	17.4	15.9	14.4	11.9	11.9	12.7
65 years and over	43.1	34.7	36.2	22.5	23.1	21.4	16.0	14.8	15.3
65–74 years	39.1	31.4	32.8	19.2	18.6	16.5	12.3	11.9	12.8
75–84 years	52.7	41.8	43.5	28.1	29.1	25.7	18.8	17.5	17.5
85 years and over	45.1	37.9	34.2	27.6	31.2	30.4	23.8	20.9	21.7
Male									
All ages, age-adjusted[b]	38.5	35.4	41.5	33.6	26.5	21.7	16.2	15.8	16.7
All ages, crude	35.4	31.8	39.7	35.3	26.7	21.3	16.3	16.0	17.0
Under 1 year	9.1	8.6	9.3	7.3	5.0	4.6	2.2	1.9	2.2
1–14 years	12.3	10.7	13.0	10.0	7.0	4.9	2.7	2.5	2.5
1–4 years	13.0	11.5	12.9	10.2	6.9	4.7	3.0	2.8	2.9
5–14 years	11.9	10.4	13.1	9.9	7.0	5.0	2.5	2.4	2.4
15–24 years	56.7	61.2	73.2	68.4	49.5	37.4	23.1	21.5	22.2
15–19 years	46.3	51.7	64.1	62.6	45.5	33.9	17.8	16.1	16.3
20–24 years	66.7	73.2	84.4	74.3	53.3	41.2	28.5	26.5	27.7
25–34 years	40.8	40.1	49.4	46.3	35.7	25.5	21.0	20.8	21.8
35–44 years	32.5	29.9	37.7	31.7	24.7	22.0	16.9	16.4	17.9
45–64 years	37.7	33.3	38.9	26.5	21.9	20.2	17.9	18.1	19.4
45–54 years	33.6	31.6	37.2	27.6	22.0	20.4	17.9	18.2	19.1
55–64 years	43.1	35.6	40.9	25.4	21.7	19.8	17.8	18.1	19.8
65 years and over	66.6	52.1	54.4	33.9	32.1	29.5	22.2	21.0	22.1
65–74 years	59.1	45.8	47.3	27.3	24.2	21.7	17.1	17.0	18.5
75–84 years	85.0	66.0	68.2	44.3	41.2	35.6	25.9	24.8	24.9
85 years and over	78.1	62.7	63.1	56.1	64.5	57.5	40.2	34.0	35.6
Female									
All ages, age-adjusted[b]	11.5	11.7	14.9	11.8	11.0	9.5	6.5	6.1	6.4
All ages, crude	10.9	11.0	14.7	12.3	11.3	9.7	6.8	6.3	6.7
Under 1 year	7.6	7.5	10.4	6.7	4.9	4.2	1.8	1.5	1.3
1–14 years	7.2	6.3	7.9	6.3	4.9	3.7	2.0	1.8	1.9
1–4 years	10.0	8.4	10.0	8.1	5.6	3.8	2.5	2.3	2.3
5–14 years	5.7	5.4	7.2	5.7	4.7	3.6	1.8	1.6	1.8
15–24 years	12.6	15.1	21.6	20.8	17.9	15.9	9.9	8.7	9.3
15–19 years	12.9	16.0	22.7	22.8	20.0	17.5	9.2	7.6	8.4
20–24 years	12.2	14.0	20.4	18.9	16.0	14.2	10.5	9.7	10.2
25–34 years	9.3	9.2	13.0	12.2	11.5	8.8	6.9	6.8	7.5
35–44 years	8.5	9.1	12.9	10.4	9.2	8.8	6.2	5.8	6.1
45–64 years	12.6	13.1	15.3	10.3	10.1	8.7	6.3	6.2	6.4
45–54 years	10.9	11.6	14.5	10.2	9.6	8.2	6.3	6.2	6.7
55–64 years	14.9	15.2	16.2	10.5	10.8	9.5	6.3	6.1	6.1
65 years and over	21.9	20.3	23.1	15.0	17.2	15.8	11.3	9.9	10.0
65–74 years	20.6	19.0	21.6	13.0	14.1	12.3	8.2	7.5	7.8
75–84 years	25.2	23.0	27.2	18.5	21.9	19.2	13.7	12.0	11.9
85 years and over	22.1	22.0	18.0	15.2	18.3	19.3	15.9	14.1	14.4
White male[c]									
All ages, age-adjusted[b]	37.9	34.8	40.4	33.8	26.3	21.8	16.7	16.1	17.0
All ages, crude	35.1	31.5	39.1	35.9	26.7	21.6	17.0	16.5	17.4
Under 1 year	9.1	8.8	9.1	7.0	4.8	4.2	2.0	1.8	1.9
1–14 years	12.4	10.6	12.5	9.8	6.6	4.8	2.7	2.4	2.5
15–24 years	58.3	62.7	75.2	73.8	52.5	39.6	24.6	23.0	23.3
25–34 years	39.1	38.6	47.0	46.6	35.4	25.1	21.4	20.8	22.1
35–44 years	30.9	28.4	35.2	30.7	23.7	21.8	17.4	16.6	18.0
45–64 years	36.2	31.7	36.5	25.2	20.6	19.7	18.3	18.3	19.5
65 years and over	67.1	52.1	54.2	32.7	31.4	29.4	22.7	21.5	22.7

TABLE 6.3

Death rates for motor vehicle-related injuries, by selected characteristics, selected years 1950–2015 [CONTINUED]

[Data are based on death certificates]

aIncludes deaths of persons who were not residents of the 50 states and the District of Columbia (D.C.).
bAge-adjusted rates are calculated using the year 2000 standard population. Prior to 2001, age-adjusted rates were calculated using standard million proportions based on rounded population numbers. Starting with 2001 data, unrounded population numbers are used to calculate age-adjusted rates.
cThe race groups, white, black, Asian or Pacific Islander, and American Indian or Alaska Native, include persons of Hispanic and non-Hispanic origin. Persons of Hispanic origin may be of any race. Death rates for Hispanic, American Indian or Alaska Native, and Asian or Pacific Islander persons should be interpreted with caution because of inconsistencies in reporting Hispanic origin or race on the death certificate (death rate numerators) compared with population figures (death rate denominators). The net effect of misclassification is an underestimation of deaths and death rates for races other than white and black.
Notes: Starting with *Health, United States, 2003*, rates for 1991–1999 were revised using intercensal population estimates based on the 1990 and 2000 censuses. For 2000, population estimates are bridged-race April 1 census counts. Starting with *Health, United States, 2012*, rates for 2001–2009 were revised using intercensal population estimates based on the 2000 and 2010 censuses. For 2010, population estimates are bridged-race April 1 census counts. Rates for 2011 and beyond were computed using 2010-based postcensal estimates. Starting with 2003 data, some states began to collect information on more than one race on the death certificate, according to 1997 Office of Management and Budget (OMB) standards. The multiple-race data for these states were bridged to the single-race categories of the 1977 OMB standards, for comparability with other states.

SOURCE: Adapted from "Table 28. Death Rates for Motor Vehicle-Related Injuries, by Sex, Race, Hispanic Origin, and Age: United States, Selected Years 1950–2015," in *Health, United States, 2016: With Chartbook on Long-Term Trends in Health*, National Center for Health Statistics, May 2017, https://www.cdc.gov/nchs/data/hus/2016/028.pdf (accessed October 17, 2017)

TABLE 6.4

Ten leading causes of nonfatal injuries, ages 65–85, 2015

Rank		Age groups
		65–85
1	Unintentional fall	3,037,550
2	Unintentional struck by/against	317,340
3	Unintentional overexertion	249,512
4	Unintentional MV-occupant	210,848
5	Unintentional cut/pierce	173,894
6	Unintentional poisoning	120,656
7	Unintentional other specified	109,583
8	Unintentional other bite/sting	103,106
9	Unintentional other transport	95,170
10	Unintentional unknown/unspecified	78,990

MV = motor vehicle.

SOURCE: "10 Leading Causes of Nonfatal Injury, United States 2015, All Races, Both Sexes, Disposition: All Cases," National Center for Injury Prevention and Control, 2017, https://webapp.cdc.gov/cgi-bin/broker.exe?_PROGRAM=wisqnf.nfilead.sas&_SERVICE=v8prod&log=0&rept=nfil&year1=2015&year2=2015&Racethn=0&Sex=0&disp=0&ranking=10&PRTFMT=FRIENDLY&lcnifmt=custom&intent=0&c_age1=65&c_age2=85&_debug=0 (accessed October 24, 2017)

- Neurologic diseases such as seizures, dementia (loss of intellectual functioning accompanied by memory loss and personality changes), multiple sclerosis (a progressive nerve disease that can result in the loss of the ability to walk or speak), Parkinson's disease (a degenerative disease that causes tremors and slowed movement and speech), peripheral neuropathy (numbness or tingling in the hands and/or feet), and residual deficits (losses or disability) resulting from stroke all may impair the driver's ability to operate a vehicle and/or exercise sufficient caution when driving.

- Psychiatric diseases, especially those mental disorders in which patients suffer hallucinations, severe anxiety, and irrational thoughts and are unable to distinguish between reality and imagination, can affect judgment and impair the driver's ability to operate a vehicle.

FIGURE 6.3

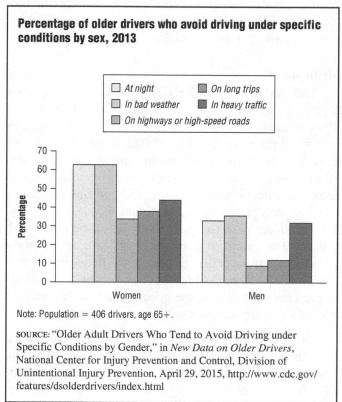

Percentage of older drivers who avoid driving under specific conditions by sex, 2013

Note: Population = 406 drivers, age 65+.

SOURCE: "Older Adult Drivers Who Tend to Avoid Driving under Specific Conditions by Gender," in *New Data on Older Drivers*, National Center for Injury Prevention and Control, Division of Unintentional Injury Prevention, April 29, 2015, http://www.cdc.gov/features/dsolderdrivers/index.html

- Metabolic diseases, such as diabetes mellitus (a condition in which there is increased sugar in the blood and urine because the body is unable to use sugar to produce energy) and hypothyroidism (decreased production of the thyroid hormone by the thyroid gland), can act to impair judgment and response time.

- Musculoskeletal disabilities, such as arthritis and injuries, can impair response time.

Driving requires a range of sophisticated cognitive skills, which is why some cognitive changes can compromise driving ability. It is not unusual for memory, attention, processing speed, and executive skills (the capacity for logical analysis) to decline with advancing age. Weakening memory may make it difficult for some older drivers to process information from traffic signs and to navigate correctly. As multiple demands are made on older drivers' attention, the AMA and the NHTSA state that "drivers must possess selective attention—the ability to prioritize stimuli and focus on only the most important—in order to attend to urgent stimuli (such as traffic signs) while not being distracted by irrelevant ones (such as roadside ads)." Selective attention problems challenge older drivers to distinguish the most critical information when they are faced with many signs and signals. Drivers have to divide their attention to concentrate "on the multiple stimuli required by most driving tasks." Processing speed affects perception-reaction time and is critical in situations where drivers must immediately choose between actions such as accelerating, braking, or steering. Executive skills enable drivers to make correct decisions after evaluating the stimuli that are related to driving, such as to stop at a red light or stop at a crosswalk when a pedestrian is crossing the street.

Medications

The AMA and the NHTSA indicate in *Physician's Guide to Assessing and Counseling Older Drivers* that many commonly used prescription and over-the-counter (nonprescription) medications can impair driving performance. In general, drugs with strong central nervous system effects, such as antidepressants, antihistamines, muscle relaxants, narcotic analgesics (painkillers), anticonvulsants (used to prevent seizures), and stimulants, have the potential to adversely affect the ability to operate a motor vehicle. The extent to which driving skills are compromised varies from person to person and between different medications that are used for the same purpose. The effects of prescription and over-the-counter medications may be intensified in combination with other drugs or alcohol.

Driving performance may also be affected by medication side effects, such as "drowsiness, dizziness, blurred vision, unsteadiness, fainting, [and] slowed reaction time." Generally, these side effects are dose-dependent and lessen over time, but older adults are often more sensitive to the effects of medications and may take longer to metabolize them, prolonging their effects. Medications such as prescription sleep aids "that cause drowsiness, euphoria, and/or anterograde amnesia may also diminish insight, and the patient may experience impairment without being aware of it."

Some Fears about Older Drivers Are Unwarranted

As the ranks of older adults swell, many states and organizations—the AMA and the NHTSA are chief among these groups—are taking action to ensure driver safety. Concern about older driver safety has intensified in recent years in response to a spate of media reports describing serious crashes involving older drivers. Some of this concern, however, may be unwarranted. In "Older Drivers: Q&As," the IIHS observes that drivers aged 60 years and older kill fewer pedestrians, bicyclists, motorcyclists, and occupants of other vehicles than do drivers aged 30 to 59 years.

These findings contradict earlier research, which predicted that older drivers would make up a substantially larger proportion of drivers in fatal crashes. The IIHS explains in "Older Drivers: Fatality Facts" that older drivers largely threaten their own safety and their passengers' safety. In 2016 about three-quarters of people killed in crashes involving drivers aged 70 years and older were either the older drivers themselves (59%) or their older passengers (15%).

Ensuring the Safety of Older Drivers

In *Physician's Guide to Assessing and Counseling Older Drivers*, the AMA and the NHTSA advocate coordinated efforts among the medical and research communities, policy makers, community planners, the automobile industry, and government agencies to achieve the common goal of safe transportation for the older population. The AMA and the NHTSA call for refined diagnostic tools to assist physicians in assessing patients' crash risk, improved access to driver assessment and rehabilitation, safer roads and vehicles, and better alternatives to driving for older adults.

Some auto insurance companies reduce payments for older adults who successfully complete driving classes such as the AARP Driver Safety program. The AARP notes in "Why Take the AARP Smart Driver Course?" (2017, https://www.aarpdriversafety.org/why-take-our-course.html?intcmp=dsp_hp_cw_learnmore) that its online refresher course provides guidance in assessing physical abilities and making adjustments accordingly. Insured drivers aged 55 years and older may be eligible for reductions in automobile insurance premium charges after completing this course. The American Automobile Association (AAA) offers a similar program called Safe Driving for Mature Operators that aims to improve the skills of older drivers. These courses address the aging process and help drivers adjust to age-related changes that can affect driving. Both organizations provide resources that help older drivers and their families determine whether they can safely continue driving.

As of February 2018, there were no upper age limits for driving. The National Institute on Aging observes that because people age at different rates, it is not possible to choose a specific age at which to suspend driving. Setting an age limit would leave some drivers on the road too long, whereas others would be forced to stop driving prematurely. Heredity, general health, lifestyle, and surroundings all influence how people age.

Many states are acting to reduce risks for older drivers by improving roadways to make driving less hazardous.

In *Older Driver Safety: Knowledge Sharing Should Help States Prepare for Increase in Older Driver Population* (2007, https://www.gao.gov/new.items/d07413.pdf), the GAO reports that several states have adopted Federal Highway Administration practices to help older drivers, including:

- Wider highway lanes

- Intersections that give drivers a longer view of oncoming traffic and allow more time for left turns

- Road signs with larger, more visible letters and numbers

- Advance street name signs before intersections

Another program to improve older drivers' safety is CarFit (2017, http://www.car-fit.org), an educational program that offers older adults an opportunity to find out how well their personal vehicles "fit" them. Developed by AAA, AARP, and the American Occupational Therapy Association, it encourages conversations between older drivers and their families about driving safety, helps older drivers maintain safe driving independence, and helps older adults feel more comfortable and safely fit behind the wheel. In "Frequently Asked Questions" (https://www.car-fit.org/carfit/FAQ), CarFit reports that the program is "highly effective on multiple fronts." A pilot program with more than 300 older driver participants found that more than one-third (37%) had a critical safety issue identified and addressed; 10% were sitting too close to the steering wheel, and about 20% did not have the necessary three-inch line of sight over the steering wheel. Participants also reported increased use of safety features in their vehicles and greater willingness to discuss their driving with family and/or health care providers.

Technology Aids Older Drivers

Along with "fit" assessments and modifications, smarter cars equipped with technology such as global positioning system navigation devices that provide turn-by-turn directions can help older adults drive more safely and comfortably. In "Safer Cars Help Keep Older Drivers on the Road" (NYTimes.com, August 28, 2017), Jane E. Brody reports that power seat adjustments, power windows and mirrors, a thicker, easy-to-grip steering wheel, keyless entry, automatic tailgate closer, and push button to start and stop the engine can make older drivers more comfortable.

High-contrast instrument panels are easier to read, and high-intensity high beams and auto-dimming rear- and side-view mirrors help minimize glare, enabling older adults with vision problems to see the road. Parking aids can help people with limited mobility, and some crash prevention systems not only alert drivers to dangers but also automatically apply the brakes if sensors detect a person or object in the vehicle's pathway.

In "Top 25 New Cars for Senior Drivers" (Consumer Reports.org, June 1, 2017), Jen Stockburger and Michelle Naranjo report on a Consumer Reports evaluation of cars based on features important for senior drivers, including front seat access, visibility, headlights, and controls. Front-seat access considerations for older drivers include wider openings and low door sills and step-in heights. Visibility pertains to the ability of drivers of different heights to see out of the front, sides, and back of the vehicle. The control category rated cars on easy-to-read gauges and interior controls for shifting gears and adjusting the radio and heating and cooling systems. The strength of headlights was also considered as a feature that "can make driving at night easier for people with decreasing or compromised vision." Consumer Reports gave the Subaru Forester, Subaru Outback, Kia Sportage, and Hyundai Sonata high marks along with cars made by Toyota, Honda, Nissan, and Ford.

PROVIDING ALTERNATIVE TRANSPORTATION AND NONEMERGENCY MEDICAL TRANSPORTATION

In *Transportation-Disadvantaged Populations* (November 6, 2013, https://www.gao.gov/assets/660/658766.pdf), the GAO considers issues and services for "transportation-disadvantaged" older adults—those who cannot drive or have limited their driving, or those who have an income restraint, disability, or medical condition that limits their ability to travel. The GAO identifies the federal programs that address this population's mobility issues, the extent to which these programs meet their mobility needs, the cost-effectiveness of service delivery, obstacles to addressing mobility needs, and strategies for overcoming these obstacles. According to the GAO, there are 80 federal programs designed to meet the transportation needs of older adults. For example, the HHS funds Community Services Block Grant programs, which provide taxicab vouchers and bus tokens that enable low-income older adults to take general trips, and Social Services Block Grants, which provide assistance for transport to and from medical or social service appointments.

The GAO reports that demand for specialized, door-to-door transport service (which costs more to operate than traditional fixed-route transit and is often used by transportation-disadvantaged populations including older adults) has increased because of the growing older population.

Another GAO report, *Transportation-Disadvantaged Populations: Nonemergency Medical Transportation Not Well Coordinated, and Additional Federal Leadership Needed* (December 2014, https://www.gao.gov/assets/670/667362.pdf) finds nonemergency medical transportation (NEMT) services poorly coordinated. Forty-two programs (funded by DOT, HHS, VA, and the US Departments of Agriculture, Education, and Housing and Urban Development) provide funding for NEMT services, although NEMT is not their primary purpose. Service delivery is fragmented, and there is overlap and duplication of services. The GAO recommends development of a strategic plan to improve coordination of this essential transportation service.

Types of Transportation for Nondrivers

Transportation for older adults can include door-to-door services such as taxis or van services, public buses that travel along fixed routes, or ride sharing in carpools. According to the AoA, in *Because We Care: A Guide for People Who Care* (2009, https://www.dshs.wa.gov/sites/default/files/ALTSA/hcs/documents/BecauseWeCare.pdf), there are three general classes of alternative transportation for older adults:

- Demand-response services generally require advance reservations and provide door-to-door service from one specific location to another. Such systems offer older adults comfortable and relatively flexible transport, with the potential for adapting to the needs of individual riders. Payment of fares for demand-response transport is usually required on a per-ride basis.

- Fixed route and scheduled services follow a predetermined route, stopping at established locations at specific times to allow passengers to board and disembark. This type of service typically requires payment of fares on a per-ride basis. Older adults are often eligible for discounted rates.

- Ride-sharing programs connect people who need rides with drivers who have room in their cars and are willing to take passengers. This system generally offers scheduled transportation to a particular destination, such as a place of employment, a senior center, or a medical center.

Meeting the Transportation Needs of Older Adults

In *Transportation-Disadvantaged Seniors: Efforts to Enhance Senior Mobility Could Benefit from Additional Guidance and Information* (August 2004, https://www.gao.gov/new.items/d04971.pdf), the GAO cites Beverly Foundation research showing the attributes necessary for alternative transportation services for older adults:

- Availability—older adults can travel to desired locations at the times they want to go.

- Accessibility—vehicles can be accessed by those with disabilities, services can be door-to-door or door-through-door as necessary, and stops are pedestrian-friendly. Door-through-door transport offers personal, hands-on assistance for older adults who may have difficulties exiting their homes, disembarking from vehicles, and/or opening doors. It is also called

assisted transportation, supported (or supportive) transportation, and escorted transportation.

- Acceptability—transport is safe, clean, and easy to use.

- Affordability—financial assistance is available if necessary.

- Adaptability—multiple trips and special equipment can be accommodated.

The GAO highlights specific unmet needs: "Seniors who rely on alternative transportation have difficulty making trips for which the automobile is better suited, such as trips that involve carrying packages; … life-enhancing needs are less likely to be met than life-sustaining needs; and … mobility needs are less likely to be met in nonurban communities (especially rural communities) than in urban communities." It also identifies obstacles to addressing transportation-disadvantaged older adults' mobility needs, potential strategies that federal and other government entities might take to better meet these needs, and trade-offs that are associated with implementing each strategy. For example, the GAO finds that older drivers are not encouraged to investigate or plan for a time when they will be unable to drive. One way to address this obstacle might be to institute educational programs that would ease older adults' transition from driver to nondriver. This strategy does, however, have the potential to increase demand for alternative transportation services and the costs that are associated with their provision.

To increase and improve alternative transportation services, the GAO suggests enlisting the aid of volunteer drivers, sponsoring demonstration programs, identifying best practices, increasing cooperation among federal programs, and establishing a central clearinghouse of information that could be accessed by stakeholders in the various programs.

Ride Sharing for Older Adults

In "7 Services Expanding Mobility for Aging Americans" (March 2, 2016, https://www.shareable.net/blog/7-services-expanding-mobility-for-aging-americans), the Shared-Use Mobility Center reports that a partnership between the ride-sharing service Lyft and the National MedTrans Network, a nonemergency medical transportation benefit manager, began in 2016. The program enables older adults to hail Lyft rides using a web-based dashboard. The dashboard also allows health care professionals to request rides for patients by entering their name, pickup location, and destination without the use of a smartphone.

SilverRide (http://www.silverride.com) is another transportation company that serves older adults. Riders book trips by telephone 24 hours in advance and pay by credit card. SilverRide also hosts monthly outings to concerts and museums to give older adults opportunities to get out and meet other SilverRide members.

CHAPTER 7
THE HEALTH AND MEDICAL PROBLEMS OF OLDER ADULTS

Among the fears many people have about aging is coping with losses—not only declining mental and physical abilities but also the prospect of failing health, chronic (long-term) illness, and disability. Although aging is associated with physiological changes, the rate and extent of these changes varies widely. One person may be limited by arthritis at age 65, whereas another is vigorous and active at age 90.

Despite the increasing proportion of active healthy older adults, it is true that the incidence (the rate of new cases of a disorder over a specified period) and prevalence (the total number of cases of a disorder in a given population at a specific time) of selected diseases as well as the utilization of health care services increase with advancing age. For example, the incidence of some diseases, such as diabetes, heart disease, breast cancer, Parkinson's disease, and Alzheimer's disease (a progressive disease that is characterized by memory loss, impaired thinking, and declining ability to function), increases with age. In contrast, the incidence of other diseases, such as human immunodeficiency virus (HIV) infection, multiple sclerosis, and schizophrenia, decreases with age.

This chapter considers the epidemiology of aging (the distribution and determinants of health and illness in the population of older adults). It describes trends in aging and the health of aging Americans; distinctions among healthy aging, disease, and disability; health promotion and prevention as applied to older people; and selected diseases and conditions that are common in old age.

GENERAL HEALTH OF OLDER AMERICANS

The proportion of adults rating their health as fair or poor increases with advancing age. In 2015, 18.7% of adults aged 55 to 64 years, 19% of adults aged 65 to 74 years, and 25.8% of adults aged 75 years and older considered themselves to be in fair or poor health, compared with just 6.3% of adults aged 18 to 44 years. (See Table 7.1.)

The Administration on Aging (AoA) indicates in *A Profile of Older Americans: 2016* (April 2017, https://www.acl.gov/sites/default/files/Aging%20and%20Disability%20in%20America/2016-Profile.pdf) that in 2015, 39% of adults aged 75 years and older considered their health to be excellent or very good, compared with 54% of those aged 45 to 64 years.

Most older people have at least one chronic condition, and many have several. According to the AoA, among adults aged 75 years and older the most frequently occurring conditions in 2015 were arthritis (53%), high cholesterol (45%), heart disease (35%), cancer (32%), and diabetes (22% in 2011–14). In "Multiple Chronic Conditions" (May 10, 2017, https://www.cms.gov/Research-Statistics-Data-and-Systems/Statistics-Trends-and-Reports/Chronic-Conditions/MCC_Main.html), the Centers for Medicare and Medicaid Services reports that in 2015, among men aged 65 years and older, 28.1% had two to three chronic conditions, 21.4% had four to five, and 15.8% had six or more chronic conditions. (See Table 7.2.) Among women aged 65 years and older, 31.4% had two to three chronic conditions, 21.7% had four to five conditions, and 16.5% had six or more chronic conditions.

The National Center for Health Statistics (NCHS) reports in *Health, United States, 2016: With Chartbook on Long-Term Trends in Health* (May 2017, https://www.cdc.gov/nchs/data/hus/hus16.pdf) that the percentage of people with difficulties performing basic actions, such as limitations in movement or in emotional, sensory, or cognitive functioning (thinking and reasoning) associated with a health problem and complex activities such as working, maintaining a household, and living independently, increase with advancing age. In 2015 the prevalence of at least one basic or complex action difficulty was higher among those aged 65 years and older (59.8%), compared with those aged 18 and 64 years (26.9%). (See Table 7.3.) The prevalence of one complex activity limitation was

TABLE 7.1

Percentage of adults who reported their health as fair or poor, by selected characteristics, selected years 1991–2015

[Data are based on household interviews of a sample of the civilian noninstitutionalized population]

Characteristic	1991[b]	1995[b]	1997	2000	2005	2010	2014	2015
	Percent of persons with fair or poor health							
All ages, age-adjusted[c, d]	10.4	10.6	9.2	9.0	9.2	9.6	8.9	9.2
All ages, crude[d]	10.0	10.1	8.9	8.9	9.3	10.1	9.8	10.1
Age								
Under 18 years	2.6	2.6	2.1	1.7	1.8	2.0	1.6	1.8
Under 6 years	2.7	2.7	1.9	1.5	1.6	1.8	1.3	1.2
6–17 years	2.6	2.5	2.1	1.8	1.9	2.2	1.8	2.1
18–44 years	6.1	6.6	5.3	5.1	5.5	6.3	6.1	6.3
18–24 years	4.8	4.5	3.4	3.3	3.3	3.9	3.7	3.8
25–44 years	6.4	7.2	5.9	5.7	6.3	7.2	7.0	7.2
45–54 years	13.4	13.4	11.7	11.9	11.6	13.3	12.8	13.5
55–64 years	20.7	21.4	18.2	17.9	18.3	19.4	18.4	18.7
65 years and over	29.0	28.3	26.7	26.9	26.6	24.4	21.7	21.8
65–74 years	26.0	25.6	23.1	22.5	23.4	21.2	19.5	19.0
75 years and over	33.6	32.2	31.5	32.1	30.2	28.3	24.9	25.8
Sex[c]								
Male	10.0	10.1	8.8	8.8	8.8	9.2	8.7	8.9
Female	10.8	11.1	9.7	9.3	9.5	10.0	9.2	9.5
Race[c, e]								
White only	9.6	9.7	8.3	8.2	8.6	8.8	8.3	8.5
Black or African American only	16.8	17.2	15.8	14.6	14.3	14.9	13.6	13.6
American Indian or Alaska Native only	18.3	18.7	17.3	17.2	13.2	17.8	14.1	16.6
Asian only	7.8	9.3	7.8	7.4	6.8	8.1	7.3	7.8
Native Hawaiian or other Pacific Islander only	—	—	—	[a]		[a]	[a]	[a]
2 or more races	—	—	—	16.2	14.5	15.6	12.8	14.4
Black or African American; white	—	—	—	14.5[a]	8.3	16.7[a]	11.9	13.7[a]
American Indian or Alaska Native; white	—	—	—	18.7	17.2	19.0	17.6	18.2
Hispanic origin and race[d, e]								
Hispanic or Latino	15.6	15.1	13.0	12.8	13.3	13.1	12.2	12.7
Mexican	17.0	16.7	13.1	12.8	14.3	13.7	13.0	12.7
Not Hispanic or Latino	10.0	10.1	8.9	8.7	8.7	9.2	8.5	8.7
White only	9.1	9.1	8.0	7.9	8.0	8.2	7.7	7.9
Black or African American only	16.8	17.3	15.8	14.6	14.4	14.9	13.6	13.4
Percent of poverty level[c, e]								
Below 100%	22.8	23.7	20.8	19.6	20.4	20.9	19.8	21.2
100%–199%	14.7	15.5	13.9	14.1	14.4	15.2	14.2	14.9
200%–399%	7.9	7.9	8.2	8.4	8.3	8.3	7.9	8.4
400% or more	4.9	4.7	4.1	4.5	4.7	4.3	3.9	4.0
Hispanic origin and race and percent of poverty level[c, e, f]								
Hispanic or Latino:								
Below 100%	23.6	22.7	19.9	18.7	20.2	19.2	18.7	21.3
100%–199%	18.0	16.9	13.5	15.3	15.3	15.6	14.1	14.4
200%–399%	10.3	10.1	10.0	10.3	10.3	10.3	9.4	9.7
400% or more	6.6	4.0	5.7	5.5	7.6	6.4	5.5	5.7
Not Hispanic or Latino:								
White only:								
Below 100%	21.9	22.8	19.7	18.8	20.1	20.9	20.3	20.7
100%–199%	14.0	14.8	13.3	13.4	13.8	14.8	14.1	15.0
200%–399%	7.5	7.3	7.7	7.9	7.9	7.7	7.4	8.0
400% or more	4.7	4.6	3.9	4.2	4.3	4.0	3.5	3.7
Black or African American only:								
Below 100%	25.8	27.7	25.3	23.8	23.3	23.9	21.8	23.3
100%–199%	17.0	19.3	19.2	18.2	17.6	18.3	16.8	17.0
200%–399%	12.0	11.4	12.2	11.7	11.2	11.2	9.8	9.8
400% or more	5.9	6.5	6.1	7.3	7.1	6.8	5.7	6.3

also higher among those aged 65 years and older (31.7%), compared with those aged 18 to 64 years (12.5).

Data from the US Census Bureau's American Community Survey reveal that 35% of adults aged 65 years and older had some sort of difficulty in hearing, vision, cognition, ambulation, self-care, or independent living in 2015.

(See Figure 7.1.) Nearly a quarter (23%) had difficulty ambulating (walking or moving from place to place).

Hospital Utilization and Physician Visits

Adults aged 65 years and older have the highest rates of inpatient hospitalization and the longest average

TABLE 7.1

Percentage of adults who reported their health as fair or poor, by selected characteristics, selected years 1991–2015 [CONTINUED]

[Data are based on household interviews of a sample of the civilian noninstitutionalized population]

Characteristic	1991[b]	1995[b]	1997	2000	2005	2010	2014	2015
				Percent of persons with fair or poor health				
Disability measure among adults 18 years and over[c, g]								
Any basic actions difficulty or complex activity limitation	—	—	27.0	27.6	28.5	28.7	28.8	29.1
Any basic actions difficulty	—	—	27.3	27.7	29.1	28.9	29.1	29.9
Any complex activity limitation	—	—	42.9	45.6	46.3	46.0	47.6	46.3
No disability	—	—	3.4	3.8	3.6	3.5	3.8	3.5
Geographic region[e]								
Northeast	8.3	9.1	8.0	7.6	7.5	7.9	7.2	8.2
Midwest	9.1	9.7	8.1	8.0	8.3	9.0	8.5	8.8
South	13.1	12.3	10.8	10.7	11.0	11.1	10.2	10.0
West	9.7	10.1	8.8	8.8	8.6	9.2	8.6	9.1
Location of residence[e, h]								
Within MSA	9.9	10.1	8.7	8.5	8.7	9.2	8.5	8.8
Outside MSA	11.9	12.6	11.1	11.1	11.2	11.9	11.4	11.8

— Data not available.

[a]Estimates are considered unreliable.

[b]Data prior to 1997 are not strictly comparable with data for later years due to the 1997 questionnaire redesign.

[c]Estimates are age-adjusted to the year 2000 standard population using six age groups: under 18 years, 18–44 years, 45–54 years, 55–64 years, 65–74 years, and 75 years and over. The disability measure is age-adjusted using the five adult age groups.

[d]Includes all other races not shown separately and unknown disability status.

[e]The race groups, white, black, American Indian or Alaska Native, Asian, Native Hawaiian or other Pacific Islander, and 2 or more races, include persons of Hispanic and non-Hispanic origin. Persons of Hispanic origin may be of any race. Starting with 1999 data, race-specific estimates are tabulated according to the 1997 Revisions to the Standards for the Classification of Federal Data on Race and Ethnicity and are not strictly comparable with estimates for earlier years. The five single-race categories plus multiple-race categories shown in the table conform to the 1997 Standards. Starting with 1999 data, race-specific estimates are for persons who reported only one racial group; the category 2 or more races includes persons who reported more than one racial group. Prior to 1999, data were tabulated according to the 1977 Standards with four racial groups, and the Asian only category included Native Hawaiian or other Pacific Islander. Estimates for single-race categories prior to 1999 included persons who reported one race or, if they reported more than one race, identified one race as best representing their race. Starting with 2003 data, race responses of other race and unspecified multiple race were treated as missing, and then race was imputed if these were the only race responses. Almost all persons with a race response of other race were of Hispanic origin.

[f]Percent of poverty level is based on family income and family size and composition using US Census Bureau poverty thresholds. Missing family income data were imputed for 1991 and beyond.

[g]Any basic actions difficulty or complex activity limitation is defined as having one or more of the following limitations or difficulties: movement difficulty, emotional difficulty, sensory (seeing or hearing) difficulty, cognitive difficulty, self-care (activities of daily living or instrumental activities of daily living) limitation, social limitation, or work limitation. Starting with 2007 data, the hearing question, a component of the basic actions difficulty measure, was revised. Consequently, data prior to 2007 are not comparable with data for 2007 and beyond.

[h]MSA is metropolitan statistical area. Starting with 2006 data, MSA status is determined using 2000 census data and the 2000 standards for defining MSAs.

Notes: Standard errors for selected years are available in the spreadsheet version of this table.

SOURCE: "Table 45. Respondent-Assessed Fair-Poor Health Status, by Selected Characteristics: United States, Selected Years 1991–2015," in *Health, United States, 2016: With Chartbook on Long-Term Trends in Health*, National Center for Health Statistics, May 2017, https://www.cdc.gov/nchs/data/hus/2016/045.pdf (accessed October 17, 2017)

---

lengths of stay. In 2015 adults aged 65 years and older were the most likely to have had one or more hospital stays during the preceding year. (See Table 7.4.)

The growing older population also uses more physician services. Visit rates increase with age among adults aged 65 years and older and were nearly three times as high as visit rates for children under the age of 18 years in 2013. (See Table 7.5.) Although women generally make more physician visits than men, the difference practically disappears among older adults.

CHRONIC DISEASES AND CONDITIONS

Chronic diseases are prolonged illnesses such as arthritis, asthma, heart disease, diabetes, and cancer that do not resolve spontaneously and are rarely cured. According to the Centers for Disease Control and Prevention (CDC), in "Chronic Disease Overview" (January 20, 2016, https://www.cdc.gov/chronicdisease/about/multiple-chronic.htm),

three out of four Americans aged 65 years and older have multiple chronic conditions, which last a year or more, require ongoing medical attention, or limit their activities. In 2015 five of the 10 leading causes of death among adults aged 65 years and older were chronic diseases: heart disease, malignant neoplasms (cancer), chronic lower respiratory diseases, cerebrovascular diseases (stroke), and diabetes mellitus (a condition in which there is increased sugar in the blood and urine because the body is unable to use sugar to produce energy). (See Table 7.6.)

Arthritis

The word *arthritis* literally means "joint inflammation," and it is applied to dozens of related diseases known as rheumatic diseases. When a joint (the point where two bones meet) becomes inflamed, swelling, redness, pain, and loss of motion occur. In the most serious forms of the disease, the loss of motion can be physically disabling.

TABLE 7.2

Percentage of adults aged 65 and older with two or more chronic conditions, by sex, 2015

State	Males 65 years and over Number of chronic conditions 2 to 3 Prevalence (%)	Males 65 years and over Number of chronic conditions 4 to 5 Prevalence (%)	Males 65 years and over Number of chronic conditions 6+ Prevalence (%)	Females 65 years and over Number of chronic conditions 0 to 1 Prevalence (%)	Females 65 years and over Number of chronic conditions 2 to 3 Prevalence (%)	Females 65 years and over Number of chronic conditions 4 to 5 Prevalence (%)	Females 65 years and over Number of chronic conditions 6+ Prevalence (%)
National	**28.1**	**21.4**	**15.8**	**30.4**	**31.4**	**21.7**	**16.5**
Alabama	29.2	24.6	18.0	24.6	32.7	24.4	18.3
Alaska	25.5	13.8	7.7	47.7	28.7	14.7	8.9
Arizona	28.3	20.1	12.8	35.5	32.2	20.0	12.3
Arkansas	28.3	21.1	14.3	30.5	32.2	21.6	15.7
California	26.9	19.7	14.2	34.7	30.2	20.3	14.8
Colorado	27.0	15.8	9.6	44.0	30.0	15.9	10.1
Connecticut	30.1	22.8	17.1	28.1	33.0	22.2	16.6
Delaware	31.6	25.9	16.8	25.1	35.4	23.8	15.7
District of Columbia	27.2	18.7	14.0	33.6	30.3	21.4	14.7
Florida	27.3	24.5	20.6	24.0	30.3	24.5	21.2
Georgia	29.0	22.9	15.7	28.3	32.4	23.0	16.3
Hawaii	30.4	21.4	11.4	31.3	34.5	23.2	11.0
Idaho	26.7	16.7	10.0	41.6	30.6	17.5	10.4
Illinois	28.7	21.2	16.3	31.0	31.8	20.8	16.4
Indiana	28.6	21.8	16.9	28.5	31.7	21.9	17.9
Iowa	29.8	19.9	12.7	34.6	33.3	19.9	12.2
Kansas	29.5	20.7	14.3	33.1	32.0	20.4	14.5
Kentucky	27.3	22.5	18.2	24.9	30.8	23.5	20.7
Louisiana	27.7	23.6	18.5	24.7	30.4	24.2	20.7
Maine	28.3	19.4	14.2	34.8	31.7	19.4	14.2
Maryland	29.7	22.8	15.7	28.7	33.1	22.7	15.5
Massachusetts	30.3	22.2	16.6	29.8	32.9	21.1	16.2
Michigan	27.5	21.9	18.6	28.4	30.1	21.9	19.6
Minnesota	25.5	16.7	11.2	40.1	30.5	17.8	11.6
Mississippi	29.0	22.0	15.8	27.4	32.3	22.9	17.5
Missouri	27.7	21.2	16.4	30.1	30.9	21.6	17.3
Montana	26.3	15.2	9.0	44.3	29.8	16.1	9.7
Nebraska	27.7	18.8	13.2	37.8	31.1	18.6	12.5
Nevada	25.9	19.2	12.8	34.9	30.8	20.2	14.0
New Hampshire	30.2	19.0	12.7	35.8	32.7	18.6	12.9
New Jersey	27.9	25.2	20.0	25.6	31.1	24.4	18.8
New Mexico	27.2	17.6	10.6	37.6	31.6	19.3	11.6
New York	27.4	23.2	18.3	27.8	30.6	23.3	18.3
North Carolina	30.2	22.0	15.0	28.3	33.4	22.4	15.9
North Dakota	27.9	19.4	13.0	35.7	31.3	19.9	13.1
Ohio	28.2	21.8	17.1	28.3	31.3	22.4	18.0
Oklahoma	27.4	22.0	16.9	29.3	30.2	22.1	18.4
Oregon	27.7	16.5	9.8	40.6	31.8	17.4	10.3
Pennsylvania	29.2	22.8	17.5	26.9	32.5	22.9	17.7
Puerto Rico	22.9	23.9	17.4	22.8	24.6	29.5	23.0
Rhode Island	29.2	23.0	17.1	25.8	33.3	23.1	17.8
South Carolina	31.3	23.1	14.5	27.7	35.2	22.8	14.3
South Dakota	26.7	17.9	12.0	37.6	31.8	18.8	11.8
Tennessee	28.6	22.1	16.3	28.5	31.7	22.3	17.5
Texas	26.6	21.5	17.3	29.5	29.3	22.1	19.1
Utah	27.4	17.6	10.5	42.1	30.6	17.0	10.4
Vermont	30.0	16.5	9.8	41.8	32.3	16.1	9.8
Virgin Islands	29.0	12.4	4.4	43.2	37.2	15.5	4.1
Virginia	30.8	21.7	14.0	30.7	33.9	21.5	14.0
Washington	27.9	17.4	10.9	41.1	30.5	17.4	11.0
West Virginia	27.2	21.9	17.4	23.5	30.9	24.6	20.9
Wisconsin	28.4	19.1	13.1	35.2	31.7	19.4	13.8
Wyoming	25.5	14.0	8.1	47.2	29.2	14.9	8.7
Unknown	9.1	5.5	2.9	77.4	11.7	7.0	3.9

SOURCE: Adapted from "Multiple Chronic Conditions Prevalence State Table: Male Fee-for-Service Beneficiaries by Age, 2015," in *Multiple Chronic Conditions*, Centers for Medicare & Medicaid Services, May 10, 2017, https://www.cms.gov/Research-Statistics-Data-and-Systems/Statistics-Trends-and-Reports/Chronic-Conditions/MCC_Main.html (accessed October 24, 2017).

More than 100 types of arthritis have been identified, but four major types affect large numbers of older Americans:

• Osteoarthritis—the most common type, generally affects people as they grow older. Sometimes called degenerative arthritis, it causes the breakdown of bones and cartilage (connective tissue that attaches to bones) and pain and stiffness in the fingers, knees, feet, hips, and back. In "Osteoarthritis" (October 31, 2017, https://emedicine.medscape.com/article/330487-overview),

TABLE 7.3

Activity limitations, by age group, selected years 1997–2015

[Data are based on household interviews of a sample of the civilian noninstitutionalized population]

Characteristic	18 years and over				18–64 years				65 years and over			
	1997	2000	2010ᵃ	2015ᵃ	1997	2000	2010ᵃ	2015ᵃ	1997	2000	2010ᵃ	2015ᵃ
	Number, in millions											
At least one basic actions difficulty or complex activity limitationᵇ·ᶜ	60.9	59.0	73.7	77.0	41.3	39.3	50.7	50.5	19.6	19.7	23.0	26.5
At least one basic actions difficultyᵇ	56.7	55.2	69.2	72.6	38.1	36.4	47.2	47.1	18.6	18.7	22.0	25.4
At least one complex activity limitationᶜ	29.0	27.2	35.0	38.6	18.1	16.7	22.9	24.2	11.0	10.5	12.1	14.4
	At least one basic actions difficulty or complex activity limitationᵇ·ᶜ Percent											
Total, age-adjustedᵈ·ᵉ	32.5	29.9	31.9	31.5	—	—	—	—	—	—	—	—
Total, crudeᵈ	31.8	29.5	32.8	33.2	25.8	23.5	27.1	26.9	62.2	60.8	61.7	59.8
	At least one basic actions difficultyᵇ Percent											
Total, age-adjustedᵈ·ᵉ	30.1	27.9	29.9	29.6	—	—	—	—	—	—	—	—
Total, crudeᵈ	29.4	27.5	30.8	31.2	23.6	21.7	25.1	25.1	58.8	58.1	59.3	57.5
	At least one complex activity limitationᶜ Percent											
Total, age-adjustedᵈ·ᵉ	15.6	13.7	14.9	15.1	—	—	—	—	—	—	—	—
Total, crudeᵈ	15.1	13.4	15.5	16.1	11.2	9.8	12.1	12.5	35.1	32.0	32.3	31.7

— Category not applicable.

ᵃStarting with 2007 data (shown in spreadsheet version), the hearing question, a component of the basic actions difficulty measure, was revised. Consequently, data for basic actions difficulty prior to 2007 are not comparable with 2007 data and beyond.

ᵇA basic actions difficulty is defined as having difficulties in one or more of the following areas of functioning: movement, emotional, sensory (seeing or hearing), or cognitive. Starting with 2007 data, the hearing question, a component of basic actions difficulty, was revised. Consequently, data prior to 2007 are not comparable with data for 2007 and beyond.

ᶜA complex activity limitation is defined as having one or more of the following limitations: maintaining independance (performing activities of daily living or instrumental activities of daily living), socializing, or working.

ᵈIncludes all other races not shown separately.

ᵉEstimates are age-adjusted to the year 2000 standard population using five age groups: 18–44 years, 45–54 years, 55–64 years, 65–74 years, and 75 years and over.

SOURCE: Adapted from "Table 42. Disability Measures among Adults Aged 18 and over, by Selected Characteristics: United States, Selected Years 1997–2015," in *Health, United States, 2016: With Chartbook on Long-Term Trends in Health*, National Center for Health Statistics, May 2017, https://www.cdc.gov/nchs/data/hus/2016/042.pdf (accessed October 24, 2017)

FIGURE 7.1

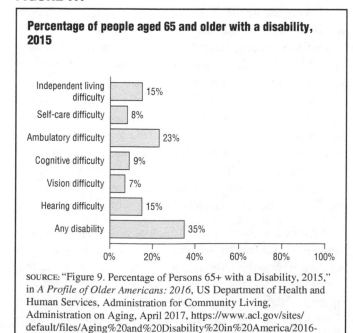

Percentage of people aged 65 and older with a disability, 2015

SOURCE: "Figure 9. Percentage of Persons 65+ with a Disability, 2015," in *A Profile of Older Americans: 2016*, US Department of Health and Human Services, Administration for Community Living, Administration on Aging, April 2017, https://www.acl.gov/sites/default/files/Aging%20and%20Disability%20in%20America/2016-Profile.pdf (accessed October 13, 2017)

Carlos J. Lozada of the University of Miami reports that more than 30 million Americans are affected by osteoarthritis, and more than half of adults aged 65 years and older are affected.

- Fibromyalgia—affects the muscles and connective tissues and causes widespread pain, as well as fatigue, sleep problems, and stiffness. Fibromyalgia also causes "tender points" that are more sensitive to pain than other areas of the body. The National Fibromyalgia Association estimates in "Prevalence" (2017, http://www.fmaware.org/about-fibromyalgia/prevalence) that 10 million Americans suffer from this condition. An estimated 8% of adults aged 80 years and older have fibromyalgia.

- Rheumatoid arthritis—an inflammatory form of arthritis caused by a flaw in the body's immune system. The result is inflammation and swelling in the joint lining, followed by damage to bone and cartilage in the hands, wrists, feet, knees, ankles, shoulders, or elbows. The Arthritis Foundation indicates in "What Is Rheumatoid Arthritis?" (2018, https://www.arthritis.org/about-arthritis/

TABLE 7.4

Hospital stays in the past year, by age, 1997–2015

[Data are based on household interviews of a sample of the civilian noninstitutionalized population]

Characteristic	One or more hospital stays[a]					Two or more hospital stays[a]				
	1997	2000	2010	2014	2015	1997	2000	2010	2014	2015
	Percent									
1 year and over, age-adjusted[b,c]	7.8	7.6	7.0	6.4	6.5	1.8	1.8	1.8	1.6	1.7
1 year and over, crude[b]	7.7	7.5	7.2	6.8	6.9	1.7	1.8	1.9	1.7	1.8
Age										
1–17 years	2.8	2.5	2.4	2.0	2.1	0.5	0.4	0.5	0.4	0.3
1–5 years	3.9	3.8	3.4	3.0	3.1	0.7	0.7	0.6	0.7	*0.4
6–17 years	2.3	1.9	1.9	1.6	1.7	0.4	0.3	0.5	0.3	0.3
18–44 years	7.4	7.0	6.3	5.8	5.8	1.2	1.1	1.3	1.1	1.2
18–24 years	7.9	7.0	5.7	4.6	4.5	1.3	1.1	1.1	0.9	0.8
25–44 years	7.3	7.0	6.6	6.2	6.3	1.2	1.2	1.3	1.1	1.3
45–64 years	8.2	8.4	8.3	7.4	7.7	2.2	2.2	2.5	2.3	2.3
45–54 years	6.9	7.3	7.3	6.1	6.4	1.7	1.8	2.1	1.9	1.8
55–64 years	10.2	10.0	9.5	8.7	9.2	2.9	2.8	2.9	2.6	2.7
65 years and over	18.0	18.2	16.1	15.3	15.2	5.4	5.8	4.9	4.3	4.9
65–74 years	16.1	16.1	13.6	13.8	12.8	4.8	4.9	3.8	4.0	4.0
75 years and over	20.4	20.7	19.0	17.5	18.8	6.2	6.8	6.2	4.8	6.2
75–84 years	19.8	20.1	18.3	16.1	17.3	6.1	6.2	6.1	4.2	5.7
85 years and over	22.8	23.4	20.8	20.9	22.5	6.2	9.0	6.6	6.3	7.3

[a]These estimates exclude hospitalizations for institutionalized persons and those who died while hospitalized, because they are outside the scope of this survey.
[b]Includes all other races not shown separately, unknown health insurance status, and unknown disability status.
[c]Estimates are for persons 1 year of age and over and are age-adjusted to the year 2000 standard population using six age groups: 1–17 years, 18–44 years, 45–54 years, 55–64 years, 65–74 years, and 75 years and over.

SOURCE: Adapted from "Table 81. Persons with Hospital Stays in the Past Year, by Selected Characteristics: United States, Selected Years 1997–2015," in *Health, United States, 2016: With Chartbook on Long-Term Trends in Health*, National Center for Health Statistics, May 2017, https://www.cdc.gov/nchs/data/hus/2016/081.pdf (accessed October 24, 2017)

types/rheumatoid-arthritis/what-is-rheumatoid-arthritis
.php) that rheumatoid arthritis affects approximately
1.5 million Americans.

- Gout—inflammation of a joint caused by an accumulation of a natural substance, uric acid, in the joint, usually the big toe, knee, or wrist. The uric acid forms crystals in the affected joint, causing severe pain and swelling. This form affects more men than women, claiming about a million sufferers.

PREVALENCE. Arthritis is a common problem and is the leading cause of disability in the United States. In "Arthritis: National Statistics" (October 25, 2017, https://www.cdc.gov/arthritis/data_statistics/national-statistics.html), the CDC reports that 54.4 million Americans (22.7% of adults) have been diagnosed with arthritis and that 23.7 million adults have activity limitations that are attributable to the disease. The CDC projects that the total number of people with arthritis will increase to 78 million by 2040. (See Figure 7.2.) At that point, about 34.6 million people with arthritis are projected to have activity limitations attributable to the disease.

Osteoporosis

Osteoporosis is a skeletal disorder characterized by compromised bone strength, which predisposes affected individuals to increased risk of fracture, especially of the hip, spine, and wrist, but any bone can be affected. Although some bone loss occurs naturally with advancing age, the stooped posture (kyphosis) and loss of height (greater than 1 to 2 inches [2.5 to 5.1 cm]) that are experienced by many older adults result from vertebral fractures caused by osteoporosis.

According to the National Osteoporosis Foundation, in "What Is Osteoporosis and What Causes It?" (2017, https://www.nof.org/patients/what-is-osteoporosis/), about 54 million Americans have osteoporosis and have low bone mass, which means they are considered to be at risk of developing the condition. The National Osteoporosis Foundation reports that one out of two women and one out of four men over the age of 50 will have an osteoporosis-related fracture in their remaining lifetime. The aging of the population and the historic lack of focus on bone health may together cause the number of fractures due to osteoporosis in the United States to exceed 3 million by 2025.

One of the goals of the treatment of osteoporosis is to maintain bone health by preventing bone loss and by building new bone. Another goal is to minimize the risk and impact of falls because they can cause fractures. Figure 7.3 shows the pyramid of prevention and treatment of osteoporosis. At its base is nutrition (with adequate intake of calcium, vitamin D, and other minerals), physical exercise, and preventive measures to reduce the risk of

TABLE 7.5

Visits to physician offices, hospital outpatient departments, and emergency departments, by age, selected years 2000–13

[Data are based on reporting by a sample of office-based physicians, hospital outpatient departments, and hospital emergency departments]

Age, sex, and race	All places[a]				Physician offices			
	2000	2010	2011	2013[b]	2000	2010	2011	2013[b]
Age				Number of visits, in thousands				
Total	**1,014,848**	**1,239,387**	**1,249,047**	—	**823,542**	**1,008,802**	**987,029**	**922,596**
Under 18 years	212,165	246,228	263,387	—	163,459	191,500	206,285	151,036
18–44 years	315,774	342,797	333,427	—	243,011	261,941	239,224	224,256
45–64 years	255,894	352,001	353,591	—	216,783	296,385	285,784	282,109
45–54 years	142,233	171,039	173,334	—	119,474	140,819	136,429	131,013
55–64 years	113,661	180,962	180,258	—	97,309	155,566	149,355	151,096
65 years and over	231,014	298,362	298,642	—	200,289	258,976	255,736	265,195
65–74 years	116,505	151,075	151,970	—	102,447	132,201	131,233	141,507
75 years and over	114,510	147,287	146,672	—	97,842	126,775	124,503	123,688
				Number of visits per 100 persons				
Total, age-adjusted[c]	**374**	**401**	**400**	—	**304**	**325**	**314**	**285**
Total, crude	**370**	**408**	**408**	—	**300**	**332**	**322**	**297**
Under 18 years	293	331	357	—	226	257	280	206
18–44 years	291	310	302	—	224	237	216	201
45–64 years	422	441	431	—	358	371	349	343
45–54 years	385	388	392	—	323	320	309	303
55–64 years	481	505	477	—	412	434	395	387
65 years and over	706	767	745	—	612	666	638	611
65–74 years	656	713	683	—	577	624	590	566
75 years and over	766	831	822	—	654	715	698	672
Sex and age								
Male, age-adjusted[c]	325	350	354	—	261	283	280	250
Male, crude	314	350	356	—	251	283	281	256
Under 18 years	302	340	372	—	231	262	294	206
18–44 years	203	205	208	—	148	151	145	137
45–54 years	316	324	322	—	260	265	250	263
55–64 years	428	460	430	—	367	396	351	359
65–74 years	614	680	655	—	539	597	566	530
75 years and over	771	871	869	—	670	760	758	679
Female, age-adjusted[c]	420	452	444	—	345	367	348	318
Female, crude	424	464	457	—	348	379	361	336
Under 18 years	285	322	341	—	221	252	265	206
18–44 years	377	415	393	—	298	323	286	263
45–54 years	451	450	459	—	384	372	364	341
55–64 years	529	546	520	—	453	469	436	413
65–74 years	692	741	707	—	609	647	611	598
75 years and over	763	804	790	—	645	685	657	667

— Data not available.

[a]All places includes visits to physician offices and hospital outpatient and emergency departments.

[b]In 2012 and 2013, data for all places and physician offices exclude visits to community health centers; in 2006–2011, data for all places and physician offices include visits to community health centers (2%–3% of visits to physician offices in 2006–2011 were to community health centers). Prior to 2006, visits to community health centers were not included in the survey.

[c]Estimates are age-adjusted to the year 2000 standard population using six age groups: under 18 years, 18–44 years, 45–54 years, 55–64 years, 65–74 years, and 75 years and over.

Notes: Rates for 1995–2000 were computed using 1990-based postcensal estimates of the civilian noninstitutionalized population as of July 1, adjusted for net underenumeration using the 1990 National Population Adjustment Matrix from the US Census Bureau. For 2001–2010 data, rates were computed using 2000-based postcensal estimates of the civilian noninstitutionalized population as of July 1. For 2011 data and beyond, rates were computed using 2010-based postcensal estimates of the civilian noninstitutionalized population as of July 1. Rates using the civilian noninstitutionalized population will be overestimated to the extent that visits by institutionalized persons are counted in the numerator (for example, hospital emergency department visits by nursing home residents) but institutionalized persons are omitted from the denominator (the civilian noninstitutionalized population). Starting with *Health, United States, 2005*, data for physician offices for 2001 and beyond use a revised weighting scheme.

SOURCE: Adapted from "Table 76. Visits to Physician Offices, Hospital Outpatient Departments, and Hospital Emergency Departments, by Age, Sex, and Race: United States, Selected Years 2000–2013," in *Health, United States, 2016: With Chartbook on Long-Term Trends in Health*, National Center for Health Statistics, May 2017, https://www.cdc.gov/nchs/data/hus/2016/076.pdf (accessed October 24, 2017)

falls. The second layer of the pyramid involves identifying and treating diseases that can cause osteoporosis, such as thyroid disease. The peak of the pyramid involves drug therapy for osteoporosis. There are two primary types of drugs used to treat osteoporosis. Antiresorptive agents act to reduce bone loss, and anabolic agents are drugs that build bone. Antiresorptive therapies include use of bisphosphonates, estrogen, selective estrogen receptor modulators, and calcitonin. They reduce bone loss, stabilize the architecture of the bone, and decrease bone turnover (the continuous process of remodeling in which bone is lost through resorption and new bone is formed).

Diabetes

Diabetes is a disease that affects the body's use of food, causing blood glucose (sugar levels in the blood) to

TABLE 7.6

Leading causes of death and numbers of deaths, by age, 1980 and 2015

[Data are based on death certificates]

Age and rank order	1980		2015	
	Cause of death	Deaths	Cause of death	Deaths
65 years and over				
Rank	All causes	1,341,848	All causes	1,992,283
1	Diseases of heart	595,406	Diseases of heart	507,138
2	Malignant neoplasms	258,389	Malignant neoplasms	419,389
3	Cerebrovascular diseases	146,417	Chronic lower respiratory diseases[a, b]	131,804
4	Pneumonia and influenza[a]	45,512	Cerebrovascular diseases	120,156
5	Chronic obstructive pulmonary diseases[b]	43,587	Alzheimer's disease	109,495
6	Atherosclerosis	28,081	Diabetes mellitus[c]	56,142
7	Diabetes mellitus	25,216	Unintentional injuries	51,395
8	Unintentional injuries	24,844	Influenza and pneumonia	48,774
9	Nephritis, nephrotic syndrome, and nephrosis	12,968	Nephritis, nephrotic syndrome, and nephrosis[c]	41,258
10	Chronic liver disease and cirrhosis	9,519	Septicemia	30,817

[a]Starting with 1999 data, the rules for selecting CLRD and Pneumonia as the underlying cause of death changed, resulting in an increase in the number of deaths for CLRD and a decrease in the number of deaths for pneumonia. Therefore, trend data for these two causes of death should be interpreted with caution.
[b]Between 1998 and 1999, the cause of death title for Chronic obstructive pulmonary diseases in the ICD–9 was renamed to Chronic lower respiratory diseases (CLRD) in ICD–10.
[c]Starting with 2011 data, the rules for selecting renal failure as the underlying cause of death were changed, affecting the number of deaths in the nephritis, nephrotic syndrome, and nephrosis and diabetes categories. These changes directly affect deaths with mention of renal failure and other associated conditions, such as diabetes mellitus with renal complications. The result is a decrease in the number of deaths for nephritis, nephrotic syndrome, and nephrosis and an increase in the number of deaths for diabetes mellitus. Therefore, trend data for these two causes of death should be interpreted with caution.

SOURCE: Adapted from "Table 20. Leading Causes of Death and Numbers of Deaths, by Age: United States, 1980 and 2015," in *Health, United States, 2016: With Chartbook on Long-Term Trends in Health*, National Center for Health Statistics, May 2017, https://www.cdc.gov/nchs/data/hus/2016/020.pdf (accessed October 24, 2017)

FIGURE 7.2

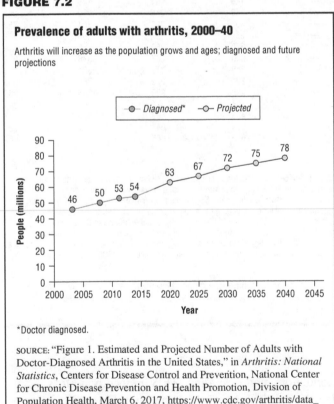

Prevalence of adults with arthritis, 2000–40

Arthritis will increase as the population grows and ages; diagnosed and future projections

*Doctor diagnosed.

SOURCE: "Figure 1. Estimated and Projected Number of Adults with Doctor-Diagnosed Arthritis in the United States," in *Arthritis: National Statistics*, Centers for Disease Control and Prevention, National Center for Chronic Disease Prevention and Health Promotion, Division of Population Health, March 6, 2017, https://www.cdc.gov/arthritis/data_statistics/national-statistics.html (accessed October 24, 2017)

the pancreas does not manufacture enough insulin, and in another type (noninsulin-dependent, or type 2), the body has insulin but cannot use the insulin effectively (this latter condition is called insulin resistance). When insulin is either absent or ineffective, glucose cannot get into the cells to be used for energy. Instead, the unused glucose builds up in the bloodstream and circulates through the kidneys. If the blood-glucose level rises high enough, the excess glucose "spills" over into the urine, causing frequent urination. This leads to an increased feeling of thirst as the body tries to compensate for the fluid that is lost through urination.

Type 2 diabetes is most often seen in adults. In type 2 diabetes the pancreas produces insulin, but it is not used effectively, and the body resists responding to it. Heredity is a predisposing factor in the genesis of diabetes, but because the pancreas continues to produce insulin in people suffering from type 2 diabetes, the disease is considered to be more of a problem of insulin resistance, in which the body is not using the hormone efficiently.

Complications can threaten the lives of diabetics. The healing process of the body is slowed and there is an increased risk of infection. Diabetics are at greater risk of heart disease; circulatory problems, especially in the legs, which are sometimes severe enough to require surgery or even amputation; diabetic retinopathy, a condition that can cause blindness; kidney disease that may require dialysis; and dental problems. Close attention to preventive health care, such as regular eye, dental, and

become too high. People with diabetes can convert food to glucose, but there is a problem with insulin. In one type of diabetes (insulin-dependent diabetes, or type 1),

FIGURE 7.3

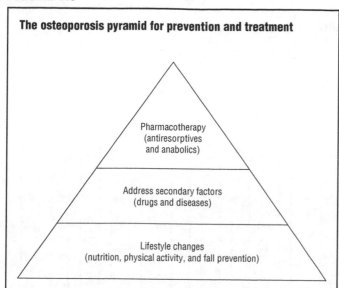

The osteoporosis pyramid for prevention and treatment

Pharmacotherapy
(antiresorptives
and anabolics)

Address secondary factors
(drugs and diseases)

Lifestyle changes
(nutrition, physical activity, and fall prevention)

Note:
The base of the pyramid: The first step in the prevention and treatment of osteoporosis and the prevention of fractures is to build a foundation of nutrition and lifestyle measures that maximize bone health. The diet should not only be adequate in calcium and vitamin D, but should have a healthy balance of other nutrients. A weight-bearing exercise program should be developed. Cigarette smoking and excessive alcohol use must be avoided. In the older individual, at high risk for fractures, the changes in lifestyle would include a plan not only to maximize physical activity, but also to minimize the risk of falls. The use of hip protectors can be considered in some high-risk patients. Diseases that increase the risk of falls by causing visual impairment, postural hypotension (a drop in blood pressure on standing, which leads to dizziness), or poor balance should be treated. Drugs that cause bone loss or increase the risk of falls should be avoided or given at the lowest effective dose.
The second level of the pyramid: The next step is to identify and treat diseases that produce secondary osteoporosis or aggravate primary osteoporosis. These measures are the foundation upon which specific pharmacotherapy is built and should never be forgotten.
The third level of the pyramid: If there is sufficiently high risk of fracture to warrant pharmacotherapy, the patient is usually started on antiresorptives. Anabolic agents are used in individuals in whom antiresorptive therapy is not adequate to prevent bone loss or fractures.

SOURCE: "Figure 9-1. The Osteoporosis Pyramid for Prevention and Treatment," in *Bone Health and Osteoporosis: A Report of the Surgeon General*, US Department of Health and Human Services, Public Health Service, Office of the Surgeon General, October 14, 2004, http://www.ncbi.nlm.nih.gov/books/NBK45501/ (accessed October 24, 2017)

foot examinations and control of blood sugar levels, can prevent or delay some of the consequences of diabetes.

The relatively recent rise in type 2 diabetes is in part attributed to rising obesity among adults. Between 1997 and 2017 the percentage of adults aged 18 years and older diagnosed with diabetes more than doubled from 5.1% to 10.5%. (See Figure 7.4.) The NCHS indicates in *Early Release of Selected Estimates Based on Data from the National Health Interview Survey, January–March 2017* (September 2017, https://www.cdc.gov/nchs/data/nhis/earlyrelease/Earlyrelease201709_14.pdf) that of all the adult age groups in 2017, the highest rate of diagnosed diabetes was among adults aged 65 years and older (21.3%). (See Figure 7.5.) Nearly a quarter (24.2%) of men and 19% of women over age 65 had been diagnosed with diabetes as of 2017.

Prostate Problems

Prostate problems typically occur after age 50. There are three common prostate disorders: prostatitis (inflammation of the prostate gland), benign prostatic hyperplasia (noncancerous enlargement of the prostate), and prostate cancer. Prostatitis causes painful or difficult urination and frequently occurs in younger men. According to the National Institute of Diabetes and Digestive and Kidney Diseases, in "Prostate Enlargement (Benign Prostatic Hyperplasia)" (September 2014, https://www.niddk.nih.gov/health-information/urologic-diseases/prostate-problems/prostate-enlargement-benign-prostatic-hyperplasia), about 50% of men between the ages of 51 and 60 and up to 90% of men aged 80 years and older have benign prostatic hyperplasia.

Prostate cancer is the second-most common cause of cancer death after lung cancer in American men, and the risk of developing the disease increases with age. Table 7.7 shows the percentage of men that will develop prostate cancer over different periods, based on the man's current age. For example, 5.8% of men who were 60 years old in 2010–12 will develop prostate cancer sometime during the next decade. This means that five or six out of every 100 men who were 60 years old in 2010–12 will be diagnosed with prostate cancer by age 70.

The American Cancer Society reports in *Cancer Facts and Figures, 2017* (2017, https://www.cancer.org/content/dam/cancer-org/research/cancer-facts-and-statistics/annual-cancer-facts-and-figures/2017/cancer-facts-and-figures-2017.pdf) that an estimated 161,360 men were diagnosed with prostate cancer in 2017, and 26,730 men died from it. When diagnosed and treated early, prostate cancer is generally not life threatening because it progresses slowly and remains localized for a long time. As a result, many men who are diagnosed late in life do not die from this disease.

Incontinence

Urinary incontinence is the uncontrollable loss of urine that is so severe that it has social or hygienic consequences. Bowel incontinence refers to accidental leakage of mucus, liquid stool, or solid stool. In *Prevalence of Incontinence among Older Americans* (June 2014, https://www.cdc.gov/nchs/data/series/sr_03/sr03_036.pdf), Yelena Gorina et al. of the CDC report that about half of adults aged 65 years and older suffer from urinary and/or bowel incontinence. The problem is more common in women than in men, although it affects men of all ages. Incontinence can lead to many complications. For example, if untreated it increases the risk of developing serious bladder and kidney infections, skin rashes, and pressure sores.

Age-related changes affect the ability to control urination. The maximum capacity of urine that the bladder can hold diminishes, as does the ability to postpone

FIGURE 7.4

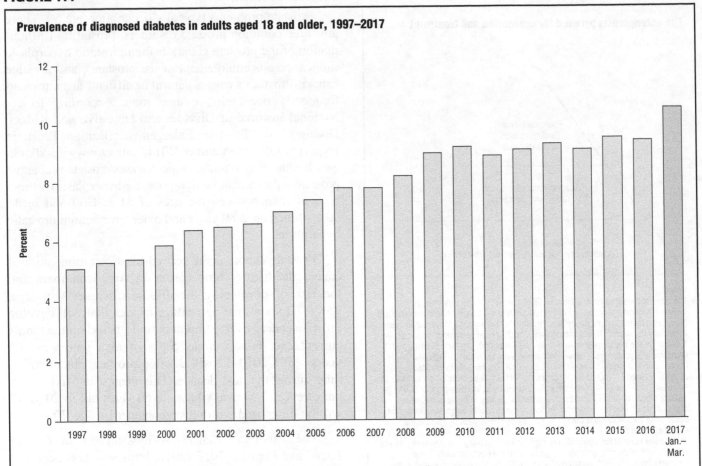

Prevalence of diagnosed diabetes in adults aged 18 and older, 1997–2017

Notes: Data are based on household interviews of a sample of the civilian noninstitutionalized population. Prevalence of diagnosed diabetes is based on self–report of ever having been diagnosed with diabetes by a doctor or other health professional. Persons reporting "borderline" diabetes status and women reporting diabetes only during pregnancy were not coded as having diabetes in the analyses. The analyses exclude persons with unknown diabetes status (about 0.1% of respondents each year).

SOURCE: "Figure 14.1. Prevalence of Diagnosed Diabetes among Adults Aged 18 and over: United States, 1997–March 2017," in *Early Release of Selected Estimates Based on Data from the National Health Interview Survey, January–March 2017*, Centers for Disease Control and Prevention, National Center for Health Statistics, September 2017, https://www.cdc.gov/nchs/data/nhis/earlyrelease/Earlyrelease201709_14.pdf (accessed October 24, 2017)

urination when a person feels the urge to urinate. As people age, the rate of urine flow out of the bladder and through the urethra slows, and the volume of urine remaining in the bladder after urination is finished increases. In women, the urethra shortens and its lining becomes thinner as the level of estrogen declines during menopause, decreasing the ability of the urinary sphincter to close tightly. Among older men, the prostate gland enlarges, sometimes blocking the flow of urine through the urethra.

Along with age, the risk factors for bowel incontinence include chronic diarrhea, inadequate fiber and water intake, and chronic constipation, diabetes, stroke, neurologic and psychiatric conditions, cognitive impairment, and mobility impairment as well as certain medications. Figure 7.6 shows the percentage of noninstitutionalized men and women aged 65 years and older that suffer from urinary and bowel incontinence.

Although incontinence is common, highly treatable, and frequently curable, it is underdiagnosed and often untreated because sufferers do not seek treatment. Many older adults are fearful, embarrassed, or incorrectly assume that incontinence is a normal consequence of growing old. The disorder exacts a serious emotional toll; sufferers are often homebound, isolated, or depressed and are more likely to report their health as fair to poor than their peers. Incontinence may lead to institutionalization because many of those afflicted have some activity limitations and because incontinence is difficult for caregivers to manage.

Malnutrition

The older population is vulnerable to nutrition-related health problems. As people age, their energy needs decline, and it is vital for them to consume nutrient-dense foods in a lower calorie diet. According to the National Resource Center on Nutrition, Physical Activity, and Aging, in "Malnutrition and Older Americans" (2018, http://nutrition.fiu.edu/aging_network/malfact2.asp), 35% to 50% of older adults in long-term care facilities and up to 65% of older adults in hospitals are at risk for malnutrition.

FIGURE 7.5

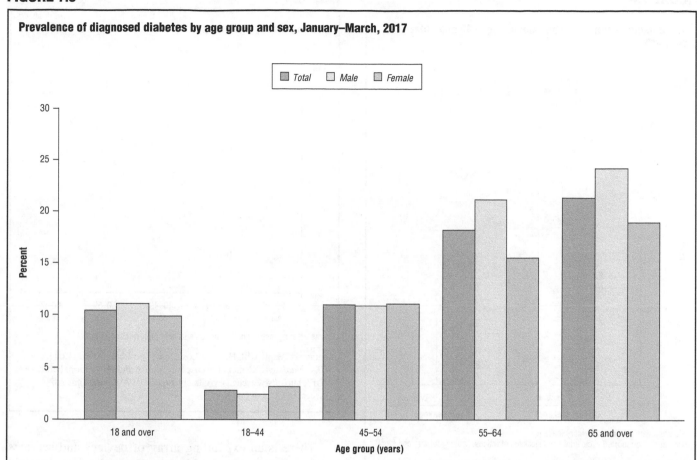

Prevalence of diagnosed diabetes by age group and sex, January–March, 2017

Notes: Data are based on household interviews of a sample of the civilian noninstitutionalized population. Prevalence of diagnosed diabetes is based on self-report of ever having been diagnosed with diabetes by a doctor or other health professional. Persons reporting "borderline" diabetes status and women reporting diabetes only during pregnancy were not coded as having diabetes in the analyses. The analyses exclude the 0.1% of persons with unknown diabetes status.

SOURCE: "Figure 14.2. Prevalence of Diagnosed Diabetes among Adults Aged 18 and over, by Age Group and Sex: United States, January–March 2017," in *Early Release of Selected Estimates Based on Data from the National Health Interview Survey, January–March 2017*, Centers for Disease Control and Prevention, National Center for Health Statistics, September 2017, https://www.cdc.gov/nchs/data/nhis/earlyrelease/Earlyrelease201709_14.pdf (accessed October 24, 2017)

TABLE 7.7

Percentage of men who develop prostate cancer over 10-, 20-, and 30-year intervals by their current age, 2010–12

Current age	10 years	20 years	30 years
30	0.01	0.32	2.31
40	0.31	2.33	7.47
50	2.09	7.41	12.50
60	5.84	11.43	13.50
70	6.91	9.46	N/A

SOURCE: "Percent of US Men Who Develop Prostate Cancer over 10-, 20-, and 30-Year Intervals according to Their Current Age, 2010–2012," in *Prostate Cancer Risk by Age*, Centers for Disease Control and Prevention, Division of Cancer Prevention and Control, December 15, 2015, https://www.cdc.gov/cancer/prostate/statistics/age.htm (accessed October 24, 2017)

An estimated 1 million homebound older adults are also at risk for malnutrition.

Older adults' nutrition may be affected by many factors, including loneliness, depression, a cognitive disorder, poor appetite, or a lack of transportation. An older adult may forgo meal preparation when there is no longer someone else to cook for or eat with, and a bereaved or frail older adult may not have the stamina or motivation to shop or cook. Malnutrition may also be the result of poverty. When faced with a fixed income and competing needs, older adults may be forced to choose between buying food or the prescription medications they need.

Hearing Loss

There are many causes of hearing loss, the most common being age-related changes in the ear's mechanism. Hearing loss is a common problem among older adults and can seriously compromise quality of life. People suffering from hearing loss may withdraw from social contact and are sometimes misdiagnosed as cognitively impaired or mentally ill. The National Institute on Deafness and Other Communication Disorders (NIDCD; one of the National Institutes of Health) reports in "Quick

FIGURE 7.6

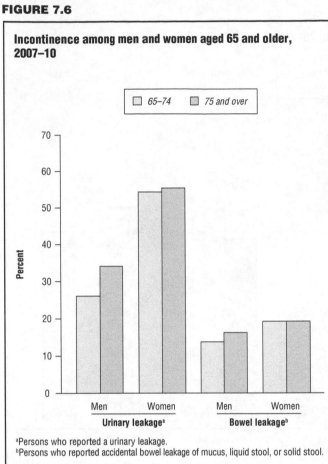

Incontinence among men and women aged 65 and older, 2007–10

aPersons who reported a urinary leakage.
bPersons who reported accidental bowel leakage of mucus, liquid stool, or solid stool.

SOURCE: Yelena Gorina et al., "Figure 2. Incontinence among Noninstitutionalized Persons Aged 65 and over, by Age and Sex: National Health and Nutrition Examination Survey, 2007–2010," in "Prevalence of Incontinence among Older Americans, *Vital and Health Statistics*, vol. 3, no. 23, June 2014, https://www.cdc.gov/nchs/data/series/sr_03/sr03_036.pdf (accessed October 24, 2017)

FIGURE 7.7

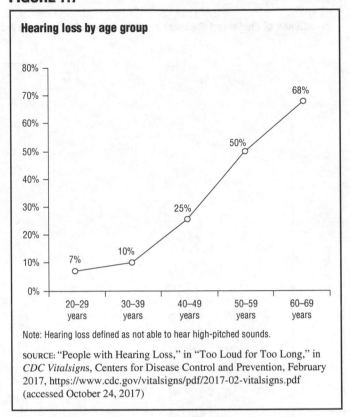

Hearing loss by age group

Note: Hearing loss defined as not able to hear high-pitched sounds.

SOURCE: "People with Hearing Loss," in "Too Loud for Too Long," in *CDC Vitalsigns*, Centers for Disease Control and Prevention, February 2017, https://www.cdc.gov/vitalsigns/pdf/2017-02-vitalsigns.pdf (accessed October 24, 2017)

Statistics about Hearing" (December 15, 2016, https://www.nidcd.nih.gov/health/statistics/quick-statistics-hearing) that the prevalence of disabling hearing loss increases with age, from 8.5% of adults aged 55 to 64 years, to 25% of those aged 65 to 74 years, and to 50% of those aged 75 years and older. The CDC finds even higher percentages of people with hearing loss. Figure 7.7 shows the percentages of adults by age group who are unable to hear high-pitched sounds.

In "Association of Hearing Loss with Hospitalization and Burden of Disease in Older Adults" (*Journal of the American Medical Association*, vol. 309, no. 22, June 12, 2013), Dane J. Genther et al. find that compared with older adults with normal hearing, older adults with hearing loss were more likely to have risk factors for heart disease and stroke. Those with hearing loss (23.8%) were more likely than those with normal hearing (18.7%) to have been hospitalized during the prior year and had more hospitalizations (1.52 on average, compared with 1.27).

There is an expanding array of devices and services to mitigate the effects of hearing loss. Hearing-impaired people may benefit from high-tech hearing aids, amplifiers for doorbells and telephones, infrared amplifiers, and even companion dogs that are trained to respond to sounds on behalf of their owner.

Medicare does not cover routine hearing examinations, hearing aids, or exams for fitting hearing aids for older adults but does cover diagnostic hearing exams ordered by a physician or other health care provider. The National Institutes of Health explains that a wide range of hearing aid technologies is available. Digital hearing aids, which require sophisticated fittings, cost from $1,500 to more than $5,000 each. The NIDCD observes that although most health insurance plans do not cover hearing aids, some nonprofit organizations provide financial assistance for hearing aids.

Vision Changes

Almost no one escapes age-related changes in vision. Over time it becomes increasingly difficult to read small print or thread a needle at the usual distance. For many older adults, night vision declines. This is often caused by a condition called presbyopia (tired eyes) and is a common occurrence. People who were previously nearsighted may actually realize some improvement in eyesight as they become slightly farsighted. In 2015, 11.9% of adults aged 65 to 74 years and 19.1% of those aged 75 years and older had vision limitations. (See Table 7.8.)

TABLE 7.8

Vision limitations by age and sex, selected years 1997–2015

[Data are based on household interviews of a sample of the civilian noninstitutionalized population]

Characteristic	Any trouble seeing, even with glasses or contacts[b]									
	1997	2000	2005	2007	2010	2011	2012	2013	2014	2015
	Percent of adults									
18 years and over, age-adjusted[c, d]	10.0	9.0	9.2	9.9	9.1	8.8	8.4	8.7	8.7	9.0
18 years and over, crude[d]	9.8	8.9	9.3	10.0	9.4	9.2	8.8	9.1	9.1	9.4
Age										
18–44 years	6.2	5.3	5.5	6.9	6.2	5.5	5.4	5.5	5.6	5.6
18–24 years	5.4	4.2	5.0	6.9	5.8	5.2	5.1	5.5	4.9	4.9
25–44 years	6.5	5.7	5.7	6.8	6.3	5.6	5.5	5.5	5.9	5.8
45–64 years	12.0	10.7	11.2	12.2	11.6	12.0	11.3	11.1	11.3	11.6
45–54 years	12.2	10.9	11.0	12.3	10.7	11.7	11.2	10.6	11.5	11.2
55–64 years	11.6	10.5	11.5	12.1	12.7	12.4	11.5	11.7	11.0	12.1
65 years and over	18.1	17.4	17.4	15.3	13.9	13.6	12.7	14.3	13.5	14.9
65–74 years	14.2	13.6	13.2	12.9	12.2	12.2	11.0	11.5	11.5	11.9
75 years and over	23.1	21.9	22.0	17.9	16.1	15.2	14.9	18.0	16.5	19.1
Sex[c]										
Male	8.8	7.9	7.9	8.5	7.9	7.6	7.1	7.5	7.6	7.4
Female	11.1	10.1	10.5	11.2	10.3	10.1	9.7	9.8	9.8	10.6
Sex and age										
Male:										
18–44 years	5.3	4.4	4.5	5.6	5.2	4.2	4.4	4.5	4.3	4.0
45–54 years	10.1	8.8	8.8	10.6	9.1	10.4	9.3	9.4	10.7	8.9
55–64 years	10.5	9.5	10.5	10.0	10.7	11.8	9.8	10.4	9.6	10.2
65–74 years	13.2	12.8	11.4	11.4	10.5	9.7	9.9	10.9	10.3	10.0
75 years and over	21.4	20.7	20.4	17.2	15.7	14.9	12.8	14.7	17.0	18.8
Female:										
18–44 years	7.1	6.2	6.5	8.1	7.1	6.9	6.4	6.5	7.0	7.1
45–54 years	14.2	12.8	13.2	13.9	12.3	13.0	12.9	11.8	12.2	13.4
55–64 years	12.6	11.5	12.4	14.2	14.6	13.0	13.1	12.9	12.3	13.8
65–74 years	15.0	14.4	14.8	14.2	13.6	14.5	11.9	12.1	12.5	13.5
75 years and over	24.2	22.7	23.0	18.4	16.4	15.4	16.4	20.3	16.1	19.4
Race[c, e]										
White only	9.7	8.8	9.1	9.9	8.8	8.6	8.4	8.7	8.5	9.0
Black or African American only	12.8	10.6	10.9	10.5	12.1	10.8	9.2	10.0	11.1	10.3
American Indian or Alaska Native only	19.2	16.6	14.9[a]	18.0	15.0	15.0	13.0	13.7	16.9	10.9[a]
Asian only	6.2	6.3	5.5	5.7	5.3	6.3	5.7	4.9	5.7	6.3
Native Hawaiian or other Pacific Islander only	—	a	a	a	a	a	a	a	a	a
2 or more races	—	16.2	16.4	16.9	13.1	12.4	15.6	11.8	11.4	12.4
Hispanic origin and race[c, e]										
Hispanic or Latino	10.0	9.7	9.6	9.9	9.2	9.4	9.4	9.7	8.8	9.3
Mexican	10.2	8.3	9.9	10.1	9.0	10.4	9.3	10.9	9.3	9.3
Not Hispanic or Latino	10.0	9.1	9.2	10.0	9.2	8.8	8.4	8.6	8.8	9.0
White only	9.8	8.9	9.1	10.1	8.9	8.6	8.4	8.6	8.5	9.1
Black or African American only	12.8	10.6	10.9	10.6	12.2	10.7	9.3	10.1	11.3	10.2
Education[f, g]										
25 years of age and over:										
No high school diploma or GED	15.0	12.2	13.5	13.4	14.1	13.9	12.9	12.8	13.1	13.4
High school diploma or GED	10.6	9.5	10.3	10.9	10.5	10.4	9.3	10.0	9.3	9.5
Some college or more	8.9	8.9	8.6	9.2	8.0	7.9	7.9	8.0	8.4	8.9
Percent of poverty level[c, h]										
Below 100%	17.0	12.9	15.3	15.0	14.8	14.2	13.7	15.6	13.2	14.2
100%–199%	12.9	11.6	11.5	13.0	12.2	11.5	10.9	11.2	10.9	11.8
200%–399%	9.1	8.8	8.9	9.4	9.0	8.7	7.9	7.6	8.8	9.4
400% or more	7.3	7.1	6.9	7.8	6.4	6.0	6.1	6.4	6.4	6.3
Hispanic origin and race and percent of poverty level[c, e, h]										
Hispanic or Latino:										
Below 100%	12.8	11.0	13.6	13.4	10.8	13.9	13.1	13.1	10.2	15.1
100%–199%	11.2	9.4	8.8	11.1	10.8	9.6	10.0	10.6	9.3	10.1
200%–399%	8.1	9.2	8.2	7.2	8.9	8.3	6.8	7.4	9.2	7.2
400% or more	8.1*	10.5	8.0	10.6	5.3	5.1	7.8	9.0	6.6	5.2

Major Eye Diseases

Cataracts, glaucoma, age-related macular degeneration, and diabetic retinopathy are the leading causes of vision impairment and blindness in older adults. Cataracts are the leading cause of blindness in the world. Glaucoma is a chronic disease that often requires lifelong treatment to

TABLE 7.8

Vision limitations by age and sex, selected years 1997–2015 [CONTINUED]

[Data are based on household interviews of a sample of the civilian noninstitutionalized population]

Characteristic	Any trouble seeing, even with glasses or contacts[b]									
	1997	2000	2005	2007	2010	2011	2012	2013	2014	2015
Not Hispanic or Latino:					Percent of adults					
White only:										
Below 100%	17.9	13.1	16.2	16.3	16.8	14.4	14.5	17.7	14.6	14.8
100%–199%	13.1	12.0	12.7	14.2	12.6	12.3	11.7	11.8	11.3	12.9
200%–399%	9.2	9.2	9.0	10.3	8.8	9.0	8.5	7.8	8.7	10.3
400% or more	7.3	7.0	6.9	7.7	6.7	5.9	6.0	6.4	6.3	6.4
Black or African American only:										
Below 100%	17.9	13.6	16.0	15.1	15.8	15.5	13.7	15.3	14.2	13.6
100%–199%	16.0	12.9	11.3	14.0	14.9	12.3	11.3	11.4	12.1	12.4
200%–399%	9.3	7.7	9.7	7.3	12.0	8.5	6.8	8.0	10.8	9.5
400% or more	7.7	8.3	6.4	6.9	6.6	8.6	6.4	6.7	8.6	6.1
Geographic region[c]										
Northeast	8.6	7.4	8.1	8.1	7.8	7.6	6.4	7.4	7.0	7.9
Midwest	9.5	9.6	9.7	10.3	9.1	8.7	8.7	9.0	9.0	9.3
South	11.4	9.2	9.8	10.1	10.6	9.4	9.1	8.9	9.1	9.4
West	9.7	9.9	8.6	10.5	8.0	9.1	8.9	9.1	9.3	8.9
Location of residence[c, i]										
Within MSA	9.5	8.5	8.6	9.6	8.6	8.6	8.2	8.4	8.4	8.7
Outside MSA	12.0	11.1	11.7	11.4	11.6	10.3	9.8	10.6	10.3	11.0

—Data not available.

[a]Estimates are considered unreliable.

[b]Respondents were asked, "Do you have any trouble seeing, even when wearing glasses or contact lenses?" Respondents were also asked, "Are you blind or unable to see at all?" In this analysis, any trouble seeing and blind are combined into one category.

[c]Estimates are age-adjusted to the year 2000 standard population using five age groups: 18–44 years, 45–54 years, 55–64 years, 65–74 years, and 75 years and over. Age-adjusted estimates in this table may differ from other age-adjusted estimates based on the same data and presented elsewhere if different age groups are used in the adjustment procedure.

[d]Includes all other races not shown separately and unknown education level.

[e]The race groups, white, black, American Indian or Alaska Native, Asian, Native Hawaiian or other Pacific Islander, and 2 or more races, include persons of Hispanic and non-Hispanic origin. Persons of Hispanic origin may be of any race. Starting with 1999 data, race-specific estimates are tabulated according to the 1997 Revisions to the Standards for the Classification of Federal Data on Race and Ethnicity and are not strictly comparable with estimates for earlier years. The five single-race categories plus multiple-race categories shown in the table conform to the 1997 Standards. Starting with 1999 data, race-specific estimates are for persons who reported only one racial group; the category 2 or more races includes persons who reported more than one racial group. Prior to 1999, data were tabulated according to the 1977 Standards with four racial groups, and the Asian only category included Native Hawaiian or other Pacific Islander. Estimates for single-race categories prior to 1999 included persons who reported one race or, if they reported more than one race, identified one race as best representing their race. Starting with 2003 data, race responses of other race and unspecified multiple race were treated as missing, and then race was imputed if these were the only race responses. Almost all persons with a race response of other race were of Hispanic origin.

[f]Estimates are for persons aged 25 and over and are age-adjusted to the year 2000 standard population using five age groups: 25–44 years, 45–54 years, 55–64 years, 65–74 years, and 75 years and over.

[g]GED is General Educational Development high school equivalency diploma.

[h]Percent of poverty level is based on family income and family size and composition using US Census Bureau poverty thresholds. Missing family income data were imputed for 1997 and beyond.

[i]MSA is metropolitan statistical area. Starting with 2006 data, MSA status is determined using 2000 census data and the 2000 standards for defining MSAs.

SOURCE: "Table 43. Vision Limitations among Adults Aged 18 and over, by Selected Characteristics: United States, Selected Years 1997–2015," in *Health, United States, 2016: With Chartbook on Long-Term Trends in Health*, National Center for Health Statistics, May 2017, https://www.cdc.gov/nchs/data/hus/2016/043.pdf (accessed October 24, 2017)

control. Age-related macular degeneration is the most common cause of blindness and vision impairment in Americans aged 60 years and older. Diabetic retinopathy is a common complication of diabetes and is considered to be a leading cause of blindness in the industrialized world.

CATARACTS. A cataract is an opacity, or clouding, of the naturally clear lens of the eye. The prevalence of cataracts increases dramatically with age and most develop slowly over time as they progressively compromise vision. Once a clouded lens develops, surgery to remove the affected lens and replace it with an artificial lens is the recommended treatment. Nissa Simon reports in "3 Eye Diseases of the Aging—Symptoms, Causes and Treatments" (May 2013, https://www.aarp.org/health/conditions-treatments/info-05-2013/eye-diseases-of-aging.html) that cataracts affect nearly 25 million

Americans over the age of 40. The National Eye Institute (one of the National Institutes of Health) projects a dramatic increase in cataracts as the US population ages. Figure 7.8 shows this projected increase by race and Hispanic origin by 2030 and 2050.

GLAUCOMA. Glaucoma is a disease that causes gradual damage to the optic nerve, which carries visual information from the eye to the brain. The loss of vision is not experienced until a significant amount of nerve damage has occurred. Because the onset is gradual, as many as half of all people with glaucoma are unaware that they have the disease. In "Glaucoma Facts and Stats" October 29, 2017, https://www.glaucoma.org/glaucoma/glaucoma-facts-and-stats.php), the Glaucoma Research Foundation indicates more than 3 million Americans have glaucoma, but just half are aware that they have it.

FIGURE 7.8

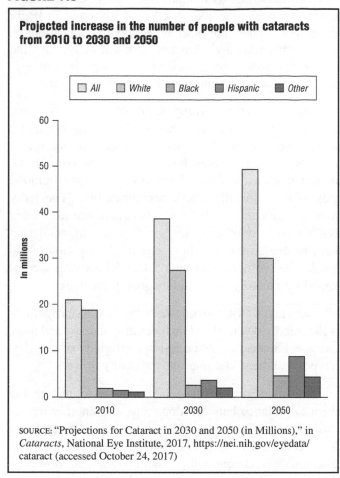

Projected increase in the number of people with cataracts from 2010 to 2030 and 2050

SOURCE: "Projections for Cataract in 2030 and 2050 (in Millions)," in *Cataracts*, National Eye Institute, 2017, https://nei.nih.gov/eyedata/cataract (accessed October 24, 2017)

FIGURE 7.9

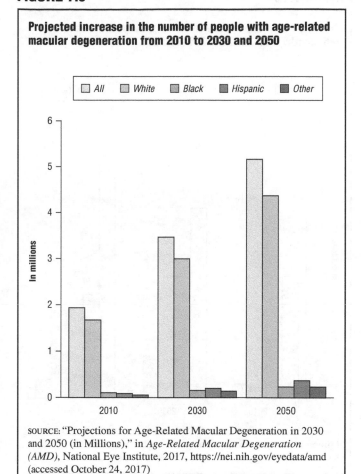

Projected increase in the number of people with age-related macular degeneration from 2010 to 2030 and 2050

SOURCE: "Projections for Age-Related Macular Degeneration in 2030 and 2050 (in Millions)," in *Age-Related Macular Degeneration (AMD)*, National Eye Institute, 2017, https://nei.nih.gov/eyedata/amd (accessed October 24, 2017)

Routine glaucoma testing is especially important for older people because people over age 60 are considered to be high risk of developing the disease. There is no cure for glaucoma and no way to restore lost vision; however, medication can generally manage the condition. At later stages, laser therapy and surgery are effective in preventing further damage.

AGE-RELATED MACULAR DEGENERATION. Age-related macular degeneration is a condition in which the macula, a specialized part of the retina that is responsible for sharp central and reading vision, is damaged. Symptoms include blurred vision, a dark spot in the center of the vision field, and vertical line distortion. The National Eye Institute reports in "Age-Related Macular Degeneration" (2018, https://nei.nih.gov/eyedata/amd) that in 2010, the most recent year for which data were available, more than 2 million adults aged 50 years and older had age-related macular degeneration.

Because the prevalence of age-related macular degeneration increases with age, rising sharply in adults over the age of 75 years, it is estimated that the number of people with age-related macular degeneration will more than double between 2010 and 2050. Although the bulk of this increase will occur in white Americans, the number of age-related macular degeneration cases in Hispanics will increase almost sixfold. (See Figure 7.9.)

DIABETIC RETINOPATHY. Diabetic retinopathy occurs when the small blood vessels in the retina become blocked, break down, leak fluid that distorts vision, and sometimes release blood into the center of the eye, causing blindness. Photocoagulation (laser treatment) can help reduce the risk of loss of vision in advanced cases. According to the National Eye Institute, in "Diabetic Retinopathy" (2018, https://nei.nih.gov/eyedata/diabetic), in 2010, the most recent year for which data were available, diabetic retinopathy affected 7.7 million Americans. The prevalence of diabetic retinopathy increases with age, reflecting the higher rates of diabetes in older people. Figure 7.10 shows that the number of cases of diabetic retinopathy is anticipated to nearly double, reaching 14.6 million by 2050.

Oral Health Problems

In "Oral Health for Older Americans" (July 10, 2013, https://www.cdc.gov/oralhealth/publications/factsheets/adult_oral_health/adult_older.htm), the CDC notes that a fourth of adults aged 60 years and older have lost all their teeth, and nearly a quarter (23%) of adults aged

FIGURE 7.10

Projected increase in the number of people with diabetic retinopathy from 2010 to 2030 and 2050

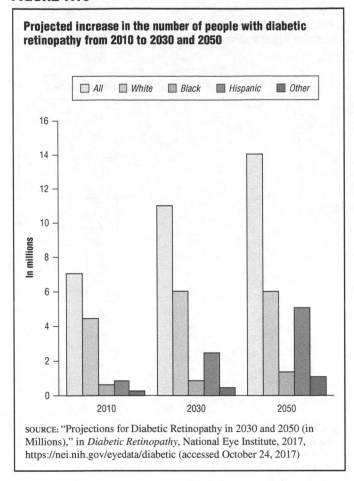

SOURCE: "Projections for Diabetic Retinopathy in 2030 and 2050 (in Millions)," in *Diabetic Retinopathy*, National Eye Institute, 2017, https://nei.nih.gov/eyedata/diabetic (accessed October 24, 2017)

65 to 74 years have periodontal (gum) disease. Older adults with the worst oral health are those who are poor and members of racial and ethnic minorities as well as those who are disabled, homebound, or institutionalized.

Parkinson's Disease

According to the Parkinson's Disease Foundation, in "Statistics" (2018, http://parkinson.org/Understanding-Parkinsons/Causes-and-Statistics/Statistics), Parkinson's disease (PD) affects about 1 million people in the United States. An estimated 60,000 people in the United States are diagnosed with PD each year and thousands of others have the disease but are not diagnosed. The incidence of PD increases with advancing age (just 4% of cases are diagnosed in people under the age of 50 years). In "Movement Disorders" (*Medical Clinics of North America*, vol. 93, no. 2, March 2009), Meghan K. Harris et al. observe that the prevalence of PD is 1% to 2% in the population aged 65 years and older and up to 4% in individuals older than age 85. PD usually begins during the 70s, but up to 10% of those affected are aged 50 years and younger.

PD is caused by the death of about half a million brain cells in the basal ganglia. These cells secrete dopamine, a neurotransmitter (chemical messenger), whose function is to allow nerve impulses to move smoothly from one nerve cell to another. These nerve cells, in turn, transmit messages to the muscles of the body to begin movement. When the normal supply of dopamine is reduced, the messages are not sent correctly, and the symptoms—mild tremor (shaking), change in walking, or a decreased arm swing—of PD begin to appear.

The four early warning signs of PD are tremors, muscle stiffness, unusual slowness (bradykinesia), and a stooped posture. Medications can control initial symptoms, but over time they become less effective. As the disease worsens, patients develop more severe tremors, causing them to fall or jerk uncontrollably. (The jerky body movements that PD patients experience are called dyskinesias.) At other times, rigidity sets in, rendering them unable to move. About one-third of patients also develop dementia (loss of intellectual functioning accompanied by memory loss and personality changes).

TREATMENT OF PARKINSON'S DISEASE. Management of PD is individualized and includes drug therapy and daily exercise. Exercise can often lessen the rigidity of muscles, prevent weakness, and improve the ability to walk.

The main goal of drug treatment is to restore the chemical balance between dopamine and another neurotransmitter, acetylcholine. Most patients are given levodopa (L-dopa), a compound that the body converts into dopamine. Treatment with L-dopa does not, however, slow the progressive course of the disease or even delay the changes in the brain that PD produces, and it may produce some unpleasant side effects such as dyskinesias.

PD patients generally have life expectancy comparable to people without the disease. Nevertheless, Rodolfo Savica et al. find in "Survival and Causes of Death among People with Clinically Diagnosed Synucleinopathies with Parkinsonism: A Population-Based Study" (*JAMA Neurology*, vol. 74, no. 7, July 1, 2017) that those with PD died about two years earlier than the general population.

INFECTIOUS DISEASES

Infectious (contagious) diseases are caused by microorganisms (viruses, bacteria, parasites, or fungi) that are transmitted from one person to another through casual contact, such as with the transmittal of influenza; through bodily fluids, such as with the transmittal of HIV; or from contaminated food, air, or water supplies. The CDC reports that in 2015 influenza and pneumonia ranked eighth among the top-10 causes of death for older adults and were responsible for 48,774 deaths of people aged 65 years and older. (See Table 7.6.) Influenza-related deaths can result from pneumonia as well as from the exacerbation of chronic diseases.

Influenza

Influenza (flu) is a contagious respiratory disease caused by a virus. The virus is expelled by an infected individual in droplets into the air and may be inhaled by anyone nearby. It can also be transmitted by direct hand contact. The flu primarily affects the lungs, but the whole body experiences symptoms. Influenza is an acute (short-term) illness characterized by fever, chills, weakness, loss of appetite, and aching muscles in the head, back, arms, and legs. The accompanying fever rises quickly—sometimes reaching 104 degrees Fahrenheit (40 degrees Celsius)—but usually subsides after two or three days. Influenza leaves the patient exhausted.

For healthy individuals, the flu is typically a moderately severe illness, but for older people who are not in good general health, the flu can be severe and even fatal. Complications such as secondary bacterial infections may develop, taking advantage of the body's weakened condition and lowered resistance. The most common bacterial complication is pneumonia, affecting the lungs, but sinuses, bronchi (larger air passages of the lungs), and inner ears can also become secondarily infected. Less common but serious complications include viral pneumonia, encephalitis (inflammation of the brain), acute renal (kidney) failure, and nervous system disorders. These complications can be fatal.

Influenza can be prevented by inoculation with a current influenza vaccine, which is formulated annually to contain the influenza viruses expected to cause the flu the upcoming year. Immunization produces antibodies to the influenza viruses, which become most effective after one or two months. The CDC advises that older adults get flu shots early in the fall because peak flu activity usually occurs around the beginning of the new calendar year. Between 1997 and 2017 the percentage of adults aged 65 years and older that received a flu shot ranged from a low of 63.1% in 1997 to a high of 71.7% during the first quarter of 2017. (See Table 7.9.) In "People at High Risk of Developing Flu-Related Complications" (January 23, 2018, https://www.cdc.gov/flu/about/disease/high_risk.htm), the CDC asserts that adults aged 65 years and older are at high risk of developing serious complications such as pneumonia should they contract the flu.

Pneumonia

Pneumonia is a serious lung infection. Symptoms of pneumonia are fever, chills, cough, shortness of breath, chest pain, and increased sputum production. Pneumonia may be caused by viruses, bacteria, or fungi; the pneumococcus bacterium, however, is the most important cause of serious pneumonia.

Older adults are two to three times more likely than other adults to develop pneumococcal infections. A single vaccination can prevent most cases of pneumococcal

TABLE 7.9

Adults aged 65 and older who received an influenza vaccination during the past 12 months, 1997–2017

Year	Total Crude percent	Total Age-adjusted percent	Men Percent	Women Percent
1997	63.2	63.1	64.8	62.1
1998	63.3	63.3	63.7	63.0
1999	65.7	65.1	67.2	64.6
2000	64.4	64.6	66.0	63.3
2001	63.1	63.2	64.8	61.8
2002	65.7	65.9	67.1	64.7
2003	65.5	65.6	66.0	65.1
2004	64.6	64.7	64.1	65.0
2005	59.7	59.7	58.9	60.2
2006	64.3	64.4	64.7	63.9
2007	66.7	66.8	66.7	66.8
2008	66.9	67.1	65.5	68.0
2009	66.7	67.0	67.3	66.3
2010	63.6	63.9	63.1	64.0
2011	67.0	67.2	66.3	67.5
2012	66.5	66.9	65.2	67.4
2013	67.9	68.4	66.4	69.2
2014	70.0	70.5	70.1	69.9
2015	69.1	69.4	70.4	68.0
2016	67.2	67.7	66.7	67.6
January–March 2017	70.3	71.1	71.7	69.1

Notes: Data are based on household interviews of a sample of the civilian noninstitutionalized population. Respondents were asked if they received a flu vaccination during the past 12 months. Starting in August 2010, questions were modified to reflect that the seasonal influenza vaccine included protection for the 2009 pandemic H1N1 virus. Prevalence of influenza vaccination during the past 12 months is different from season-specific coverage. Advisory Committee on Immunization Practices recommendations regarding who should receive an influenza vaccination have changed over the years, and changes in coverage estimates may reflect changes in recommendations (4–8). The analyses exclude the 2.0% of persons with unknown influenza vaccination status.

SOURCE: "Table 4.1b. Percentage of Adults Aged 65 and over Who Received an Influenza Vaccination during the Past 12 Months, by Sex: United States, 1997—March 2017," in *Early Release of Selected Estimates Based on Data from the National Health Interview Survey, January—March 2017*, Centers for Disease Control and Prevention, National Center for Health Statistics, September 2017, https://www.cdc.gov/nchs/data/nhis/earlyrelease/Early release201709_04.pdf (accessed October 24, 2017)

pneumonia. The CDC recommends that all people aged 65 years and older receive the pneumococcal vaccine, and increasing percentages of adults aged 65 years and older report having been vaccinated. (See Figure 7.11.)

MANDATORY IMMUNIZATION FOR NURSING HOME RESIDENTS. Nursing home residents are required to be immunized against influenza and pneumonia; nursing homes that fail to enforce this requirement risk losing reimbursement from Medicare (a federal health insurance program for people aged 65 years and older and people with disabilities) and Medicaid (a state and federal health insurance program for low-income people). The regulation, which was issued by the Centers for Medicare and Medicaid Services in August 2005, intends to ensure that the most vulnerable older adults receive their flu and pneumococcal vaccinations. People aged 65 years and older are among the most vulnerable, especially those in the close quarters of nursing homes, where infection can spread more easily.

FIGURE 7.11

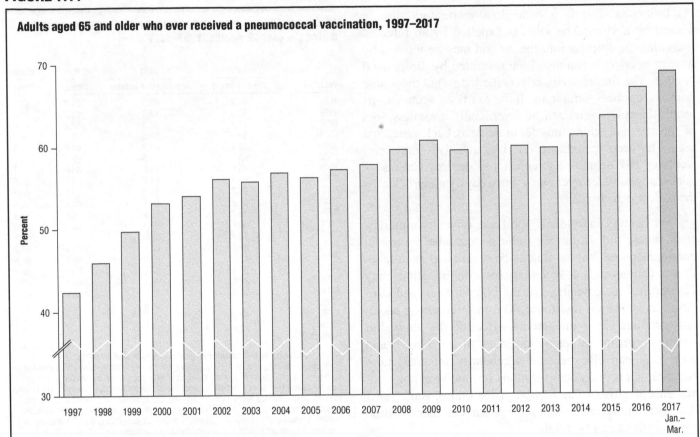

Adults aged 65 and older who ever received a pneumococcal vaccination, 1997–2017

Notes: Data are based on household interviews of a sample of the civilian noninstitutionalized population. The analyses exclude those with unknown pneumococcal vaccination status (about 5% of respondents each year). Advisory Committee on Immunization Practices recommendations regarding who should receive pneumococcal vaccination have changed over the years, and changes in coverage estimates may reflect changes in recommendations. Of particular note, beginning in 2014, all adults aged 65 and over are recommended to receive both the 13-valent pneumococcal conjugate vaccine (PCV13) and the 23-valent pneumococcal polysaccharide vaccine (PPSV23) in series (9–11). The National Health Interview Survey (NHIS) question on receipt of pneumococcal vaccination does not distinguish between the type of vaccine received.

SOURCE: "Figure 5.1. Percentage of Adults Aged 65 and over Who Had Ever Received a Pneumococcal Vaccination: United States, 1997—March 2017," in *Early Release of Selected Estimates Based on Data from the National Health Interview Survey, January—March 2017*, Centers for Disease Control and Prevention, National Center for Health Statistics, September 2017, https://www.cdc.gov/nchs/data/nhis/earlyrelease/Earlyrelease201709_05.pdf (accessed October 24, 2017)

DISABILITY IN THE OLDER POPULATION

Americans are not only living longer but also are developing fewer chronic diseases and disabilities. The current cohort (a group of individuals that shares a common characteristic such as birth years and is studied over time) of older Americans are defying the stereotype that aging is synonymous with increasing disability and dependence.

The Federal Interagency Forum on Aging-Related Statistics discusses in *Older Americans 2016: Key Indicators of Well-Being* (August 2017, https://agingstats.gov/docs/LatestReport/Older-Americans-2016-Key-Indicators-of-WellBeing.pdf) the types of functional limitations (disabilities) that older adults experience. Figure 7.12 shows that between 2010 and 2014 the percentage of adults aged 65 years and older with hearing difficulties increased, while the percentage with mobility difficulties decreased. In 2014 more women (24%) reported having functional limitations than did men (19%). Difficulties with mobility (e.g., walking or climbing stairs) were the most frequently reported disability, affecting 17% of women and 11% of men.

The Federal Interagency Forum on Aging-Related Statistics observes that disability increases with age. In 2014, 17% of adults aged 65 to 74 years reported any disability, compared with 42% of those aged 85 years and older.

DRUG USE AMONG OLDER ADULTS

Prescription drug use increased between 1988–94 and 2011–14. (See Table 7.10.) The percentage of adults aged 65 years and older that took at least one prescription drug during the past 30 days rose from 73.6% in 1988–94 to 90.6% in 2011–14, and the percentage that took three or more prescription drugs grew from 35.3% to 66.8%.

Older Adults Respond Differently to Drugs

Many factors influence the efficacy (the ability of an intervention to produce the intended diagnostic or therapeutic effect in optimal circumstances), safety, and success

FIGURE 7.12

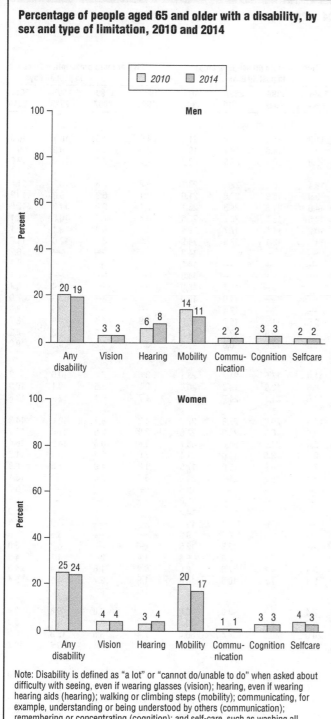

Percentage of people aged 65 and older with a disability, by sex and type of limitation, 2010 and 2014

☐ 2010 ▨ 2014

Men

Women

Note: Disability is defined as "a lot" or "cannot do/unable to do" when asked about difficulty with seeing, even if wearing glasses (vision); hearing, even if wearing hearing aids (hearing); walking or climbing steps (mobility); communicating, for example, understanding or being understood by others (communication); remembering or concentrating (cognition); and self-care, such as washing all over or dressing (self-care). Any disability is defined as having difficulty with at least one of these activities.
Data labels in this chart are based on rounded values.
Reference population: These data refer to the civilian noninstitutionalized population.

SOURCE: "Percentage of People Age 65 and over with a Disability, by Sex and Functional Domain, 2010 and 2014," in *Older Americans 2016: Key Indicators of Well-Being*, Federal Interagency Forum on Aging-Related Statistics, August 2016, https://agingstats.gov/docs/LatestReport/Older-Americans-2016-Key-Indicators-of-WellBeing.pdf (accessed October 13, 2017)

distribution, metabolism, and excretion of drugs). Of the four, absorption is the least affected by aging. In older people, absorption is generally complete, just slower. The distribution of most medications is related to body weight and composition changes that occur with aging, such as decreased lean muscle mass, increased fat mass, and decreased total body water.

Health professionals who care for older adults know that drug dosages must often be modified based on changing organ function and estimates of lean body mass. They coined the adage "start low and go slow" to guide prescribing drugs for older adults. For example, some initial doses of drugs should be lower because older adults have decreased total body water, which might increase the concentration of the drug. Fat-soluble drugs may also have to be administered in lower doses because they may accumulate in fatty tissues, resulting in longer durations of action. The mechanism used to clear a drug via metabolism in the liver or clearance (excretion) through the kidneys changes with aging and is affected by interactions with other medications. Pharmacodynamics (tissue sensitivity to drugs) also changes with advancing age. Among older adults, the complete elimination of a drug from body tissues, including the brain, can take weeks longer than it might in younger people.

Adherence, Drug-Drug Interactions, and Polypharmacy

Adherence (taking prescription medications regularly and correctly) is a challenge for older people who may suffer from memory loss, impaired vision, or arthritis. In "Improving Medication Adherence and Health Outcomes in Older Adults: An Evidence-Based Review of Randomized Controlled Trials" (*Drugs Aging*, vol. 34, no. 3, March 2017), Zachary A. Marcum, Joseph T. Hanlon, and Michael D. Murray note that about half of older adults fail to take their medications at the right times and in the right amounts. Strategies to improve adherence include behavioral and educational interventions, telephone counseling, weekly pill boxes, calendars, and easy-to-open bottles with large-print labels.

Drug-drug interactions are more frequent among older adults because they are more likely than people of other ages to be taking multiple medications. Dangerous drug-drug interactions may occur when two or more drugs act together to either intensify or diminish one another's potency and effectiveness or when in combination they produce adverse side effects. For example, a person who takes heparin, a blood-thinning medication, should not take aspirin, which also acts to thin the blood. Similarly, antacids can interfere with the absorption of certain drugs that are used to treat Parkinson's disease, hypertension, and heart disease.

of drug therapy with older patients. These factors include the effects of aging on pharmacokinetics (the absorption,

TABLE 7.10

Prescription drug use in past 30 days, by age group, selected years 1988–94 to 2011–14

[Data are based on a sample of the civilian noninstitutionalized population]

Sex, race and Hispanic origin[b], and age	At least one prescription drug in past 30 days				Three or more prescription drugs in past 30 days				Five or more prescription drugs in past 30 days			
	1988–1994	1999–2002	2007–2010	2011–2014	1988–1994	1999–2002	2007–2010	2011–2014	1988–1994	1999–2002	2007–2010	2011–2014
All ages, age-adjusted[c]					Percent of population							
Both sexes[d]	39.1	45.2	47.5	46.9	11.8	17.8	20.8	21.5	4.0	7.5	10.1	10.9
Male	32.7	39.8	42.8	42.6	9.4	14.8	19.1	19.7	2.9	6.1	9.2	9.7
Female	45.0	50.3	52.0	51.2	13.9	20.4	22.5	23.2	4.9	8.7	11.0	12.0
Not Hispanic or Latino:												
White only	41.1	48.7	52.8	51.9	12.4	18.9	22.4	23.1	4.2	7.8	10.7	11.5
White only, male	34.2	43.0	47.5	46.8	9.9	15.9	20.6	21.0	3.1	6.3	9.8	10.2
White only, female	47.6	54.3	57.9	57.0	14.6	21.8	24.3	25.1	5.1	9.2	11.6	12.8
Black or African American only	36.9	40.1	42.3	44.2	12.6	16.5	20.7	22.5	3.8	7.7	10.8	12.1
Black or African American only, male	31.1	35.4	36.7	38.3	10.2	14.5	17.7	19.4	2.9	6.4	9.1	10.1
Black or African American only, female	41.4	43.8	46.8	49.0	14.3	18.1	22.9	24.9	4.5	8.7	12.0	13.7
Asian only	—	—	—	34.3	—	—	—	14.3	—	—	—	6.2
Asian only, male	—	—	—	31.9	—	—	—	14.1	—	—	—	6.2
Asian only, female	—	—	—	36.3	—	—	—	14.6	—	—	—	6.1
Hispanic or Latino	—	—	35.2	35.7	—	—	15.7	16.0	—	—	8.4	8.4
Hispanic or Latino, male	—	—	31.7	32.1	—	—	14.0	15.0	—	—	7.3	7.9
Hispanic or Latina, female	—	—	38.8	39.2	—	—	17.4	17.1	—	—	9.5	8.8
Mexican origin	31.7	31.7	33.9	34.2	9.0	11.2	15.0	15.9	2.9	4.4	7.9	8.7
Mexican origin, male	27.5	25.8	31.0	31.8	7.0	9.5	13.4	14.9	2.0	3.5	7.2	8.2
Mexican origin, female	36.0	37.8	37.0	36.9	11.0	12.8	16.6	17.0	3.7	5.2	8.7	9.2
All ages, crude												
Both sexes[d]	37.8	45.0	48.5	48.9	11.0	17.6	21.7	23.1	3.6	7.4	10.6	11.9
Male	30.6	38.6	43.0	43.7	8.3	13.9	19.0	20.4	2.5	5.6	9.1	10.0
Female	44.6	51.1	53.8	53.9	13.6	21.1	24.2	25.8	4.7	9.1	12.1	13.6
Not Hispanic or Latino:												
White only	41.4	50.7	56.2	57.0	12.5	20.6	25.8	27.7	4.2	8.7	12.6	14.3
White only, male	33.5	43.8	50.3	51.4	9.5	16.5	22.9	24.6	2.9	6.6	11.0	12.1
White only, female	48.9	57.5	61.8	62.4	15.4	24.5	28.6	30.7	5.4	10.8	14.2	16.4
Black or African American only	31.2	36.0	40.2	42.8	9.2	13.5	18.6	21.1	2.6	6.2	9.4	11.2
Black or African American only, male	25.5	30.7	33.9	36.3	7.0	10.9	15.0	17.5	1.8	4.8	7.5	8.9
Black or African American only, female	36.2	40.6	45.7	48.5	11.1	15.7	21.7	24.2	3.3	7.4	11.1	13.1
Asian only	—	—	—	34.0	—	—	—	13.6	—	—	—	5.7
Asian only, male	—	—	—	30.5	—	—	—	12.6	—	—	—	5.5
Asian only, female	—	—	—	37.1	—	—	—	14.5	—	—	—	6.0
Hispanic or Latino	—	—	28.6	29.5	—	—	10.3	10.9	—	—	5.0	5.3
Hispanic or Latino, male	—	—	24.9	25.4	—	—	8.4	9.3	—	—	3.8	4.6
Hispanic or Latina, female	—	—	32.5	33.5	—	—	12.3	12.6	—	—	6.2	6.0
Mexican origin	24.0	23.6	26.4	27.0	4.8	6.1	9.0	9.8	1.4	2.1	4.1	4.9
Mexican origin, male	20.1	18.8	23.7	24.9	3.4	4.8	7.6	9.0	0.9	1.6	3.4	4.6
Mexican origin, female	28.1	28.9	29.4	29.3	6.4	7.5	10.6	10.8	1.9	2.7	4.9	5.4
Both sexes												
Under 18 years	20.5	23.8	24.0	21.5	2.4	4.1	3.8	3.9	[a]	0.8[a]	0.8	0.8
18–44 years	31.3	35.9	38.7	37.1	5.7	8.4	9.7	10.1	1.2	2.3	3.1	3.9
45–64 years	54.8	64.1	66.2	69.0	20.0	30.8	34.4	36.4	7.4	13.3	16.8	18.3
65 years and over	73.6	84.7	89.7	90.6	35.3	51.8	66.6	66.8	13.8	27.1	39.7	40.7
Male												
Under 18 years	20.4	25.7	24.5	21.1	2.6	4.3	4.4	4.3	[a]	[a]	0.8	0.9
18–44 years	21.5	27.1	29.5	28.8	3.6	6.7	7.1	7.5	0.8[a]	1.7	2.1	3.0
45–64 years	47.2	55.6	61.3	65.6	15.1	23.6	30.4	33.0	4.8	9.5	14.4	15.7
65 years and over	67.2	80.1	88.8	88.7	31.3	46.3	66.8	65.2	11.3	24.7	39.5	38.4
Female												
Under 18 years	20.6	21.7	23.5	22.0	2.3	3.9	3.1	3.5	[a]	0.8[a]	0.7[a]	[a]
18–44 years	40.7	44.6	47.6	45.3	7.6	10.2	12.2	12.6	1.7	2.8	4.0	4.8
45–64 years	62.0	72.0	70.8	72.1	24.7	37.5	38.1	39.4	9.7	16.8	19.1	20.7
65 years and over	78.3	88.1	90.4	92.1	38.2	55.9	66.4	68.1	15.6	28.9	39.8	42.6

Polypharmacy is the use of many medications at the same time. It also refers to prescribing more medication than is needed or a medication regimen that includes at least one unnecessary medication. The major risk associated with polypharmacy is the potential for adverse drug reactions and interactions. Drug-induced adverse events may masquerade as other illnesses or precipitate confusion, falls, and incontinence, potentially prompting the physician to prescribe yet another drug. This "prescribing cascade" is easily prevented. It requires that physicians ensure that all medications prescribed are appropriate, safe, effective, and taken correctly.

[Data are based on a sample of the civilian noninstitutionalized population]

—Data not available.
[a]Estimates are considered unreliable.
[b]Persons of Hispanic and Mexican origin may be of any race. Starting with 1999 data, race-specific estimates are tabulated according to the 1997 Revisions to the Standards for the Classification of Federal Data on Race and Ethnicity and are not strictly comparable with estimates for earlier years. The non-Hispanic race categories shown in the table conform to the 1997 Standards. Starting with 1999 data, race-specific estimates are for persons who reported only one racial group. Prior to data year 1999, estimates were tabulated according to the 1977 Standards. Estimates for single-race categories prior to 1999 included persons who reported one race or, if they reported more than one race, identified one race as best representing their race.
[c]Estimates are age-adjusted to the year 2000 standard population using four age groups: under 18 years, 18–44 years, 45–64 years, and 65 years and over. Age-adjusted estimates in this table may differ from other age-adjusted estimates based on the same data and presented elsewhere if different age groups are used in the adjustment procedure.
[d]Includes persons of all races and Hispanic origins, not just those shown separately.

SOURCE: "Table 79. Prescription Drug Use in the Past 30 Days, by Sex, Race and Hispanic Origin, and Age: United States, Selected Years 1988–1994 through 2011–2014," in *Health, United States, 2016: With Chartbook on Long-Term Trends in Health*, National Center for Health Statistics, May 2017, https://www .cdc.gov/nchs/data/hus/2016/079.pdf (accessed October 24, 2017)

Gretchen I. Riker and Stephen M. Setter find in "Polypharmacy in Older Adults at Home: What It Is and What to Do about It—Implications for Home Healthcare and Hospice" (*Home Healthcare Nurse*, vol. 30, no. 8, September 2012) that increasing prescription drug use increases the likelihood of polypharmacy. Because polypharmacy is potentially dangerous, Riker and Setter suggest that "periodic medication reviews and effective and constant communication between healthcare providers and patients can help to identify potentially inappropriate medications."

LEADING CAUSES OF DEATH

The number of deaths among people aged 65 years and older attributable to heart disease and cerebrovascular diseases decreased between 1980 and 2015, whereas deaths attributable to malignant neoplasms increased. (See Table 7.6.)

Heart Disease

Although deaths from heart disease have declined, it still kills more Americans than any other single disease. According to the American Heart Association, in "Older Americans and Cardiovascular Diseases" (2016, https:// www.heart.org/idc/groups/heart-public/@wcm/@sop/@ smd/documents/downloadable/ucm_483970.pdf), 80% of people who die of heart disease are aged 65 years and older. Among adults aged 60 to 79 years, 19.9% of men and 9.7% of women have heart disease. Among those aged 80 years and older the percentages increase to 32.2% of men and 17.3% of women. The average age of a first heart attack is 65 for men and 72 for women. Because women are generally older when they suffer heart attacks, they are more likely to die within weeks of the attack.

Table 7.6 shows the decrease in the numbers of deaths from heart disease and cerebrovascular diseases between 1980 and 2015. Several factors account for the decreasing numbers of deaths from heart disease, including better control of hypertension and cholesterol levels

and changes in exercise and diet. The increasing ranks of trained paramedics and the widespread use of cardiopulmonary resuscitation and immediate treatment have also increased the likelihood of surviving an initial heart attack.

The growing use of statin drugs (drugs that reduce blood cholesterol levels) to reduce the risk of heart disease as well as procedures such as cardiac catheterization, coronary bypass surgery, pacemakers, angioplasty (a procedure to open narrowed or blocked blood vessels of the heart), and stenting (using wire scaffolds that hold arteries open) have improved the quality, and in some instances extended the lives, of people with heart disease.

Nonetheless, the Mayo Clinic explains in "Statins: Are These Cholesterol-Lowering Drugs Right for You?" (April 8, 2015, https://www.mayoclinic.org/diseases-conditions/ high-blood-cholesterol/in-depth/statins/art-20045772) that statin use may produce side effects such as joint and muscle pain, nausea, diarrhea, and constipation. Although these common side effects often subside with continued use of the drugs, less frequent but serious side effects such as liver and kidney damage, severe muscle pain, and elevated blood sugar may occur with statin treatment.

Cancer

Cancer is the second-leading cause of death among older adults. (See Table 7.6.) The American Cancer Society indicates in *Cancer Facts and Figures, 2017* that about 87% of all cancers are diagnosed after age 50. The likelihood of dying of cancer increases every decade after the age of 30. In 2015, among adults aged 65 to 74 years, there were 594.3 cancer deaths per 100,000 people; for adults aged 75 to 84 years, this rate was 1,100.8 deaths per 100,000 people; and for adults aged 85 years and older, it was 1,628.6 deaths per 100,000 people. (See Table 7.11.)

Cancer risk increases with advancing age because some age-related changes such as diminished immunity,

TABLE 7.11

Death rates for malignant neoplasms, selected characteristics, selected years 1950–2015

[Data are based on death certificates]

Sex, race, Hispanic origin, and age	1950[a, b]	1960[a, b]	1970[b]	1980[b]	1990[b]	2000[c]	2014[c]	2015[c]
				Deaths per 100,000 resident population				
All persons								
All ages, age-adjusted[d]	193.9	193.9	198.6	207.9	216.0	199.6	161.2	158.5
All ages, crude	139.8	149.2	162.8	183.9	203.2	196.5	185.6	185.4
Under 1 year	8.7	7.2	4.7	3.2	2.3	2.4	1.3	1.3
1–4 years	11.7	10.9	7.5	4.5	3.5	2.7	2.0	2.2
5–14 years	6.7	6.8	6.0	4.3	3.1	2.5	2.1	2.1
15–24 years	8.6	8.3	8.3	6.3	4.9	4.4	3.6	3.4
25–34 years	20.0	19.5	16.5	13.7	12.6	9.8	8.3	8.4
35–44 years	62.7	59.7	59.5	48.6	43.3	36.6	27.8	26.9
45–54 years	175.1	177.0	182.5	180.0	158.9	127.5	103.2	99.7
55–64 years	390.7	396.8	423.0	436.1	449.6	366.7	287.6	284.1
65–74 years	698.8	713.9	754.2	817.9	872.3	816.3	603.1	594.3
75–84 years	1,153.3	1,127.4	1,169.2	1,232.3	1,348.5	1,335.6	1,125.9	1,100.8
85 years and over	1,451.0	1,450.0	1,320.7	1,594.6	1,752.9	1,819.4	1,632.9	1,628.6
Male								
All ages, age-adjusted[d]	208.1	225.1	247.6	271.2	280.4	248.9	192.9	189.2
All ages, crude	142.9	162.5	182.1	205.3	221.3	207.2	198.4	198.3
Under 1 year	9.7	7.7	4.4	3.7	2.4	2.6	1.1	1.5
1–4 years	12.5	12.4	8.3	5.2	3.7	3.0	2.2	2.4
5–14 years	7.4	7.6	6.7	4.9	3.5	2.7	2.3	2.2
15–24 years	9.7	10.2	10.4	7.8	5.7	5.1	4.2	3.9
25–34 years	17.7	18.8	16.3	13.4	12.6	9.2	8.2	8.2
35–44 years	45.6	48.9	53.0	44.0	38.5	32.7	24.0	23.0
45–54 years	156.2	170.8	183.5	188.7	162.5	130.9	102.9	99.4
55–64 years	413.1	459.9	511.8	520.8	532.9	415.8	330.3	325.5
65–74 years	791.5	890.5	1,006.8	1,093.2	1,122.2	1,001.9	711.9	701.7
75–84 years	1,332.6	1,389.4	1,588.3	1,790.5	1,914.4	1,760.6	1,387.5	1,355.8
85 years and over	1,668.3	1,741.2	1,720.8	2,369.5	2,739.9	2,710.7	2,250.4	2,220.2
Female								
All ages, age-adjusted[d]	182.3	168.7	163.2	166.7	175.7	167.6	138.1	135.9
All ages, crude	136.8	136.4	144.4	163.6	186.0	186.2	173.2	172.9
Under 1 year	7.6	6.8	5.0	2.7	2.2	2.3	1.6	1.1
1–4 years	10.8	9.3	6.7	3.7	3.2	2.5	1.8	2.0
5–14 years	6.0	6.0	5.2	3.6	2.8	2.2	1.8	2.0
15–24 years	7.6	6.5	6.2	4.8	4.1	3.6	2.9	2.8
25–34 years	22.2	20.1	16.7	14.0	12.6	10.4	8.5	8.6
35–44 years	79.3	70.0	65.6	53.1	48.1	40.4	31.6	30.7
45–54 years	194.0	183.0	181.5	171.8	155.5	124.2	103.4	100.0
55–64 years	368.2	337.7	343.2	361.7	375.2	321.3	247.9	245.4
65–74 years	612.3	560.2	557.9	607.1	677.4	663.6	507.5	499.8
75–84 years	1,000.7	924.1	891.9	903.1	1,010.3	1,058.5	928.0	906.4
85 years and over	1,299.7	1,263.9	1,096.7	1,255.7	1,372.1	1,456.4	1,311.7	1,315.8
White male[e]								
All ages, age-adjusted[d]	210.0	224.7	244.8	265.1	272.2	243.9	193.0	189.7
All ages, crude	147.2	166.1	185.1	208.7	227.7	218.1	214.4	214.7
25–34 years	17.7	18.8	16.2	13.6	12.3	9.2	8.4	8.4
35–44 years	44.5	46.3	50.1	41.1	35.8	30.9	24.0	23.1
45–54 years	150.8	164.1	172.0	175.4	149.9	123.5	102.3	98.8
55–64 years	409.4	450.9	498.1	497.4	508.2	401.9	323.5	320.5
65–74 years	798.7	887.3	997.0	1,070.7	1,090.7	984.3	707.6	698.7
75–84 years	1,367.6	1,413.7	1,592.7	1,779.7	1,883.2	1,736.0	1,400.4	1,369.4
85 years and over	1,732.7	1,791.4	1,772.2	2,375.6	2,715.1	2,693.7	2,279.7	2,251.6
Black or African American male[e]								
All ages, age-adjusted[d]	178.9	227.6	291.9	353.4	397.9	340.3	231.9	224.8
All ages, crude	106.6	136.7	171.6	205.5	221.9	188.5	165.1	163.8
25–34 years	18.0	18.4	18.8	14.1	15.7	10.1	8.3	8.7
35–44 years	55.7	72.9	81.3	73.8	64.3	48.4	28.8	26.3
45–54 years	211.7	244.7	311.2	333.0	302.6	214.2	128.8	123.8
55–64 years	490.8	579.7	689.2	812.5	859.2	626.4	450.5	437.4
65–74 years	636.5	938.5	1,168.9	1,417.2	1,613.9	1,363.8	925.8	895.8
75–84 years[f]	853.5	1,053.3	1,624.8	2,029.6	2,478.3	2,351.8	1,569.4	1,526.9
85 years and over	—	1,155.2	1,387.0	2,393.9	3,238.3	3,264.8	2,378.6	2,316.0

decreased ability of the hormone insulin to regulate blood sugar, and chronic inflammation may spur the growth of cancer. Older adults may also be more susceptible to cancer-causing agents in the environment such as second-hand smoke and chemical pollutants (e.g., asbestos and radiation).

TABLE 7.11

Death rates for malignant neoplasms, selected characteristics, selected years 1950–2015 [CONTINUED]

[Data are based on death certificates]

—Data not available.
Note: Rates based on fewer than 20 deaths are considered unreliable and are not shown.
[a]Includes deaths of persons who were not residents of the 50 states and the District of Columbia (D.C.).
[b]Underlying cause of death was coded according to the 6th Revision of the International Classification of Diseases (ICD) in 1950, 7th Revision in 1960, 8th Revision in 1970, and 9th Revision in 1980–1998.
[c]Starting with 1999 data, cause of death is coded according to ICD–10.
[d]Age-adjusted rates are calculated using the year 2000 standard population. Prior to 2001, age-adjusted rates were calculated using standard million proportions based on rounded population numbers. Starting with 2001 data, unrounded population numbers are used to calculate age-adjusted rates.
[e]The race groups, white, black, Asian or Pacific Islander, and American Indian or Alaska Native, include persons of Hispanic and non-Hispanic origin. Persons of Hispanic origin may be of any race. Death rates for Hispanic, American Indian or Alaska Native, and Asian or Pacific Islander persons should be interpreted with caution because of inconsistencies in reporting Hispanic origin or race on the death certificate (death rate numerators) compared with population figures (death rate demominators). The net effect of misclassification is an underestimation of deaths and death rates for races other than white and black.
Detailed discussion of sources of bias in death rates by race and Hispanic origin.
[f]In 1950, rate is for the age group 75 years and over.

SOURCE: Adapted from "Table 24. Death Rates for Malignant Neoplasms, by Sex, Race, Hispanic Origin, and Age: United States, Selected Years 1950–2015," in *Health, United States, 2016: With Chartbook on Long-Term Trends in Health*, National Center for Health Statistics, May 2017, https://www.cdc.gov/nchs/data/hus/2016/024.pdf (accessed October 24, 2017)

Success in treating certain cancers, such as Hodgkin's disease and some forms of leukemia, has been offset by the rise in rates of other cancers, such as breast and lung cancers. Table 7.6 shows that the number of cancer deaths among adults aged 65 years and older rose sharply from 258,389 in 1980 to 419,389 in 2015. Progress in treating cancer has largely been related to screenings, early diagnoses, and new drug therapies.

Stroke

Stroke (cerebrovascular disease or "brain attack") is the fourth-leading cause of death and is the principal cause of disability among older adults. (See Table 7.6.) In "Older Americans and Cardiovascular Diseases," the American Heart Association reports that among adults aged 60 to 79 years the risk of stroke is 6.1% for men and 5.2% for women. Among those aged 80 years and older, the risk rises to 15.8% for men and 14% for women.

According to the NCHS, in *Health, United States, 2016*, strokes killed 146,417 people aged 65 years and older in 1980. (Table 7.6.) In 2015, among people aged 65 years and older, 120,156 deaths were attributable to stroke. The death rate for people aged 65 to 74 years declined as well, from 219 per 100,000 population in 1980 to 75.5 per 100,000 population in 2015. (See Table 7.12.) There was a comparable decline for people aged 75 to 84 years. There were 273 deaths from stroke per 100,000 population for this age group in 2015, down from 786.9 deaths per 100,000 population in 1980. The improvement was even greater for people aged 85 years and older. There were 975.8 deaths from stroke per 100,000 population for this age group in 2015, less than half the rate of 2,283.7 per 100,000 population in 1980.

In "Stroke Rehab to Regain Arm Movement" (February 15, 2017, https://www.webmd.com/stroke/ss/slideshow-stroke), WebMD observes that about 80% of stroke victims suffer some weakness or paralysis on the opposite side of the body from where the stroke occurred in the brain. Although stroke rehabilitation improves the chances of recovery, some stroke survivors must learn to live with disability.

HEALTHY AGING

According to the CDC, ample research demonstrates that healthy lifestyles have a greater effect than genetic factors in helping to prevent the deterioration that is traditionally associated with aging. People who are physically active, eat a healthy diet, and do not smoke reduce their risk for chronic diseases, have half the rate of disability of those who do not, and can delay disability by as many as 10 years.

Among the recommended health practices for older adults is participating in early detection practices such as screenings for hypertension, cancer, diabetes, and depression. Screening detects diseases early in their course, when they are most treatable; however, many older adults do not obtain the recommended screenings.

Because falls are the most common cause of injuries in older adults, injury prevention is a vitally important way to prevent disability. The CDC reports in "Important Facts about Falls" (February 10, 2017, https://www.cdc.gov/HomeandRecreationalSafety/Falls/adultfalls.html) that more than a quarter of adults aged 65 years and older fall each year, and of those who fall, 20% suffer broken bones or other injuries that impair mobility and independence. The death rate from unintentional falls has climbed steadily between 2005 and 2014. (See Figure 7.13.) Removing tripping hazards in the home, such as rugs, and installing grab bars in bathrooms are simple measures that can greatly reduce older Americans' risk for falls and fractures.

The current cohort of older adults is better equipped to prevent the illness, disability, and death associated

TABLE 7.12

Death rates for cerebrovascular disease, by age group, selected years 1950–2015

[Data are based on death certificates]

Sex, race, Hispanic origin, and age	1950[b, c]	1960[b, c]	1970[c]	1980[c]	1990[c]	2000[d]	2014[d]	2015[d]
All persons				Deaths per 100,000 resident population				
All ages, age-adjusted[e]	180.7	177.9	147.7	96.2	65.3	60.9	36.5	37.6
All ages, crude	104.0	108.0	101.9	75.0	57.8	59.6	41.7	43.7
Under 1 year	5.1	4.1	5.0	4.4	3.8	3.3	2.4	2.2
1–4 years	0.9	0.8	1.0	0.5	0.3	0.3	0.2	0.3
5–14 years	0.5	0.7	0.7	0.3	0.2	0.2	0.2	0.2
15–24 years	1.6	1.8	1.6	1.0	0.6	0.5	0.4	0.4
25–34 years	4.2	4.7	4.5	2.6	2.2	1.5	1.3	1.3
35–44 years	18.7	14.7	15.6	8.5	6.4	5.8	4.3	4.4
45–54 years	70.4	49.2	41.6	25.2	18.7	16.0	12.3	12.3
55–64 years	194.2	147.3	115.8	65.1	47.9	41.0	29.3	29.6
65–74 years	554.7	469.2	384.1	219.0	144.2	128.6	74.5	75.5
75–84 years	1,499.6	1,491.3	1,254.2	786.9	498.0	461.3	265.7	273.0
85 years and over	2,990.1	3,680.5	3,014.3	2,283.7	1,628.9	1,589.2	929.7	975.8
Male								
All ages, age-adjusted[e]	186.4	186.1	157.4	102.2	68.5	62.4	36.9	37.8
All ages, crude	102.5	104.5	94.5	63.4	46.7	46.9	35.3	36.8
Under 1 year	6.4	5.0	5.8	5.0	4.4	3.8	2.6	2.6
1–4 years	1.1	0.9	1.2	0.4	0.3	a	a	0.3
5–14 years	0.5	0.7	0.8	0.3	0.2	0.2	0.2	0.2
15–24 years	1.8	1.9	1.8	1.1	0.7	0.5	0.5	0.4
25–34 years	4.2	4.5	4.4	2.6	2.1	1.5	1.5	1.4
35–44 years	17.5	14.6	15.7	8.7	6.8	5.8	5.0	4.9
45–54 years	67.9	52.2	44.4	27.2	20.5	17.5	14.0	13.6
55–64 years	205.2	163.8	138.7	74.6	54.3	47.2	35.2	35.4
65–74 years	589.6	530.7	449.5	258.6	166.6	145.0	85.1	86.3
75–84 years	1,543.6	1,555.9	1,361.6	866.3	551.1	490.8	272.8	282.2
85 years and over	3,048.6	3,643.1	2,895.2	2,193.6	1,528.5	1,484.3	832.0	863.3
Female								
All ages, age-adjusted[e]	175.8	170.7	140.0	91.7	62.6	59.1	35.6	36.9
All ages, crude	105.6	111.4	109.0	85.9	68.4	71.8	47.9	50.3
Under 1 year	3.7	3.2	4.0	3.8	3.1	2.7	2.1	1.9
1–4 years	0.7	0.7	0.7	0.5	0.3	0.4	a	a
5–14 years	0.4	0.6	0.6	0.3	0.2	0.2	0.2	0.2
15–24 years	1.5	1.6	1.4	0.8	0.6	0.5	0.3	0.4
25–34 years	4.3	4.9	4.7	2.6	2.2	1.5	1.2	1.1
35–44 years	19.9	14.8	15.6	8.4	6.1	5.7	3.7	3.9
45–54 years	72.9	46.3	39.0	23.3	17.0	14.5	10.7	11.0
55–64 years	183.1	131.8	95.3	56.8	42.2	35.3	23.8	24.3
65–74 years	522.1	415.7	333.3	188.7	126.7	115.1	65.2	66.0
75–84 years	1,462.2	1,441.1	1,183.1	740.1	466.2	442.1	260.3	266.0
85 years and over	2,949.4	3,704.4	3,081.0	2,323.1	1,667.6	1,632.0	980.6	1,035.3

[a]Rates based on fewer than 20 deaths are considered unreliable and are not shown.
[b]Includes deaths of persons who were not residents of the 50 states and the District of Columbia (D.C.).
[c]Underlying cause of death was coded according to the 6th Revision of the International Classification of Diseases (ICD) in 1950, 7th Revision in 1960, 8th Revision in 1970, and 9th Revision in 1980–1998.
[d]Starting with 1999 data, cause of death is coded according to ICD-10.
[e]Age-adjusted rates are calculated using the year 2000 standard population. Prior to 2001, age-adjusted rates were calculated using standard million proportions based on rounded population numbers. Starting with 2001 data, unrounded population numbers are used to calculate age-adjusted rates.

SOURCE: Adapted from "Table 23. Death Rates for Cerebrovascular Diseases, by Sex, Race, Hispanic Origin, and Age: United States, Selected Years 1950–2015," in *Health, United States, 2016: With Chartbook on Long-Term Trends in Health*, National Center for Health Statistics, May 2017, https://www.cdc.gov/nchs/data/hus/2016/023.pdf (accessed October 24, 2017)

with many chronic diseases than any previous generation. They are less likely to smoke, drink, or experience detrimental stress than younger people, and older adults have better eating habits than their younger counterparts. For example, the percentage of men aged 65 years and older who smoke cigarettes declined from 28.5% in 1965 to 9.7% in 2015. (See Table 7.13.) In contrast, the percentage of women the same age who smoke remained relatively constant during this period, decreasing slightly from 9.6% to 7.5%.

Smoking

Data from the 2017 National Health Interview Survey reveal that adults aged 65 years and older were the least likely to be current smokers—just 8.8%, compared with 14.8% of adults aged 18 to 44 years and 18.2% of those aged 45 to 64 years. (See Figure 7.14.)

The US surgeon general explains that even older adult smokers realize health benefits from quitting. For example, a smoker's risk of heart disease begins to

FIGURE 7.13

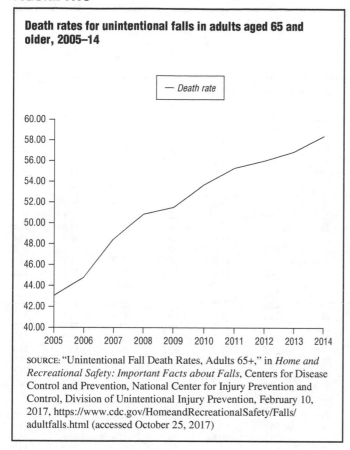

Death rates for unintentional falls in adults aged 65 and older, 2005–14

— Death rate

SOURCE: "Unintentional Fall Death Rates, Adults 65+," in *Home and Recreational Safety: Important Facts about Falls*, Centers for Disease Control and Prevention, National Center for Injury Prevention and Control, Division of Unintentional Injury Prevention, February 10, 2017, https://www.cdc.gov/HomeandRecreationalSafety/Falls/adultfalls.html (accessed October 25, 2017)

decline almost immediately after quitting, regardless of how long the person smoked.

Maintaining a Healthy Weight

The United States is in the throes of an obesity epidemic. Obesity is defined as a body mass index (a number that shows body weight adjusted for height) greater than or equal to 30 kilograms per meters squared. In 2017, 31.1% of adults aged 60 years and older were obese, and the group of adults aged 40 to 59 years that will soon join the ranks of older Americans reported the highest rate of obesity, at 38%. (See Figure 7.15.)

Obesity increases the risk for multiple health problems, including hypertension, high cholesterol, type 2 diabetes, coronary heart disease, congestive heart failure, stroke, arthritis, obstructive sleep apnea, and other serious conditions.

Physical Activity

Regular physical activity comes closer to being a fountain of youth than any prescription medicine. Along with helping older adults to remain mobile and independent, exercise can lower the risk of obesity, heart disease, stroke, diabetes, and some cancers. It can also delay osteoporosis and arthritis, reduce symptoms of depression, and improve sleep quality and memory. Despite these benefits, older adults are less likely to exercise than younger adults. In 2017, 28.1% of adults aged 75 years and older met the 2008 federal physical activity guidelines for aerobic activity (150 minutes a week of moderate-intensity aerobic physical activity, or 75 minutes a week of vigorous-intensity aerobic physical activity, or an equivalent combination of moderate- and vigorous-intensity aerobic activity) through leisure-time activity. (See Figure 7.16.) Increasing evidence suggests that behavior change, even late in life, is beneficial and can improve disease control and enhance quality of life.

Use of Preventive Health Services

More widespread use of preventive services is a key to preserving and extending the health and quality of life of older Americans. Screening for early detection of selected cancers (such as breast, cervical, and colorectal) as well as diabetes, cardiovascular disease, and glaucoma can save lives and slow the progress of chronic disease. People with a regular source of medical care are more likely to receive basic medical services, such as routine checkups, which present the opportunity to receive preventive services. In 2017, 96.6% of adults aged 65 years and older reported having a regular source of medical care. (See Figure 7.17.) Given that Medicare covers a comprehensive range of preventive services and screenings, such as screening for heart disease, cancer, diabetes, glaucoma, and depression, it seems unlikely that cost prevents older adults from obtaining these services. Data from the 2017 National Health Interview Survey reveal that just 2.9% of respondents aged 65 years and older reported that they failed to obtain needed medical care because of cost during the 12 months preceding the interview. (See Figure 7.18.)

SEXUALITY IN AGING

Despite the popular belief that sexuality is exclusively for the young, sexual interest, activity, and capabilities are often lifelong. Although the growing population of older adults will likely spur additional research, to date there are scant data about the levels of sexual activity among older adults. The data that are available are often limited to community-dwelling older adults, so there is nearly no information about the sexual behavior of institutionalized older adults.

After age 50 sexual responses slow; however, very rarely does this natural and gradual diminution cause older adults to end all sexual activity. More important in terms of curtailing older adults' sexual activity is the lack of available partners, which limits opportunities for sexual expression, especially for older women. Another issue is the greater incidence of illness and progression of chronic diseases that occurs with advancing age. Medical problems with the potential to adversely affect sexual function include diabetes, hypothyroidism (a condition in which the thyroid is underactive—producing too little

TABLE 7.13

Current cigarette smoking by age and sex, selected years 1965–2015

[Data are based on household interviews of a sample of the civilian noninstitutionalized population]

Sex, race, and age	1965[a]	1979[a]	1985[a]	1990[a]	2000	2005	2010	2012	2013	2014	2015
18 years and over, age-adjusted[b]					Percent of adults who were current cigarette smokers[c]						
All persons	41.9	33.3	29.9	25.3	23.1	20.8	19.3	18.2	17.9	17.0	15.3
Male	51.2	37.0	32.2	28.0	25.2	23.4	21.2	20.6	20.5	19.0	16.8
Female	33.7	30.1	27.9	22.9	21.1	18.3	17.5	15.9	15.5	15.1	13.8
White male[d]	50.4	36.4	31.3	27.6	25.4	23.3	21.4	20.7	20.5	18.8	16.8
Black or African American male[d]	58.8	43.9	40.2	32.8	25.7	25.9	23.3	22.0	21.8	21.7	20.3
White female[d]	33.9	30.3	27.9	23.5	22.0	19.1	18.3	16.9	16.3	16.0	14.8
Black or African American female[d]	31.8	30.5	30.9	20.8	20.7	17.1	16.6	14.2	14.9	13.4	13.2
18 years and over, crude											
All persons	42.4	33.5	30.1	25.5	23.2	20.9	19.3	18.1	17.8	16.8	15.1
Male	51.9	37.5	32.6	28.4	25.6	23.9	21.5	20.5	20.5	18.8	16.7
Female	33.9	29.9	27.9	22.8	20.9	18.1	17.3	15.8	15.3	14.8	13.6
White male[d]	51.1	36.8	31.7	28.0	25.7	23.6	21.4	20.3	20.3	18.5	16.5
Black or African American male[d]	60.4	44.1	39.9	32.5	26.2	26.5	24.3	22.0	21.9	21.8	20.6
White female[d]	34.0	30.1	27.7	23.4	21.4	18.7	17.9	16.6	15.9	15.5	14.3
Black or African American female[d]	33.7	31.1	31.0	21.2	20.8	17.3	17.0	14.7	15.1	13.5	13.1
All males											
18–44 years	57.9	40.4	35.2	31.4	29.2	27.1	23.9	24.0	22.9	21.7	18.5
18–24 years	54.1	35.0	28.0	26.6	28.1	28.0	22.8	20.1	21.9	18.5	15.0
25–34 years	60.7	43.9	38.2	31.6	28.9	27.7	26.1	28.0	24.4	23.7	21.3
35–44 years	58.2	41.8	37.6	34.5	30.2	26.0	22.5	22.8	22.1	22.0	18.3
45–64 years	51.9	39.3	33.4	29.3	26.4	25.2	23.2	20.2	21.9	19.4	17.9
45–54 years	55.9	42.0	34.9	32.1	28.8	28.1	25.2	21.4	21.4	19.9	18.3
55–64 years	46.6	36.4	31.9	25.9	22.6	21.1	20.7	18.8	22.6	18.8	17.5
65 years and over	28.5	20.9	19.6	14.6	10.2	8.9	9.7	10.6	10.6	9.8	9.7
All females											
18–44 years	42.1	34.7	31.4	25.6	24.5	21.2	19.1	16.9	16.6	16.6	14.5
18–24 years	38.1	33.8	30.4	22.5	24.9	20.7	17.4	14.5	15.4	14.8	11.0
25–34 years	43.7	33.7	32.0	28.2	22.3	21.5	20.6	19.4	17.9	17.5	15.0
35–44 years	43.7	37.0	31.5	24.8	26.2	21.3	19.0	16.1	16.3	17.0	16.5
45–64 years	32.0	30.7	29.9	24.8	21.7	18.8	19.1	18.9	18.1	16.8	16.1
45–54 years	37.5	32.6	32.4	28.5	22.2	20.9	21.3	21.3	20.6	18.7	18.4
55–64 years	25.0	28.6	27.4	20.5	20.9	16.1	16.5	16.2	15.2	14.8	13.7
65 years and over	9.6	13.2	13.5	11.5	9.3	8.3	9.3	7.5	7.5	7.5	7.5

[a]Data prior to 1997 are not strictly comparable with data for later years due to the 1997 questionnaire redesign.
[b]Estimates are age-adjusted to the year 2000 standard population using five age groups: 18–24 years, 25–34 years, 35–44 years, 45–64 years, and 65 years and over. Age-adjusted estimates in this table may differ from other age-adjusted estimates based on the same data and presented elsewhere if different age groups are used in the adjustment procedure.
[c]Starting with 1993 data, current cigarette smokers were defined as ever smoking 100 cigarettes in their lifetime and smoking now every day or some days.
[d]The race groups, white and black, include persons of Hispanic and non-Hispanic origin. Starting with 1999 data, race-specific estimates are tabulated according to the 1997 Revisions to the Standards for the Classification of Federal Data on Race and Ethnicity and are not strictly comparable with estimates for earlier years. The single-race categories shown in the table conform to the 1997 Standards. Starting with 1999 data, race-specific estimates are for persons who reported only one racial group. Prior to 1999, data were tabulated according to the 1977 Standards. Estimates for single-race categories prior to 1999 included persons who reported one race or, if they reported more than one race, identified one race as best representing their race. Starting with 2003 data, race responses of other race and unspecified multiple race were treated as missing, and then race was imputed if these were the only race responses. Almost all persons with a race response of other race were of Hispanic origin.

source: Adapted from "Table 47. Current Cigarette Smoking among Adults Aged 18 and over, by Sex, Race, and Age: United States, Selected Years 1965—2015," in *Health, United States, 2016: With Chartbook on Long-Term Trends in Health*, National Center for Health Statistics, May 2017, https://www.cdc.gov/nchs/data/hus/2016/047.pdf (accessed October 24, 2017).

thyroid hormones), neuropathy (a disease or abnormality of the nervous system), cardiovascular disease, urinary tract infections, prostate cancer, incontinence, arthritis, depression, and dementia. Many pharmacological treatments for chronic illnesses have sexual side effects that range from diminished libido (sexual desire and drive) to erectile dysfunction. For example, some medications (e.g., antihypertensives, antidepressants, diuretics, steroids, anticonvulsants, and beta-blockers) have high rates of sexual side effects.

Despite these changes, research reveals that long-married couples still have active sex lives. In fact, couples married for 50 years actually experience a slight increase in their sex lives. In "Marital Characteristics and the Sexual Relationships of U.S. Older Adults: An Analysis of National Social Life, Health, and Aging Project Data" (*Archives of Sexual Behavior*, vol. 44, no. 1, January 2015), Samuel Stroope, Michael J. McFarland, and Jeremy E. Uecker explain this finding by observing that "relationship permanency may drive the greater sexual activity."

One of the biggest recent changes in the sex lives of older adults is older men's use of potency drugs for erectile dysfunction (Viagra, Cialis, and Levitra) to enhance their performance. Since the 1998 debut of Viagra, these pharmaceutical solutions to erectile changes affecting older men have enjoyed tremendous popularity.

FIGURE 7.14

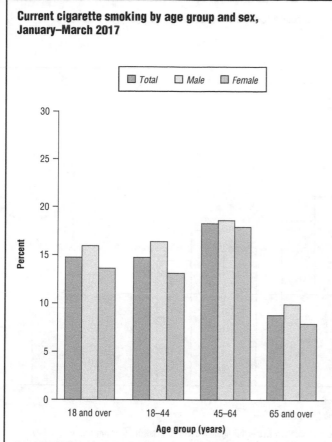

Current cigarette smoking by age group and sex, January–March 2017

Notes: Data are based on household interviews of a sample of the civilian noninstitutionalized population. Current cigarette smokers were defined as those who had smoked more than 100 cigarettes in their lifetime and now smoke every day or some days. The analyses exclude the 0.4% of persons with unknown cigarette smoking status.

SOURCE: "Figure 8.3. Prevalence of Current Cigarette Smoking among Adults Aged 18 and over, by Age Group and Sex: United States, January–March 2017," in *Early Release of Selected Estimates Based on Data from the National Health Interview Survey, January–March 2017*, Centers for Disease Control and Prevention, National Center for Health Statistics, September 2017, https://www.cdc.gov/nchs/data/nhis/earlyrelease/Earlyrelease201709_08.pdf (accessed October 24, 2017)

FIGURE 7.15

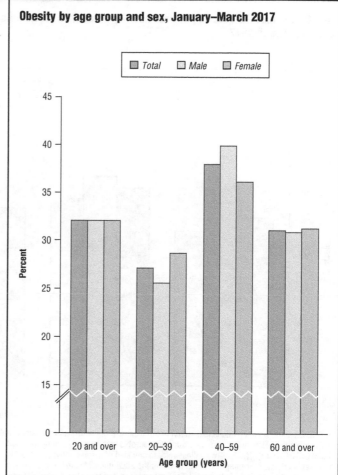

Obesity by age group and sex, January–March 2017

Notes: Data are based on household interviews of a sample of the civilian noninstitutionalized population. Obesity is defined as a body mass index of 30 kg/m² or more. The measure is based on self-reported height (m) and weight (kg). Estimates of obesity are restricted to adults aged 20 and over for consistency with the Healthy People 2020 (3) initiative. The analyses exclude the 3.6% of persons with unknown height or weight.

SOURCE: "Figure 6.2. Prevalence of Obesity among Adults Aged 20 and over, by Age Group and Sex: United States, January–March 2017," in *Early Release of Selected Estimates Based on Data from the National Health Interview Survey, January–March 2017*, Centers for Disease Control and Prevention, National Center for Health Statistics, September 2017, https://www.cdc.gov/nchs/data/nhis/earlyrelease/Earlyrelease201709_06.pdf (accessed October 24, 2017)

Sexually Transmitted Infections

Mark Stibich reports in "Sexual Activity among Older Populations" (Verywell.com, December 20, 2017) that a British study finds that 60% of men in their 70s and 80s are sexually active. Research conducted at Indiana University's Center for Sexual Health Promotion finds that 43% of men and 22% of women between the ages of 70 and 80 years engage in sexual intercourse. Because older women no longer require protection against pregnancy, many older adults do not practice safe sex. As a result, there has been an increase in sexually transmitted infections among older adults.

Data from the 2017 National Health Interview Survey reveal that adults aged 65 years and older were the least likely to have ever had an HIV test of any age group. Just 21.7% of men and 19% of women aged 65 years and older reported having had an HIV test. (See Figure 7.19.)

THE SHORTAGE OF SPECIALISTS IN GERIATRIC MEDICINE

In 1909 the American physician Ignatz L. Nascher (1863–1944) coined the term *geriatrics* from the Greek *geras* (old age) and *iatrikos* (physician). Geriatricians are physicians trained in internal medicine or family practice who obtain additional training and medical board certification in the diagnosis and treatment of older adults.

The American Geriatrics Society observes in "Who We Are" (https://www.americangeriatrics.org/about-us/who-we-are) that in 2017 there were about 6,000 board-certified

FIGURE 7.16

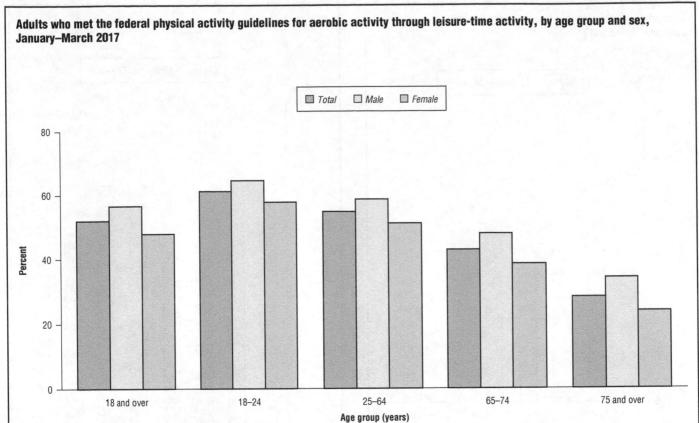

Adults who met the federal physical activity guidelines for aerobic activity through leisure-time activity, by age group and sex, January–March 2017

Notes: Data are based on household interviews of a sample of the civilian noninstitutionalized population. Estimates in this figure are limited to leisure-time physical activity only. This measure reflects an estimate of leisure-time aerobic activity motivated by the 2008 federal Physical Activity Guidelines for Americans, which are being used for Healthy People 2020 Objectives (3). The 2008 guidelines refer to any kind of aerobic activity, not just leisure-time aerobic activity, so the leisure-time aerobic activity estimates in this figure may underestimate the percentage of adults who met the 2008 guidelines for aerobic activity. This figure presents the percentage of adults who met the 2008 federal guidelines for aerobic activity. The 2008 federal guidelines recommend that for substantial health benefits, adults perform at least 150 minutes a week of moderate-intensity aerobic physical activity, 75 minutes a week of vigorous-intensity aerobic physical activity, or an equivalent combination of moderate- and vigorous-intensity aerobic activity. The 2008 guidelines state that aerobic activity should be performed in episodes of at least 10 minutes and preferably should be spread throughout the week. The analyses exclude the 2.0% of persons with unknown physical activity participation.

SOURCE: "Figure 7.2. Percentage of Adults Aged 18 and over Who Met the 2008 Federal Physical Activity Guidelines for Aerobic Activity through Leisure-Time Aerobic Activity, by Age Group and Sex: United States, January–March 2017," in *Early Release of Selected Estimates Based on Data from the National Health Interview Survey, January–March 2017*, Centers for Disease Control and Prevention, National Center for Health Statistics, September 2017, https://www.cdc.gov/nchs/data/nhis/earlyrelease/Earlyrelease201709_07.pdf (accessed October 24, 2017)

geriatricians, which is fewer than half of the estimated need. The shortage of specially trained physicians will intensify as the baby boom generation (people born between 1946 and 1964) joins the ranks of older adults. The American Geriatrics Society contends that financial disincentives pose the greatest barrier to new physicians entering geriatrics.

In "As Population Ages, Where Are the Geriatricians?" (NYTimes.com, January 25, 2016), Katie Hafner reports that there were about 7,000 geriatricians in practice in 2016, with a projected need for an additional 6,250 by 2030, which is about 450 more per year than are trained at the current rate.

FIGURE 7.17

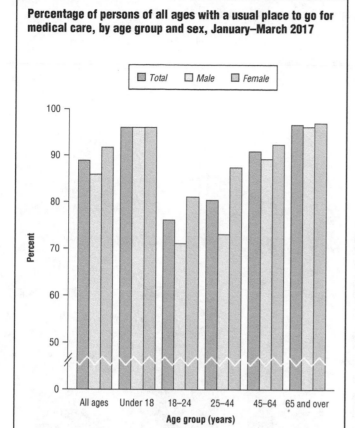

Percentage of persons of all ages with a usual place to go for medical care, by age group and sex, January–March 2017

Notes: Data are based on household interviews of a sample of the civilian noninstitutionalized population. The usual place to go for medical care does not include a hospital emergency room. The analyses excluded the 0.7% of persons with an unknown usual place to go for medical care.

SOURCE: "Figure 2.2. Percentage of Persons of All Ages with a Usual Place to Go for Medical Care, by Age Group and Sex: United States, January–March 2017," in *Early Release of Selected Estimates Based on Data from the National Health Interview Survey, January–March 2017*, Centers for Disease Control and Prevention, National Center for Health Statistics, September 2017, https://www.cdc.gov/nchs/data/nhis/earlyrelease/Earlyrelease201709_02.pdf (accessed October 24, 2017)

FIGURE 7.18

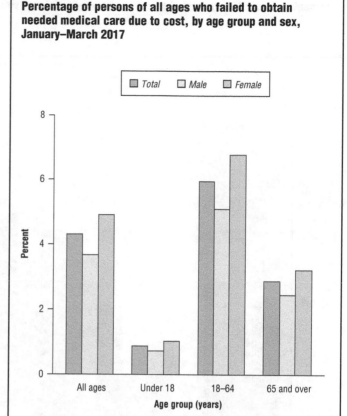

Percentage of persons of all ages who failed to obtain needed medical care due to cost, by age group and sex, January–March 2017

Notes: Data are based on household interviews of a sample of the civilian noninstitutionalized population. The analyses exclude the <0.1% of persons with unknown responses to the question on failure to obtain needed medical care due to cost.

SOURCE: "Figure 3.2. Percentage of Persons of All Ages Who Failed to Obtain Needed Medical Care Due to Cost at Some Time during the Past 12 Months, by Age Group and Sex: United States, January–March 2017," in *Early Release of Selected Estimates Based on Data from the National Health Interview Survey, January–March 2017*, Centers for Disease Control and Prevention, National Center for Health Statistics, September 2017, https://www.cdc.gov/nchs/data/nhis/earlyrelease/Earlyrelease201709_03.pdf (accessed October 24, 2017)

FIGURE 7.19

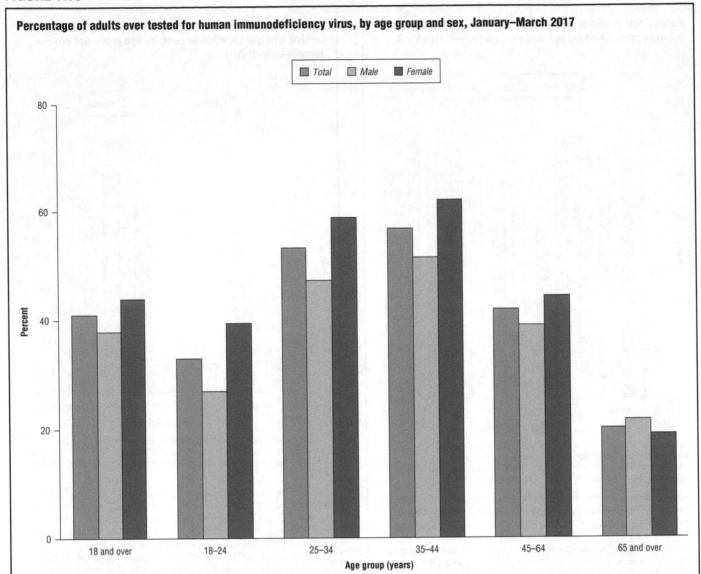

Percentage of adults ever tested for human immunodeficiency virus, by age group and sex, January–March 2017

Notes: Data are based on household interviews of a sample of the civilian noninstitutionalized population. Persons who received human immunodeficiency virus (HIV) testing solely as a result of blood donation were considered not to have been tested for HIV. The AIDS Knowledge and Attitudes section of the National Health Interview Survey (NHIS) was dropped in 2011; only the HIV testing question was retained, and it was moved to the Adult Access to Health Care and Utilization section of the Sample Adult questionnaire. In 2013, the HIV testing question was moved again to the Adult Selected Items section of the Sample Adult questionnaire and is not comparable with 2011–2012. Differences observed in estimates based on 2010 and earlier NHIS, 2011–2012 NHIS, and 2013 and later NHIS may be partially or fully attributable to these changes in placement of the HIV testing question in the NHIS questionnaire. The analyses exclude the 5.2% of adults with unknown HIV test status.

SOURCE: "Figure 10.2. Percentage of Adults Aged 18 and over Who Had Ever Been Tested for HIV, by Age Group and Sex: United States, January–March 2017," in *Early Release of Selected Estimates Based on Data from the National Health Interview Survey, January—March 2017*, Centers for Disease Control and Prevention, National Center for Health Statistics, September 2017, https://www.cdc.gov/nchs/data/nhis/earlyrelease/Earlyrelease201709_10 .pdf (accessed October 24, 2017).

CHAPTER 8
MENTAL HEALTH AND MENTAL ILLNESS

Changes in mental capabilities are among the most feared aspects of aging. Mental health problems that impair functioning are among the most common age-related changes. They are cause for concern because cognitive impairment (loss of intellectual functioning accompanied by memory loss and personality changes) is associated with increased risk for disability and progression to dementia (chronic disorder characterized by impaired reasoning, judgment, and language skills caused by damage to or death of nerve cells in the brain).

The aging population has spurred interest in age-related problems in cognition (the process of thinking, learning, and remembering). Cognitive difficulties much milder than those that are associated with organic brain diseases, such as Alzheimer's disease (AD; a type of dementia), affect a significant proportion of older adults. Organic brain diseases, often referred to as organic brain syndromes, refer to physical disorders of the brain that produce mental health problems as opposed to psychiatric conditions, which may also cause mental health problems.

In "Screening for Cognitive Impairment in Older Adults: U.S. Preventive Services Task Force Recommendation Statement" (*Annals of Internal Medicine*, vol. 160, no. 11, June 3, 2014), Virginia A. Moyer of the US Preventive Services Task Force in Rockville, Maryland, indicates that estimates of the prevalence (the total number of cases of a disorder in a given population at a specific time) of mild cognitive impairment among adults aged 65 years and older vary, ranging from 3% to 42%. Between 2.4 million and 5.5 million Americans suffer from dementia. The prevalence of dementia increases with age, from 5% in people aged 71 to 79 years, to 24% in those aged 80 to 89 years, and to 37% in those aged 90 years and older.

Because the number of people with cognitive impairments and dementia is anticipated to increase as the population ages, and older adults with cognitive impairment are at risk for institutionalization, the economic burden for society is expected to escalate. As such, the mental health and illness of older adults is an increasingly important public health issue.

MENTAL HEALTH

Mental health may be measured in terms of an individual's abilities to think and communicate clearly, learn and grow emotionally, deal productively and realistically with change and stress, and form and maintain fulfilling relationships with others. Mental health is a key component of wellness (self-esteem, resilience, and the ability to cope with adversity), which influences how people feel about themselves.

When mental health is defined and measured in terms of the absence of serious psychological distress, then older adults fare quite well compared with other age groups. The 2017 National Health Interview Survey, conducted by the Centers for Disease Control and Prevention (CDC), questioned whether respondents had experienced serious psychological distress within the 30 days preceding the interview. Adults aged 65 years and older were the least likely to have experienced serious psychological distress (2.8%) in early 2017, compared with adults aged 45 to 64 years (4.6%) and adults aged 18 to 44 years (3.1%). (See Figure 8.1.) Earlier research, however, finds that more than more than one-quarter (27.3%) of people aged 65 years and older with serious psychological distress also had limitations in activities of daily living. (See Figure 8.2.)

Experience Shapes Mental Health in Old Age

One theory of aging, called continuity theory and explained by Robert C. Atchley in *The Social Forces in Later Life: An Introduction to Social Gerontology* (1985), posits that people who age most successfully are those who carry forward the habits, preferences, lifestyles, and relationships from midlife into late life. This theory has

FIGURE 8.1

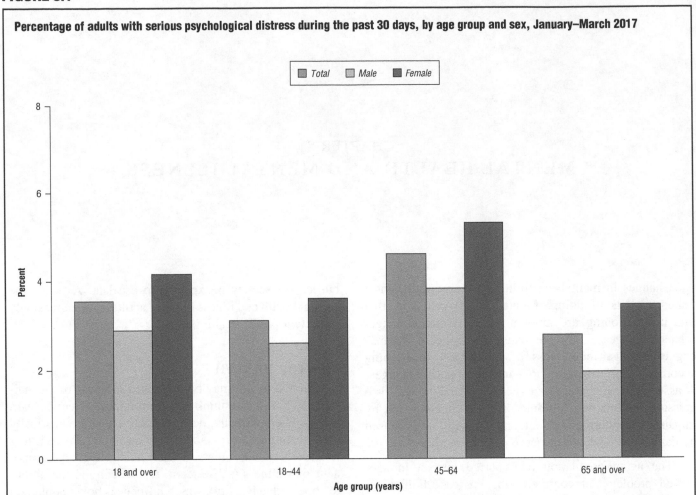

Percentage of adults with serious psychological distress during the past 30 days, by age group and sex, January–March 2017

Notes: Data are based on household interviews of a sample of the civilian noninstitutionalized population. Six psychological distress questions are included in the Sample Adult Core component of the National Health Interview Survey (NHIS). These questions ask how often a respondent experienced certain symptoms of psychological distress during the past 30 days. The response codes (0–4) of the six items for each person are summed to yield a scale with a 0–24 range. A value of 13 or more for this scale is used here to define serious psychological distress (12). In 2013, the six psychological distress questions were moved to the Adult Selected Items section of the Sample Adult questionnaire. Differences observed in estimates based on 2012 and earlier NHIS and 2013 and later NHIS may be partially or fully attributable to this change in placement of the six psychological distress questions in the NHIS questionnaire. The analyses exclude the 3.5% of persons with unknown serious psychological distress status.

SOURCE: "Figure 13.2. Percentage of Adults Aged 18 and over Who Experienced Serious Psychological Distress during the Past 30 Days, by Age Group and Sex: United States, January–March 2017," in *Early Release of Selected Estimates Based on Data from the National Health Interview Survey, January–March 2017*, Centers for Disease Control and Prevention, National Center for Health Statistics, September 2017, https://www.cdc.gov/nchs/data/nhis/earlyrelease/Earlyrelease201709_13.pdf (accessed October 24, 2017)

gained credence from research studies that find that traits measured in midlife are strong predictors of outcomes in later life and that many psychological and social characteristics are stable across the life span. For most people, old age does not represent a radical departure from the past; changes often occur gradually and sometimes unnoticeably. Most older adults adapt to the challenges and changes associated with later life using well-practiced coping skills that were acquired earlier in life.

Adults who have struggled with mental health problems or mental disorders throughout their life often continue to suffer these same problems in old age. Few personal problems disappear with old age, and many progress and become more acute. Marital problems, which may have been kept at bay because one or both

spouses were away at work, may intensify when a couple spends more time together in retirement. Reduced income, illness, and disability in retirement can aggravate an already troubled marriage and can strain even healthy interpersonal, marital, and other family relationships.

Older age can be a period of regrets, which can lead to mutual recriminations. With life expectancy rising, married couples can now expect to spend many years together in retirement. Most older couples manage the transition, but some have problems.

Coping with losses of friends, family, health, and independence may precipitate mental health problems. Hearing loss is common, and close correlations have been found between loss of hearing and depression. Visual impairment limits mobility and the ability to read and

FIGURE 8.2

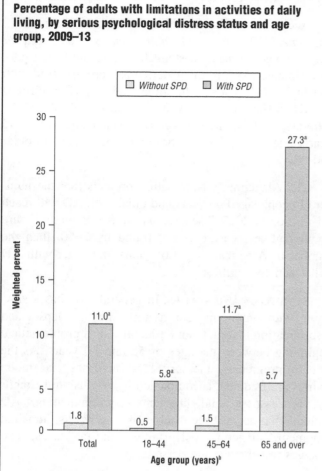

Percentage of adults with limitations in activities of daily living, by serious psychological distress status and age group, 2009–13

[Legend: □ Without SPD ■ With SPD]

Total: 1.8, 11.0[a]
18–44: 0.5, 5.8[a]
45–64: 1.5, 11.7[a]
65 and over: 5.7, 27.3[a]

Weighted percent (y-axis)
Age group (years)[b] (x-axis)

[a]Significant difference from adults without serious psychological distress.
[b]Significant increasing linear trend by age group.
Note: SPD is serious psychological distress.

SOURCE: Judith Weissman et al. "Figure 4. Percentage of Adults Aged 18 and over with Limitations in Activities of Daily Living at Interview, by Serious Psychological Distress Status and Age: United States, 2009–2013," in "Serious Psychological Distress among Adults: United States, 2009<en>2013," *NCHS Data Brief*, no. 203, Centers for Disease Control and Prevention, National Center for Health Statistics, May 2015, https://www.cdc.gov/nchs/data/databriefs/db203.htm (accessed October 25, 2017)

watch television. Loss of sight or hearing can cause perceptual disorientation, which in turn may lead to depression, paranoia, fear, and alienation.

A constant awareness of the imminence of death can also become a problem for older adults. Although most older adults resolve their anxieties and concerns about death, some live in denial and fear. How well older adults accept the inevitability of death is a key determinant of satisfaction and emotional well-being in old age.

Memory

Because memory is a key component of cognitive functioning, declining memory that substantially impairs older adults' functioning is a major risk factor for institutionalization. In "Self-Reported Increased Confusion or Memory Loss and Associated Functional Difficulties among Adults Aged ≥60 Years—21 States, 2011" (*Morbidity and Mortality Weekly Report*, vol. 62, no. 18, May 10, 2013), Mary L. Adams et al. report that an analysis of data from the 2011 Behavioral Risk Factor Surveillance System survey finds that 12.7% of older adults reported increased confusion or memory loss in the 12 months preceding the survey. Of those reporting increased confusion or memory loss, more than one-third (35.2%) described experiencing functional difficulties. The percentage reporting confusion or memory loss was significantly higher among people aged 85 years and older (15.6%), compared with those aged 60 to 64 years (12%) and 65 to 74 years (11.9%) and retirees (12.3%).

ORGANIC BRAIN DISEASES—DEMENTIAS

Dementia refers to a range of mental and behavioral changes caused by cerebrovascular or neurological diseases that permanently damage the brain, impairing the activity of brain cells. These changes can affect memory, speech, and the ability to perform the activities of daily living.

Occasional forgetfulness and memory lapses are not signs of dementia. Dementia is caused by disease and is not the inevitable result of growing older. Many disorders may cause or simulate dementia, which is not a single disorder; dementia refers to a condition that is caused by a variety of diseases and disorders, a small proportion of which are potentially reversible.

Furthermore, research suggests that although people with cognitive impairment have an increased risk for dementia, not all people with mild cognitive impairment will progress over time to dementia. In "Neuropsychological Measures That Predict Progression from Mild Cognitive Impairment to Alzheimer's Type Dementia in Older Adults: A Systematic Review and Meta-analysis" (*Neuropsychology Review*, vol. 27, no. 4, December 2017), Sylvie Belleville et al. conducted a large meta-analysis (a review that looks at the findings of many studies) and report that although older adults with mild cognitive impairment have a 10-fold greater risk of progression to dementia than the general population, not all individuals who meet the criteria for mild cognitive impairment will progress to dementia. The researchers show that performance on cognitive tests can predict whether patients with mild cognitive impairment will progress to dementia at least three years before the time when the diagnosis of dementia is made.

Multi-infarct Dementia

The National Institute of Neurological Disorders and Stroke indicates in "Multi-infarct Dementia Information Page" (2017, https://www.ninds.nih.gov/Disorders/All-Disorders/Multi-Infarct-Dementia-Information-Page) that multi-infarct dementia is a common cause of memory loss and progressive dementia. Multi-infarct dementia is caused by a series of small strokes that disrupt blood flow and damage or destroy brain tissue. Sometimes these small strokes are "silent," meaning that they produce no obvious symptoms and are detected only on imaging studies, such as computed tomography (CT) or magnetic resonance imaging (MRI) scans of the brain. An older adult may have a number of small strokes before experiencing noticeable changes in memory, reasoning, or other signs of multi-infarct dementia.

Because strokes occur suddenly, the loss of cognitive skills and memory present quickly, although some affected individuals may appear to improve for short periods, then decline again after having more strokes. Establishing the diagnosis of multi-infarct dementia is challenging because its symptoms are difficult to distinguish from those of Alzheimer's disease. Treatment cannot reverse the damage already done to the brain. Instead, it focuses on preventing further damage by reducing the risk of additional strokes. This entails treating the underlying causes of stroke, such as hypertension (high blood pressure), diabetes, high cholesterol, and heart disease. Surgical procedures to improve blood flow to the brain, such as carotid endarterectomy (a surgical procedure that removes blockages from the carotid arteries, which supply blood to the brain), angioplasty (a procedure that opens narrowed or blocked blood vessels of the heart), or stenting (using wire scaffolds that hold arteries open), as well as medications to reduce the risk of stroke are used to treat this condition.

PEOPLE WITH DIABETES ARE AT INCREASED RISK. Ralph N. Martins explains in "Understanding the Link between Dementia and Diabetes" (*Journal of Alzheimer's Disease*, vol. 59, no. 2, May 2017) that people with type 2 diabetes are at an increased risk for developing dementia. Although the exact way that diabetes increases risk for dementia is not yet known, evidence from imaging studies show increased brain wasting (atrophy) and greater impairment in brain function in type 2 diabetics compared with nondiabetics. Research also points to a relationship between the insulin resistance seen in diabetes and the accumulation of proteins associated with Alzheimer's disease (AD) as well as inflammatory changes common to both type 2 diabetes and AD.

Alzheimer's Disease

Alzheimer's disease (AD) is the most common form of dementia among older adults. It is characterized by severely compromised thinking, reasoning, behavior, and memory, and it may be among the most fearsome of age-related disorders because it challenges older adults' ability to live independently. The disease was named after Alois Alzheimer (1864–1915), the German neurologist who first described the anatomical changes in the brain—the plaques and tangles that are the characteristic markers of this progressive, degenerative disease.

According to the Alzheimer's Association, in *2017 Alzheimer's Disease Facts and Figures* (2017, https://www.alz.org/documents_custom/2017-facts-and-figures.pdf), an estimated 5.5 million Americans were afflicted with AD in 2017. The overwhelming majority (5.3 million) of AD sufferers were aged 65 years and older. An estimated 10% of people aged 65 years and older and nearly one-third (32%) of those aged 85 years and older had AD.

The Alzheimer's Association projects that the number of people aged 65 years and older with AD will reach 7.1 million in 2025. The association asserts that if a cure or preventive measure is not found by 2050, then the number of Americans aged 65 years and older with AD will reach 13.8 million.

SYMPTOMS AND STAGES. In general, AD has a slow onset, with symptoms such as mild memory lapses and disorientation that may not be identified as problematical beginning between the ages of 55 and 80 years. As the disease progresses, memory loss increases and mood swings are frequent, accompanied by confusion, irritability, restlessness, and problems communicating. AD patients may experience trouble finding words, impaired judgment, difficulty performing familiar tasks, and changes in behavior and personality.

In "Stages of Alzheimer's" (2017, https://www.alz.org/alzheimers_disease_stages_of_alzheimers.asp), the Alzheimer's Association describes how AD progresses. In the early stage, there is no and then little apparent cognitive decline, with mild lapses of memory, which are often discernible to family, friends, and coworkers. During moderate or middle-stage AD, cognitive decline is apparent. For example, AD patients may have diminished recall of recent activities or their own address or telephone number.

Ultimately, the disease progresses to severe or late-stage AD, when patients are entirely unable to care for themselves. In their terminal stages, AD victims require around-the-clock care and supervision. They no longer recognize family members, other caregivers, or themselves, and they require assistance with daily activities such as eating, dressing, bathing, and using the toilet. Eventually, they may become incontinent, blind, completely unable to communicate, and have difficulty swallowing.

According to the Alzheimer's Association, in *2017 Alzheimer's Disease Facts and Figures*, in 2017 an estimated 700,000 people died with AD, and it was the sixth-leading cause of death in people of all ages and the fifth-leading cause of death among adults aged 65 years and older.

GENETIC ORIGINS OF AD. AD is not a normal consequence of growing older. It is a disease of the brain that develops in response to genetic predisposition and nongenetic causative factors. Scientists have identified some genetic components of the disease and have observed the different patterns of inheritance, ages of onset, genes, chromosomes, and proteins that are linked to the development of AD.

In "The *mec-4* Gene Is a Member of a Family of *Caenorhabditis elegans* Genes That Can Mutate to Induce Neuronal Degeneration" (*Nature*, vol. 349, no. 6310, February 14, 1991), Monica Driscoll and Martin Chalfie of Columbia University reported their discovery that a mutation in a single gene could cause AD. The defect was in the gene that directs cells to produce a substance called amyloid protein. The researchers also found that low levels of acetylcholine, a neurotransmitter that is involved in learning and memory, contribute to the formation of hard deposits of amyloid protein that accumulate in the brains of AD patients. In healthy people, the protein fragments are broken down and excreted by the body.

In 1995 three more genes linked to AD were identified. Two genes are involved with forms of early-onset AD, which can begin as early as age 30. The third gene, known as apolipoprotein E (apoE), regulates lipid metabolism and helps redistribute cholesterol. In the brain, apoE participates in repairing nerve tissue that has been injured. According to the National Institute on Aging (NIA), in the press release "Cortex Area Thinner in Youth with Alzheimer's-Related Gene" (April 24, 2007, https://www.nimh.nih.gov/news/science-news/2007/cortex-area-thinner-in-youth-with-alzheimers-related-gene.shtml), 40% of late-onset AD patients have at least one apoE-4 gene, whereas only 10% to 25% of the general population has an apoE-4 gene. The NIA notes in "Alzheimer's Disease Fact Sheet" (August 17, 2016, https://www.nia.nih.gov/health/alzheimers-disease-fact-sheet) that research confirms that the apoE-4 gene increases the risk of developing AD, but it is not yet known how it acts to increase this risk. Inheriting the apoE-4 gene does not necessarily mean that a person will develop AD and the absence of the gene does not ensure that an individual will not develop AD.

In 2011 two studies published in *Nature Genetics* (vol. 43, no. 5)—Adam C. Naj et al.'s "Common Variants at MS4A4/MS4A6E, CD2AP, CD33, and EPHA1 Are Associated with Late-Onset Alzheimer's Disease" and Paul Hollingworth et al.'s "Common Variants at ABCA7, MS4A6A/MS4A4E, EPHA1, CD33, and CD2AP Are Associated with Alzheimer's Disease"— identified five additional genes that are implicated in increasing the risk of developing the disease and the course of the disease. It should be noted, however, that none of the recently identified genes plays as important a role as apoE; the newly identified genes increase risk by just 10% to 15%, compared with apoE, which confers a 400-fold increase in risk of developing AD.

In 2012 two groups of researchers—Harold Neumann and Mark J. Daly in "Variant *TREM2* as Risk Factor for Alzheimer's Disease," and Rita Guerreiro et al. in "*TREM2* Variants in Alzheimer's Disease" (both published in *New England Journal of Medicine*, vol. 368, no. 2, January 10, 2013)—identified mutations in the TREM2 gene, which is thought to interfere with the brain's ability to prevent the buildup of plaque. This discovery is important because it identifies a potential way to alter the course of AD.

Paola Piscopo et al. report in "SORL1 Gene Is Associated with the Conversion from Mild Cognitive Impairment to Alzheimer's Disease" (*Journal of Alzheimer's Disease*, April 16, 2015) that the sortilin-related receptor gene (SORL1), which is known to increase susceptibility for AD, may also be useful for identifying which people with mild cognitive impairment are at high risk for developing AD.

In 2017 Gerard D. Schellenberg et al. identified two additional genes that increase a person's risk of developing AD in "Rare Coding Variants in PLCG2, ABI3, and TREM2 Implicate Microglial-Mediated Innate Immunity in Alzheimer's Disease" (*Nature Genetics*, vol. 49, no. 9, September 2017). The research also identified a number of other genes and proteins that are likely to be important in the development of AD. These genes suggest that immune cells in the brain play a key role in the disease and may prove to be good targets for potential drug treatment to combat the disease.

As of February 2018, there were two ongoing, long-term NIA initiatives: the Alzheimer's Disease Genetics Study (2016, https://clinicaltrials.gov/ct2/show/NCT00064870), which began in 2003 and collects blood samples and deoxyribonucleic acid (DNA) for researchers to use, and the Alzheimer's Disease Genetics Consortium (2017, http://www.adgenetics.org), which aims to compare genetic material from 10,000 people with AD to genetic material from 10,000 people without the disease. In "Alzheimer's Disease Genetics Fact Sheet" (August 30, 2015, https://www.nia.nih.gov/health/alzheimers-disease-fact-sheet), the NIA reports that these initiatives have helped identify "key steps in the formation of brain abnormalities typical of Alzheimer's disease" and the variation in the age at which the disease begins. This research has spurred development of imaging tests that detect accumulation of amyloid and tau in the brain. The NIA also participates in the Dominantly Inherited Alzheimer Network, an international research project that studies early-onset AD in adult children of a parent with a mutated gene.

DIAGNOSTIC TESTING. Historically, the only sure way to diagnose AD was to examine brain tissue under a microscope. The brain of a patient who has died of AD reveals a characteristic pattern that is the hallmark of the disease: tangles of fibers (neurofibrillary tangles) and clusters of degenerated nerve endings (neuritic plaques) in areas of the brain that are crucial for memory and intellect.

Evaluation of people with cognitive changes involves obtaining a thorough medical history and a physical examination to rule out cognitive changes that may result from an underlying illness such as diabetes, a psychiatric disorder such as depression, or a reaction to medication. Physicians ask patients a series of questions to assess their memory, thinking, reasoning, and problem-solving capabilities. Although a complete medical history, physical examination, and psychiatric and neurological assessment do not provide as definitive a diagnosis of AD as an examination of the brain, they can usually produce an accurate diagnosis by ruling out other potential causes of cognitive impairment. Diagnostic tests for AD may also include analysis of blood and spinal fluid as well as the use of brain scans (CT and MRI) to detect strokes or tumors and to measure the volume of brain tissue in the areas used for memory and cognition. Brain scans assist to accurately identify people with AD and predict who may develop AD in the future.

Osama Sabri et al. describe in "Florbetaben PET Imaging to Detect Amyloid Beta Plaques in Alzheimer Disease: Phase 3 Study" (*Alzheimer's and Dementia*, March 28, 2015) the successful use of positron emission tomography (PET) imaging to detect the amyloid beta deposits that form in the brains of AD patients. In "Alzheimer-Signature MRI Biomarker Predicts AD Dementia in Cognitively Normal Adults" (*Neurology*, vol. 76, no. 16, April 19, 2011), Brad C. Dickerson et al. used MRI to measure the thickness of the cerebral cortex (the outer portion of the brain that is responsible for higher-order functions such as information processing and language) to help predict which cognitively normal people would develop AD. The researchers hypothesized that the cortical thinning observed in patients with mild AD might be present in cognitively normal adults who will develop AD before they have any symptoms of the disease. Dickerson et al. find that cognitively normal adults who went on to develop AD had thinner cortical areas and those in the highest third of cortical thickness never developed AD. The researchers conclude that "this measure [is] a potentially important imaging biomarker of early neurodegeneration."

The NIA explains in "Alzheimer's Disease Genetics Fact Sheet" that apoE testing is used as a research tool to identify research subjects who may have an increased risk of developing AD. Investigators are then able to look for early brain changes in research subjects and compare the effectiveness of treatments for people with different apoE profiles. Because the apoE test does not accurately predict who will or will not develop AD, it is useful for

studying AD risk in populations but not for determining any one individual's specific risk.

Simon Lovestone of the University of Oxford observes in "Blood Biomarkers for Alzheimer's Disease" (*Genome Medicine*, vol. 6, no. 8, 2014) that progress has been made in the identification of biomarkers for AD in cerebrospinal fluid and that "prospects for identifying blood-derived markers for early diagnosis and prognosis are very good." He is less certain that blood biomarkers will be able to be used to monitor the progression of AD. Instead, Lovestone suggests that this will be done using multiple assessments, including imaging studies such as PET and MRI, electrophysiology (electrical activity in the brain), clinical cognitive measures, and molecular tests of cerebrospinal fluid and blood.

In July 2014 Tafu Chen et al. confirmed the utility of a test biomarker for amyloid beta and tau proteins in plasma in "Blood Biomarker for Diagnosing Mild Cognition Impairment and Alzheimer's Disease Using Biofunctionalized Magnetic Nanoparticles" (*Alzheimer's and Dementia*, vol. 10, no. 4). The researchers note that it may be feasible to use blood tests to distinguish between mild cognitive impairment and AD.

In "Amyloid Beta and Tau as Alzheimer's Disease Blood Biomarkers: Promise from New Technologies" (*Neurology and Therapy*, vol. 6, suppl. 1, July 2017), Lih-Fen Lue, Andre Guerra, and Douglas G. Walker described two ultrasensitive new technologies that promise to establish amyloid beta (Aβ) and tau as blood biomarkers for AD. A series of studies has shown promising correlations between the blood tests and PET imaging of amyloid and tau.

A simple and accurate test, such as a blood-based biomarker, that distinguishes people with AD from those with cognitive problems or dementias arising from other causes will prove useful for scientists, physicians, and other clinical researchers. However, because advances in detection have outpaced treatment options, the availability of tests to predict who may develop AD raises ethical and practical questions: Do people really want to know their risks of developing AD? Is it helpful to predict a condition that is not yet considered preventable or curable?

DIAGNOSTIC GUIDELINES AND CRITERIA FOR AD. In 2011 the NIA and the Alzheimer's Association established new guidelines for diagnosing AD, and Guy M. McKhann et al. summarize the details in "The Diagnosis of Dementia Due to Alzheimer's Disease: Recommendations from the National Institute on Aging and the Alzheimer's Association Workgroup" (*Alzheimer's and Dementia*, vol. 7, no. 3, May 2011). The guidelines update diagnostic criteria and aim to detect the disease earlier than ever before. They also acknowledge that imaging and biomarkers should not "be used routinely in clinical diagnosis without further testing and validation."

The updated guidelines explain AD as a continuum of mental decline that may begin many years before the first symptoms arise. Furthermore, they describe the first of three phases: preclinical, which occurs absent symptoms; mild cognitive impairment, which involves noticeable memory problems without loss of ability to function independently; and Alzheimer's dementia, with its characteristic decline in reasoning and function.

New criteria for determining cognitive impairment caused by AD were also created, and Marilyn S. Albert et al. outline the details in "The Diagnosis of Mild Cognitive Impairment Due to Alzheimer's Disease: Recommendations from the National Institute on Aging and Alzheimer's Association Workgroup" (*Alzheimer's and Dementia*, vol. 7, no. 3, May 2011). Two sets of new criteria were developed: one for use by health care providers without access to advanced imaging techniques or blood and cerebrospinal fluid analysis and one for use by clinical researchers. The second set of criteria describe the use of biomarkers that are based on imaging and blood and cerebrospinal fluid measures and establish four levels of confidence, depending on the presence and character of the biomarker findings.

TREATMENT. There is no cure or prevention for AD, and treatment focuses on managing symptoms. Medication may slow the appearance of some symptoms and can lessen others, such as agitation, anxiety, unpredictable behavior, and depression. Physical exercise and good nutrition are important, as is a calm and highly structured environment. The objective is to help the AD patient maintain as much comfort, normalcy, and dignity for as long as possible.

According to the Alzheimer's Association, in "Current Alzheimer's Treatments" (https://www.alz.org/research/science/alzheimers_disease_treatments.asp), in 2017 there were five prescription drugs (Aricept, Razadyne, Namenda, Exelon, and Namzaric) for the treatment of AD that had been approved by the US Food and Drug Administration, and National Institutes of Health (NIH) affiliates and pharmaceutical companies were involved in clinical trials of new drugs to treat AD. All the drugs being tested were intended to improve the symptoms of AD and slow its progression, but none was expected to cure AD. Investigational drugs aim to address three aspects of AD: to improve cognitive function in people with early-stage AD, to slow or postpone the progression of the disease, and to control behavioral problems of patients with AD such as wandering, aggression, and agitation.

In 2011 a new method of drug delivery, a transdermal patch that delivers the drug through the skin, compared favorably with oral drug administration. Pam Harrison

reports in "Transdermal Patch for Alzheimer's Gets Caregiver Thumbs-Up: Delivery Method May Reduce Caregiver Stress, Enhance Patient Response" (Medscape.com, March 30, 2011) that Pablo Martinez-Lage et al. said that some patient caregivers felt the patch slowed, or even stopped, the deterioration that is the hallmark of AD. They opined that the continuous drug delivery offered by the patch might account for the reported improvement in the patients' behavior. Many caregivers found administering the patch easier and less stressful than administering oral medication to potentially combative or uncooperative patients.

As use of the transdermal patch continued to increase, Steven Ferris, Xiangyi Meng, and Drew Velting wondered whether caregivers' preferences for this easy-to-administer treatment would improve AD patients' functional and cognitive outcomes. In "Caregiver Treatment Preference/Satisfaction and Efficacy among Patients in the Optimising Transdermal Exelon in Mild-to-Moderate Alzheimer's Disease (OPTIMA) Study" (*Aging, Dementia, Cognitive, and Behavioral Neurology: Clinical Trials*, vol. 84, no. 14, suppl. P7.104, April 6, 2015), the researchers conclude, "Caregiver treatment preference/satisfaction is associated with positive functional and cognitive outcomes in mild-to-moderate AD; this highlights the importance of easy-to-use therapies that aid effective AD management."

CARING FOR THE AD PATIENT. Caring for a patient with AD has significant implications for members of the patient's family. Although medication may suppress some symptoms and occasionally slow the progression of the disease, eventually most AD patients require constant care and supervision. In the past, nursing homes and residential care facilities were not equipped to provide this kind of care, and if they accepted AD patients at all, they admitted only those in the earliest stages of the disease. Since 2000 a growing number of nursing homes have welcomed AD patients, even though they are more difficult and costly to care for than older adults without AD. This change is in some respects financially motivated because nursing home occupancy rates dropped in response to the growth of alternative housing for older adults.

The Alzheimer's Association indicates in *2017 Alzheimer's Disease Facts and Figures* that in 2016, 15.9 million caregivers provided nearly 18.2 billion hours of unpaid care valued at $230.1 billion. Many relatives of AD patients care for the affected family member at home as long as possible because they cannot afford institutional care or they feel an obligation to do so. No matter how devoted the caregiver, the time, patience, and resources required to provide care are immense, and the task is often overwhelming. As the patient's condition progresses, caregivers often find themselves socially isolated. Caregiving has been linked to increased rates of depression, compromised immune function, and a greater use of medication, particularly medications that are used to relieve symptoms of mental distress.

Caregivers who participate in support groups and make use of home health aides, adult day care, and respite care (facilities where patients stay for a limited number of days) not only feel healthier but also are better able to care for AD patients and maintain them at home longer than those who do not.

In *2017 Alzheimer's Disease Facts and Figures*, the Alzheimer's Association describes the growing burden that AD imposes on families, caregivers, and the US health care system. The total cost of health and long-term care for people with AD was an estimated $259 billion in 2017 and is expected to exceed $1 trillion in 2050.

MENTAL ILLNESS

Older people with mental illnesses were once considered senile—that is, mentally debilitated as a result of old age. Serious forgetfulness, emotional disturbances, and other behavioral changes do not, however, occur as a normal part of aging. They may be caused by chronic illnesses such as heart disease, thyroid disorders, or anemia; infections, poor diet, or lack of sleep; or prescription drugs, such as narcotic painkillers, sedatives, and antihistamines. Social isolation, loneliness, boredom, or depression may also cause memory lapses. When accurately diagnosed and treated, these types of problems can frequently be reversed.

Mental illness refers to all identifiable mental health disorders and mental health problems. In the landmark study *Mental Health: A Report of the Surgeon General, 1999* (1999, https://profiles.nlm.nih.gov/ps/retrieve/ResourceMeta data/NNBBHS), the US surgeon general defines mental disorders as "health conditions that are characterized by alterations in thinking, mood, or behavior (or some combination thereof) associated with distress and/or impaired functioning." The surgeon general distinguishes mental health problems from mental health disorders, describing the signs and symptoms of mental health problems as less intense and of shorter duration than those of mental health disorders, but acknowledges that both mental health problems and disorders may be distressing and disabling.

The surgeon general observes that nearly 20% of people aged 55 years and older experience mental disorders that are not part of normal aging. The most common disorders, in order of estimated prevalence rates, are anxiety (11.4%), severe cognitive impairment (6.6%), and mood disorders (4.4%) such as depression. The surgeon general also points out that mental disorders in older adults are frequently unrecognized, underreported, and undertreated.

Diagnosing mental disorders in older adults is challenging because their symptoms may be different from that of other adults. For example, many older adults complain about physical as opposed to emotional or psychological problems, and they present symptoms that are not typical of depression or anxiety disorders. Accurately identifying, detecting, and diagnosing mental disorders in older adults is also complicated by the following:

- Mental disorders often coexist with other medical problems.

- The symptoms of some chronic diseases may imitate or conceal psychological disorders.

- Older adults are more likely to report physical symptoms than psychological ones because there is less stigma associated with physical health or medical problems than with mental health problems.

The Growing Mental Health Needs of Older Adults

Stephen J. Bartels and John A. Naslund of the Dartmouth Institute for Health Policy and Clinical Practice in Lebanon, New Hampshire, report in "The Underside of the Silver Tsunami—Older Adults and Mental Health Care" (*New England Journal of Medicine*, vol. 368, no. 6, February 7, 2013) that between 5.6 million and 8 million adults aged 65 years and older have mental health or substance-use disorders and that by 2030 their ranks will grow to between 10.1 million and 14.4 million. Older adults with mental health disorders are more disabled than those with physical illness alone, and they make more hospital and emergency department visits, resulting in costs that are between 47% and 200% higher than their age peers without mental illness.

Depression

Symptoms of depression are an important indicator of physical and mental health in older adults because people who experience symptoms of depression are also more likely to report higher rates of physical illness, disability, and health service utilization.

The prevalence of clinically relevant depressive symptoms (as distinguished from brief periods of sadness or depressed mood) increases with advancing age. According to the CDC, in "Depression Is Not a Normal Part of Growing Older" (January 31, 2017, https://www.cdc.gov/aging/mentalhealth/depression.htm), an estimated 1% to 5% of healthy older adults living in the community are depressed, and 13.5% of older adults who require home health care and 11.5% of older hospital patients are depressed.

Often, illness itself can trigger depression by altering the chemicals in the brain. Examples of illnesses that can touch off depression are diabetes, hypothyroidism (a condition in which the thyroid is underactive—producing too little thyroid hormones), kidney or liver dysfunction, heart disease, and infection. In patients with these ailments, treating the underlying disease usually eliminates the depression. David M. Clarke and Kay C. Currie find in "Depression, Anxiety, and Their Relationship with Chronic Diseases: A Review of the Epidemiology, Risk, and Treatment Evidence" (*Medical Journal of Australia*, vol. 190, no. 7, April 6, 2009) not only strong evidence for the association of physical illness, depression, and anxiety but also their effects on outcomes (how well patients fare). The researchers indicate that people with disabling chronic illnesses such as arthritis, stroke, and pulmonary diseases are likely to become depressed. Furthermore, Clarke and Currie note that some prescription medications, as well as over-the-counter (nonprescription) drugs, may also cause depression.

Depression causes some older adults to deliberately neglect or disregard their medical needs by eating poorly and failing to take prescribed medication or taking it incorrectly. These may be covert acts of suicide. Actual suicide, which is frequently a consequence of serious depression, is highest among older adults relative to all other age groups. In 2015 the death rate for suicide among people aged 75 to 84 years was 17.5 per 100,000 resident population and among adults aged 85 years and older was 19.3 per 100,000. (See Table 8.1.) Older men had the highest rates—35.2 per 100,000 resident population for those aged 75 to 84 years and 49.9 per 100,000 for those aged 85 years and older.

TREATMENT OF DEPRESSION. According to the surgeon general, in *Mental Health*, despite the availability of effective treatments for depression, a substantial fraction of affected older adults do not receive treatment, largely because they either do not seek it or their depression is not identified or accurately diagnosed. For example, although many older patients respond well to antidepressants, some physicians do not prescribe them to older patients already taking many drugs for chronic medical conditions because they do not want to risk drug–drug interactions or add another drug to an already complicated regimen. As a result, only a minority of older adults diagnosed with depression receives the appropriate drug dose and duration of treatment.

Treatment for depression includes psychotherapy, with or without the use of antidepressant medications, and electroconvulsive therapy (ECT). Psychotherapy is most often used to treat mild to moderate depression and is prescribed for a limited, defined period, generally ranging from 10 to 20 weeks. ECT is used for life-threatening depression that does not respond to treatment with antidepressant drugs.

In "Long Term Effect of Depression Care Management on Mortality in Older Adults: Follow-Up of Cluster Randomized Clinical Trial in Primary Care" (*BMJ*, vol. 3, no. 10, June 2013), a five-year study of 1,226 older patients, Joseph J. Gallo et al. not only find that depression is independently associated with mortality risk in older adults but also confirm that treatment for depression reduces this risk. Of the total number of subjects, about 600 were determined to be suffering from major or minor depression. During the five-year follow-up, subjects who received treatment for depression were 24% less likely to die than those who were not treated.

Anxiety Disorders

Anxiety disorders (extreme nervousness and apprehension or sudden attacks of fear without apparent external causes) can be debilitating. Symptoms may include a "knot" in the stomach, sweating, or elevated blood pressure. If the anxiety is severe and long lasting, more serious problems may develop. People suffering from anxiety over extended periods may have headaches, ulcers, irritable bowel syndrome, insomnia, or depression. Because anxiety tends to create various other emotional and physical symptoms, a cascade effect can occur in which these new problems produce even more anxiety.

Unrelenting anxiety that appears unrelated to specific environments or situations is called generalized anxiety disorder. People suffering from this disorder worry excessively about the events of daily life and the future. They are also more likely to experience physical symptoms such as shortness of breath, dizziness, rapid heart rate, nausea, stomach pains, and muscle tension than people who are afflicted with other panic disorders, social phobias, or agoraphobia (fear of being in an open space or a place where escape is difficult).

The surgeon general estimates in *Mental Health* the prevalence of anxiety disorder as about 11.4% of adults aged 55 years and older. Phobic anxiety disorders such as social phobia, which causes extreme discomfort in social settings, are among the most common mental disturbances in late life. In contrast, some disorders have low rates of prevalence among older adults, such as panic disorder (0.5%) and obsessive-compulsive disorder (1.5%). Generalized anxiety disorder, rather than specific anxiety syndromes, may be more prevalent in older people.

Effective treatment for anxiety involves medication, primarily benzodiazepines such as Valium, Librium, and Xanax, as well as psychotherapy. Like other medications, the effects of benzodiazepines may last longer in older adults, and their side effects may include drowsiness, fatigue, physical impairment, memory or other cognitive impairment, confusion, depression, respiratory problems, abuse or dependence problems, and withdrawal reactions.

Nondrug treatment may also be effective for older adults suffering from debilitating anxiety. In "Antidepressant Medication Augmented with Cognitive-Behavioral Therapy for Generalized Anxiety Disorder in

TABLE 8.1

Death rates for suicide, by selected characteristics, selected years 1950–2015

[Data are based on death certificates]

Sex, race, Hispanic origin, and age	1950[a,b]	1960[a,b]	1970[b]	1980[b]	1990[b]	2000[c]	2010[c]	2014[c]	2015[c]
All persons				Deaths per 100,000 resident population					
All ages, age-adjusted[d]	13.2	12.5	13.1	12.2	12.5	10.4	12.1	13.0	13.3
All ages, crude	11.4	10.6	11.6	11.9	12.4	10.4	12.4	13.4	13.7
Under 1 year	—	—	—	—	—	—	—	—	—
1–4 years	—	—	—	—	—	—	—	—	—
5–14 years	0.2	0.3	0.3	0.4	0.8	0.7	0.7	1.0	1.0
15–24 years	4.5	5.2	8.8	12.3	13.2	10.2	10.5	11.6	12.5
15–19 years	2.7	3.6	5.9	8.5	11.1	8.0	7.5	8.7	9.8
20–24 years	6.2	7.1	12.2	16.1	15.1	12.5	13.6	14.2	15.1
25–44 years	11.6	12.2	15.4	15.6	15.2	13.4	15.0	15.8	16.4
25–34 years	9.1	10.0	14.1	16.0	15.2	12.0	14.0	15.1	15.7
35–44 years	14.3	14.2	16.9	15.4	15.3	14.5	16.0	16.6	17.1
45–64 years	23.5	22.0	20.6	15.9	15.3	13.5	18.6	19.5	19.6
45–54 years	20.9	20.7	20.0	15.9	14.8	14.4	19.6	20.2	20.3
55–64 years	26.8	23.7	21.4	15.9	16.0	12.1	17.5	18.8	18.9
65 years and over	30.0	24.5	20.8	17.6	20.5	15.2	14.9	16.7	16.6
65–74 years	29.6	23.0	20.8	16.9	17.9	12.5	13.7	15.6	15.2
75–84 years	31.1	27.9	21.2	19.1	24.9	17.6	15.7	17.5	17.9
85 years and over	28.8	26.0	19.0	19.2	22.2	19.6	17.6	19.3	19.4
Male									
All ages, age-adjusted[d]	21.2	20.0	19.8	19.9	21.5	17.7	19.8	20.7	21.1
All ages, crude	17.8	16.5	16.8	18.6	20.4	17.1	19.9	21.1	21.5
Under 1 year	—	—	—	—	—	—	—	—	—
1–4 years	—	—	—	—	—	—	—	—	—
5–14 years	0.3	0.4	0.5	0.6	1.1	1.2	0.9	1.3	1.2
15–24 years	6.5	8.2	13.5	20.2	22.0	17.1	16.9	18.2	19.4
15–19 years	3.5	5.6	8.8	13.8	18.1	13.0	11.7	13.0	14.2
20–24 years	9.3	11.5	19.3	26.8	25.7	21.4	22.2	22.9	24.2
25–44 years	17.2	17.9	20.9	24.0	24.4	21.3	23.6	24.4	25.2
25–34 years	13.4	14.7	19.8	25.0	24.8	19.6	22.5	23.8	24.7
35–44 years	21.3	21.0	22.1	22.5	23.9	22.8	24.6	25.0	25.9
45–64 years	37.1	34.4	30.0	23.7	24.3	21.3	29.2	29.7	29.5
45–54 years	32.0	31.6	27.9	22.9	23.2	22.4	30.4	30.0	30.1
55–64 years	43.6	38.1	32.7	24.5	25.7	19.4	27.7	29.4	28.9
65 years and over	52.8	44.0	38.4	35.0	41.6	31.1	29.0	31.4	31.0
65–74 years	50.5	39.6	36.0	30.4	32.2	22.7	23.9	26.6	26.2
75–84 years	58.3	52.5	42.8	42.3	56.1	38.6	32.3	34.9	35.2
85 years and over	58.3	57.4	42.4	50.6	65.9	57.5	47.3	49.9	48.2
Female									
All ages, age-adjusted[d]	5.6	5.6	7.4	5.7	4.8	4.0	5.0	5.8	6.0
All ages, crude	5.1	4.9	6.6	5.5	4.8	4.0	5.2	6.0	6.2
Under 1 year	—	—	—	—	—	—	—	—	—
1–4 years	—	—	—	—	—	—	—	—	—
5–14 years	0.1	0.1	0.2	0.2	0.4	0.3	0.4	0.7	0.8
15–24 years	2.6	2.2	4.2	4.3	3.9	3.0	3.9	4.6	5.3
15–19 years	1.8	1.6	2.9	3.0	3.7	2.7	3.1	4.2	5.1
20–24 years	3.3	2.9	5.7	5.5	4.1	3.2	4.7	5.0	5.5
25–44 years	6.2	6.6	10.2	7.7	6.2	5.4	6.4	7.2	7.5
25–34 years	4.9	5.5	8.6	7.1	5.6	4.3	5.3	6.3	6.6
35–44 years	7.5	7.7	11.9	8.5	6.8	6.4	7.5	8.2	8.4
45–64 years	9.9	10.2	12.0	8.9	7.1	6.2	8.6	9.8	10.2
45–54 years	9.9	10.2	12.6	9.4	6.9	6.7	9.0	10.7	10.7
55–64 years	9.9	10.2	11.4	8.4	7.3	5.4	8.0	8.9	9.7
65 years and over	9.4	8.4	8.1	6.1	6.4	4.0	4.2	5.0	5.1
65–74 years	10.1	8.4	9.0	6.5	6.7	4.0	4.8	5.9	5.7
75–84 years	8.1	8.9	7.0	5.5	6.3	4.0	3.7	4.3	4.6
85 years and over	8.2	6.0	5.9	5.5	5.4	4.2	3.3	3.4	4.2

Older Adults" (*American Journal of Psychiatry*, vol. 170, no. 7, July 1, 2013), Julie L. Wetherell et al. compare cognitive behavioral therapy (CBT; treatment that focuses on changing thoughts to solve psychological problems), drug treatment alone, a combination of the two, and a placebo (a pill that contains no active drug) as treatment for generalized anxiety disorder in older adults. The researchers find that although both drug treatment and CBT relieved anxiety and prevented relapse when compared with a placebo, CBT alone provided long-term relief from anxiety. Wetherell et al. conclude that although medication prevents relapse, CBT is able to prevent recurrences without the need for long-term drug treatment.

Nondrug relaxation interventions also have proven effective for older adults. In "Effects of Relaxation

TABLE 8.1

Death rates for suicide, by selected characteristics, selected years 1950–2015 [CONTINUED]

[Data are based on death certificates]

—Category not applicable.

[a]Includes deaths of persons who were not residents of the 50 states and the District of Columbia (D.C.).

[b]Underlying cause of death was coded according to the 6th Revision of the International Classification of Diseases (ICD) in 1950, 7th Revision in 1960, 8th Revision in 1970, and 9th Revision in 1980–1998.

[c]Starting with 1999 data, cause of death is coded according to ICD–10.

[d]Age-adjusted rates are calculated using the year 2000 standard population. Prior to 2001, age-adjusted rates were calculated using standard million proportions based on rounded population numbers. Starting with 2001 data, unrounded population numbers are used to calculate age-adjusted rates.

[e]The race groups, white, black, Asian or Pacific Islander, and American Indian or Alaska Native, include persons of Hispanic and non-Hispanic origin. Persons of Hispanic origin may be of any race. Death rates for Hispanic, American Indian or Alaska Native, and Asian or Pacific Islander persons should be interpreted with caution because of inconsistencies in reporting Hispanic origin or race on the death certificate (death rate numerators) compared with population figures (death rate denominators). The net effect of misclassification is an underestimation of deaths and death rates for races other than white and black.

Notes: Starting with *Health, United States, 2003*, rates for 1991–1999 were revised using intercensal population estimates based on the 1990 and 2000 censuses. For 2000, population estimates are bridged-race April 1 census counts. Starting with *Health, United States, 2012*, rates for 2001–2009 were revised using intercensal population estimates based on the 2000 and 2010 censuses. For 2010, population estimates are bridged-race April 1 census counts. Rates for 2011 and beyond were computed using 2010-based postcensal estimates. Figures for 2001 include September 11–related deaths for which death certificates were filed as of October 24, 2002. Age groups were selected to minimize the presentation of unstable age-specific death rates based on small numbers of deaths and for consistency among comparison groups. Starting with 2003 data, some states began to collect information on more than one race on the death certificate, according to 1997 Office of Management and Budget (OMB) standards. The multiple-race data for these states were bridged to the single-race categories of the 1977 OMB standards, for comparability with other states. Data for additional years are available. Some data have been revised and differ from previous editions of *Health, United States*.

SOURCE: Adapted from "Table 30. Death Rates for Suicide, by Sex, Race, Hispanic Origin, and Age: United States, Selected Years 1950–2015," in *Health, United States, 2016: With Chartbook on Long-Term Trends in Health*, National Center for Health Statistics, May 2017, https://www.cdc.gov/nchs/data/hus/2016/030.pdf (accessed October 24, 2017)

Interventions on Depression and Anxiety among Older Adults: A Systematic Review" (*Aging & Mental Health*, vol. 19, no. 12, January 2015), Piyanee Klainin-Yobas et al. reviewed 27 studies that assessed the effects of relaxation programs for older adults. The researchers find that older adults who received relaxation interventions experienced greater reductions in depression and anxiety than those who did not receive these interventions. Progressive muscle relaxation training, music therapy, and yoga had the strongest effects on depression and anxiety symptoms among older adults.

Schizophrenia

Schizophrenia is an extremely disabling form of mental illness. Its symptoms include hallucinations, paranoia, delusions, and social isolation. People suffering from schizophrenia "hear voices," and over time the voices take over in the schizophrenic's mind, obliterating reality and directing all kinds of erratic behaviors. Suicide attempts and violent attacks are common in the lives of schizophrenics. In an attempt to escape the torment inflicted by their brains, many schizophrenics turn to drugs. The National Institute of Mental Health indicates in *What Is Schizophrenia?* (2015, https://www.nimh.nih.gov/health/topics/schizophrenia/index.shtml) that most symptoms of schizophrenia emerge early in life (the late teens or 20s) and rarely begin after age 45.

In *Mental Health*, the surgeon general notes that the prevalence of schizophrenia among adults aged 65 years and older is estimated to be 0.6%, less than half of the 1.3% that is estimated for the population aged 18 to 54 years. However, the economic burden of late-life schizophrenia is high.

Drug treatment of schizophrenia in older adults is complicated. The medications that are used to treat schizophrenia, such as Haldol, effectively reduce symptoms (e.g., delusions and hallucinations) in many older patients, but they also have a high risk of disabling side effects, such as tardive dyskinesias (involuntary, rhythmic movements of the face, jaw, mouth, tongue, and trunk). Even newer atypical antipsychotic medications that are used to treat the symptoms of schizophrenia, such as Abilify, can produce troubling side effects, including tremors, restlessness, shakes, muscle stiffness, or other involuntary movements.

MISUSE OF ALCOHOL AND PRESCRIPTION DRUGS

The surgeon general observes in *Mental Health* that older adults are more likely to misuse, as opposed to abuse, alcohol and prescription drugs. The surgeon general estimates that the prevalence of heavy drinking (12 to 21 drinks per week) in the cohort (a group of individuals that shares a common characteristic such as birth years and is studied over time) of older adults is 3% to 9%. The prevalence rates are expected to rise as the baby boomer (people born between 1946 and 1964) cohort, with its history of alcohol and illegal drug use, joins the ranks of older adults. In "Substance Use Disorder among Older Adults in the United States in 2020" (*Addiction*, vol. 104, no. 1, January 2009), Beth Han et al. forecast that the number of adults aged 50 years and older with substance use disorder (alcohol/illicit drug dependence or abuse) is projected to double from an average of 2.8 million per year in 2006 to 5.7 million in 2020. The current group of older adults is more likely to suffer

FIGURE 8.3

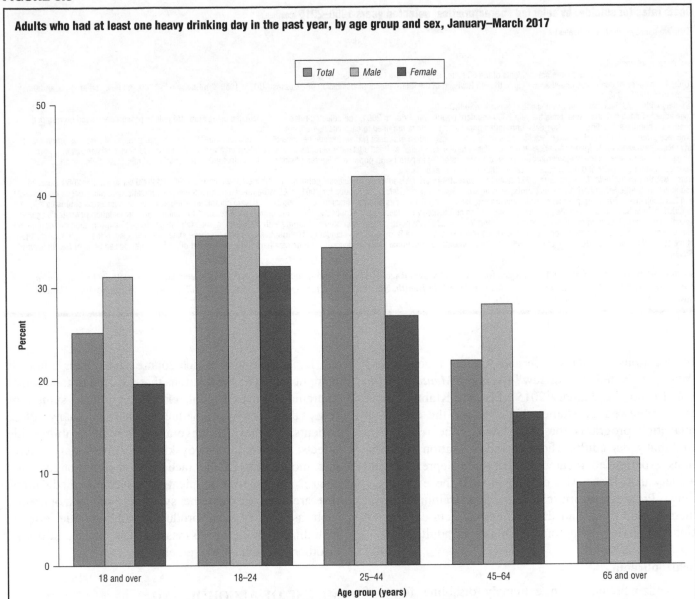

Adults who had at least one heavy drinking day in the past year, by age group and sex, January–March 2017

Notes: Data are based on household interviews of a sample of the civilian noninstitutionalized population. Heavy drinking days are defined as days in which men consumed five or more drinks and women consumed four or more drinks. The analyses exclude the 1.2% of adults with unknown alcohol consumption.

SOURCE: "Figure 9.2. Percentage of Adults Aged 18 and over Who Had at Least 1 Heavy Drinking Day in the Past Year, by Age Group and Sex: United States, January–March 2017," in *Early Release of Selected Estimates Based on Data from the National Health Interview Survey, January–March 2017*, Centers for Disease Control and Prevention, National Center for Health Statistics, September 2017, https://www.cdc.gov/nchs/data/nhis/earlyrelease/ Earlyrelease201709_09.pdf (accessed October 27, 2017).

substance misuse problems, such as drug dependence, arising from underuse, overuse, or erratic use of prescription and over-the-counter medications.

Figure 8.3 shows that adults aged 65 years and older (8.8%) had the lowest rate of excessive alcohol consumption of all age groups. Older men (11.5%) were much more likely than older women (6.7%) to have met the National Health Interview Survey criteria for excessive alcohol consumption (at least one heavy drinking day in the past year, defined as five or more drinks for a man and four or more drinks for a woman).

Prevalence of Types of Older Problem Drinkers

In *Module 10C: Older Adults and Alcohol Problems* (March 2005, https://pubs.niaaa.nih.gov/publications/ social/Module10COlderAdults/Module10C.html), the National Institute on Alcohol Abuse and Alcoholism describes the prevalence of three types of problem drinkers: at-risk drinkers, problem drinkers, and alcohol-dependent drinkers.

- *At-risk drinking* is alcohol use that increases the risk of developing alcohol-related problems and complications. People over the age of 65 years who drink more than seven drinks per week (one per day) are considered at risk of developing health, social, or emotional problems caused by alcohol.

- *Problem drinkers* have already suffered medical, psychological, family, financial, self-care, legal, or social consequences of alcohol abuse.

- *Alcohol-dependent drinkers* suffer from a medical disorder that is characterized by a loss of control over consumption, preoccupation with alcohol, and continued use despite adverse health, social, legal, and financial consequences.

Figure 8.4 shows the estimated prevalence rates of these different types of drinkers as well as the majority (65%) of older adults that abstains from alcohol consumption.

Types of Older Problem Drinkers

Another way to characterize older problem drinkers is by the duration and patterns of their drinking histories. The first group consists of those over the age of 60 years who have been drinking for most of their life. Members of this group are called survivors or early-onset problem drinkers. They have beaten the statistical odds by living to old age despite heavy drinking, but they are most likely to suffer from cirrhosis of the liver (a chronic degenerative disease of the liver marked by scarring of liver tissue and eventually liver failure) and mental health disorders such as depression.

FIGURE 8.4

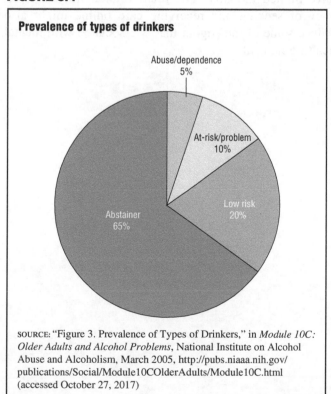

Prevalence of types of drinkers

Abuse/dependence 5%

At-risk/problem 10%

Low risk 20%

Abstainer 65%

SOURCE: "Figure 3. Prevalence of Types of Drinkers," in *Module 10C: Older Adults and Alcohol Problems*, National Institute on Alcohol Abuse and Alcoholism, March 2005, http://pubs.niaaa.nih.gov/publications/Social/Module10COlderAdults/Module10C.html (accessed October 27, 2017)

The second group, intermittents, has historically engaged in binge drinking interspersed with periods of relative sobriety. These drinkers are at risk for alcohol abuse because they are more likely than others to self-medicate with alcohol to relieve physical pain and emotional distress or to assuage loneliness and social isolation.

Reactors or late-onset problem drinkers make up the third group. The stresses of later life, particularly the loss of work or a spouse, may precipitate heavy drinking. These people show few of the physical consequences of prolonged drinking and fewer disruptions in their life.

Alcohol-Related Issues Unique to Older Adults

Older adults generally have a decreased tolerance to alcohol. Consumption of a given amount of alcohol by older adults usually produces higher blood-alcohol levels than it would in a younger population. Chronic medical problems such as cirrhosis may be present, but older adults are less likely to require detoxification and treatment of alcohol-withdrawal problems. One possible explanation is that few lifelong alcohol abusers survive to old age.

Because older adults usually take more medication than people in other age groups, they are more susceptible to drug–alcohol interactions. Alcohol reduces the safety and effectiveness of many medications and, in combination with some drugs, may produce coma or death. Adverse consequences of alcohol consumption in older adults are not limited to problem drinkers. Older adults with medical problems, including diabetes, heart disease, liver disease, and central nervous system degeneration, may also suffer adverse reactions from alcohol consumption.

SCREENING, DIAGNOSIS, AND TREATMENT. The National Institute on Alcohol Abuse and Alcoholism advocates screening to identify at-risk drinkers, problem drinkers, and dependent drinkers to determine the need for further diagnostic evaluation and treatment. Furthermore, in *Module 10C* it provides a screening protocol that recommends:

- All adults aged 60 years and older should be screened for alcohol and prescription drug use/abuse as part of any medical examination or application for health or social services.

- Annual rescreening should be performed if certain physical symptoms emerge or if the individual is undergoing major life changes, stresses, or transitions.

- These screening criteria apply to any health, social, work, or recreation setting that serves older adults and are not limited to medical care and substance treatment settings.

Diagnosis of problem drinking in the older population is complicated by the fact that many psychological, behavioral, and physical symptoms of problem drinking also occur in people who do not have drinking problems. For example, brain damage, heart disease, and gastrointestinal disorders often develop in older adults independent of alcohol use, but may also occur with drinking. In addition, mood disorders, depression, and changes in employment, economic, or marital status often accompany aging but can also be symptoms of alcoholism. Alcohol-induced organic brain syndrome is characterized by cognitive impairment (memory lapses, confusion, and disorientation). As a result, some older alcoholics may be incorrectly diagnosed as suffering from dementia or other mental illness.

Older problem drinkers make up a relatively small proportion of the total number of clients seen by most agencies for treatment of alcohol abuse. Little data about the effectiveness of intervention and treatment, which usually consists of some combination of counseling and education, in the older population exist. Nonetheless, the chances for recovery among older drinkers are considered good because older clients tend to complete the full course of therapy more often than younger clients.

There are indications that the number of older adults with alcohol and substance abuse problems will increase in the coming years. For example, in "Substance Abuse and Misuse in Older Adults" (Winter 2015, https://mhao fnyc.org/wp-content/uploads/2014/11/Substance-Abuse-BHN-Winter15.pdf), Michael B. Friedman and Kimberly A. Williams observe that as the baby boomers become "elder boomers," the number of older adults with substance use problems will at least double by 2030 and will likely outpace the growth of the older population. The researchers note that misuse of prescription and over-the-counter drugs is increasing, especially painkillers and sleep aids. There is also growing misuse of psychoactive medications, including antidepressants and antipsychotics. Because many substance abuse problems of older adults are not detected by family, friends, or health professionals, Friedman and Williams call for public education programs to increase awareness of the problem.

WHO WILL TREAT THIS GROWING PROBLEM? Just as there is a serious shortage of geriatricians (physicians who are specially trained to care for older adults), there is a comparable shortfall of geriatric mental health providers. More than half of the available training slots for geriatric psychiatrists go unfilled each year, and few psychologists focus on treating older adults. Friedman and Williams concur and add that other access problems exist. For example, providers and programs that do exist are overloaded or unavailable in some geographic areas or they are not affordable.

In "Expanding the Geriatric Mental Health Workforce through Utilization of Non-licensed Providers" (*Aging & Mental Health*, vol. 21, no. 9, May 2016), Mark E. Kunik et al. suggest increasing the mental health workforce by using supervised, non-licensed providers trained to treat geriatric mental health and substance-use disorders. Furthermore, Kunik et al. assert, "Licensed and non-licensed providers have achieved similar improvements for generalized anxiety disorder among patients, although non-licensed providers did so at a lower cost."

Other potential solutions might be internet-based technologies, which may provide opportunities for screening and treatment for older adults who are unable to seek or access care because they lack transportation or have limited mobility. The relative anonymity and privacy of seeking and receiving care online might also reduce some of the stigma that is associated with mental health treatment.

CHAPTER 9
CARING FOR OLDER ADULTS: CAREGIVERS

In the United States most long-term care of older adults is provided by families as opposed to nursing homes, assisted living facilities, social service agencies, or government programs. The continuing commitment to family care of older adults in the community is remarkable in view of relatively recent changes in the fabric of American society. American family life has undergone significant changes in the past four decades. Most households require two incomes, and greater numbers of women participate in the workforce. Delayed marriage and childbearing has produced a so-called sandwich generation of family caregivers that is simultaneously caring for two generations: their children and their parents. For the first time in US history, adults may spend more years caring for a parent than for a child. Increased geographic separation of families further compounds the difficulties of family caregiving.

Another challenge is that the supply of caregivers is not keeping pace with the growth in the older population. The number of older adults for every 100 adults of working age (aged 20 to 64 years) is called the dependency ratio. The US Bureau of Labor Statistics (BLS) estimates in "Economic Dependency Ratio" (October 24, 2017, https://www.bls.gov/emp/ep_table_307.htm) that in 2016 there were an estimated 24.9 older adults for every 100 working-age adults. Projections suggest the figure will rise from 25.4 older adults per 100 people of working age in 2018 to 34.9 per 100 in 2030. (See Table 9.1.)

In *Occupational Outlook Handbook* (October 24, 2017, https://www.bls.gov/ooh/healthcare/home-health-aides-and-personal-care-aides.htm), the BLS predicts changes in employment for all occupations. For example, the BLS projects that between 2016 and 2026 the number of home health aides will increase 47%, and the number of personal care aides will increase 39%. No single occupation is projected to add more workers than personal care aides, who help older adults with activities of daily living such as shopping, bathing, and cooking. Together with home health aides, these two occupations are projected to add 1.2 million new jobs between 2016 and 2026, which is about 10% of the total 11.5 million jobs that the BLS expects the economy to add. By 2026 an estimated 1.3 million home health aides and 2.8 million personal care aides will be employed.

FAMILY CAREGIVERS

According to the Family Caregiver Alliance, in "Where Do People Receive Long-Term Care and from Whom?" (January 31, 2015, https://www.caregiver.org/selected-long-term-care-statistics), most adults who receive long-term care at home rely exclusively on informal caregivers such as family and friends. Every year, 65.7 million Americans devote billions of hours providing this care, which includes help with tasks such as bathing, meal preparation, and managing medications, enabling older adults to remain in the community and age in place (remain in their own home rather than relocating to an assisted living facility or other supportive housing). Approximately 44 million caregivers provide care for adults aged 50 years and older, and of this group 14.9 million care for an older adult suffering from dementia (loss of intellectual functioning accompanied by memory loss and personality changes).

Caregiving in the United States

In "Women and Caregiving: Facts and Figures" (February 2015, https://www.caregiver.org/women-and-caregiving-facts-and-figures), the Family Caregiver Alliance describes the average caregiver as a 49-year-old, married, working woman who spends three or more years caring for a parent who does not live with her. Caregivers shop, prepare food, clean house, do laundry, provide transportation, and administer medication. They also assist with personal care, such as feeding, dressing, bathing, and toileting. In addition, caregivers research disease

TABLE 9.1

Age dependency ratios, 2018–30

	Population (in thousands)				Dependency ratio (number of dependents per 100 persons of working age)		
Year	Total	Children (0–19)	Working age (20–64)	Older persons (65–65+)	All dependents	Children (0–19)	Older persons (65–65+)
2018	334,497	86,859	197,405	50,233	69.4	44.0	25.4
2019	336,892	87,247	197,826	51,819	70.3	44.1	26.2
2020	339,270	87,547	198,213	53,510	71.2	44.2	27.0
2021	341,626	87,736	198,642	55,248	72.0	44.2	27.8
2022	343,958	87,883	199,059	57,016	72.8	44.1	28.6
2023	346,255	88,003	199,475	58,777	73.6	44.1	29.5
2024	348,514	88,233	199,736	60,545	74.5	44.2	30.3
2025	350,729	88,597	199,789	62,343	75.5	44.3	31.2
2026	352,871	88,942	199,847	64,082	76.6	44.5	32.1
2027	354,936	89,266	199,965	65,705	77.5	44.6	32.9
2028	356,946	89,574	200,139	67,233	78.3	44.8	33.6
2029	358,898	89,863	200,347	68,688	79.1	44.9	34.3
2030	360,794	90,133	200,644	70,017	79.8	44.9	34.9

SOURCE: Adapted from Laura B. Shrestha, "Appendix Table 1. Age Dependency Ratios, United States, 1950–2080," in *Age Dependency Ratios and Social Security Solvency*, Congressional Research Service, The Library of Congress, October 27, 2006, http://congressionalresearch.com/RL32981/document.php?study=Age+Dependency+Ratios+and+Social+Security+Solvency (accessed October 27, 2017)

care and treatment as well as coordinate physician visits and manage finances.

Caregiving can take a toll on physical and mental health and well-being. Research reveals that caregivers may suffer a range of health problems, including:

- Elevated blood pressure and insulin levels, which in turn increase the risk of developing cardiovascular disease

- High levels of physical and emotional stress and impaired immune function, which renders them less able to defend against illness

- Depression, anxiety, anger, and other emotional problems

The Economics of Caregiving

Most of the costs and responsibility for long-term care for older adults rest with family caregivers. The shift toward increasing reliance on this informal system of care was spurred by changes in the health care financing system that resulted in shorter hospital stays, rising costs of nursing home care, older adults preferring home care over institutional care, and a shortage of long-term care workers. Taken together, these factors continue to increase the likelihood that frail, disabled, and ill older adults will be cared for by relatives.

The Family Caregiver Alliance notes in "Women and Caregiving: Facts and Figures" that caregiving reduces paid work hours for women by about 41% and that its negative effect on caregivers' retirement funds is about $40,000 more for women than it is for men. Female caregivers are less likely than male caregivers to receive a pension, and of those women who do receive a pension, they receive about half as much as what men receive.

Employers also shoulder many of the costs of caregiving. They spend about $3.3 billion to replace women who leave their job to become a caregiver, and absenteeism among female caregivers costs businesses nearly $270 million. Long lunch breaks and leaving work early or arriving late to accommodate caregiving has been estimated at $327 million, and interruptions during the workday add another $3.8 billion to the business tab.

Measuring the Emotional, Financial, and Physical Costs of Caregiving

In "A National Profile of Family and Unpaid Caregivers Who Assist Older Adults with Health Care Activities" (*JAMA Internal Medicine*, vol. 176, no. 3, March 2016), Jennifer L. Wolff et al. report the results of the first nationally representative study to examine caregiving-related effects for family caregivers who assist with health care activities. Wolff et al. find that unpaid and family caregivers help nearly 8 million older adults with disabilities. An analysis of data from two nationally representative, population-based studies enabled Wolff et al. to measure physical, financial, and emotional difficulties associated with providing care as well as participation restrictions, a term that refers to "activities reported as being very or somewhat important to the caregiver that were limited in the prior month because of caregiving." The researchers also studied work productivity and attendance issues (missed time from work) because of caregiving in the prior month among caregivers who were working for pay.

Wolff et al. find caregivers who provided substantial assistance with health care (coordinating care and managing medication and physician visits) were more likely to report physical and emotional difficulties, missed work, and reduced participation in one or more valued activities because of caregiving compared with caregivers who provided little or no help with health care. Although caregivers who provide substantial assistance with health care were more likely to use supportive services than caregivers who provided some or no help, overall just one in four caregivers receives supportive services.

The Effects of the Patient Protection and Affordable Care Act on Informal Caregivers

In 2010 President Barack Obama (1961–) signed into law the Patient Protection and Affordable Care Act (ACA), commonly known as Obamacare. The law reformed health care delivery to improve access to care. In "Transforming the System of Care for Older Adults: The Affordable Care Act Five Years Later" (March 2015, http://www.thescan foundation.org/sites/default/files/tsf_perspectives_aca5years .pdf), Bruce Chernof of the SCAN Foundation explains that the law recognizes the need for home care services and offers incentives for the states to provide these services through Medicaid for older adults with low incomes (up to 300% of the maximum Supplemental Security Income payment). One way these services are provided is via the Community First Choice option, which enables states to use Medicaid funds to provide community-based attendant services to older adults who meet Medicaid and level-of-care eligibility standards. In *Report to Congress: Community First Choice—Interim Report to Congress as Required by the Patient Protection and Affordable Care Act of 2010* (2015, https:// www.medicaid.gov/medicaid/hcbs/downloads/cfc-final-report-to-congress.pdf), the US Department of Health and Human Services notes that, as of July 2015, seven states were participating in the Community First Choice program (California, Connecticut, Maryland, Montana, Oregon, Texas, and Washington), and two states (Minnesota and New York) were in the process of setting up a plan.

The SCAN Foundation exhorts in the policy brief *System Transformation in California: Coordinating Health Care and Long-Term Services and Supports* (July 2015, http://www.thescanfoundation.org/sites/default/ files/tsf_policy_brief_ca_ltss_transformation_july_2015.pdf) that the "importance of family caregivers needs to be acknowledged, with corresponding strategies to support their needs in the community," and observes that many states have already "established legal and system supports for family caregivers in addition to existing federal policies."

According to Lynn Feinberg and Allison M. Reamy, in the fact sheet *Health Reform Law Creates New Opportunities to Better Recognize and Support Family Caregivers* (October 2011, https://assets.aarp.org/rgcenter/ppi/ ltc/fs239.pdf), the ACA promotes models of care that better recognize the family caregiver as a key partner in care and provides more support for family caregivers, especially those who are caring for people with multiple chronic conditions. This support includes Aging and Disability Resource Center initiatives, which serve as entry points for older adults in need of long-term care services, and geriatric education centers to offer free or low-cost training to family caregivers.

The Effects of the ACA on Paid and Unpaid Caregivers

The ACA redirects reimbursement to incentivize health professionals to care for people with chronic conditions in the community rather than in hospitals. It created the Community-Based Care Transitions Program to assist Medicare beneficiaries to return to their home following hospital discharge. It also created the Independence at Home Medical Practice Pilot Program that in 2012 began providing coordinated, primary care services at home to Medicare beneficiaries with multiple chronic conditions.

ACA provisions aimed at increasing the numbers of health care workers include:

- Grant funding and other incentives to encourage students and health professionals to train in primary care, geriatrics, chronic care, and long-term care

- Funding to train health care workers who are direct-service providers such as home health aides and other providers of long-term and community-based services

- Establishing the Personal Care Attendants Workforce Advisory Panel to assess and advise on issues involving direct-care workers, including salaries, wages, and benefits

- Launching the National Health Care Workforce Commission to advise on ways to better meet the growing need for health care workers

Although the ACA created the National Health Care Workforce Commission to recommend national health care workforce priorities, goals, and policies, as of February 2018 Congress had not funded the commission.

Everette James and Meredith Hughes, in "Embracing the Role of Family Caregivers in the US Health System" (Health Affairs, September 8, 2016, https://www.health affairs.org/do/10.1377/hblog20160908.056387/full/), report that the importance of supporting family caregiving has become "more central to post–Affordable Care Act health policymaking." About half the states require providers to identify and train caregivers during the hospital discharge planning process. Making certain that family caregivers are informed and trained to provide appropriate home care can help avoid rehospitalizations.

The Effects of Repeal or Rollback of the ACA on Caregivers

The National Association of Area Agencies on Aging policy brief "What Would ACA Repeal Mean for Older

Adults, Caregivers and the Aging Network?" (January 2017, https://www.n4a.org/files/ACA_PolicyBrief_Jan 2017_final.pdf) asserts that rolling back or eliminating many provisions of the ACA could imperil older adults and their caregivers. For example, ending spousal impoverishment protections under Medicaid, which currently assure that spousal caregivers do not have to exhaust their personal assets in order to obtain Medicaid long-term support services for their partners, could jeopardize older adults' financial stability.

THE CONTINUUM OF FORMAL SERVICES

As the older population increases, the segment of the population that is available to provide unpaid care, generally consisting of family members, has decreased. Because the availability of caregivers has diminished, increasing numbers of older adults in need of assistance will rely on a combination of family caregiving and paid professional services or on professional services alone.

Home Health Care

Home health care agencies provide a variety of services. Services range from helping with activities of daily living, such as bathing, housekeeping, and meals, to skilled nursing care. Home health care agencies employ registered nurses, licensed practical nurses, and home health aides to deliver the bulk of these services. Other personnel involved in home health care include physical therapists, social workers, and speech-language pathologists.

Since the 1990s home health care has been one of the fastest growing segments of health services. Its growth is attributable to the fact that in many cases caring for patients at home is preferable to and more cost effective than care that is provided in a hospital, nursing home, or other residential facility.

Before 2000 Medicare coverage for home health care was limited to patients immediately following discharge from the hospital. By 2000 Medicare covered beneficiaries' home health care services with no requirement for prior hospitalization. There were also no limits to the number of professional visits or to the length of coverage. As long as the patient's condition warranted it, the following services were provided:

- Part-time or intermittent skilled nursing and home health aide services

- Speech-language pathology services

- Physical and occupational therapy

- Medical social services

- Medical supplies

- Durable medical equipment (with a 20% co-payment)

Since 2000 the population receiving home care services has changed. Although ACA provisions increase community-based chronic and long-term care for older adults, by 2018 much of home health care was associated with rehabilitation from critical illnesses, and fewer users were long-term patients with long-term conditions. Compared with postacute care users, long-term patients are older, more functionally disabled, more likely to be incontinent, and more expensive to serve.

Respite Care and Adult Day Care

Respite care enables caregivers to take much-needed breaks from the demands of caregiving. It offers relief for families who may be overwhelmed and exhausted by the demands of caregiving and may be neglecting their own needs for rest and relaxation.

Respite care takes many forms. In some cases the respite worker comes to the home to take care of the older adult so that the caregiver can take a few hours off for personal needs, relaxation, or rest. Inpatient respite care, which is offered by some nursing homes and board-and-care facilities, provides an alternative to in-home care. Respite care is also available for longer periods, so that caregivers can recuperate from their own illnesses or even take vacations.

Adult day care programs, which are freestanding or based in hospitals, provide structured programs where older adults may receive the social, health, and recreational services they need to restore or maintain optimal functioning. Although they are not specifically intended to provide respite for caregivers, adult day care programs temporarily relieve families of the physical and emotional stress of caregiving.

Community Services

Besides home health care services, many communities offer a variety of services to help older adults and their caregivers:

- Home care aides assist with chores such as housecleaning, grocery shopping, or laundry, as well as with the activities of daily living

- Repair services help with basic home maintenance, as well as minor changes to make homes secure and safe, such as the installation of grab bars in bathrooms, special seats in the shower, or ramps for wheelchairs

- Home-delivered meal programs deliver nutritious meals to those who can no longer cook or shop for groceries

- Companion and telephone reassurance services keep in touch with older adults living alone (volunteers make regular visits or phone calls to check on and maintain contact with isolated older adults)

- Trained postal or utility workers spot signs of trouble at the homes of older people

- Emergency Response Systems devices allow older adults to summon help during emergencies (when the user pushes the button on the wearable device, it sends a message to a response center or police station)

- Senior centers offer recreation programs, social activities, educational programs, health screenings, and meals

- Communities provide transportation to help older adults run errands and attend medical appointments (these services are often subsidized or free of charge)

- Adult day care centers care for older adults who need supervised assistance (services may include health care, recreation, meals, rehabilitative therapy, and respite care)

Home and Community-Based Services

Home and community-based services refer to the entire array of supportive services that help older people live independently in their home and community. In 1981 federal law implemented the Medicaid home and community-based services (HCBS) waiver program. Before the passage of this legislation, Medicaid long-term care benefits were primarily limited to nursing homes. The HCBS legislation enabled states to offer services not otherwise available through Medicaid to serve people in their own home, thereby preserving their independence and ties to family and friends at a cost no higher than that of institutional care.

Seven specific services may be provided under HCBS waivers:

- Case management services

- Homemaker services

- Home health aide services

- Personal care services

- Adult day care/health care services

- Respite care services

- Rehabilitation services

Other services may be provided at the request of the state if approved by the federal government. Services must be cost effective and necessary for the prevention of institutionalization. States have flexibility in designing their waiver programs; this allows them to tailor their programs to the specific needs of the populations they want to serve.

In the fact sheet "Home and Community-Based Services" (January 10, 2014, https://www.cms.gov/Newsroom/MediaReleaseDatabase/Fact-sheets/2014-Fact-sheets-items/2014-01-10-2.html), the Centers for Medicare and Medicaid Services (CMS) describes how the ACA provides flexibility and enables expansion of HCBS. It details the key provisions and requirements for implementing HCBS under a final rule that was issued in 2014. These provisions are intended to improve the quality of services delivered. For example, one provision requires that service planning for participants in Medicaid HCBS programs "must be developed through a person-centered planning process that addresses health and long-term services and support needs in a manner that reflects individual preferences and goals."

In the press release "CMS Announces Extension for States under Medicaid Home and Community-Based Settings Criteria" (May 5, 2017, https://www.cms.gov/Newsroom/MediaReleaseDatabase/Press-releases/2017-Press-releases-items/2017-05-09.html), the CMS announced a three-year extension for state Medicaid programs to meet the HCBS settings requirements. This extension was granted in response to states' request for more time to demonstrate compliance with the regulatory requirements.

The National Aging Network

The National Aging Network (November 17, 2017, https://eldercare.acl.gov/Public/About/Aging_Network/Index.aspx), which is funded by the Older Americans Act, provides funds for supportive home and community-based services to 622 area agencies on aging, more than 260 Native American organizations, 56 state units on aging, and tens of thousands of service providers. It awards funds for disease prevention/health promotion services, elder rights programs, the National Family Caregiver Support Program, and the Native American Caregiver Support Program. All Americans aged 60 years and older may receive services through the act, but it specifically targets vulnerable older populations—those older adults who are disadvantaged by social or health disparities.

Eldercare Locator

The US Administration on Aging sponsors the Eldercare Locator Directory (December 13, 2017, https://eldercare.acl.gov/Public/Index.aspx), a nationwide toll-free and online service that helps older adults and their caregivers find local services. The Eldercare Locator program connects those who contact it to an information specialist who has access to multiple databases, including the National Aging Network.

BenefitsCheckUp

The National Council on Aging offers the online BenefitsCheckUp program (2018, https://www.benefitscheckup.org), which examines a database of more than 2,500 programs to determine older adults' eligibility for federal, state, and local private and public benefits and programs. Users respond to a few questions and then the program lists which federal, state, and local programs they might be eligible for and how to apply. It is the first online service that is designed to help older Americans, their families, and caregivers determine quickly and easily which benefits they qualify for and how to claim them.

In each state, there are approximately 70 programs available to individuals. Among the programs included are those that help older adults find income support, prescription drug savings, government health programs, energy assistance, property tax relief, nutrition programs, in-home services, veterans' programs, and volunteer, educational, and training programs. As of February 2018, the BenefitsCheckUp program had helped approximately 6.5 million people find benefits worth $23.5 billion to which they were entitled.

Women's Institute for a Secure Retirement

Founded in 1996 with a grant from the Heinz Family Philanthropies, the Women's Institute for a Secure Retirement (WISER; http://www.wiserwomen.org) works to help women understand and plan for retirement income. WISER publications help women navigate the complexities of Social Security, divorce, pensions, savings and investments, banking, homeownership, long-term care, and disability insurance. WISER also conducts research and workshops to identify opportunities for women to secure adequate retirement income.

Geriatric Care Managers Help Older Adults Age in Place

The increasing complexity of arranging care for older adults, especially when families live at a distance from the older adults in need of care, has given rise to a new service profession: geriatric care management. Geriatric care managers have varied educational backgrounds and professional credentials. They may be gerontologists (professionals who study the social, psychological, and biological aspects of aging), nurses, or social workers who specialize in issues that are related to aging and services for older adults. Geriatric care managers work with a formal or informal network of social workers, nurses, psychologists, elder law attorneys, advocates, and agencies that serve older adults.

Geriatric care managers work with families and increasingly with corporations wishing to assist employees to create flexible plans of care to meet the needs of older adults. They oversee home health staffing needs, monitor the quality of in-home services and equipment, and serve as liaisons for families at a distance from their older relatives.

Hired homemakers/caregivers, transportation services, home modifications, and other services are also available. The total monthly cost of services varies. An older adult who needs light housekeeping or companionship for three hours twice a week might spend about $300 per month, whereas someone who needs 24-hour-per-day supervision might pay $5,000 per month or more. Costs can be even higher if care from a certified home health aide or licensed vocational nurse is required.

Geriatric care management is especially important for older adults with dementia. Amy Benson et al. find in "Change in Burden and Distress among Caregivers of Community-Dwelling Older Adults with Dementia Enrolled in Care Management" (*American Journal of Geriatric Psychiatry*, vol. 21, no. 3, March 2013) that care managers help ease caregivers' distress, especially during particularly trying periods such as when medication is used to control troubling behavioral symptoms. The researchers suggest that caregiver access to education, support, and care management "may help improve caregiver well-being and ability to cope with patient symptoms, enabling caregivers to provide at-home care for longer periods prior to nursing home placement."

CHAPTER 10
HEALTH CARE USE, EXPENDITURES, AND FINANCING

Health care use and expenditures tend to be concentrated among older adults. Because older adults often suffer multiple chronic conditions, they are hospitalized more frequently, use the most prescription and over-the-counter (nonprescription) drugs, make the highest number of physician visits, and require care from more physician specialists and other health care providers—such as podiatrists and physical therapists—than any other age group.

Nearly all older Americans have health insurance through Medicare, which covers inpatient hospitalization, outpatient care, physician services, home health care, short-term skilled nursing facility care, hospice (end-of-life care) services, and prescription drugs. Historically, older adults' use of health care services has changed in response to physician practice patterns, advances in medical technology, and Medicare reimbursement for services. For example, advances in medical technology and physician practice patterns have shifted many medical procedures once performed in hospitals to outpatient settings such as ambulatory surgery centers.

Older adults are responsible for disproportionate health care expenditures. For example, the Centers for Medicare and Medicaid Services (CMS) notes in "NHE Fact Sheet" (June 14, 2017, https://www.cms.gov/research-statistics-data-and-systems/statistics-trends-and-reports/nationalhealthexpenddata/nhe-fact-sheet.html) that health care expenditures for adults aged 65 years and older were $18,988 per person in 2012, over five times higher than spending per child ($3,552) and approximately three times the spending per working-age person ($6,632). (See Table 10.1.)

In "The State of Aging and Health in America 2013" (2013, https://www.cdc.gov/aging/pdf/State-Aging-Health-in-America-2013.pdf), the Centers for Disease Control and Prevention explains that these disproportionate expenses are in part attributable to the fact that two out of three older adults have multiple chronic health conditions, and

treatment for this population accounts for 66% of the country's health care budget. The CMS projects that the national health expenditure will grow to $5.3 trillion by 2025. (See Table 10.2; note that because these numbers are projections, they differ from numbers presented in other tables and figures.) Medicare is projected to reach $1.3 trillion by 2025, accounting for 25% of all health care expenditures.

FINANCING HEALTH CARE FOR OLDER ADULTS

The Patient Protection and Affordable Care Act (ACA) of 2010, often called Obamacare, contains about 165 provisions that affect Medicare. By reducing costs, increasing revenues, strengthening certain benefits, combating fraud and abuse, and conducting research to identify and strengthen provider payment mechanisms and health care delivery systems, these provisions are intended to improve the quality of health care for beneficiaries and reduce its costs.

The ACA expanded Americans' access to health care. It also addressed aspects of health care reform, including:

- Improving the quality and efficiency of health care—there is special emphasis placed on improving clinical outcomes (how patients fare as a result of treatment) for people receiving care through government entitlement programs

- Prevention of chronic disease and improving public health—the ACA established a national prevention and health promotion strategy; it also established the Prevention and Public Health Investment Fund to support national investment in prevention and public health

- Health care workforce—increasing the supply, training, and quality of health care workers

TABLE 10.1

Per capita personal health care spending by age group and sex, selected years 2002–12

[In dollars]

Age group	Levels						Average annual growth				
	2002	2004	2006	2008	2010	2012	2002–04	2004–06	2006–08	2008–10	2010–12
Total	4,758	5,428	6,054	6,629	7,102	7,564	6.8%	5.6%	4.6%	3.5%	3.2%
0–18	2,024	2,398	2,747	3,032	3,300	3,552	8.8%	7.0%	5.1%	4.3%	3.8%
19–64	4,193	4,792	5,366	5,831	6,238	6,632	6.9%	5.8%	4.2%	3.4%	3.1%
19–44	2,766	3,193	3,576	3,908	4,156	4,458	7.4%	5.8%	4.5%	3.1%	3.6%
45–64	6,504	7,218	7,922	8,456	9,000	9,513	5.3%	4.8%	3.3%	3.2%	2.8%
65+	13,537	15,112	16,434	17,786	18,544	18,988	5.7%	4.3%	4.0%	2.1%	1.2%
65–84	12,119	13,509	14,623	15,776	16,425	16,872	5.6%	4.0%	3.9%	2.0%	1.4%
85+	23,702	26,339	28,521	30,827	31,903	32,411	5.4%	4.1%	4.0%	1.7%	0.8%
Males	4,149	4,747	5,318	5,858	6,334	6,788	7.0%	5.8%	5.0%	4.0%	3.5%
0–18	2,095	2,490	2,840	3,136	3,418	3,698	9.0%	6.8%	5.1%	4.4%	4.0%
19–64	3,596	4,103	4,619	5,043	5,445	5,822	6.8%	6.1%	4.5%	3.9%	3.4%
19–44	2,080	2,387	2,664	2,901	3,119	3,352	7.1%	5.6%	4.4%	3.7%	3.7%
45–64	6,130	6,786	7,493	8,048	8,624	9,203	5.2%	5.1%	3.6%	3.5%	3.3%
65+	12,955	14,446	15,656	16,995	17,849	18,251	5.6%	4.1%	4.2%	2.5%	1.1%
65–84	12,146	13,528	14,606	15,753	16,532	16,890	5.5%	3.9%	3.9%	2.4%	1.1%
85+	21,500	23,756	25,594	28,243	29,244	29,922	5.1%	3.8%	5.0%	1.8%	1.2%
Females	5,349	6,089	6,771	7,380	7,844	8,315	6.7%	5.5%	4.4%	3.1%	3.0%
0–18	1,950	2,301	2,649	2,923	3,176	3,399	8.6%	7.3%	5.1%	4.2%	3.5%
19–64	4,789	5,479	6,111	6,616	7,019	7,430	7.00%	5.60%	4.10%	3.00%	2.90%
19–44	3,469	4,017	4,507	4,934	5,204	5,579	7.60%	5.90%	4.60%	2.70%	3.50%
45–64	6,862	7,633	8,335	8,849	9,358	9,808	5.50%	4.50%	3.00%	2.80%	2.40%
65+	13,954	15,597	17,011	18,383	19,072	19,558	5.70%	4.40%	4.00%	1.90%	1.30%
65–84	12,099	13,495	14,637	15,795	16,338	16,857	5.60%	4.10%	3.90%	1.70%	1.60%
85+	24,621	27,461	29,848	32,045	33,192	33,662	5.60%	4.30%	3.60%	1.80%	0.70%

SOURCE: "Table 7. Total Personal Health Care Per-Capita Spending by Gender and Age Group, Calendar Years 2002, 2004, 2006, 2008, 2010, 2012 Level (Dollars)," in "Age and Gender Tables," in *NHE Fact Sheet*, Centers for Medicare & Medicaid Services, June 2017, https://www.cms.gov/research-statistics-data-and-systems/statistics-trends-and-reports/nationalhealthexpenddata/nhe-fact-sheet.html (accessed October 30, 2017)

- Transparency and program integrity—providing public information and combating fraud and abuse

- Community living assistance services and supports— the ACA instituted the Community Living Assistance Services and Supports Independence Benefit Plan, a voluntary, self-funded long-term care (LTC) insurance program, to help older adults pay for community living assistance services

Of the many changes that occurred under the ACA, several are particularly relevant to older adults. For example, the ACA eliminated lifetime and unreasonable limits on benefits, prohibited cancellation of health insurance policies, and enabled people with preexisting conditions to acquire insurance coverage. The act increased Medicare provider fees in rural areas and extended Medicare bonus payments for ground and air ambulance services in rural areas. It also created an independent Medicare Advisory Board to present Congress with proposals to reduce costs and improve quality for Medicare beneficiaries.

The Health Care and Education Affordability Reconciliation Act of 2010 amended the ACA. It contains provisions that are important for older adults, including closing the gap in Medicare prescription drug benefits known as the "donut hole." The CMS explains in "Costs in the Coverage Gap" (2017, https://www.medicare.gov/part-d/costs/coverage-gap/part-d-coverage-gap.html) that the donut hole is a coverage gap in the Medicare Part D program. The coverage gap begins when beneficiaries and their drug plans together have spent a certain amount for covered drugs. In 2018 beneficiaries in the coverage gap pay 35% of the plan's cost for covered brand-name drugs and 44% of the plan's cost for covered generic drugs until they reach the end of the coverage gap. Beneficiaries who receive help paying for Medicare Part D, which is the prescription drug plan, do not enter the coverage gap.

The ACA has been decreasing the donut hole by reducing beneficiaries' co-payments, with the intention of completely closing the hole by 2020. By 2020 beneficiaries will pay 25% for covered brand-name and generic drugs during the gap; this is the same percentage they pay from the time they meet their health plan deductible (if any) until they reach the out-of-pocket spending limit.

MEDICARE

The spirit in which this law is written draws deeply upon the ancient dreams of all mankind. In Leviticus, it is written, "Thou shall rise up before the hoary head, and honor the face of an old man."

—Senator Russell B. Long (1918–2003; D-LA) at the original vote for Medicare in 1965

TABLE 10.2

National health expenditures by source of funds, 2009–25

Year	Total	Out-of-pocket payments	Health insurance[a]					Other third party payers[c]
			Total	Private health insurance	Medicare	Medicaid	Other health insurance programs[b]	
Historical estimates					Amount in billions			
2009	$2,355.7	$293.1	$1,796.1	$832.6	$498.9	$374.4	$90.3	$266.5
2010	2,453.7	298.7	1,875.1	863.1	519.3	397.2	95.6	279.8
2011	2,538.4	308.5	1,948.2	895.1	546.3	406.7	100.1	281.8
2012	2,642.2	317.6	2,019.6	925.1	569.5	422.7	102.2	305.0
2013	2,724.5	325.1	2,086.3	944.9	590.4	445.4	105.6	313.1
2014	2,878.4	329.7	2,228.2	1,000.0	618.5	497.2	112.6	320.5
2015	3,050.8	338.1	2,384.5	1,072.1	646.2	545.1	121.1	328.2
Projected								
2016	3,200.1	350.4	2,508.5	1,135.4	678.6	565.5	129.0	341.2
2017	3,375.4	365.8	2,652.0	1,208.8	718.7	586.5	138.1	357.6
2018	3,574.2	382.7	2,816.5	1,280.4	767.9	621.8	146.4	375.0
2019	3,784.9	401.2	2,990.1	1,351.3	824.9	658.1	155.8	393.6
2020	4,006.2	424.3	3,168.8	1,416.0	890.5	696.7	165.6	413.2
2021	4,240.8	446.2	3,360.6	1,488.6	958.8	737.1	176.1	433.9
2022	4,488.2	468.7	3,564.5	1,564.9	1,033.2	779.7	186.6	455.0
2023	4,748.4	492.0	3,779.6	1,643.9	1,113.9	824.9	196.9	476.8
2024	5,018.6	516.6	4,002.5	1,725.9	1,196.1	873.2	207.2	499.5
2025	5,299.9	542.3	4,234.1	1,809.1	1,277.8	929.0	218.1	523.5
Historical estimates					Per capita amount			
2009	$7,687	$957	d	d	d	d	d	d
2010	7,942	967	d	d	d	d	d	d
2011	8,158	991	d	d	d	d	d	d
2012	8,427	1,013	d	d	d	d	d	d
2013	8,625	1,029	d	d	d	d	d	d
2014	9,041	1,035	d	d	d	d	d	d
2015	9,508	1,054	d	d	d	d	d	d
Projected			d					
2016	9,884	1,082	d	d	d	d	d	d
2017	10,331	1,120	d	d	d	d	d	d
2018	10,838	1,161	d	d	d	d	d	d
2019	11,369	1,205	d	d	d	d	d	d
2020	11,922	1,263	d	d	d	d	d	d
2021	12,504	1,316	d	d	d	d	d	d
2022	13,115	1,370	d	d	d	d	d	d
2023	13,754	1,425	d	d	d	d	d	d
2024	14,411	1,483	d	d	d	d	d	d
2025	15,091	1,544	d	d	d	d	d	d
Historical estimates					Percent distribution			
2009	100.0	12.4	76.2	35.3	21.2	15.9	3.8	11.3
2010	100.0	12.2	76.4	35.2	21.2	16.2	3.9	11.4
2011	100.0	12.2	76.7	35.3	21.5	16.0	3.9	11.1
2012	100.0	12.0	76.4	35.0	21.6	16.0	3.9	11.5
2013	100.0	11.9	76.6	34.7	21.7	16.3	3.9	11.5
2014	100.0	11.5	77.4	34.7	21.5	17.3	3.9	11.1
2015	100.0	11.1	78.2	35.1	21.2	17.9	4.0	10.8
Projected								
2016	100.0	10.9	78.4	35.5	21.2	17.7	4.0	10.7
2017	100.0	10.8	78.6	35.8	21.3	17.4	4.1	10.6
2018	100.0	10.7	78.8	35.8	21.5	17.4	4.1	10.5
2019	100.0	10.6	79.0	35.7	21.8	17.4	4.1	10.4
2020	100.0	10.6	79.1	35.3	22.2	17.4	4.1	10.3
2021	100.0	10.5	79.2	35.1	22.6	17.4	4.2	10.2
2022	100.0	10.4	79.4	34.9	23.0	17.4	4.2	10.1
2023	100.0	10.4	79.6	34.6	23.5	17.4	4.1	10.0
2024	100.0	10.3	79.8	34.4	23.8	17.4	4.1	10.0
2025	100.0	10.2	79.9	34.1	24.1	17.5	4.1	9.9

The major government health care entitlement programs are Medicare and Medicaid. They provide financial assistance for people aged 65 years and older, the poor, and people with disabilities. Before the existence of these programs, many older Americans could not afford adequate medical care. For older adult beneficiaries, the Medicare program provides reimbursement for hospital and physician care, whereas Medicaid pays for the cost of nursing home care.

The Medicare program, which was enacted under Title XVIII (Health Insurance for the Aged) of the Social

Year	Total	Out-of-pocket payments	Total	Private health insurance	Medicare	Medicaid	Other health insurance programs[b]	Other third party payers[c]
					Health insurance[a]			
				Annual percent change from previous year shown				
Historical estimates								
2009	—	—	—	—	—	—	—	—
2010	4.2	1.9	4.4	3.7	4.1	6.1	5.9	5.0
2011	3.5	3.3	3.9	3.7	5.2	2.4	4.7	0.7
2012	4.1	2.9	3.7	3.4	4.3	3.9	2.2	8.2
2013	3.1	2.4	3.3	2.1	3.7	5.4	3.3	2.7
2014	5.6	1.4	6.8	5.8	4.8	11.6	6.6	2.4
2015	6.0	2.6	7.0	7.2	4.5	9.7	7.5	2.4
Projected								
2016	4.9	3.6	5.2	5.9	5.0	3.7	6.5	4.0
2017	5.5	4.4	5.7	6.5	5.9	3.7	7.0	4.8
2018	5.9	4.6	6.2	5.9	6.8	6.0	6.1	4.9
2019	5.9	4.8	6.2	5.5	7.4	5.8	6.4	5.0
2020	5.8	5.8	6.0	4.8	8.0	5.9	6.3	5.0
2021	5.9	5.2	6.1	5.1	7.7	5.8	6.4	5.0
2022	5.8	5.0	6.1	5.1	7.8	5.8	5.9	4.9
2023	5.8	5.0	6.0	5.0	7.8	5.8	5.5	4.8
2024	5.7	5.0	5.9	5.0	7.4	5.9	5.3	4.8
2025	5.6	5.0	5.8	4.8	6.8	6.4	5.2	4.8

[a]Includes Private Health Insurance (Employer Sponsored Insurance and other private insurance, which includes Marketplace plans), Medicare, Medicaid, Children's Health Insurance Program (Titles XIX and XXI), Department of Defense, and Department of Veterans' Affairs.
[b]Children's Health Insurance Program (Titles XIX and XXI), Department of Defense, and Department of Veterans' Affairs.
[c]Includes worksite health care, other private revenues, Indian Health Service, workers' compensation, general assistance, maternal and child health, vocational rehabilitation, other federal programs, Substance Abuse and Mental Health Services Administration, other state and local programs, and school health.
[d]Calculation of per capita estimates is not applicable.
Note: Per capita amounts based on estimates that reflect the US Bureau of Census definition for resident-based population (which includes all persons who usually reside in one of the fifty states or the District of Columbia, but excludes (i) residents living in Puerto Rico and areas under US sovereignty, and (ii) US Armed Forces overseas and US citizens whose usual place of residence is outside of the United States) plus a small (typically less than 0.2% of population) adjustment to reflect Census undercounts. Projected estimates reflect the area population growth assumptions found in the Medicare Trustees Report. Numbers and percents may not add to totals because of rounding.

SOURCE: "Table 4. Health Consumption Expenditures; Aggregate and Per Capita Amounts, Percent Distribution and Annual Percent Change by Source of Funds: Calendar Years 2009–2025," in *National Health Expenditures Projections 2016–2025*, Centers for Medicare and Medicaid Services, March 21, 2017, https://www.cms.gov/Research-Statistics-Data-and-Systems/Statistics-Trends-and-Reports/NationalHealthExpendData/NationalHealthAccountsProjected.html (accessed October 30, 2017)

Security Act, was signed into law by President Lyndon B. Johnson (1908–1973) and went into effect on July 1, 1966. That year 19 million older adults entered the program. In 2016, 56.8 million people were enrolled in Medicare. (See Table 10.3.) By 2030 the Medicare population is projected to increase by 47%, to 81.8 million.

The establishment of the Medicare program in 1966 served to improve equity in health care. Before the creation of Medicare about half of the older population was uninsured, and the insured population was often limited to benefits of just $10 per day. Furthermore, because poverty rates among older adults hovered at about 30%, some of the older population could not be expected to pay for private health insurance. The Medicare program extended health care coverage to a population that had growing health needs and little income.

The Medicare program consists of several parts:

- Part A provides hospital insurance. Coverage includes physicians' fees, nursing services, meals, semiprivate rooms, special care units, operating room costs, laboratory tests, and some drugs and supplies. Part A also covers rehabilitation services, posthospital skilled nursing facility care, home health care, and hospice care for the terminally ill.

- Part B (Supplemental Medical Insurance) is elective medical insurance; enrollees must pay premiums to get coverage. It covers private physicians' services, diagnostic tests, outpatient hospital services, outpatient physical therapy, speech pathology services, home health services, and medical equipment and supplies.

- The third part of Medicare, sometimes known as Part C, is the Medicare Advantage program, which was established by the Balanced Budget Act of 1997 to expand beneficiaries' options and allow them to participate in private-sector health plans. The ACA restructured payments to the Medicare Advantage plans in response to geographic differences in fees and rewards plans that demonstrate quality with bonuses.

- Part D, the Medicare prescription drug benefit, was enacted after Congress passed the Prescription Drug, Improvement, and Modernization Act of 2003.

Medicare enrollment, selected years 1970–2091

[In thousands]

Calendar year	HI Part A	SMI Part B	SMI Part D	Part C	Total[a]
Historical data:					
1970	20,104	19,496	—	—	20,398
1975	24,481	23,744	—	—	24,864
1980	28,002	27,278	—	—	28,433
1985	30,621	29,869	—	1,271	31,081
1990	33,747	32,567	—	2,017	34,251
1995	37,175	35,641	—	3,467	37,594
2000	39,257	37,335	—	6,856	39,688
2005	42,233	39,752	1,841	5,794	42,606
2010	47,365	43,882	34,772	11,692	47,720
2011	48,549	44,917	35,720	12,383	48,896
2012	50,540	46,477	37,448	13,588	50,874
2013	52,169	47,952	39,103	14,843	52,504
2014	53,777	49,413	40,499	16,243	54,115
2015	55,205	50,744	41,804	17,492	55,542
2016	56,463	52,088	43,191	18,391	56,800
Intermediate estimates:					
2017	58,287	53,525	44,461	19,778	58,625
2018	59,999	55,038	46,074	20,780	60,337
2019	61,839	56,648	47,806	21,695	62,178
2020	63,720	58,325	49,224	22,393	64,060
2021	65,595	59,993	50,658	23,150	65,937
2022	67,489	61,680	52,110	24,011	67,832
2023	69,338	63,342	53,527	24,839	69,683
2024	71,134	64,946	54,904	25,624	71,482
2025	72,955	66,570	56,298	26,391	73,305
2026	74,723	68,163	57,655	27,133	75,075
2030	80,866	73,689	62,329	28,890	81,223
2035	85,823	78,064	66,029	30,613	86,178
2040	88,453	80,399	68,004	31,474	88,803
2045	90,103	81,843	69,226	[b]	90,452
2050	92,261	83,772	70,857	[b]	92,616
2055	95,127	86,298	72,994	[b]	95,492
2060	98,669	89,522	75,721	[b]	99,048
2065	102,023	92,591	78,317	[b]	102,410
2070	105,765	96,004	81,204	[b]	106,159
2075	109,705	99,619	84,262	[b]	110,104
2080	112,157	101,928	86,215	[b]	112,551
2085	115,201	104,646	88,513	[b]	115,587
2090	119,583	108,572	91,835	[b]	119,961
2091	120,459	109,368	92,507	[b]	120,835

[a]Number of beneficiaries with HI and/or SMI coverage.
[b]The Trustees do not explicitly project enrollment in Part C beyond 2040.
Notes: HI = Hospital Insurance. SMI = Supplementary Medical Insurance.

SOURCE: "Table V.B4. Medicare Enrollment," in *2017 Annual Report of the Boards of Trustees of the Federal Hospital Insurance and Federal Supplementary Medical Insurance Trust Funds*, Centers for Medicare & Medicaid Services, 2017, https://www.cms.gov/Research-Statistics-Data-and-Systems/Statistics-Trends-and-Reports/ReportsTrustFunds/Downloads/TR2017.pdf (accessed October 30, 2017)

As reported in the *2017 Annual Report of the Boards of Trustees of the Federal Hospital Insurance and Federal Supplementary Medical Insurance Trust Funds* (2017, https://www.cms.gov/Research-Statistics-Data-and-Systems/Statistics-Trends-and-Reports/Reports TrustFunds/Downloads/TR2017.pdf), in 2016, $678.7 billion was projected to be spent to provide coverage for the 56.8 million people who were enrolled in Medicare. (See Table 10.2 and Table 10.3.) The majority of Medicare recipients were aged 65 years and older.

Reimbursement under Medicare

Historically, Medicare reimbursed physicians on a fee-for-service basis (paid for each visit, procedure, or treatment delivered), as opposed to per capita or per member per month (PMPM). In response to the increasing administrative burden of paperwork, reduced compensation, and delays in reimbursements, some physicians opt out of Medicare participation; they do not provide services under the Medicare program and choose not to accept Medicare patients into their practice. Others continue to provide services to Medicare beneficiaries, but they do not "accept assignment"; that is, their patients must pay out of pocket for services and then seek reimbursement from Medicare.

The Tax Equity and Fiscal Responsibility Act of 1982 authorized a "risk managed care" option for Medicare, based on agreed-on prepayments. Beginning in 1985 CMS contracted to pay providers, such as health maintenance organizations (HMOs) or other prepaid plans, to serve Medicare and Medicaid patients. These groups were paid a predetermined amount per enrollee for their services. These became known as Medicare-risk HMOs.

During the 1980s and 1990s the federal government, employers that provided health coverage for retirees, and many states sought to control costs by encouraging Medicare and Medicaid beneficiaries to enroll in HMOs. HMOs kept costs down because, essentially, the federal government paid them fixed fees (a predetermined dollar amount PMPM). For this fixed fee, Medicare recipients were to receive a comprehensive array of benefits. The PMPM payment provided a financial incentive for HMO physicians to control costs, unlike physicians who were reimbursed on a fee-for-service basis.

Although Medicare recipients were generally satisfied with these HMOs (even when enrolling meant they had to change physicians and thereby end long-standing relationships with their family doctors), many of the health plans did not fare well. The plans suffered for several reasons: some had underestimated the service utilization rates of older adults, and some were unable to provide the stipulated range of services. For other plans, the PMPM payment was not sufficient to enable them to cover all the clinical services and administrative overhead.

Regardless, the health plans providing these "senior HMOs" competed to enroll older adults. Some plans feared that closing their Medicare-risk programs would be viewed negatively by employer groups, which, when faced with the choice of plans that offered coverage for both younger workers and retirees or that covered only the younger workers, would choose the plans that covered both. Despite losing money, most health plans maintained their Medicare-risk programs to avoid alienating the employers they depended on to enroll workers who were younger, healthier, and less expensive to serve than the older adults.

Approximately 10 years into operations, some Medicare-risk programs faced challenges that proved insurmountable. Their enrollees had aged and required more health care services than they had previously. For example, a member who had joined as a healthy 65-year-old could now be a frail 75-year-old with multiple chronic health conditions requiring costly health care services. The PMPM had increased over the years, but for some health plans it was simply insufficient to cover their costs. Many health plans, especially the smaller ones, ended their Medicare-risk programs abruptly, leaving thousands of older adults scrambling to join other health plans. Others endured, offering older adults comprehensive care and generating substantial cost savings for employers and the federal government.

Medicare Advantage

The Balanced Budget Act of 1997 replaced the Medicare-risk plans with Medicare+Choice, which later became known as Medicare Advantage. These plans offer Medicare beneficiaries a wider range of managed care plan options than just HMOs—older adults can join preferred provider organizations and provider-sponsored organizations that generally offer greater freedom of choice of providers (physicians and hospitals) than is available through HMO membership. Table 10.4 compares original Medicare with Medicare Advantage.

When older adults join the Medicare Advantage plans that have entered into contracts with the CMS, the plans are paid a fixed amount PMPM, which represents Medicare's share of the cost of the services. Members no longer have to pay the regular Medicare deductibles and co-payments for covered services. Some plans charge modest monthly premiums and/or nominal co-payments as services are used, but there are no other charges by the plan for physician visits, hospitalization, or use of other covered services. However, members of the Medicare Advantage plans must continue to pay the Medicare Part B monthly premium. Federal payments to Medicare Advantage plans were gradually reduced by the ACA to bring them into line with payments for traditional Medicare programs.

Insurance to Supplement Medicare Benefits

In 2013, 12.1 million (27.4%) adults aged 65 and older had private insurance obtained through the workplace to supplement their Medicare coverage. (See Table 10.5.) The most popular private insurance is supplemental insurance known as Medigap insurance. Federal regulations mandate that all Medigap policies sold offer a standard minimum set of benefits, but there are variations that offer additional coverage and benefits. As Table 10.5 shows, the percentage of older adults with Medigap

TABLE 10.4

Comparing original Medicare to Medicare Advantage, 2018

Original Medicare		Medicare Advantage
There's **no limit** on how much you pay out-of pocket per year unless you have supplemental coverage.	Cost	Plans have a **yearly limit** on your out-of-pocket costs. If you join a Medicare Advantage Plan, once you reach a certain limit, you'll **pay nothing** for covered services for the rest of the year.
Medicare **covers medical** services and supplies in hospitals, doctors' offices, and other health care settings. Services are either covered under Part A or Part B.	Coverage*	Plans must cover all of the services that Original Medicare covers. Plans may **offer benefits** that Original Medicare doesn't cover like **vision, hearing, or dental**.
You **can add** a Medigap policy to help pay your out-of-pocket costs in Original Medicare, like your deductible and coinsurance.	Supplemental coverage	It may be more cost effective for you to join a Medicare Advantage Plan because your **cost sharing is lower (or included)**. You can't use (and can't be sold) a Medigap policy if you're in a Medicare Advantage Plan.
You'll **need to join** a Medicare Prescription Drug Plan to get drug coverage.	Prescription drugs*	Most Medicare Advantage Plans **include drug coverage**.
You can **go to any doctor** that accepts Medicare.	Doctor and hospital choice	You may need to use health care providers who participate in the **plan's network.** If so, find out how close the network's doctor or pharmacies are to your home. Some plans offer out-of-network coverage.
You can get a snapshot of the quality of care health care providers (and facilities) give their patients by visiting **Medicare.gov.**	Quality of care	The Medicare Plan Finder at **Medicare.gov/find-a-plan** features a **star rating system** for Medicare plans.
Original Medicare generally **doesn't cover care outside the US** You may be able to buy supplemental insurance that offers travel coverage.	Travel	Plans **usually don't cover care** you get outside of the US

*If you have other types of health or prescription drug coverage, check to see how it works with the type of coverage you're considering before you make any decisions or changes.

SOURCE: "Things to Consider When Choosing Your Medicare Coverage," in *Medicare & You 2018*, Centers for Medicare and Medicaid Services, 2017, https://www.medicare.gov/pubs/pdf/10050-Medicare-and-You.pdf (accessed October 30, 2017)

insurance declined from 33.9% in 1992 to 18.7% in 2013, whereas the percentage with only Medicare rose from 9.9% in 1992 to 14.6% in 2013.

Besides Medigap policies, older adults may also purchase Medicare supplement health insurance, which offers essentially the same coverage as Medigap policies but requires use of preferred providers (specific hospitals and in some cases plan physicians) to receive full benefits. Although these policies restrict older adults' choices, they are generally less expensive than Medigap policies.

A less popular option is hospital indemnity coverage—insurance that pays a fixed cash amount for each day of hospitalization for a designated number of days. Some

TABLE 10.5

Health insurance coverage for persons aged 65 and older, by type of coverage and selected characteristics, selected years 1992–2013

[Data are based on household interviews of a sample of noninstitutionalized Medicare beneficiaries]

Characteristic	Medicare Advantage plan[b]					Medicaid[c]				
	1992	1995	2000	2012	2013	1992	1995	2000	2012	2013
Age					Number, in millions					
65 years and over	1.1	2.6	5.9	12.4	13.8	2.7	2.8	2.7	3.6	3.6
					Percent distribution					
65 years and over	3.9	8.9	19.3	29.1	31.2	9.4	9.6	9.0	8.5	8.1
65–74 years	4.2	9.5	20.6	29.1	30.3	7.9	8.8	8.5	7.6	7.2
75–84 years	3.7	8.3	18.5	30.1	33.8	10.6	9.6	8.9	9.2	8.6
85 years and over	a	7.3	16.3	26.3	29.4	16.6	13.6	11.2	10.3	11.4
Sex										
Male	4.6	9.2	19.3	28.9	30.0	6.3	6.2	6.3	5.6	5.7
Female	3.4	8.6	19.3	29.2	32.3	11.6	12.0	10.9	10.7	10.1
Race and Hispanic origin										
White, not Hispanic or Latino	3.6	8.4	18.4	26.9	29.1	5.6	5.4	5.1	5.1	4.9
Black, not Hispanic or Latino	a	7.9	20.7	30.3	33.4	28.5	30.3	23.6	19.0	17.8
Hispanic	a	15.5	27.5	45.5	46.7	39.0	40.5	28.7	20.2	20.1
Percent of poverty level[d]										
Below 100%	3.6	7.7	18.4	—	—	22.3	17.2	15.9	—	—
100%–less than 200%	3.7	9.5	23.4	—	—	6.7	6.3	8.4	—	—
200% or more	4.2	10.1	18.0	—	—	a	a	a	—	—
Marital status										
Married	4.6	9.5	18.7	28.6	30.2	4.0	4.3	4.3	3.9	3.5
Widowed	2.3	7.7	19.4	28.6	31.2	14.9	15.0	13.6	13.8	12.5
Divorced	a	9.7	24.4	32.4	35.2	23.4	24.5	20.2	15.7	16.0
Never married	a	a	15.8	27.4	32.1	19.2	19.0	17.0	14.5	17.9

Characteristic	Employer-sponsored plan[e]					Medigap[f]				
	1992	1995	2000	2012	2013	1992	1995	2000	2012	2013
Age					Number, in millions					
65 years and over	12.5	11.3	10.7	12.0	12.1	9.9	9.5	7.6	8.0	8.2
					Percent distribution					
65 years and over	42.8	38.6	35.2	28.1	27.4	33.9	32.5	25.0	18.9	18.7
65–74 years	46.9	41.1	36.6	29.8	29.5	31.4	29.9	21.7	17.5	17.5
75–84 years	38.2	37.1	35.0	25.9	24.4	37.5	35.2	27.8	20.2	19.8
85 years and over	31.6	30.2	29.4	26.1	24.9	38.3	37.6	31.1	22.1	21.1
Sex										
Male	46.3	42.1	37.7	30.2	29.1	30.6	30.0	23.4	17.2	17.2
Female	40.4	36.0	33.4	26.4	25.9	36.2	34.4	26.2	20.3	19.9
Race and Hispanic origin										
White, not Hispanic or Latino	45.9	41.3	38.6	30.6	29.5	37.2	36.2	28.3	22.4	22.1
Black, not Hispanic or Latino	25.9	26.7	22.0	27.4	26.7	13.6	10.2	7.5	5.7	5.3
Hispanic	20.7	16.9	15.8	13.1	13.9	15.8	10.1	11.3	6.3	5.6
Percent of poverty level[d]										
Below 100%	29.0	32.1	28.1	—	—	30.8	29.8	22.6	—	—
100%–less than 200%	37.5	32.0	27.0	—	—	39.3	39.1	28.4	—	—
200% or more	58.4	52.8	49.0	—	—	32.8	32.2	26.2	—	—
Marital status										
Married	49.9	44.6	41.0	32.9	33.0	33.0	32.6	25.6	20.1	19.6
Widowed	34.1	30.3	28.7	22.6	21.3	37.5	35.2	26.7	19.9	19.9
Divorced	27.3	26.6	22.4	19.7	17.2	27.9	24.1	16.9	13.0	14.8
Never married	38.0	35.1	28.5	24.3	21.5	29.1	26.2	21.9	16.7	13.1

coverage may have added benefits such as surgical benefits or skilled nursing home benefits. Most policies have a maximum annual number of days or a lifetime maximum payment.

The Prescription Drug, Improvement, and Modernization Act

In 2003 Congress passed the Prescription Drug, Improvement, and Modernization Act, the largest expansion of Medicare since its creation in 1965. The legislation established a Medicare prescription drug benefit. The benefit took full effect in 2006. Among other things, it provides help for low-income beneficiaries and those with the highest drug costs.

Medicare Prescription Drug Coverage

Enrollees in the Medicare prescription drug program, called Part D, pay a monthly premium, which varies by

TABLE 10.5

Health insurance coverage for persons aged 65 and older, by type of coverage and selected characteristics, selected years 1992–2013 [CONTINUED]

[Data are based on household interviews of a sample of noninstitutionalized Medicare beneficiaries]

Characteristic	Medicare fee-for-service only or Other[f]				
	1992	1995	2000	2012	2013
Age			Number, in millions		
65 years and over	2.9	3.1	3.5	6.6	6.4
			Percent distribution		
65 years and over	9.9	10.5	11.5	15.5	14.6
65–74 years	9.7	10.7	12.6	16.0	15.5
75–84 years	10.1	9.9	9.9	14.6	13.5
85 years and over	10.8	11.3	11.3	15.1	13.3
Sex					
Male	12.2	12.6	13.3	18.0	18.0
Female	8.3	8.9	10.2	13.4	11.9
Race and Hispanic origin					
White, not Hispanic or Latino	7.7	8.7	9.6	15.1	14.3
Black, not Hispanic or Latino	26.7	25.0	26.1	17.6	16.8
Hispanic	18.3	17.1	16.7	14.9	13.7
Percent of poverty level[c]					
Below 100%	14.3	13.3	15.1	—	—
100%–less than 200%	12.9	13.1	12.7	—	—
200% or more	4.0	4.5	6.3	—	—
Marital status					
Married	8.5	9.0	10.5	14.6	13.8
Widowed	11.2	11.9	11.6	15.1	15.2
Divorced	15.7	15.1	16.1	19.3	16.9
Never married	[a]	13.1	16.8	17.2	15.4

—Data not available.

[a]Estimates are considered unreliable if the sample cell size is 50 or fewer.

[b]Enrollee has a Medicare Advantage plan regardless of other insurance. Medicare Advantage plans include health maintenance organizations, preferred provider organizations, private fee-for-service plans, special needs plans, and Medicare medical savings account plans. Starting with 2013 data, the term Medicare Risk Health Maintenance Organization was replaced with Medicare Advantage plan.

[c]Enrolled in Medicaid and not enrolled in a Medicare Advantage plan.

[d]Percent of poverty level is based on family income and family size and composition using US Census Bureau poverty thresholds.

[e]Private insurance plans purchased through employers (own, current, or former employer, family business, union, or former employer or union of spouse) and not enrolled in a Medicare Advantage plan or Medicaid.

[f]Supplemental insurance purchased privately or through organizations such as American Association of Retired Persons or professional organizations, and not enrolled in a Medicare Advantage plan, Medicaid, or employer-sponsored plan.

Notes: Data for noninstitutionalized Medicare beneficiaries. Insurance categories are mutually exclusive. Persons with more than one type of coverage are categorized according to the order in which the health insurance categories appear in the table.

SOURCE: "Table 106. Health Insurance Coverage of Noninstitutionalized Medicare Beneficiaries Aged 65 Years and over, by Type of Coverage and Selected Characteristics: United States, Selected Years 1992–2013," in *Health, United States, 2016: With Chartbook on Long-Term Trends in Health*, National Center for Health Statistics, May 2017, https://www.cdc.gov/nchs/data/hus/2016/106.pdf (accessed October 24, 2017)

plan, and a yearly deductible that in 2017 was no more than $400. They also pay part of the cost of their prescriptions, including a co-payment or coinsurance. Costs vary among the different drug plans; some plans offer more coverage and access to a wider range of drugs for a higher monthly premium. According to the Kaiser Family Foundation, in "The Medicare Prescription Drug Benefit Fact Sheet" (October 2, 2017, https://www.kff.org/medicare/fact-sheet/the-medicare-prescription-drug-benefit-fact-sheet/), in 2018 the monthly Part D premiums ranged from $12.60 to $197. Older adults with limited incomes may not have to pay premiums or deductibles for the drug coverage.

THE MEDICARE PRESCRIPTION DRUG, IMPROVEMENT, AND MODERNIZATION ACT AIMS TO REFORM MEDICARE. The Medicare Prescription Drug, Improvement, and Modernization Act of 2003 was intended to introduce private-sector enterprise into a Medicare model in urgent need of reform. Under the act, premiums and deductibles may rise quickly because they are indexed to the growth in per capita Medicare expenditures.

Older adults with substantial incomes face increasing premium costs. According to the CMS, in "Medicare 2018 Costs at a Glance" (2018, https://www.medicare.gov/your-medicare-costs/costs-at-a-glance/costs-at-glance.html), in 2018 older adults with annual incomes of $85,000 or less or couples earning $170,000 or less paid the standard premium, $134 per month, for Medicare Part B. Individuals and couples with higher incomes paid higher income-adjusted amounts monthly, ranging from $187.50 to $428.60 per month.

The act also expanded coverage of preventive medical services. According to the CMS, new beneficiaries receive a free physical examination along with laboratory tests to screen for heart disease and diabetes.

Medicare Faces Challenges

Like Social Security, the Medicare program's continuing financial viability is in jeopardy. The Social Security and Medicare trust funds are examined annually by the Social Security and Medicare Boards of Trustees, which publish annual reports on the current and projected financial status of the programs. The *2017 Annual Report of the Board of Trustees of the Federal Old-Age and Survivors Insurance and Federal Disability Insurance Trust Funds* (July 13, 2017, https://www.ssa.gov/oact/tr/2017/tr2017.pdf) forecasts that Medicare costs will outpace Social Security costs because per capita health care costs will continue to grow faster than the per capita gross domestic product (GDP; the total value of goods and services that are produced by the United States) in the future.

The Medicare program has two separate trust funds, the Hospital Insurance (HI) Trust Fund and the Supplementary Medical Insurance Trust Fund. The trustees project that the HI Trust Fund will be depleted in 2029. Medicare costs will exceed the GDP through the 2030s in response to population aging caused by baby boomers (people born between 1946 and 1964) entering retirement and lower-birth-rate generations entering employment. Figure 10.1 shows how Social Security (Federal Old-Age and Survivors Insurance [OASI], and disability insurance [DI]) and Medicare's HI and Supplementary Medical Insurance will grow. The growth in expenditures per Medicare beneficiary exceeds growth in per capita GDP. Medicare costs increase from 3.6% of GDP in 2017 to 5.4% of GDP in 2035 largely because of the greater number of beneficiaries. The 5.9% increase by 2091 is attributed to an increase in health care cost per beneficiary. Table 10.6 shows that the OASI, DI, and HI trust funds will be depleted by the mid-2030s. The OASI and DI Trust Funds are separate and operate independently. OASDI is the designation for the two trust funds and is used to illustrate the actuarial status of the program as whole.

Solving Medicare's Problems

In "Medicare: Insolvency Projections" (August 16, 2017, https://fas.org/sgp/crs/misc/RS20946.pdf), Patricia A. Davis of the Congressional Research Service notes that media reports sometimes mistakenly describe Medicare as being on the verge of bankruptcy. Medicare's outlays can exceed its income and the trust funds may be depleted, but the federal government is not a private business and as such, will not face bankruptcy. In fact,

FIGURE 10.1

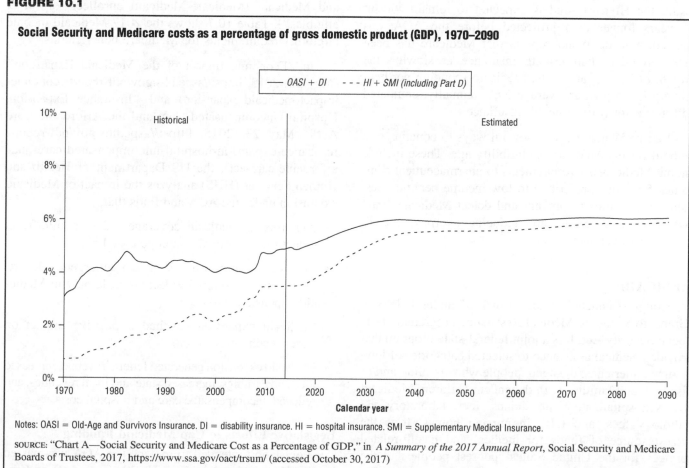

Social Security and Medicare costs as a percentage of gross domestic product (GDP), 1970–2090

Notes: OASI = Old-Age and Survivors Insurance. DI = disability insurance. HI = hospital insurance. SMI = Supplementary Medical Insurance.

SOURCE: "Chart A—Social Security and Medicare Cost as a Percentage of GDP," in *A Summary of the 2017 Annual Report*, Social Security and Medicare Boards of Trustees, 2017, https://www.ssa.gov/oact/trsum/ (accessed October 30, 2017)

TABLE 10.6

Projected dates that the Social Security and Medicare trust funds will be depleted

	OASI	DI	OASDI	HI
First year cost exceeds income excluding interest	2010	2022	2010	2021
First year cost exceeds total income	2022	2019	2022	2023
Year trust funds are depleted	2035	2028	2034	2029

OASI = Old-Age and Survivors Insurance. DI = disability insurance. OASDI = The two trust funds considered together, Old-Age and Survivors Insurance and Disability Insurance. HI = hospital insurance.
Notes: Dates indicate the first year a condition is projected to occur and to persist annually thereafter through 2090.

SOURCE: "Key Dates for the Trust Funds," in *A Summary of the 2017 Annual Reports*," Social Security and Medicare Boards of Trustees, 2017, https://www.ssa.gov/oact/trsum/ (accessed October 30, 2017)

TABLE 10.7

Medicaid income eligibility requirements for Medicare beneficiaries, 2017

[Monthly income limits: (100% FPL + $20)*]

	Individual	Couple
All states and DC (except Alaska & Hawaii)	$1,025	$1,374
Alaska	$1,275	$1,711
Hawaii	$1,175	$1,576
Asset limits	$7,390	$11,090

*$20 = Amount of the monthly SSI income disregard.
SSI = Supplemental Security Income.
FPI = Federal poverty level.

SOURCE: "2017 Dual Eligible Standards (Based on Percentage of Federal Poverty Level) Qualified Medicare Beneficiary (QMB)," in *Seniors & Medicare and Medicaid Enrollees*, Centers for Medicare & Medicaid Services, 2017, https://www.medicaid.gov/medicaid/eligibility/medicaid-enrollees/index.html (accessed October 30, 2017)

Congress has already increased the trust fund's revenues or reduced its outlays when the HI fund faced insolvency.

In "Medicare Is Not 'Bankrupt'" (July 24, 2017, https://www.cbpp.org/research/health/medicare-is-not-bankrupt), Paul N. Van de Water of the Center on Budget and Policy Priorities explains that the anticipated shortfall in 2029 will have to be addressed by increasing revenues or slowing the growth of costs or a combination of both. He notes that the ACA has "significantly improved Medicare's financial outlook, boosting revenues and making the program more efficient." As a result, the HI trust fund is expected to remain solvent 11 years longer than projected before the ACA was enacted. Van de Water reports that Medicare has been more effective than private insurance at slowing the growth of health care costs. Medicare spending per beneficiary has grown an average 5.6% annually, compared with 6.9% for private health insurance.

Van de Water suggests several ways to contain costs without raising Medicare's eligibility age. These include ending Medicare's overpayments to pharmaceutical companies for drugs prescribed to low-income beneficiaries, increasing actions to prevent and detect Medicare fraud and wasteful spending, and reducing overpayments to Medicare Advantage plans.

MEDICAID

Congress enacted Medicaid in 1965 under Title XIX (Grants to States for Medical Assistance Programs) of the Social Security Act. It is a joint federal-state program that provides medical assistance to selected categories of low-income Americans: the aged, people who are blind and/or disabled, and families with dependent children. Medicaid covers hospitalization, physicians' fees, laboratory and radiology fees, and LTC in nursing homes. It is the largest source of funds for medical and health-related services for the United States' poorest people and the second-largest public payer of health care costs, after

Medicare. In 2017 Medicaid provided additional coverage for more than 4.6 million Medicare beneficiaries aged 65 years and older.

Medicaid covers services beyond those provided under Medicare, including eyeglasses, hearing aids, and nursing facility care beyond the Medicare 100-day limit. The ACA created a new office within the CMS, the Medicare-Medicaid Coordination Office, to coordinate care for individuals who are eligible for both Medicaid and Medicare (Medicare-Medicaid enrollees, or "dual eligibles"). Table 10.7 shows the 2017 Medicaid income eligibility requirements for Medicare beneficiaries.

In "Economic Impact of the Medicaid Expansion" (May 23, 2015, https://aspe.hhs.gov/pdf-report/economic-impact-medicaid-expansion) and "Insurance Expansion, Hospital Uncompensated Care and the Affordable Care Act" (May 23, 2015, https://aspe.hhs.gov/pdf-report/insurance-expansion-hospital-uncompensated-care-and-affordable-care-act), the US Department of Health and Human Services (HHS) analyzes the impact of Medicaid expansion under the ACA and finds that:

- Increases in Medicaid coverage led to a significant reduction in hospital uncompensated care.

- The volume of uninsured/self-pay emergency department visits substantially decreased, largely in Medicaid expansion states.

- Medicaid expansion has had a positive impact on states' economies.

- Medicaid expansion generated federal revenue, increased jobs and earnings, increased state and local revenues, and reduced uncompensated care and hospital costs.

Legislative Efforts to Cap Medicaid Funding

Legislation intended to replace the ACA was passed by the House (the American Health Care Act) and the

Senate (Better Care Reconciliation Act) in 2017. Each of these bills, although not enacted into law at the time, included provisions that would cap Medicaid funding. In *Medicaid Funding Reform: Impact on Dual Eligible Beneficiaries* (June 2017, http://avalere-health-production .s3.amazonaws.com/uploads/pdfs/1498661372_20170628 _TSF_Report_on_Dual_Eligibles_and_Capped_Medicaid _Funding_BCRA_Update.pdf), Avalere Health notes that capping Medicaid funding would not only adversely affect dual-eligible older adults but also would increase Medicare spending. Because nearly one-quarter (24%) of Medicaid spending is for long-term care for dual-eligible people, cuts to Medicaid could increase hospitalizations, increasing Medicare spending.

Another attempt to cap Medicaid funding was included in Senate Amendment 1030, submitted in September 2017 and sponsored by the US senators Lindsey Graham (1955–; R-SC) and Bill Cassidy (1957–; R-LA). Known as the Graham-Cassidy amendment, S. 1030 proposed to cap federal payments for Medicaid, among other provisions, such as repealing individual and employer mandates for health insurance, loosening regulations regarding preexisting conditions, and eliminating many subsidies. The amendment did not generate the necessary support to advance through the approval process. Sara R. Collins of the Commonwealth Fund notes in "What Are the Potential Effects of the Graham-Cassidy ACA Repeal-and-Replace Bill? Past Estimates Provide Some Clues" (September 20, 2017, http://www.commonwealth fund.org/publications/blog/2017/sep/potential-effects-of-graham-cassidy) that if approved, the amendment would have made "the deepest cuts in the Medicaid program since its inception in 1965."

VETERANS' BENEFITS

People who served in the US military are entitled to medical treatment at any veterans' facility in the nation. The US Department of Veterans Affairs (VA) reports in "Selected Veterans Health Administration Characteristics: FY 2002 to FY 2015" (August 10, 2017, https://www .va.gov/vetdata/Utilization.asp) that in fiscal year 2015 approximately 9 million veterans made 95.2 million outpatient visits, and had nearly 700,000 inpatient hospital admissions. (See Table 10.8.)

The Veterans Millennium Health Care and Benefits Act of 1999 extended benefits and services for veterans. Among the health care programs that were stipulated by the act, the requirement to provide extended care and LTC were especially relevant to older veterans.

The number of veterans aged 65 years and older who received health care from the Veterans Health Administration increased steadily between 1990 and 2015. This increase may be attributable in part to the fact that Veterans Health Administration benefits cover services that

TABLE 10.8

Veterans' outpatient visits and inpatient hospital admissions, 2002–15

Fiscal year	Total enrollees[a] (in millions)	Outpatient visits[b] (in millions)	Inpatient admissions (in thousands)
2002	6.8	46.5	564.7
2003	7.1	49.8	567.3
2004	7.3	54.0	589.8
2005	7.7	57.5	585.8
2006	7.9	59.1	568.9
2007	7.8	62.3	589.0
2008	7.8	67.7	641.4
2009	8.1	74.9	662.0
2010	8.3	80.2	682.3
2011	8.6	79.8	692.1
2012	8.8	83.6	703.5
2013	8.9	86.4	694.7
2014	9.1	92.4	707.4
2015	9.0	95.2	699.1

[a]Includes non-enrolled Veteran patients.
[b]Includes fee visits.

SOURCE: "Selected Veterans Health Administration Characteristics: FY 2002 to FY 2015," in *National Center for Veterans Analysis and Statistics: Utilization*, US Department of Veterans Affairs, August 10, 2017, https://www.va.gov/vetdata/Utilization.asp (accessed October 30, 2017)

are not covered by Medicare, such as prescription drugs (Medicare coverage began in 2006), mental health care, LTC (nursing home and community-based care), and specialized services for people with disabilities. Figure 10.2 shows that even though the veteran population has declined since 1986, the number of veterans with a service-connected disability has increased.

The VA offers many health services that are designed to meet older veterans' unique health care needs, such as post-traumatic stress disorder (a mental health condition that is marked by severe anxiety, uncontrollable thoughts, and nightmares that are triggered by a terrifying event such as violence).

Benefits for older veterans also include job training and allowances to pursue higher education, vocational skills training, or apprenticeships. For example, monthly allowances help veterans to attend college; the allowances increase for veterans who have dependents, enabling them to care for their dependents while they attend school.

Veterans and their families can receive respite care to relieve family caregivers of veterans, nursing home services through three national programs (VA-owned and -operated community living centers, state veterans' homes owned and operated by the states, and the contract community nursing home program), home care services for veterans who require regular aid and assistance, home loan assistance, disability compensation for those with service-related disabilities, and nonservice-connected pensions for low-income, war-era veterans. Veterans and their dependents may qualify for education and training programs, and there is a college fee

FIGURE 10.2

Veteran population and veterans with a service-connected disability, 1986–2014

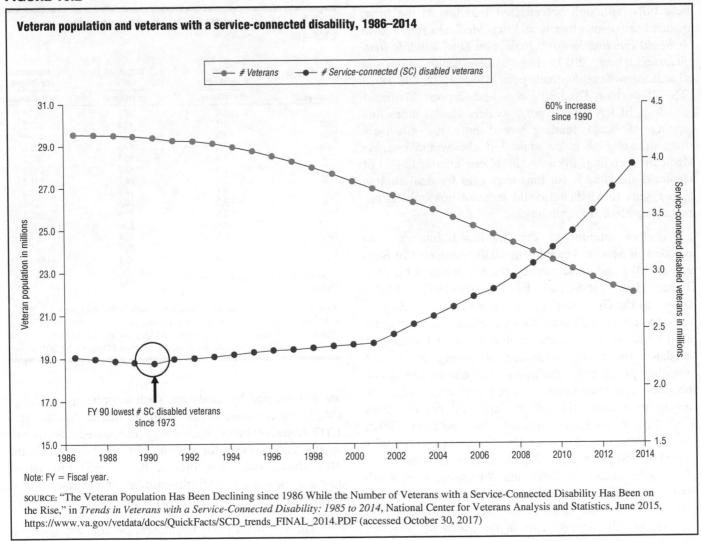

Note: FY = Fiscal year.

SOURCE: "The Veteran Population Has Been Declining since 1986 While the Number of Veterans with a Service-Connected Disability Has Been on the Rise," in *Trends in Veterans with a Service-Connected Disability: 1985 to 2014*, National Center for Veterans Analysis and Statistics, June 2015, https://www.va.gov/vetdata/docs/QuickFacts/SCD_trends_FINAL_2014.PDF (accessed October 30, 2017)

waiver for eligible dependents. Surviving families of veterans who served during times of war may be helped by burial cost reimbursement and death pensions.

LONG-TERM CARE

The options for quality, affordable LTC in the United States are limited but improving. Nursing home costs range from $50,000 to more than $200,000 per year, depending on services and location. In "Monthly Costs: National Median (2017)" (2015, https://www.genworth.com/corporate/about-genworth/industry-expertise/cost-of-care.html), Genworth Financial notes that in 2017 nursing home care cost an average of $8,121 per month for a private room. Medicaid is the largest payer of long-term services, which includes home and community-based services.

In fiscal year 2015 Medicaid expenditures for nursing home care were about $55 billion. Figure 10.3 shows the growth in Medicaid expenditures for institutional and home-based services for older adults and people with disabilities between 1995 and 2012.

Although nursing home care may seem cost prohibitive, Genworth Financial reports that in 2017 homemaker services and home health aide care cost an average of about $4,000 per month.

Medicare, Medicaid, and Long-Term Care

Medicare does not cover custodial or long-term nursing home care but, under specific conditions, it pays for short-term rehabilitative stays in nursing homes and for some home health care. (Custodial care is nonmedical care that helps individuals with their activities of daily living.) Medicaid is the only public program with LTC coverage.

Medicaid, however, does not work like private insurance, which offers protection from catastrophic expense. Medicaid is a means-tested program, so middle-income people needing nursing home care become eligible for Medicaid only after they spend down their own personal income and assets.

Even then, Medicaid will not necessarily pay the entire nursing home bill. Nursing home residents must also meet

FIGURE 10.3

Medicaid long-term care expenditures for institutional and community-based care, 1995–2015

[In billions]

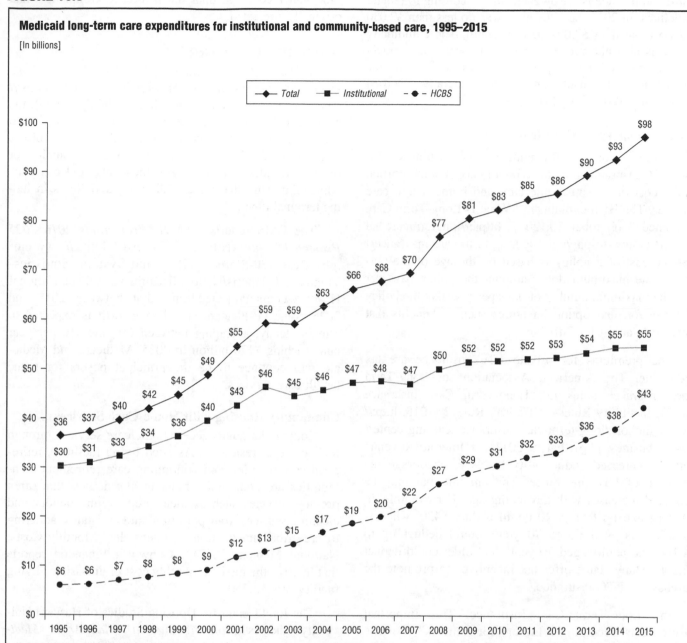

Notes: Institutional includes nursing facilities.

HCBS includes personal care, home health, community first choice, PACE, private duty nursing, self-directed personal assistance services, and HCBS targeting older adults and people with physical disabilities in section 1915(c) waivers, state plan HCBS, health homes, and in a fee-for-service 1115 demonstration or a managed care program (e.g., a section 1915(b) waiver) that were not authorized under another state plan or waiver authority. HCBS = Home & Community Based Services.

SOURCE: Steve Eiken et al., "Figure 11. Medicaid LTSS Expenditures Targeted to Older People and People with Physical Disabilities, by Service Category, FY 1995–2015 (in Billions)," in *Medicaid Expenditures for Long-Term Services and Supports (LTSS) in FY 2015*, Centers for Medicare & Medicaid Services, April 14, 2017, https://www.medicaid.gov/medicaid/ltss/downloads/reports-and-evaluations/ltssexpendituresffy2015final.pdf (accessed October 30, 2017)

income eligibility standards. In some states, older adults with incomes too high for regular Medicaid eligibility, but with substantial medical bills, are allowed to spend down to become income-eligible for Medicaid. They must incur medical bills until their income for a given period, minus the medical expenses, falls below the Medicaid threshold.

Although every state's Medicaid program covers LTC, each makes different choices about the parameters

of its program. Eligibility rules and protection for the finances of spouses of nursing home residents vary, but federal law requires states to allow the community spouse to retain enough of the institutionalized spouse's income to maintain a monthly allowance for minimum living costs. The CMS indicates in "2017 SSI and Spousal Impoverishment Standards" (2017, https://www.medicaid.gov/medicaid/eligibility/downloads/spousal-impoverishment/2017-ssi-and-spousal-impoverishment-standards.pdf) that the allowance is set by each state according to federal guidelines. In 2017 the allowance was no less than $2,030 and no more than $3,022.50 per month. The community spouse is also allowed to retain joint assets—an amount equal to half of the couple's resources at the time the spouse enters the institution, up to a federally specified maximum ($120,900 in 2017).

Private Long-Term Care Insurance

Another source of financing is LTC insurance. Private LTC insurance policies typically cover some portion of the cost of nursing home care and home health care services. The HHS explains in "What Is Long-Term Care Insurance?" (October 10, 2017, https://longtermcare.acl.gov/costs-how-to-pay/what-is-long-term-care-insurance/) that the cost of a policy is based on the age of the purchaser, the maximum dollar amount the policy pays per day, the maximum number of days per year that the policy will pay for, and optional features such as benefits that increase to adjust for inflation.

The premiums for private LTC insurance are tax deductible. The American Association for Long-Term Care Insurance notes in "Long-Term Care Insurance Tax-Deductibility Rules—LTC Tax Rules" (2018, http://www.aaltci.org/long-term-care-insurance/learning-center/tax-for-business.php) that in 2011 the Internal Revenue Service increased deductibility levels to encourage the purchase of LTC insurance. The amount that may be deducted increases with advancing age. For example, in 2018 people up to age 40 could deduct $420, whereas older adults aged 60 to 70 years could deduct up to $4,160 and adults aged 70 years and older could deduct $5,200. Many states offer tax incentives to promote the purchase of LTC insurance.

In "Long-Term Care Insurance: This Important Insurance Is Becoming a Luxury for Retirees" (Fortune.com, April 2017), Jeff Bukhari reports that the average annual LTC insurance premium was $2,727 in 2015, up 19% from 2010. The escalating premiums reflect more than the rising costs of health care. They are also the result of some insurance companies abandoning the LTC market and others recalculating their premiums as their insured live longer and require more time under coverage than the insurance companies' had originally projected.

HOME HEALTH CARE

In *National Home and Hospice Care Survey: Home Health—Data Highlights* (November 6, 2015, https://www.cdc.gov/nchs/nhhcs/nhhcs_home_highlights.htm), the National Center for Health Statistics describes home health care as "provided to individuals and families in their places of residence for the purpose of promoting, maintaining, or restoring health or for maximizing the level of independence while minimizing the effects of disability and illness, including terminal illness."

The CMS reports in *NHE Projections 2016–2025 Projected–Tables* (November 21, 2017, https://www.cms.gov/Research-Statistics-Data-and-Systems/Statistics-Trends-and-Reports/NationalHealthExpendData/NationalHealthAccountsProjected.html) that between 2018 and 2025 home health care spending growth is expected to remain steady, averaging between 6% and 7% per year and reaching $170 billion in 2025. Medicare and Medicaid will continue to be the principal payers for home health care services.

Community Housing with Home Care Services

Some older adults access home care services through their place of residence. Assisted living facilities, retirement communities, and continuing care retirement communities are community housing alternatives that often provide services such as meal preparation, laundry and cleaning services, transportation, and assistance adhering to prescribed medication regimens. In "Monthly Costs: National Median (2017)," Genworth Financial reports that in 2017 the median monthly cost of an assisted living facility was $3,750.

The Joint Center for Housing Studies of Harvard University indicates in *Housing America's Older Adults: Meeting the Needs of an Aging Population* (2014, https://www.aarp.org/content/dam/aarp/livable-communities/documents-2014/Harvard-Housing-Americas-Older-Adults-2014.pdf) that although just 2% of older adults live in group care settings, 37% of adults aged 65 years and older will receive care in an institutional facility at some point during their life, with an average stay of one year.

CHAPTER 11
CRIME AND ABUSE OF OLDER ADULTS

Each year, an estimated 5 million older adults are abused, neglected, or exploited. Older Americans lose an estimated $2.6 billion or more annually due to elder financial abuse and exploitation, funds that could be used to pay for basic needs such as housing, food, and medical care. It is estimated that only one in five of these crimes are discovered.

—Administration for Community Living in "World Elder Abuse Awareness Day" (June 15, 2017)

Elder abuse, as defined by the Centers for Disease Control and Prevention (CDC) in "Elder Abuse: Definitions" (June 8, 2017, https://www.cdc.gov/violenceprevention/elderabuse/definitions.html), is "an intentional act, or failure to act, by a caregiver or another person in a relationship involving an expectation of trust that causes or creates a risk of harm" to an adult aged 60 years or older. Elder abuse encompasses physical and sexual abuse, emotional or psychological abuse, financial abuse, and neglect; it may have negative effects on victims' health, security, independence, and dignity. The CDC explains that few studies have examined the long-term consequences of elder abuse, but in addition to obvious wounds and injuries, the likely physical effects include sleep disturbances, nutrition and hydration issues, exacerbation of existing health conditions, increased susceptibility to disease, and increased risk of premature death. The CDC notes that psychological effects may include high levels of distress and depression, fear, anxiety, learned helplessness, and post-traumatic stress disorder.

CRIME AGAINST OLDER ADULTS

Older adults have lower rates of violent crime than other age groups, and their rate of serious violent victimization (rape or sexual assault, robbery, and aggravated assault) decreased 24% from 6.8 per 1,000 individuals in 1995 to 5.2 per 1,000 in 2015. (See Figure 11.1.) The rate of violent victimization among older women (6.7 per 1,000) was more than twice that of older men (3.2 per

1,000) in 2015. (See Figure 11.2.) Jennifer L. Truman and Rachel E. Morgan of the Bureau of Justice Statistics (BJS) note in *Criminal Victimization, 2015* (October 2016, https://www.bjs.gov/content/pub/pdf/cv15.pdf) that in 2015 older adults had the lowest rate of violent victimization of any age group among those aged 12 years and older. (See Table 11.1.)

The Physical and Emotional Impact of Crime

According to the BJS, most older Americans who are the victims of violent crime are not physically injured. Physical injuries, however, do not tell the whole story. Victimization and fear of victimization can have far more serious effects on the quality of older adults' lives than they might for younger people.

Older adults are often less resilient than younger people. Even so-called nonviolent crimes, such as purse snatching, vandalism, or burglary, can be devastating. Stolen or damaged articles and property are often irreplaceable because of their sentimental value. Furthermore, nonviolent crimes leave victims with a sense of violation and heightened vulnerability.

Older People Are Considered Easy Prey

Because of their physical limitations, older adults are often considered easy prey. They are less likely than younger victims to resist criminal attacks. Their reluctance to resist may be based on awareness that they lack the strength to repel a younger aggressor and that they are physically frail and at risk of injuries that could permanently disable them. The BJS reports that crime victims over the age of 65 years who try to protect themselves most often use nonphysical actions, such as arguing, reasoning, or screaming. Younger victims are more likely to use physical action, such as attacking, resisting, or running from or chasing offenders.

FIGURE 11.1

Violent victimization of adults aged 65 and older, 1995–2015

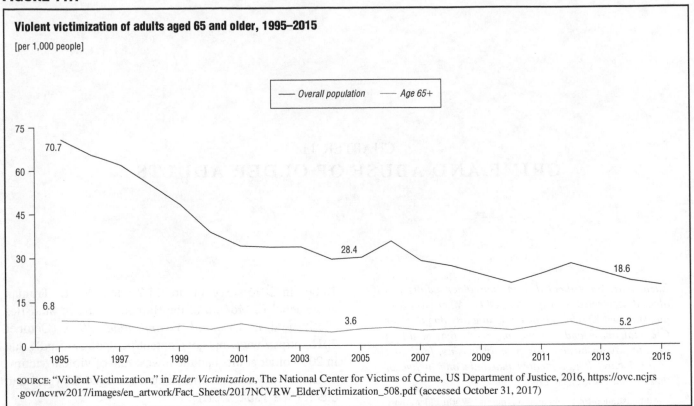

[per 1,000 people]

SOURCE: "Violent Victimization," in *Elder Victimization*, The National Center for Victims of Crime, US Department of Justice, 2016, https://ovc.ncjrs .gov/ncvrw2017/images/en_artwork/Fact_Sheets/2017NCVRW_ElderVictimization_508.pdf (accessed October 31, 2017)

FIGURE 11.2

Violent victimization of adults aged 65 and older, by sex, 1995–2015

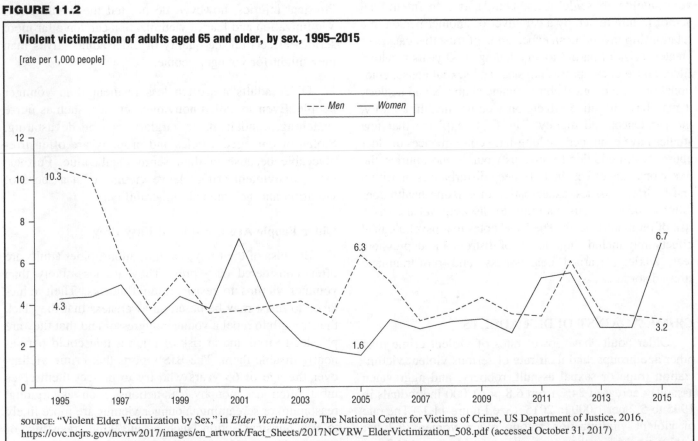

[rate per 1,000 people]

SOURCE: "Violent Elder Victimization by Sex," in *Elder Victimization*, The National Center for Victims of Crime, US Department of Justice, 2016, https://ovc.ncjrs.gov/ncvrw2017/images/en_artwork/Fact_Sheets/2017NCVRW_ElderVictimization_508.pdf (accessed October 31, 2017)

TABLE 11.1

Rates of violent victimization by age group, 2014 and 2015

Victim demographic characteristic	Violent crime[a]		Serious violent crime[b]	
	2014	2015	2014	2015
Total	**20.1**	**18.6**	**7.7**	**6.8**
Sex				
Male	21.1	15.9	8.3	5.4
Female	19.1	21.1	7.0	8.1
Race/Hispanic origin				
White[c]	20.3	17.4	7.0	6.0
Black[c]	22.5	22.6	10.1	8.4
Hispanic	16.2	16.8	8.3	7.1
Other[c,d]	23.0	25.7	7.7	10.4
Age				
12–17	30.1	31.3	8.8	7.8
18–24	26.8	25.1	13.6	10.7
25–34	28.5	21.8	8.6	9.3
35–49	21.6	22.6	8.9	7.8
50–64	17.9	14.2	7.0	5.7
65 or older	3.1	5.2	1.3	1.5
Marital status				
Never married	27.9	26.2	10.7	9.4
Married	12.4	9.9	4.0	3.5
Widowed	8.7	8.5	2.9	2.9
Divorced	30.3	35.3	14.2	13.0
Separated	52.8	39.5	27.7	20.6
Household income[e]				
$9,999 or less	39.7	39.2	18.7	17.7
$10,000–$14,999	36.0	27.7	16.8	12.0
$15,000–$24,999	25.3	25.9	8.4	8.2
$25,000–$34,999	19.7	16.3	8.3	5.5
$35,000–$49,999	19.0	20.5	8.1	7.1
$50,000–$74,999	16.4	16.3	5.4	5.9
$75,000 or more	15.1	12.8	4.7	4.5

[a]Includes rape or sexual assault, robbery, aggravated assault, and simple assault. Excludes homicide because the NCVS is based on interviews with victims and therefore cannot measure murder.
[b]In the NCVS, serious violent crime includes rape or sexual assault, robbery, and aggravated assault.
[c]Excludes persons of Hispanic or Latino origin.
[d]Includes American Indian and Alaska Natives; Asian, Native Hawaiian, and Other Pacific Islanders; and persons of two or more races.
[e]Household income was imputed for 2014 and 2015.
Note: Victimization rates are per 1,000 persons age 12 or older.

SOURCE: Jennifer L. Truman, and Rachel E. Morgan, "Table 7. Rate of Violent Victimization, by Victim Demographic Characteristics, 2014 and 2015," in *Criminal Victimization, 2015*, US Department of Justice, Bureau of Justice Statistics, October 2016, https://www.bjs.gov/content/pub/pdf/cv15.pdf (accessed October 31, 2017)

FRAUD

Older adults are considered easy prey for fraud, deception, and exploitation. They are more readily accessible to con artists than other age groups because they are likely to be at home to receive visits from door-to-door salespeople or phone calls from telemarketers. Older adults who are homebound or otherwise isolated may not have regular contact with others who might help them to identify possible schemes or frauds. Law enforcement officials and consumer advocates assert that older people are targeted because:

- They are more likely than younger people to have substantial financial savings, home equity, or credit, all of which are tempting to fraud perpetrators.

- They are often reluctant to be rude to others, so they may be more likely to hear out a con's story. They may also be overly trusting.

- They are less likely to report fraud because they are embarrassed, they do not know how or to whom to report the crime, or they fear appearing incapable of handling their personal finances.

- Older adults who do report fraud may not make good witnesses. Their memories may fade over the span of time between the crime and the trial, and on the witness stand they may be unable to provide detailed enough information to lead to a conviction.

In "Prevalence of Financial Fraud and Scams among Older Adults in the United States: A Systematic Review and Meta-analysis" (*American Journal of Public Health*, August 2017), David Burnes et al. estimate that the prevalence of fraud among older adults is 5.6%. In 12 studies of 41,711 older adults, the researchers find that fraud, financial exploitation, and victimization are associated with poor physical and mental health and higher rates of hospitalization and death.

The Federal Trade Commission (FTC) is the government's lead consumer protection agency. FTC authority extends over much of the economy, including business and consumer transactions via telephone and the internet. The FTC's consumer mission includes prohibiting unfair or deceptive acts or practices.

The US Food and Drug Administration (FDA) and the FTC actively work to prevent health fraud and scams. These agencies identify products with substandard or entirely useless ingredients as well as those with fraudulent or misleading advertising to prevent the dissemination of unsubstantiated or deceptive claims about the benefits of particular products or services.

Health Fraud

Older adults may be particularly susceptible to false or misleading claims about the safety and/or efficacy (the ability of an intervention to produce the intended diagnostic or therapeutic effect in optimal circumstances) of over-the-counter (nonprescription) drugs, devices, foods, and dietary supplements because the marketing of such products often relates to conditions that are associated with aging. Also, many of these unproven treatments promise false hope and offer immediate cures for chronic (long-term) diseases or complete relief from pain. It is understandable that older adults who are frightened or in pain might be seduced by false promises of quick cures.

Working together, the FDA and the FTC combat deceptive advertising for health products such as false and unsubstantiated claims for dietary supplements. One example of an FDA action is described in the press release "FTC, New York State Charge the Marketers of

Prevagen with Making Deceptive Memory, Cognitive Improvement Claims" (January 9, 2017, https://www.ftc.gov/news-events/press-releases/2017/01/ftc-new-york-state-charge-marketers-prevagen-making-deceptive). The FTC explains that it moved to stop the marketers of the dietary supplement Prevagen from "making false and unsubstantiated claims that the product improves memory, provides cognitive benefits, and is 'clinically shown' to work." Jessica Rich, director of the FTC's Bureau of Consumer Protection, asserts that "the marketers of Prevagen preyed on the fears of older consumers experiencing age-related memory loss."

Financial Fraud, Abuse, and Exploitation

Financial crimes against older adults are largely underreported but are estimated to total losses of at least $3 billion each year. Of those who reported both crimes and their age to the FTC in 2016, adults aged 60 to 69 years made 20% of fraud complaints, and those aged 70 years and older made 17% of complaints. (See Figure 11.3.)

This section presents findings from *The True Link Report on Elder Financial Abuse 2015* (2015, http://documents.truelinkfinancial.com/True-Link-Report-On-Elder-Financial-Abuse-012815.pdf), a study about reported instances of elder financial abuse conducted by the True Link Financial data science team and Laurie Orlov, an industry analyst.

The study's principal findings include:

- Approximately 36.9% of seniors are affected by financial abuse in any five-year period. Financial

exploitation, defined as misleading or confusing language and tactics that take advantage of older adults' memory or cognitive impairment, results in nearly $17 billion in losses per year.

- Criminal fraud, which is illegal activity such as financial scams or identity theft, accounts for nearly $13 billion lost annually.

- Almost $7 billion is lost per year to caregiver abuse—deceit or theft by a family member, paid helper, friend, accountant, or other trusted individual.

- Because risk of abuse equals vulnerability plus exposure, older adults who are urban and college educated are more likely to be victims than the very old and those with memory and cognitive impairment.

- Friendly older adults are at higher risk because they may seem more approachable, and financially savvy older adults lose more to fraud because they more readily move large amounts of money.

- An older adult who suffers even small financial losses is likely to be vulnerable to other types of fraud.

The researchers note that a significant portion of elder financial abuse goes unreported. Among survey respondents less than one-third (29%) of people who lost money to financial abuse had reported it to banks or law enforcement; 71% had not made a report. This is especially important because the study finds that in addition to financial ruin, elder financial abuse compromises physical health and increases rates of mental health issues among older adults.

Medicare Fraud

Every year Medicare (the federal health insurance program for people aged 65 years and older and people with disabilities) loses millions of dollars due to fraud and abuse. In "The Department of Health and Human Services and the Department of Justice Health Care Fraud and Abuse Control Program Annual Report for Fiscal Year 2016" (January 2017, https://oig.hhs.gov/publications/docs/hcfac/FY2016-hcfac.pdf), the Health Care Fraud and Abuse Control Program reports that in 2016 it recovered $1.7 billion for Medicare. This figure brought to $17.9 billion the amount of Medicare funds recovered since fiscal year 2009 and $31 billion since 1997, the year the program was established.

The Patient Protection and Affordable Care Act (ACA) of 2010, commonly called Obamacare, expanded actions to prevent fraud including:

- New rules and harsher sentences for crimes resulting in more than $1 million in losses

- Additional scrutiny of providers and suppliers that may pose a higher risk of fraud or abuse

FIGURE 11.3

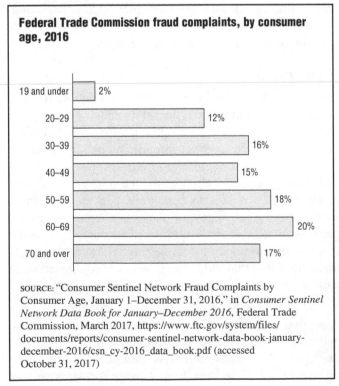

Federal Trade Commission fraud complaints, by consumer age, 2016

Age	Percentage
19 and under	2%
20–29	12%
30–39	16%
40–49	15%
50–59	18%
60–69	20%
70 and over	17%

SOURCE: "Consumer Sentinel Network Fraud Complaints by Consumer Age, January 1–December 31, 2016," in *Consumer Sentinel Network Data Book for January–December 2016*, Federal Trade Commission, March 2017, https://www.ftc.gov/system/files/documents/reports/consumer-sentinel-network-data-book-january-december-2016/csn_cy-2016_data_book.pdf (accessed October 31, 2017)

- Improved application of technology "to target resources to highly suspect behaviors"

- Increased funding to intensify antifraud efforts by the Centers for Medicare & Medicaid Services (CMS)

Besides the Health Care Fraud and Abuse Control Program, other government fraud-fighting initiatives are the Healthcare Fraud Prevention Partnership and the Health Care Fraud Prevention and Enforcement Action Team, which includes the Medicare Fraud Strike Force, an interagency task force team composed of analysts, investigators, and prosecutors from the US Department of Health and Human Services (HHS), US Department of Justice (DOJ), and Office of the Inspector General. In a media release, "The Health Care Fraud and Abuse Control Program Protects Consumers and Taxpayers by Combating Health Care Fraud" (January 18, 2017, https://www.cms.gov/Newsroom/MediaReleaseDatabase/Factsheets/2017-Fact-Sheet-items/2017-01-18-2.html), the CMS reports, "Since 2007, the Medicare Fraud Strike Force has charged over 3,018 individuals involved in more than $10.8 billion in fraud."

To combat Medicare fraud at the beneficiary level, the Administration on Aging (AoA) provides grants to local organizations to help older Americans become more vigilant health care consumers so that they can identify and prevent fraudulent health care practices. The Senior Medicare Patrol program trains community volunteers, many of whom are retired professionals, such as doctors, nurses, accountants, investigators, law enforcement personnel, attorneys, and teachers, to help Medicare beneficiaries become better health care consumers.

The HHS indicates in *2016 Performance Data for the Senior Medicare Patrol Projects* (June 8, 2017, https://oig.hhs.gov/oei/reports/oei-02-17-00220.pdf) that 53 Senior Medicare Patrol projects were conducted in 2016. During these projects, 6,126 volunteers held 195,386 one-on-one counseling sessions and 26,220 group education sessions. Recoveries attributable to the projects in 2016 included $163,904 in cost avoidance on behalf of Medicare, Medicaid, or other beneficiaries, $53,449 in savings to beneficiaries and others, and $2,672 in Medicare recoveries. Information provided to federal prosecutors from Senior Medicare Patrol projects contributed to settlements totaling an additional $9.2 million in expected Medicare recoveries.

ABUSE AND MISTREATMENT OF OLDER ADULTS

Domestic violence against older adults first gained publicity during the late 1970s when the US representative Claude Denson Pepper (1900–1989; D-FL) held widely publicized hearings about the mistreatment of older adults. Since those hearings, policy makers, health professionals, social service personnel, and advocates for older Americans have sought ways to protect the older population from physical, psychological, and financial abuse.

Magnitude of the Problem

It is difficult to determine exactly how many older adults are victims of abuse or mistreatment. As with child abuse and domestic violence, the number of actual cases is larger than the number of reported cases. There is consensus among professionals and agencies that deal with issues of elder abuse that it is far less likely than child or spousal abuse to be reported. The challenge of estimating the incidence (the rate of new cases of a disorder over a specified period) and prevalence (the total number of cases of a disorder in a given population at a specific time) of this problem is further compounded by the varying definitions of abuse and reporting practices used by the voluntary, state, and federal agencies, as well as by the fact that comprehensive national data are not collected. Furthermore, research suggests that abuse often occurs over long periods and that only when it reaches a critical juncture, such as instances of severe injury, will the neglect or abuse become evident to health, social service, or legal professionals.

Although the magnitude of the problem of abuse of older adults is unknown, its social and moral importance is obvious. Abuse and neglect of older individuals in society violate a sacred trust and moral commitment to protect vulnerable individuals and groups from harm and to ensure their well-being and security.

High-profile cases of elder abuse and the media's spotlight on the problem have helped increase Americans' awareness that it is a pervasive problem. In "Old and Alone: The Epidemic of Elder Abuse in America" (Vice.com, September 20, 2016), Jamie Loftus reports elder abuse is a widespread problem that affects people of all races, ethnicities, incomes, and educational attainment and has historically been neglected and underreported. Loftus notes that the DOJ estimates just one in 23 cases are reported.

Greater Efforts Are Needed to Combat Elder Abuse

In her testimony *Elder Justice: Stronger Federal Leadership Could Help Improve Response to Elder Abuse* (March 2, 2011, https://www.gao.gov/new.items/d11384t.pdf) before the US Senate's Special Committee on Aging, Kay E. Brown of the US Government Accountability Office (GAO) stated that the estimated 14.1% rate of elder abuse among noninstitutionalized older Americans (people who are not in the US military, school, jail, or mental health facilities) was probably a low estimate of prevalence.

The committee also heard testimony from Mickey Rooney (1920–2014; https://www.aging.senate.gov/imo/media/doc/hr230mr.pdf), an American actor and World War II (1939–1945) veteran, who suffered from elder abuse. Rooney described the loss of control he experienced:

> In my case, I was eventually and completely stripped of the ability to make even the most basic decisions in my own life. Over the course of time, my daily life became unbearable. Worse, it seemed to happen out of nowhere. At first, it was something small, something I could control. But then it became something sinister that was completely out of control. I felt trapped, scared, used, and frustrated. But above all, I felt helpless. For years I suffered silently. I couldn't muster the courage to seek the help I knew I needed. Even when I tried to speak up, I was told to be quiet. It seemed like no one believed me.

His testimony underscored the observation that any older adult can fall victim to abuse and that this problem is not limited exclusively to older adults in nursing homes or to those who suffer from cognitive impairments.

Brown concluded in her testimony that many state adult protective service programs charged with addressing elder abuse have struggled to keep pace with growing caseloads because they lack the funding and leadership to effectively fulfill their responsibilities. She called for stronger and more effective federal guidance for adult protective service programs. Among the many actions to combat such abuse, Brown recommended that the HHS develop an effective method for national surveillance of elder abuse and the collection of data as well as a system for compiling and disseminating these data nationwide. Her testimony shone a spotlight on the issue and spurred subsequent strengthening of federal, state, and local protections and development of *The Elder Justice Roadmap: A Stakeholder Initiative to Respond to an Emerging Health, Justice, Financial and Social Crisis* described in the next section.

A National Strategy to Combat Abuse

The GAO explains in *Elder Abuse* (2017, https://www.gao.gov/key_issues/elder_abuse/issue_summary) that coordination between federal, state, and local social service, criminal justice, and consumer protection systems is important. Figure 11.4 shows the Consumer Financial Protection Bureau and other federal agencies that work to prevent and identify elder abuse, to protect consumers, or to respond to consumer inquiries.

A joint initiative of the DOJ and HHS, *The Elder Justice Roadmap: A Stakeholder Initiative to Respond to an Emerging Health, Justice, Financial and Social Crisis* (July 2014, https://www.justice.gov/file/852856/download) delineates the top-five priorities for understanding and combating elder abuse and promoting health and justice for older adults:

- Increase public awareness of elder abuse

- Conduct research on cognitive loss and mental health, which are critical factors for both victims and perpetrators

- Determine the costs of elder abuse, which involves financial incentives and exacts huge fiscal costs to victims, families, and society

- Provide better support and training for paid and unpaid caregivers who play a critical role in preventing elder abuse

- Devote more resources to services, education, research, and enhancing knowledge to reduce elder abuse

In 2016 the US senators Susan Collins (1952–; R-ME) and Richard Blumenthal (1946–; D-CT) of the Senate Special Committee on Aging introduced a bipartisan resolution designating June 15, 2016, as World Elder Abuse Awareness Day. The Senate approved the resolution, which calls attention to the problem of elder abuse around the nation, and honors all those that fight for justice for victims. The media release "Senate Unanimously Approves Collins, Blumenthal Resolution Recognizing World Elder Abuse Awareness Day" (June 16, 2016, https://www.aging.senate.gov/press-releases/senate-unanimously-approves-collins-blumenthal-resolution-recognizing-world-elder-abuse-awareness-day) explains that the resolution "recognizes judges, lawyers, adult protective services professionals, law enforcement officers, long-term-care regulators, social workers, health care providers, professional guardians, advocates for victims, and other professionals and agencies for their efforts to advance awareness of elder abuse; and encourages members of the public and professionals who work with older adults to act as catalysts to promote awareness and long-term prevention of elder abuse by reaching out to local adult protective services agencies, long-term care ombudsman programs, and the National Center on Elder Abuse, and by learning to recognize, detect, report, and respond to elder abuse."

Types of Mistreatment

Most documented instances of elder abuse involve maltreatment of an older person by someone who has a special relationship with the older adult, such as a spouse, sibling, child, friend, or caregiver. Until recently, most data indicated that adult children were the most common abusers of older family members, but the National Center for Victims of Crime indicates in *Elder Victimization* (2016, https://ovc.ncjrs.gov/ncvrw2017/images/en_artwork/Fact_Sheets/2017NCVRW_ElderVictimization_508.pdf) that spouses are the most common perpetrators of abuse and mistreatment. Figure 11.5 shows that after partners/spouses, acquaintances, children/grandchildren, and other relatives are perpetrators of physical mistreatment of older adults.

FIGURE 11.4

Federal agencies involved in combating elder abuse

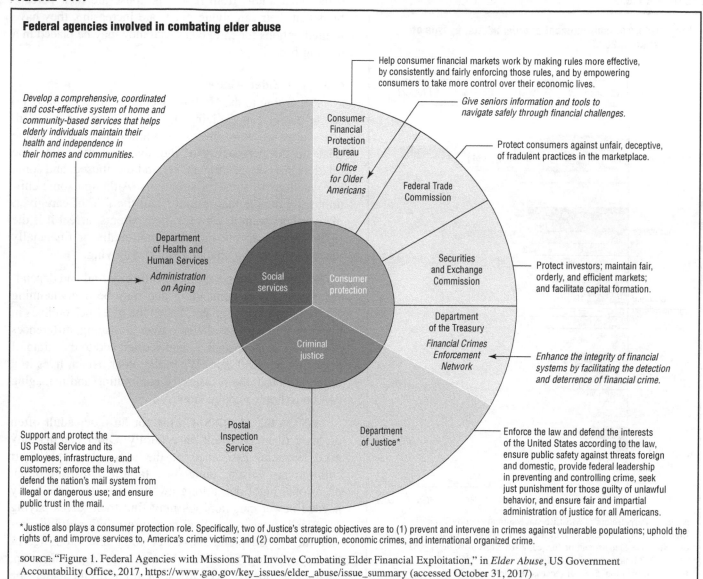

Develop a comprehensive, coordinated and cost-effective system of home and community-based services that helps elderly individuals maintain their health and independence in their homes and communities.

Help consumer financial markets work by making rules more effective, by consistently and fairly enforcing those rules, and by empowering consumers to take more control over their economic lives.

Give seniors information and tools to navigate safely through financial challenges.

Protect consumers against unfair, deceptive, of fradulent practices in the marketplace.

Protect investors; maintain fair, orderly, and efficient markets; and facilitate capital formation.

Enhance the integrity of financial systems by facilitating the detection and deterrence of financial crime.

Enforce the law and defend the interests of the United States according to the law, ensure public safety against threats foreign and domestic, provide federal leadership in preventing and controlling crime, seek just punishment for those guilty of unlawful behavior, and ensure fair and impartial administration of justice for all Americans.

Support and protect the US Postal Service and its employees, infrastructure, and customers; enforce the laws that defend the nation's mail system from illegal or dangerous use; and ensure public trust in the mail.

*Justice also plays a consumer protection role. Specifically, two of Justice's strategic objectives are to (1) prevent and intervene in crimes against vulnerable populations; uphold the rights of, and improve services to, America's crime victims; and (2) combat corruption, economic crimes, and international organized crime.

SOURCE: "Figure 1. Federal Agencies with Missions That Involve Combating Elder Financial Exploitation," in *Elder Abuse*, US Government Accountability Office, 2017, https://www.gao.gov/key_issues/elder_abuse/issue_summary (accessed October 31, 2017)

The major types of elder abuse and mistreatment include:

- Physical abuse—inflicting physical pain or bodily injury

- Sexual abuse—nonconsensual sexual contact of any kind with an older person

- Emotional or psychological abuse—inflicting mental anguish by, for example, name calling, humiliation, threats, or isolation

- Neglect—willful or unintentional failure to provide basic necessities, such as food and medical care, as a result of caregiver indifference, inability, or ignorance

- Material or financial abuse—exploiting or misusing an older person's funds or assets

- Abandonment—the desertion of an older adult by an individual who has physical custody of the elder or who has assumed responsibility for providing care for the older person

- Self-neglect—behaviors of an older person that threaten his or her own health or safety

Reporting Abuse

Like child abuse and sexual assault crimes, many crimes against older adults are not reported because the victims are physically or mentally unable to summon help or because they are reluctant or afraid to publicly accuse relatives or caregivers. Loneliness or dependency prevents many victims from reporting the crimes, even when they are aware of them, because they are afraid to lose the companionship and care of the perpetrator. When financial abuse is reported, the source of the information is likely to be someone other than the victim: a police officer, ambulance attendant, bank teller, neighbor, or other family member.

FIGURE 11.5

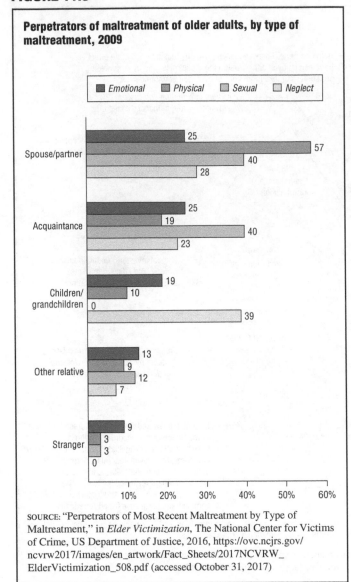

Perpetrators of maltreatment of older adults, by type of maltreatment, 2009

Legend: ■ Emotional ■ Physical ■ Sexual □ Neglect

Spouse/partner
- Emotional: 25
- Physical: 57
- Sexual: 40
- Neglect: 28

Acquaintance
- Emotional: 25
- Physical: 19
- Sexual: 40
- Neglect: 23

Children/grandchildren
- Emotional: 19
- Physical: 10
- Sexual: 0
- Neglect: 39

Other relative
- Emotional: 13
- Physical: 9
- Sexual: 12
- Neglect: 7

Stranger
- Emotional: 9
- Physical: 3
- Sexual: 3
- Neglect: 0

(x-axis: 10% 20% 30% 40% 50% 60%)

SOURCE: "Perpetrators of Most Recent Maltreatment by Type of Maltreatment," in *Elder Victimization*, The National Center for Victims of Crime, US Department of Justice, 2016, https://ovc.ncjrs.gov/ncvrw2017/images/en_artwork/Fact_Sheets/2017NCVRW_ElderVictimization_508.pdf (accessed October 31, 2017)

The National Center for Victims of Crime estimates in *Elder Victimization* that less than 5% of adults aged 65 years and older report their victimization to the police. In 2015 less than half (45%) of victims of violent crime over the age of 65 years reported the crimes to the police.

In "Examining Barriers to Self-Reporting of Elder Physical Abuse in Community-Dwelling Older Adults" (*Geriatric Nursing*, vol. 35, no. 2, March–April 2014), Carolyn E. Ziminski Pickering and Veronica F. Rempush-eski explain that although one out of 10 older adults experiences elder abuse during their lifetime, less than one-third of cases are reported. The researchers interviewed older adults to identify barriers to reporting abuse. They find that older adults' perceptions of abuse vary by both the abusive act and their relationship to the perpetrator. For example, acts by a paid caregiver were more likely to be viewed as abusive than the same acts committed by an adult child serving as caregiver. Other fears that prevent some older adults from reporting abuse are their perceptions that their caregiving needs are increasing, they have limited options for caregivers, and they may be placed in a nursing home.

Causes of Elder Abuse

According to the National Center on Elder Abuse, no single theory can explain why older people are abused. The causes of abuse are diverse and complicated. Some relate to the personality of the abuser, some reflect the relationship between the abuser and the abused, and some are reactions to stressful situations. Although some children truly dislike their parents and the role of caregiver, many others want to care for their parents or feel it is the right thing to do but may be emotionally or financially unable to meet the challenges of caregiving.

STRESS. Meeting the daily needs of a frail and dependent older adult is demanding and may be overwhelming for some family caregivers. When the older person lives in the same household as the caregiver, crowding, differences of opinion, and constant demands often add to the strain of providing physical care. When the older person lives in a different house, the pressure of commuting and managing two households may be stressful.

FINANCIAL BURDEN. Caring for an older adult often places a financial strain on a family. Older parents may need financial assistance at the same time that their children are raising their own families. Instead of an occasional night out, a long-awaited vacation, or a badly needed newer car, families may find themselves paying for ever-increasing medical care, prescription drugs, special dietary supplements, extra food and clothing, or therapy. Saving for their children's college education, for their children's weddings, or for retirement may be difficult or impossible.

CYCLE OF ABUSE. One theory of the causation of abuse of older adults posits that people who abuse an older parent or relative were themselves abused as children. The National Council on Child Abuse and Family Violence confirms this pattern of abuse in "Elder Abuse Information" (2017, https://www.nccafv.org/elder-abuse), stating, "In a family where there is a tendency to physically harm members who are weak or dependent, the aging members of society, who are among the most vulnerable, become the next victims in the cycle of intergenerational family violence." The council cautions that "it is important to remember that violence and its related behaviors are learned and often passed from one generation to the next. A child who is abused by a parent may become an adult who uses violence toward a spouse or child then, as caretaker for an aging parent, extends the abuse to his/her parent or relative."

INVASION OF PRIVACY. Trevor John Mills of the University of California, Davis, School of Medicine indicates in "Elder Abuse" (February 15, 2015, https://emedi cine.medscape.com/article/805727-overview) that a shared living arrangement is a major risk factor for mistreatment of older adults, with older people living alone at the lowest risk for abuse. A shared residence increases the opportunities for contact, conflict, and mistreatment. When the home must be shared, there is an inevitable loss of a certain amount of control and privacy. Movement may be restricted, habits may need to change, and rivalries between generations may follow. Frustration and anxiety may result as both older parent and supporting child try to suppress anger, with varying degrees of success.

SOCIAL ISOLATION. Mills notes that social isolation is linked to abuse and the mistreatment of older adults. It may be that socially isolated families are better able to hide unacceptable behaviors from friends and neighbors who might report the abuse. Although there are no data to support the corollary to this finding, it is hypothesized that mistreatment is less likely in families that are rooted in strong social networks.

ALZHEIMER'S DISEASE OR OTHER DEMENTIA. According to Xinqi Dong, Ruijia Chen, and Melissa A. Simon, in "Elder Abuse and Dementia: A Review of the Research and Health Policy" (*Health Affairs*, vol. 33, no. 4, April 2014), older adults with dementia may be at a greater risk for mistreatment. The researchers find that psychological abuse was the most common form of abuse among older adults, affecting 27.9% to 62.3%. Between 3.5% and 23.1% of older adults with dementia experienced physical abuse, and many older adults experienced multiple forms of abuse simultaneously. Dong, Chen, and Simon also find that the risk of death from abuse may be higher in older adults with greater levels of cognitive impairment.

REVERSE DEPENDENCY. Some sources believe that abusers may be quite dependent, emotionally and financially, on their victims for housing, financial assistance, and transportation. They appear to have fewer resources and are frequently unable to meet their own basic needs. Rather than having power in the relationship, they are relatively powerless. From these observations, some researchers speculate that abusing caregivers may not always be driven to violence by the physical and emotional burden of caring for a seriously disabled older person but may have mental health problems of their own that can lead to violent behavior. Several studies specifically point to depression as a characteristic of perpetrators of elder mistreatment.

Intimate Partner Violence: The Abusive Spouse

The US Preventive Services Task Force indicates in "Screening for Intimate Partner Violence and Abuse of Elderly and Vulnerable Adults" (January 2013, https://www.uspreventiveservicestaskforce.org/Page/Document/ RecommendationStatementFinal/intimate-partner-violence-and-abuse-of-elderly-and-vulnerable-adults-screening) that intimate partner violence and abuse of older and vulnerable adults is common but often undetected. Nearly 31% of women and 26% of men report some form of intimate partner violence during their lifetime. As many as 25% of older adults experience abuse.

The high rate of spousal abuse among the older population is possibly because many older adults live with their spouses, so the opportunity for spousal violence is great. Violence against an older spouse may be the continuation of an abusive relationship that began years earlier—abuse does not end simply because a couple ages. Sometimes, however, the abuse may not begin until later years, in which case it is often associated with mental illness, alcohol abuse, unemployment, postretirement depression, and/or loss of self-esteem.

There are many reasons the problem of spousal abuse among older adults may be underestimated and underreported. For example, in "Perceptions of Intimate Partner Violence, Age, and Self-Enhancement Bias" (*Journal of Elder Abuse and Neglect*, vol. 23, no. 1, January 2011), Michael N. Kane, Diane Green, and Robin J. Jacobs find that students preparing for careers in human services such as social work, psychology, and criminal justice were less likely to take allegations of domestic violence between older adults seriously. The students mistakenly assumed that a 30-year-old couple was more likely to engage in conflict and violence than a 75-year-old couple. Kane, Green, and Jacobs opine that these are ageist beliefs and call for increased awareness and sensitivity to the issue, stating that "raising awareness may help students to identify the possibility of intimate partner abuse when the bruises on the 70-year-old face of Aunt Rose are not attributable to being clumsy but are attributable to 72-year-old Uncle Frank."

Intervention and Prevention

All 50 states and the District of Columbia have laws that address abuse of older adults, but like laws aiming to prevent and reduce child abuse and domestic violence among younger people, they are often ineffective. The effectiveness of these laws varies from state to state and even from county to county within a given state. No standard definition of abuse exists among enforcement agencies. In many cases authorities cannot legally intervene and terminate an abusive condition unless a report is filed, the abuse is verified, and the victim files a formal complaint. An older adult could understandably be reluctant, physically unable, or too fearful to accuse or prosecute an abuser.

Clearly, the best way to stop elder abuse is to prevent its occurrence. Older people who know that they will eventually need outside help should carefully analyze the potential challenges of living with their family and, if necessary and possible, make alternate arrangements. Furthermore, older adults should take action to protect their money and assets to ensure that their valuables cannot be easily taken from them.

Families or individuals who serve as caregivers for older adults, voluntarily or otherwise, must be helped to realize that their frustration and despair do not have to result in abuse. Health and social service agencies offer interventions including group support programs and counseling to help caregivers and their families. Many communities allocate resources to assist families to offset the financial burden of elder care, for example, through tax deductions or subsidies for respite care.

Multidisciplinary Teams Can Help Prevent and Identify Elder Abuse

A range of support services including criminal justice, health care, mental health care, victim services, civil legal services, adult protective services, financial counseling and long-term care are involved in preventing and identifying elder abuse. In "Elder Abuse: Global Situation, Risk Factors, and Prevention Strategies" (*Gerontologist*, vol. 56, suppl. 2, April 1, 2016), Karl Pillemer et al. observe that coordinating available services improves their effectiveness. The use of multidisciplinary teams composed of representatives of these key services has proven to be an "effective response to coordinating care and reducing fragmentation, leveraging resources, increasing professional knowledge, and improving outcomes." Besides multidisciplinary teams, Pillemer et al. cite helplines for potential victims, financial management services for older adults at risk of financial exploitation, caregiver support interventions and emergency shelter for victims as the most promising strategies to effectively prevent and intervene in elder abuse.

INSTITUTIONAL ABUSE: A FORGOTTEN POPULATION?

Abuse of the older population can and does occur in the institutions (nursing homes, board-and-care facilities, and retirement homes) that are charged with, and compensated for, caring for the nation's older population. The term *institutional abuse* generally refers to the same forms of abuse as domestic abuse crimes but is perpetrated by people who have legal or contractual obligations to provide older adults with care. Although the Omnibus Budget Reconciliation Act of 1987 states that nursing homes must take steps to attain or maintain the "highest practicable physical, mental, and psychosocial well-being of each resident," too many residents are victims of neglect or abuse by these facilities or their employees.

Older adult residents of long-term care facilities or supportive housing are thought to be at higher risk for abuse and neglect than community-dwelling older

adults. They are particularly vulnerable because most suffer from one or more chronic diseases that impair their physical and cognitive functioning, rendering them dependent on others. Furthermore, many are either unable to report abuse or neglect or are fearful that reporting may generate reprisals from the facility staff or otherwise adversely affect their life. Others are unaware of the availability of help.

There are federal laws and regulations that govern nursing homes, but there is no federal oversight of residential care facilities, such as personal care homes, adult congregate living facilities, residential care homes, homes for the aged, domiciliary care homes, board-and-care homes, and assisted living facilities. As a result, it is more difficult than with nursing homes to estimate the prevalence or nature of abuse or neglect in these facilities.

Studies of elder abuse in long-term care facilities—such as Lawrence B. Schiamberg et al.'s "Physical Abuse of Older Adults in Nursing Homes: A Random Sample Survey of Adults with an Elderly Family Member in a Nursing Home" (*Journal of Elder Abuse and Neglect*, vol. 24, no. 1, 2012), Linda R. Phillips and Guifang Gao's "Mistreatment in Assisted Living Facilities: Complaints, Substantiations, and Risk Factors" (*Gerontologist*, vol. 51, no. 3, January 2011), and Radka Buzgová and Katerina Ivanová's "Violation of Ethical Principles in Institutional Care for Older People" (*Nursing Ethics*, vol. 18, no. 1, January 2011)—find that it is associated with high staff turnover, which in turn may reflect unsatisfactory working conditions or other organizational problems as well as the use of unlicensed or poorly trained personnel.

Types of Abuse and Neglect

Institutional neglect and abuse can take many forms. In *Elder Victimization*, the National Center for Victims of Crime reports that a study of nursing homes found that more than half of staff admitted that they had abused or neglected older patients. The National Center for Victims of Crime also notes that more than one-fifth of the complaints filed against nursing homes in 2012 were about resident-on-resident physical or sexual abuse. Figure 11.6 shows the estimated prevalence rates of complaints about various types of staff abuse of residents from that study.

Resident Risk Factors

Although there has been scant research describing the factors that contribute to risk for abuse of institutionalized older adults, some studies indicate that the risk for abuse increases in direct relationship to the older resident's dependence on the facility's staff for safety, protection, and care. For example, Diana K. Harris and Michael L. Benson, in *Maltreatment of Patients in Nursing Homes: There Is No Safe Place* (2006), and Mark Miller, a New York State long-term care ombudsman, in "Ombudsmen

FIGURE 11.6

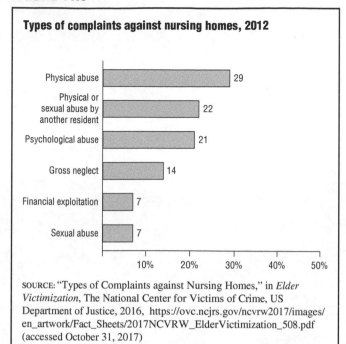

Types of complaints against nursing homes, 2012

Type	Percentage
Physical abuse	29
Physical or sexual abuse by another resident	22
Psychological abuse	21
Gross neglect	14
Financial exploitation	7
Sexual abuse	7

SOURCE: "Types of Complaints against Nursing Homes," in *Elder Victimization*, The National Center for Victims of Crime, US Department of Justice, 2016, https://ovc.ncjrs.gov/ncvrw2017/images/en_artwork/Fact_Sheets/2017NCVRW_ElderVictimization_508.pdf (accessed October 31, 2017)

on the Front Line: Improving Quality of Care and Preventing Abuse in Nursing Homes" (*Generations*, vol. 2, no. 4, July–August 2001), suggest that residents with Alzheimer's disease or dementia are at greater risk for abuse in the average nursing home population. In "Elder Abuse and Neglect in Long-Term Care" (*Clinics in Geriatric Medicine*, vol. 21, no. 2, May 2005), Seema Joshi and Joseph H. Flaherty of the St. Louis Veterans Administration Medical Center indicate that residents with behavioral symptoms, such as physical aggressiveness, appear to be at higher risk for abuse by staff; this finding is supported by interviews with certified nursing assistants.

In "Decision-Making Ability and Elder Mistreatment" (2017, http://ltcombudsman.org/uploads/files/issues/ncea-decision-making.pdf), the National Center on Elder Abuse explains that decision-making ability is "of special concern for the field of elder mistreatment because impaired decision-making can lead to an increased risk for abuse and exploitation among older people." Once impaired decision-making capacity is identified, steps may be taken to protect affected older adults from exploitation and abuse. For example, older adults may enter into a supported decision-making agreement in which they choose a trusted family member or friend to help them get information they need to make informed decisions about important issues such as the medical care they wish to receive and communicate their decisions to others.

Social isolation and powerlessness may also increase the risk for abuse. Residents who have no visitors are especially vulnerable because they lack family or friends who could oversee their care, bear witness to and report any abuses, and advocate on their behalf.

Efforts to Identify and Reduce Abuse

In an effort to improve the quality of care and eliminate abuse in nursing homes, government regulations and laws have been enacted that require greater supervision and scrutiny of nursing homes. President Ronald Reagan (1911–2004) signed the Omnibus Budget Reconciliation Act of 1987, which included protections for patient rights and treatment. The law went into effect in 1990, but compliance with the law varies from state to state and from one nursing facility to another.

In 1987 the AoA established the Prevention of Elder Abuse, Neglect, and Exploitation program. This program trains law enforcement officers, health care workers, and other professionals about how to identify and respond to elder abuse and supports education campaigns to increase public awareness of elder abuse and how to prevent it.

Many states have adopted additional legislation to help stem instances of institutional abuse and neglect. For example, in 1998 the state of New York enacted Kathy's Law, which created the new felony-level crime of "abuse of a vulnerable elderly person." At the state level, there are many agencies involved in identifying and investigating cases of abuse and neglect. These agencies differ across states but may include ombudsmen (offices that assist patients who have complaints), adult protective services, the state survey agency responsible for licensing nursing homes, the state agency responsible for the operation of the nurse aide registry, Medicaid fraud units in the attorney general's office, and professional licensing boards.

Raising public awareness of the problem is vital for preventing it. The National Center on Elder Abuse encourages adult children to discuss mistreatment, abuse, and exploitation with their parents and other older adults and to take specific steps to reduce the risk of abuse, such as by carefully screening prospective caregivers.

LONG-TERM CARE OMBUDSMAN PROGRAM. Long-term care ombudsmen are advocates for residents of nursing homes, board-and-care homes, assisted living facilities, and other adult care facilities. The Long-Term Care Ombudsman Program was established under the Older Americans Act of 1965, which is administered by the AoA's Administration for Community Living.

In "Data Show Extensive Services Provided to Persons in LTC Facilities" (September 6, 2017, https://www.acl.gov/programs/protecting-rights-and-preventing-abuse/long-term-care-ombudsman-program), the Administration for Community Living reports that 7,734 volunteers and 1,300 paid ombudsmen worked to resolve 199,238 complaints in fiscal year 2015. About two-thirds (67%) of all nursing homes and more than a quarter (27%) of all board-and-care, assisted living, and similar homes were visited regularly by state and local ombudsmen.

IMPORTANT NAMES
AND ADDRESSES

AARP (formerly the American Association of Retired Persons)
601 E St. NW
Washington, DC 20049
1-888-687-2277
URL: https://www.aarp.org/

ACAPcommunity
PO Box 8278
Morganton, NC 28680
1-877-599-2227
Email: info@ACAPcommunity.org
URL: http://www.acapcommunity.org

Administration for Community Living
330 C St. SW
Washington, DC 20201
(202) 401-4634
URL: https://www.acl.gov/

Alliance for Aging Research
1700 K St. NW, Ste. 740
Washington, DC 20006
(202) 293-2856
FAX: (202) 955-8394
Email: info@agingresearch.org
URL: http://www.agingresearch.org/

Alzheimer's Association
225 N. Michigan Ave., 17th Floor
Chicago, IL 60601-7633
(312) 335-8700
1-800-272-3900
FAX: 1-866-699-1246
URL: https://www.alz.org/

American Association for Geriatric Psychiatry
6728 Old McLean Village Dr.
McLean, VA 22101
(703) 556-9222
FAX: (703) 556-8729
Email: main@aagponline.org
URL: http://www.aagponline.org/

American Geriatrics Society
40 Fulton St., 18th Floor
New York, NY 10038
(212) 308-1414
FAX: (212) 832-8646
Email: info.amger@americangeriatrics.org
URL: https://www.americangeriatrics.org/

American Heart Association
7272 Greenville Ave.
Dallas, TX 75231
1-800-242-8721
URL: https://www.heart.org/

ARCH National Respite Network and Resource Center
800 Eastowne Dr., Ste. 105
Chapel Hill, NC 27514
(703) 256-2084
FAX: (703) 256-0541
URL: https://archrespite.org/

Argentum
1650 King St., Ste. 602
Alexandria, VA 22314
(703) 894-1805
FAX: (703) 894-1831
URL: https://www.argentum.org/

Arthritis Foundation
1355 Peachtree St. NE, Ste. 600
Atlanta, GA 30309
(404) 872-7100
URL: https://www.arthritis.org/

Caregiver Action Network (formerly the National Family Caregivers Association)
1150 Connecticut Ave. NW, Ste. 501
Washington, DC 20036-3904
(202) 454-3970
Email: info@caregiveraction.org
URL: http://caregiveraction.org/

Centers for Disease Control and Prevention
1600 Clifton Rd.
Atlanta, GA 30329-4027

1-800-232-4636
URL: https://www.cdc.gov/

Centers for Medicare and Medicaid Services
7500 Security Blvd.
Baltimore, MD 21244
(410) 786-3000
1-877-267-2323
URL: https://www.cms.gov/

Eldercare Locator Directory
1-800-677-1116
URL: https://eldercare.acl.gov/Public/Index.aspx

Encore.org
PO Box 29542
San Francisco, CA 94129
(415) 430-0141
FAX: (415) 430-0144
URL: https://encore.org/

Family Caregiver Alliance
235 Montgomery St., Ste. 950
San Francisco, CA 94104
(415) 434-3388
1-800-445-8106
URL: https://www.caregiver.org/

Gerontological Society of America
1220 L St. NW, Ste. 901
Washington, DC 20005
(202) 842-1275
URL: https://www.geron.org/

Insurance Institute for Highway Safety
1005 N. Glebe Rd., Ste. 800
Arlington, VA 22201
(703) 247-1500
FAX: (703) 247-1588
URL: http://www.iihs.org/

Justice in Aging (formerly the National Senior Citizens Law Center)
1444 Eye St. NW, Ste. 1100
Washington, DC 20005

(202) 289-6976
URL: http://www.justiceinaging.org/

LeadingAge
2519 Connecticut Ave. NW
Washington, DC 20008
(202) 783-2242
Email: info@leadingage.org
URL: http://leadingage.org/

Medicare Rights Center
1444 I St. NW, Ste. 1105
Washington, DC 20005
(202) 637-0961
1-800-333-4114
FAX: (202) 637-0962
URL: https://www.medicarerights.org/

**National Academy of Elder Law
Attorneys**
1577 Spring Hill Rd., Ste. 310
Vienna, VA 22182
(703) 942-5711
FAX: (703) 563-9504
URL: https://www.naela.org/

National Alliance for Caregiving
4720 Montgomery Ln., Ste. 205
Bethesda, MD 20814
(301) 718-8444
FAX: (301) 951-9067
Email: info@caregiving.org
URL: http://www.caregiving.org/

**National Association for Home Care and
Hospice**
228 Seventh St. SE
Washington, DC 20003
(202) 547-7424
FAX: (202) 547-3540
URL: https://www.nahc.org/

**National Caucus and Center on Black
Aging**
1220 L St. NW, Ste. 800
Washington, DC 20005
(202) 637-8400
FAX: (202) 347-0895
URL: http://www.ncba-aged.org/

National Center for Health Statistics
Division of Data Services
3311 Toledo Rd.
Hyattsville, MD 20782
1-800-232-4636
URL: https://www.cdc.gov/nchs/

National Center on Elder Abuse
University of Southern California
Keck School of Medicine
Department of Family Medicine and
Geriatrics
1000 S. Fremont Ave., Unit 22, Bldg. A-6
Alhambra, CA 91803
1-855-500-3537

FAX: (626) 457-4090
URL: https://ncea.acl.gov/

**National Consumer Voice for Quality
Long-Term Care (formerly the National
Citizens' Coalition for Nursing Home
Reform)**
1001 Connecticut Ave. NW, Ste. 632
Washington, DC 20036
(202) 332-2275
FAX: 1-866-230-9789
Email: info@theconsumervoice.org
URL: http://theconsumervoice.org/

National Council on Aging
251 18th St. South, Ste. 500
Arlington, VA 22202
(571) 527-3900
URL: https://www.ncoa.org/

National Hispanic Council on Aging
2201 12th St. NW, Ste. 101
Washington, DC 20009
(202) 347-9733
FAX: (202) 347-9735
URL: http://www.nhcoa.org/

**National Hospice and Palliative Care
Organization**
1731 King St.
Alexandria, VA 22314
(703) 837-1500
FAX: (703) 837-1233
URL: https://www.nhpco.org/

National Indian Council on Aging
8500 Menaul Blvd. NE
Albuquerque, NM 87112
(505) 292-2001
FAX: (505) 292-1922
URL: https://nicoa.org/

National Institute on Aging
Bldg. 31, Rm. 5C27
31 Center Dr., MSC 2292
Bethesda, MD 20892
(301) 496-1752
FAX: (301) 496-1072
URL: https://www.nia.nih.gov/

National Osteoporosis Foundation
251 18th St. S, Ste. 630
Arlington, VA 22202
(202) 223-2226
1-800-231-4222
FAX: (202) 223-2237
URL: https://www.nof.org/

National PACE Association
675 N. Washington St., Ste. 300
Alexandria, VA 22314
(703) 535-1565
FAX: (703) 535-1566
Email: info@npaonline.org
URL: https://www.npaonline.org/

**National Society for American Indian
Elderly**
PO Box 50070
Phoenix, AZ 85076
(602) 424-0542
Email: info@nsaie.org
URL: http://www.nsaie.org/

OWL The Voice of Women 40+
1625 K St. NW, Ste. 1275
Washington, DC 20006
(202) 450-8986
Email: owl@owl-national.org
URL: https://statusofwomendata.org/
partners/owl-the-voice-of-women-40/

**Pension Benefit Guaranty
Corporation**
1200 K St. NW
Washington, DC 20005
1-800-400-7242
URL: https://www.pbgc.gov/

Pension Rights Center
1730 M St. NW, Ste. 1000
Washington, DC 20036
(202) 296-3776
1-888-420-6550
URL: http://www.pensionrights.org/

SeniorNet
5237 Summerlin Commons Blvd., Ste. 314
Fort Myers, FL 33907
(239) 275-2202
FAX: (239) 275-2501
URL: http://www.seniornet.org/

**Service Corps of Retired Executives
(SCORE)**
1175 Herndon Pkwy., Ste. 900
Herndon, VA 20170
1-800-634-0245
URL: https://www.score.org/

Social Security Administration
Office of Public Inquiries
1100 W. High Rise
6401 Security Blvd.
Baltimore, MD 21235
1-800-772-1213
URL: https://www.ssa.gov/

US Census Bureau
4600 Silver Hill Rd.
Washington, DC 20233
(301) 763-4636
1-800-923-8282
URL: https://www.census.gov/

**US Department of Veterans
Affairs**
810 Vermont Ave. NW
Washington, DC 20420
1-800-827-1000
URL: https://www.va.gov/

RESOURCES

Many of the demographic data cited in this text were drawn from US Census Bureau and US Bureau of Labor Statistics publications, including "Older Americans Month: May 2017" (April 2017), "Population by Age and Sex: 2012, 2035 and 2060" (December 2012), "An Aging Nation" (April 2017), *2014 National Population Projections* (December 2014), and *An Aging World: 2015* (2016). The Guinness World Records provided information about centenarians.

The report *A Profile of Older Americans: 2016* (April 2017) by the Administration on Aging (AoA) and the data collected by the Federal Interagency Forum on Aging-Related Statistics provided useful information about older adults, as did population data from the Central Intelligence Agency's *The World Factbook: United States* (January 2018).

Many of the findings and statistics cited are drawn from data collected by the following federal entities: Administration for Community Living; AoA; Agency for Healthcare Research and Quality; Census Bureau; Centers for Medicare and Medicaid Services; Employee Benefits Security Administration; National Center for Health Statistics (Centers for Disease Control and Prevention); National Institute on Aging; Office of Research, Evaluation, and Statistics; Office of Statistical and Science Policy; Office of the Assistant Secretary for Planning and Evaluation (US Department of Health and Human Services); Social Security Administration; Substance Abuse and Mental Health Services Administration; US Bureau of Labor Statistics; US Department of Agriculture; US Department of Housing and Urban Development; US Department of Veterans Affairs; and US Environmental Protection Agency.

The Pew Research Center's *Facts on U.S. Immigrants, 2015* (Gustavo López and Jynnah Radford, May 2017) and the Pew Forum on Religion and Public Life's *2014 U.S. Religious Landscape Study* (2018) offered insight into the opinions, concerns, and the role of religion in the lives of older adults. In *Tech Adoption Climbs among Older Adults* (Monica Anderson and Andrew Perrin, May 2017), the Pew Research Center reported the rates of internet use by older adults. The *Milliman 2017 Corporate Pension Funding Study* (Zorast Wadia, Alan H. Perry, and Charles J. Clark, April 2017) described recent trends in corporate pension plans. The Institute for Tomorrow (2018) described the thoughts and behaviors of members of the baby boomer generation. In *Encore Careers: The Persistence of Purpose* (2014), Encore.org reported that millions of Americans aged 50 to 70 years are interested in launching so-called encore careers to address social needs.

The National Highway Traffic Safety Administration (NHTSA) confirms in "Alternative Transportation—It Could Work for You" (2017) that older adult nondrivers rely on rides from family or friends, public transportation, walking, or senior vans or taxicabs. In *Older Drivers* (2017), the NHTSA documented the increasing numbers of older drivers. The Insurance Institute for Highway Safety reported in "Older Drivers: Q&As" (September 2017) that in 2014 motor vehicle crashes accounted for less than 1% of fatalities among people aged 70 years and older and that fatal crash rates increase markedly at ages 70 to 74 years and are highest among drivers 85 years and older. In "Older Adult Drivers" (November 2017), the Centers for Disease Control and Prevention reported that older drivers take fewer risks than younger drivers. The American Medical Association and the NHTSA developed the *Physician's Guide to Assessing and Counseling Older Drivers* (2010) and the American Geriatrics Society published the *Clinician's Guide to Assessing and Counseling Older Drivers* (2015), both of which detail medical conditions and their potential effects on driving skills.

The National Coalition on Homelessness noted in "Elder Homelessness" (2018) an increase in the proportion of older adults in the homeless population. The National Low Income Housing Coalition documented in *Out of Reach 2017* (Andrew Aurand et al., June 2017) income and rental housing cost data for the 50 states, the District of Columbia, and Puerto Rico. The National Center for Health described in *Long-Term Care Providers and Services Users in the United States: Data from the National Study of Long-Term Care Providers, 2013–2014* (Lauren Harris-Kojetin et al., February 2016) characteristics of long-term care facilities and residents. The Genworth 2017 Cost of Care Survey (August 2017) reported the national average rates for long-term care facilities.

The Social Security Administration provided information about the history and future of Social Security and Medicare as well as benefits and eligibility in publications such as *Fast Facts and Figures about Social Security, 2016* (August 2016) and *The 2017 Annual Report of the Board of Trustees of the Federal Old-Age and Survivors Insurance and Federal Disability Insurance Trust Funds* (July 2017).

Many organizations and publications provided information on specific health and medical problems of older adults. Among the many publications cited in this text were the American Heart Association's "Older Americans and Cardiovascular Diseases" (2016), the American Cancer Society's *Cancer Facts and Figures, 2017* (2017), and the Alzheimer's Association's *2017 Alzheimer's Disease Facts and Figures* (2017). The US Department of Veterans Affairs provided demographic projections of the health and other needs of older veterans.

Similarly, many agencies, organizations, and professional organizations, notably the American Geriatrics Society, the Family Caregiver Alliance, the Kaiser Family Foundation, the Mature Workers Employment Alliance, and the National Center for Education Statistics, offered data and analyses of myriad issues of importance to older Americans.

Professional medical journals publish research findings and information about health and disease among older adults as well as health service utilization and financing. Articles from the following journals were cited in this text: *Addiction*; *Aging, Dementia, Cognitive, and Behavioral Neurology: Clinical Trials*; *Alzheimer's and Dementia*; *American Journal of Geriatric Psychiatry*; *American Journal of Psychiatry*; *American Journal of Public Health*; *Annals of Internal Medicine*; *Archives of Sexual Behavior*; *BMJ*; *Clinics in Geriatric Medicine*; *Drugs Aging*; *Genome Medicine*; *Geriatric Nursing*; *Gerontologist*; *Health Affairs*; *Home Healthcare Nurse*; *International Social Science Review*; *JAMA Neurology*; *Journal of Alzheimer's Disease*; *Journal of Elder Abuse and Neglect*; *Journal of Epidemiology*; *Journal of Personality and Social Psychology*; *Journal of the American Medical Association*; *Journals of Gerontology*; *Medica Press*; *Medical Clinics of North America*; *Medical Journal of Australia*; *Nature*; *Nature Genetics*; *Neurology*; *Neurology and Therapy*; *Neuropsychology Review*; *New England Journal of Medicine*; *Nursing Ethics*; *PLOS One*; *Proceedings of the National Academy of Sciences*; and *Psychology and Aging*.

Because the aging population affects nearly every aspect of society, from employment and housing to health care and politics, consumer publications frequently feature articles about and of interest to older adults. Articles cited in this volume were drawn from Associated Press, Atlantic.com, CNN.com, ConsumerReports.org, Forbes.com, Fortune.com, Huffingtonpost.com, NYTimes.com, Reuters, USNews.com, WashingtonPost.com, and WSJ.com.

Information about abuse and mistreatment of older adults was found in *The True Link Report on Elder Financial Abuse 2015* (2015); "Screening for Intimate Partner Violence and Abuse of Elderly and Vulnerable Adults" (January 2013) by the US Preventive Services Task Force; *Elder Victimization* (2016) by the National Center for Victims of Crime; and *The Elder Justice Roadmap: A Stakeholder Initiative to Respond to an Emerging Health, Justice, Financial and Social Crisis* (July 2014) by the US Departments of Justice and Health and Human Services. The Bureau of Justice Statistics' *Criminal Victimization, 2015* (Jennifer L. Truman and Rachel E. Morgan, October 2016) provided data about fraud, abuse, and violent victimization of older adults.

We are very grateful to Gallup, Inc., for permitting us to present the results of its renowned opinion polls.

INDEX

Community housing with home care services, 158
Community Living Assistance Services, 146
Community-Based Care Transitions Program, 141
Companion services, 142
Condominiums, 55
Confusion, 127
Congressional representatives, 83–84
Console, Stephen, 68
Console Mattiacci Law, LLC, 68
Consumer Financial Protection Bureau, 164
Consumer expenditures, 25–26, 29, 87t
Consumer fraud, 161–162
Consumer price index, 25, 31
Consumer Reports, 93
Continuing care retirement communities, 51–52, 158
Continuing education, 29, 46
Continuity theory of aging, 125–127
Conyers, John, Jr., 84
Corporation for National and Community Service, 69–70
Cost-of-living adjustments (COLAs), 31, 33
Costs
    Alzheimer's disease care, 132
    assisted living, 158
    driving, 85–86
    expenditures, by category, 87t
    failure to obtain needed medical care due to cost, 123(f7.18)
    gasoline expenditures, 88f
    hearing aids, 106
    home caregivers, 144
    home ownership and renting a home, 53–54
    long-term care, 156
    Medicare, 152, 154
    myths about older workers, 63–64
    preventive health services, 119
    transportation services, 94
    See also Expenditures
Court cases
    Gross v. FBL Financial Services, Inc., 68
    Meacham et al. v. Knolls Atomic Power Laboratory, 68
    Smith v. City of Jackson, 68
Create the Good program, 71
Crime
    elder abuse, 159, 163–169, 166f, 169f
    fraud, 161–163, 162f
    pension fraud, 22
    violent crime, 160f, 161t
Crist, Charlie, 34
Cultural issues, 13
Culture change in nursing homes, 45–47
Cycle of abuse, 166

D
Death
    awareness of imminence of, 127
    from falls, 117, 119f
    leading causes of, 102t, 115–117, 118t, 128
    motor vehicle accidents, 87, 89f, 90t–91t, 92
    rates, 2, 3
    suicide, 134t–135t
    See also Mortality
Death pensions, veterans', 156
Deceptive advertising, 161–162
Defined benefit plans, 19
Defined contribution plans, 19
Del Webb communities, 52–53
Delirium, 89
Demand-response transportation services, 94
Dementia
    Alzheimer's disease, 128–132
    elder abuse, 167, 169
    geriatric care managers, 144
    long-term care facilities with dementia care units, 45, 45(f3.5)
    multi-infarct dementia, 127–128
    prevalence, 125
Democrats, 83, 84
Demographics
    absenteeism, worker, 65t
    death rates for motor vehicle-related injuries, 90t–91t
    demographic transitions, 2
    employment tenure, 66t
    family income, 23t
    family net worth, 24t
    health insurance, by type of coverage, 151t–152t
    labor force, 63t–64t
    older adults, 5–6, 8–9
    population, by marital status, 9f
    population projections, 7t–8t, 8f
    poverty, 17t–18t, 26t–27t
    smoking, 120t, 121(f7.14)
    suicide, 134t–135t
    vision limitations, 107t–108t
    volunteers, 70t, 71t–72t, 73t–74t
Denmark, 52
Developing countries, life expectancy in, 3–4
Diabetes, 91, 101–103, 104f, 105f, 128
Diabetic retinopathy, 107, 109, 110f
Diagnosing Alzheimer's disease, 129–131
Disability
    activity limitations, 95–96
    by age group, 99t
    disability claims, 15–16
    home adaptations, 55
    mental health, 126–127

    prevalence, 99f, 112, 113f
    psychological distress, 127f
    stroke, 117
    veterans, 156f
Discrimination, employment, 58–59, 65–66, 68
Disparate impact theory, 68
Dominantly Inherited Alzheimer Network, 129
Donut hole, Medicare coverage, 146
Door-to-door transport services, 93, 94
Driving
    accidents, 87–88
    age-related changes, 88–89, 91–92
    avoidance of driving under specific conditions, 91
    death rates for motor vehicle-related injuries, 90t–91t
    gasoline expenditures, 88f
    licensed drivers, 85, 86t
    speeding drivers in fatal crashes, by age and gender, 89f
    technology aids, 93
Drug interactions, 113, 114, 133, 137
Drugs, prescription. *See* Medications

E
Early retirement, 66
Earnings test, Social Security, 31–32, 32(t2.10)
Easter Seals Inc., 87
Eastern District of Pennsylvania, 68
ECHO (elder cottage housing opportunity) units, 52
Economic and financial issues
    age dependency ratio, 139, 140t
    Alzheimer's disease costs, 132
    assisted living costs, 51
    caregiving, 131, 140
    changes in the US economy, 59–60
    community housing with home care services, costs of, 158
    consumer expenses, 25–26
    driving, 85–86
    expenditures, by category, 87t
    failure to obtain needed medical care due to cost, 123(f7.18)
    family households aged 65 and over reporting income, 18(f2.2)
    family income, by demographic characteristics, 23t
    family net worth, by demographic characteristics, 24t
    financial abuse, 165
    financial fraud, 162
    gasoline expenditures, 88f
    Great Recession, 15–16
    health care expenditures, 145, 146t, 147t–148t
    hearing aids, 106

Impairment of driving skills, 88–89, 90–91

Income
    aggregate income, by source, 19f
    encore careers, 69
    family households aged 65 and over reporting income, 18(f2.2)
    family income, by demographic characteristics, 23t
    income distribution, 16
    interest rates, 23–24
    median income of older adults, 25
    Medicaid income eligibility requirements, 154(t10.7)
    pension funds, 18–22
    percentage of older adults receiving income, by source, 21f
    reported income, 28f
    reverse mortgages, 53–54
    Social Security, 18(f2.3)
    Social Security benefit amounts, by retirement age, 30–31, 30t
    Social Security benefits, by gender, 31t
    sources, 16–17
    Supplemental Security Income, 32(t2.9), 33t, 34t
    Women's Institute for a Secure Retirement, 144
    workers with retirement plan benefits, 20t–21t

Incontinence, 103–104, 106(f7.6)

Independence at Home Medical Practice Pilot Program, 141

Indiana University, 121

Individual retirement plans, 22

Industrialization, 59–60

Infectious diseases, 110–111

Influenza, 111, 111t

Information age, 60

Injuries
    crime victims, 159
    falls, 117
    leading causes of, 91(t6.4)
    motor vehicle-related, 87, 90t–91t

Innovation, 64–65

Innovations Exchange Program, 46

Instagram, 83

Institutional abuse, 168–169

Insurance. See Auto insurance; Health insurance; Long-term care insurance; Medicaid; Medicare

Insurance Institute for Highway Safety, 85, 87, 92

Intentional communities, 52

Interactions, drug, 113, 114, 133, 137

Interagency Coordinating Council on Access and Mobility, 87

Interest rates, 23–24

Intergenerational cohousing, 52

Intergenerational family violence, 166

Intermediate care facilities, 43

Internal Revenue Service, 158

International issues
    life expectancy, 3–4, 6t
    population aging, 2(f1.2)

Internet use, 80

Internet-based mental health services, 138

Interpersonal relationships, 13

Intimate partner violence, 167

Iron Workers Local 17 pension fund, 22

J

Job training, veterans', 155

Johnson, Lyndon B., 148

Johnson, Sam, 33

Judges, 59

K

Kaiser Family Foundation, 174

Kang, Navnoor, 22

Kathy's Law (New York), 169

Kennedy, John F., 69

Keys Amendment, 49

Knolls Atomic Power Laboratory, Meacham et al. v., 68

L

Labor force. *See* Employment

Labor unions, 22

Law enforcement officers, 169

Lawsuits, discrimination, 66, 67t, 68

L-dopa, 110

Leading causes of death. *See* Death, leading causes of

Legislation
    Age Discrimination in Employment Act, 58–59, 59–60, 65, 66, 67t, 68
    American Health Care Act (proposed), 154–155
    Balanced Budget Act of 1997, 148, 150
    Economic Opportunity Act, 69
    Employee Retirement Income Security Act, 19, 21
    Federal Insurance Contributions Act (FICA), 30
    Graham-Cassidy amendment (proposed), 155
    Health Care and Education Affordability Reconciliation Act, 146
    Housing Act, 55
    Kathy's Law (New York), 169
    Keys Amendment, 49
    Older Americans Act, 49, 143, 169
    Older Workers Benefit Protection Act, 59, 65
    Omnibus Budget Reconciliation Act of 1987, 169
    Patient Protection and Affordable Care Act, 141–142, 143, 145
    Pension Protection Act, 22

Prescription Drug, Improvement, and Modernization Act, 148, 151, 152–153

Providing Choice for Social Security Retirees Act (proposed), 33–34

Retirement Equity Act, 21

Save Social Security Act (proposed), 34–35

Seniors Tax Hike Prevention Act (proposed), 84

Social Security Act, 29

Social Security Amendments, 31

Supportive Housing for the Elderly Act, 55–56

Tax Equity and Fiscal Responsibility Act, 149

Title XIX, Social Security Act, 154

Title XVIII, Social Security Act, 147–148

Veterans Millennium Health Care and Benefits Act, 155

See also Affordable Care Act

Liberalism, political, 83

Licensed drivers, 86t

Licensing of assisted living facilities, 49

Life care communities, 42, 51–52

Life expectancy
    homelessness, 40
    increase in, 3
    international comparisons, 6t
    Parkinson's disease, 110
    perceptions of aging and longevity, 12–13
    Social Security solvency, 33, 35t

Lifelong learning, 29, 75, 77, 79–80

Lifestyle, 28, 117

Living arrangements, 40f
    assisted living, 47–51
    continuing care retirement communities, 51–52
    costs of community housing with home care services, 158
    elder cottage housing opportunity units, 52
    homelessness, 39–40, 42f
    homeownership, 54t
    hospice services offered by nursing homes, 45(f3.4)
    householders, age of, 37, 38t–39t, 39f
    long-term care and supportive housing, 40–42
    long-term care providers, by age of recipients, 48(f3.6)
    long-term care providers, by gender of recipients, 48(f3.7)
    long-term care providers, by race/ethnicity of recipients, 49f
    long-term care users needing assistance with activities of daily living, 50f
    Medicaid as payer source for long-term care services, 51(f3.11)
    multigenerational households, 37–39, 42t

nursing home complaint rates, 50–51, 51(*f*3.10)

nursing homes, 42–47, 43*t*–44*t*

owning and renting homes, 53, 53*f*, 54*t*

public housing, 55–56

residential care communities, by bed numbers, 50*t*

retirement communities, 52–53

shared housing and cohousing, 52

shared residences and privacy issues, 166–167

Lockheed Martin, 68

Longevity and perceptions of aging, 12–13

Long-term care

assisted living facilities, 47–49

board-and-care facilities, 49

Community Living Assistance Services and Supports Independence Benefit Plan, 146

costs, 158

dementia care, 45(*f*3.5)

elder abuse, 168–169, 169*f*

health care, 156–158

hospice services, 45(*f*3.4)

immunizations, 111

insurance, 146, 158

living arrangements, 40–42

Medicaid, 51(*f*3.11), 154, 157*f*

nursing home complaint rates, 51(*f*3.10)

nursing homes, 42–47, 43*t*–44*t*

nursing homes complaint rates, 50–51

providers, by age of recipients, 48(*f*3.6)

providers, by gender of recipients, 48(*f*3.7)

providers, by race/ethnicity of recipients, 49*f*

residential care communities, by bed numbers, 50*t*

residents needing assistance with activities of daily living, 50*f*

veterans, 155

Long-Term Care Ombudsman Program, 49, 169

Low Income Home Energy Assistance Program, 25–26

Low-income individuals. *See* Poverty and low-income individuals

Lyft, 94

M

Macular degeneration, 107, 109, 109(*f*7.9)

Maine, 9

Malnutrition, 104–105

Mandatory retirement, 58–59

Marital status, 41*t*

demographics of older US adults, 6, 8, 9*f*

health insurance, by type of coverage, 151*t*–152*t*

volunteers, 70*t*, 73*t*–74*t*

Marketing to older consumers, 27–29

Markwood, Sandy, 85

Marriage

Medicaid rules, 157–158

mental health, 126

sexuality, 120

working women, 61–62

Mattiacci, Laura, 68

Mature Workers Employment Alliance, 174

McCain, John, 57

Meacham et al. v. Knolls Atomic Power Laboratory, 68

Mead, Margaret, 57

Meal delivery programs, 142

Means testing Social Security, 33

Measures, poverty, 24–25

Media portrayals, 13, 14

Median income of older adults, 25

Medicaid

Affordable Care Act, 142

Community First Choice program, 141

fraud, 169

home and community-based services program, 143

immunizations, 111

income eligibility requirements, 154(*t*10.7)

long-term care, 51(*f*3.11), 156–158

provisions and coverage, 154–155

risk managed care, 149

Medical transportation services, 143

Medicalization of aging, 14

Medicare

Affordable Care Act, 146

age for benefits to begin, 3

compared to Medicare Advantage, 150*t*

costs, 153*f*

enrollment, 149*t*

fraud, 162–163

future of, 153–154, 154(*t*10.6)

health care use, 145

history, 146–148

home health care, 142

immunizations, 111

long-term health care, 156

Medicaid income eligibility requirements, 154(*t*10.7)

Medicare Advantage, 150

politics, 84

prescription drug coverage, 151–153

Prescription Drug, Improvement, and Modernization Act, 151

preventive health services, 119

provisions, 148–149

reimbursement under, 149–150

Medicare Advantage, 150*t*

Medicare Advisory Board, 146

Medicare Fraud Strike Force, 163

Medicare-Medicaid Coordination Office, CMS, 154

Medications

alcohol interactions, 137

Alzheimer's disease, 131

anxiety disorders, 133–134

for depression, 133

depression as a side effect of, 133

driving impairment, 92

effect on sexuality, 120

Medicare, 146, 148, 151–153

misuse, 135–138

osteoporosis, 101

Parkinson's disease, 110

schizophrenia, 135

statins, 115

use of, 112–115, 114*t*–115*t*

Medigap policies, 150–151

Memory, 13–14, 127

See also Dementia

Memphis, TN, 15–16

Mental health and illness

of caregivers, 140–141

continuity theory, 125–127

crime impacts, 159

dementia, 127–132

depression, 132–133

disability and psychological distress, 127*f*

driving impairment, 91

elder abuse, 165, 166

financial abuse effects, 162

happiness and attitudes about aging, 9–13

homelessness, 40

nursing homes, 46–47

psychological distress, 125, 126*f*

self-reported memory issues and confusion, 127

substance abuse, 135–138, 136*f*, 137*f*

veterans, 155

video games, 83

Mercedes-Benz, 29

Metabolic diseases, 91

Michigan, 9

Midlife and continuity theory, 125–127

Mild cognitive impairment, 125, 127

Mixed-use redevelopment projects, 56

Moral values, 83

Mortality, 2, 3

See also Death

Multidisciplinary teams for elder abuse prevention, 168

Multigenerational households, 37–39, 42*t*

Multi-infarct dementia, 127–128

Musculoskeletal disabilities, 91

Myths and stereotypes

older drivers, 92

older workers, 62–65

Prevention of Elder Abuse, Neglect, and Exploitation program, 169
Preventive health services utilization, 119
Privacy issues and elder abuse, 166–167
Private long-term care insurance, 158
Private pension funds, 19, 21
Problem drinking, 135–138
Projections, population, 2(f1.1), 3
Prostate problems, 103, 105t
Providing Choice for Social Security Retirees Act (proposed), 33–34
Psychological abuse, 165
Psychological distress, 125, 126f, 127f
Psychotherapy, 133–134
Public health, 145
Public housing, 55–56
Public opinion and attitudes
  religion, 9
  social issues, 83
  Social Security, concern about, 35–36
Public pension funds, 19, 21
Public transportation, 94

Q

Quality of care, 45–46, 145, 169
Quality of life, 14, 46, 86, 105

R

Race/ethnicity
  absenteeism, worker, 65t
  age-related macular degeneration, 109(f7.9)
  cancer, 116t–117t
  cataracts, 109(f7.8)
  death rates for motor vehicle-related injuries, 90t–91t
  demographics of older US adults, 6
  diabetic retinopathy, 110f
  educational attainment, 75
  family income, by demographic characteristics, 23t
  family net worth, 24t
  health insurance, by type of coverage, 151t–152t
  income, 16
  labor force, 63t–64t
  long-term care, by type of provider, 49f
  long-term care recipients, 47
  population projections, 8f
  poverty, 17t–18t, 26t–27t
  prescription drug use, 114t–115t
  vision limitations, 107t–108t
  volunteers, 70t, 73t–74t
Reagan, Ronald, 169
Rehabilitation, stroke, 117
Relationships, 13
Relaxation therapies, 134–135
Religion, 9
Relocation and older adults, 9

Renters, home, 53, 54–55
Repair services help, 142
Reporting, elder abuse, 162, 165–166
Republicans, 83, 84
Residential care communities. *See* Long-term care
Respite care, 45, 142
Retinopathy, 107, 109, 110f
Retired and senior volunteers programs, 69
Retirement
  defining and redefining, 57–58
  economics of caregiving, 140
  mandatory retirement, 58–59
  pressure to retire, 66
  Social Security benefit amounts, by retirement age, 30–31, 30t
  volunteerism, 69–71
  See also Pensions
Retirement communities, 42, 51–53, 158
Retirement Confidence Survey, 22
Retirement Equity Act, 21
Reverse dependency, 167
Reverse mortgages, 53–54
Rheumatoid arthritis, 99–100
Rich, Jessica, 162
Richmond, VA, 56
Ride Connection, 86
Ride sharing, 94
Risk managed care, 149
Road Scholar program, 75, 77, 79–80
Robert Wood Johnson Foundation, 47
Rooney, Mickey, 164
Roosevelt, Franklin D., 15, 29
Roth IRAs, 22
Rural areas, 87, 94, 146

S

Safe Driving for Mature Operators program, 92
Safety
  driving, 92–93
  home safety, 55
Sale/leaseback with life tenancy, 54
San Diego County, CA, 10
Sandwich generation, 139
Save Social Security Act (proposed), 34–35
Savings, 22, 23–24
SBA (Small Business Administration), 70
Schizophrenia, 135
SCORE (Service Corps of Retired Executives), 70
Screening
  health, 117, 119
  substance abuse, 137
Seizures, 89
Self-employed individuals, 22
Self-neglect, 165
Self-reported health status, 95, 96t–97t

Self-reported memory issues and confusion, 127
Senate Special Committee on Aging, 164
Senior centers, 143
Senior Community Service Employment program, 69
Senior Companion program, 69
Senior Corps, 69
Senior Medicare Patrol program, 163
Senior Transportation programs, 86–87
Seniors Tax Hike Prevention Act (proposed), 84
Service Corps of Retired Executives (SCORE), 70
Service organizations, 69–71
Service-learning programs, 79–80
Sexual abuse, 165
Sexuality, 119–121
Sexually transmitted infections, 121, 123f, 124f
Shared housing, 52
Shared-Use Mobility Center, 94
Silent Generation, 8, 83
Silent strokes, 128
SilverRide, 94
Skilled nursing facilities, 43
Small Business Administration (SBA), 70
Smart cars, 93
Smart homes, 55
Smartphones, 80
Smith, Adrian, 33
Smith v. City of Jackson, 68
Smoking, 118–119, 120t, 121(f7.14)
Social change, 28–29
Social isolation and elder abuse, 169
Social issues, 83
Social media, 80, 83
Social Security
  age for benefits to begin, 3
  average benefits, by gender, 31t
  benefit amounts, by retirement age, 30–31, 30t
  costs, 153f
  earnings test, 31–32
  eligibility age, 60
  future of, 32–36, 154(t10.6)
  history, 29–30
  as income source, 16–17
  politics, 84
  public concern over changes to, 35–36
  reliance on, 15, 18(f2.3)
Social Security Act, 29, 147–148, 154
Social Security Amendments, 31
Social service careers, 68–69
Speeding, 89, 89f
Spousal violence, 167
Stairs, 55
States
  adult protective service programs, 164
  assisted living facilities, 48

OCT - - 2018

CPSIA information can be obtained
at www.ICGtesting.com
Printed in the USA
FFHW01n2017121018
48792253-52926FF

9 781410 325518